MW01101838

FORGING FREEDOM

The Life of Cerf Berr of Médelsheim

Margaret R. O'Leary

iUniverse, Inc.
Bloomington

Forging Freedom
The Life of Cerf Berr of Médelsheim

Copyright © 2012 Margaret R. O'Leary

iUniverse books may be ordered through booksellers or by contacting:

iUniverse
1663 Liberty Drive
Bloomington, IN 47403
www.iuniverse.com
1-800-Authors (1-800-288-4677)

Front cover photo credit: Eighteenth-century oil-on-canvas portrait of Cerf Berr of Médelsheim, property of the Hospice Elisa in Strasbourg. The portrait hangs in the Musée Historique de Strasbourg. The photograph of the portrait is by Rama, Wikimedia Commons, Cc-by-sa-2.0-fr.

ISBN: 978-1-4759-1013-1 (sc)
ISBN: 978-1-4759-1014-8 (hc)
ISBN: 978-1-4759-1015-5 (e)

Printed in the United States of America

iUniverse rev. date: 05/30/2012

CONTENTS

CHAPTER ONE:
The Old Man of Alsace

In the early afternoon of December 7, 1793, an old man fell beneath the scythe of death. Silence wrapped his timber-framed, black-and-white Alsatian house along the Quai Finkwiller in Strasbourg. Outside the old man's house, both along the murky waterfront and in the twisted back streets of old Strasbourg, the bloody French Revolution raged. Maximilien Robespierre, Louis Antoine Léon of Saint-Just, and other macabre members of the Committee of Public Safety in Paris, ordered Strasbourg authorities to intimidate, imprison, and randomly execute Alsatian residents. The rationale for the Reign of Terror was to persuade disaffected provincials to conform to the revolutionary creed and fight. The sadistic Mayor Monet of Strasbourg terrorized the old man by imprisoning him for reasons unknown in a dank, dirty jail during the cold autumn of 1793. In sixteen days, the old man of Alsace was dead.

In the late afternoon of the passing of the old man, his relatives gently closed his plain wooden coffin, covered it with a black sheet, and waited for night to bury him in the forbidden Rosenwiller Jewish Cemetery. Thirteen days earlier, atheist and deist leaders of the French Revolutionary Government in Paris had ordered destruction of the Rosenwiller Jewish Cemetery. All future decedents of the revealed faiths (Christianity, Judaism, and Islam) in France were to receive burials in civil cemeteries stripped of all religious symbols and decorated with new Cult of Reason signs that read, "Death is an eternal sleep."

Despite the ravaged state of the Rosenwiller Jewish Cemetery, the old man's kin were determined to bury him there. Who *was* this old man? How did the particular set of circumstances of his death come about? What did he accomplish during his life that commended him to such extraordinary efforts by his kin after his death? Were his kin successful in burying him in Rosenwiller Jewish Cemetery? Was the old man born in Alsace? If not, where did he come from? Did he always live in Strasbourg?

Why did French revolutionaries destroy religious cemeteries throughout France? Who were the Ashkenazim? Where did they come from? What was the status of the Ashkenazim in Alsace during the lifetime of the old man? What was his line of work? Who was his family? Why did many Alsatian Christians tyrannize the Ashkenazim in Alsace?

The name of the old man was Cerf Berr of Médelsheim (pronounced Serf BARE of MAY-del-shime), the hero of this book. He lived most of his extraordinary life near the eternal Rhine River, which tumbles out of the Alps to race through a north-south-trending trench, rift, or graben cut deeply into the earth's crust. This Rhine graben is a classic of geologic structures. The Rhine graben belongs to an intercontinental belt of related grabens known as the Rhine graben rift system, which traverses Europe from near Marseille on the southern coast of France, to near Rotterdam on the coast of the Netherlands. The pulling apart of the earth's crust at these grabens began in the Middle Eocene epoch about forty million years ago.[1-2]

The main surface of the Rhine graben is the floor of the Rhine Valley. Beneath this floor are miles of layered sediments under which a giant pillow of molten rock boils.[1-3] The Rhine graben rift system is seismically active. The last major earthquake associated with the Rhine graben occurred on October 18, 1356 at its south end, near present-day Basel, Switzerland. This earthquake destroyed most of Basel and emitted shock waves felt as far west and east as Paris and Prague, respectively.[4]

The Kaiserstuhl Mountains (maximum elevation around eighteen hundred feet above sea level) on the Rhine Valley floor near the City of Freiburg were originally active volcanoes.[5] The valley floor and lateral edges of the Rhine graben were sinking and spreading, respectively, during Cerf Berr's lifetime, and they continue to do so today.

The heights of the Vosges (France) and the Black Forest (Germany) form the western and eastern boundaries of the Rhine graben, respectively. These heights appear as rounded mountain chains; however, they are actually the upthrown shoulders of the downthrown Rhine graben. The Vosges extend in a north-northeast direction between the French cities of Belfort and Saverne. The highest peak in the Vosges is the Grand Ballon (around forty-seven hundred feet above sea level). The Jura Mountains near Basel form the natural southern boundary of the Rhine graben. The northern aspect of the Rhine graben lacks a natural boundary and yawns to the North Sea.

What is the location of the Rhine River Valley in Europe? The dominant territorial feature of Europe is its vast west-to-east, upward-trending plain—the Great European Plain—which stretches without interruption for over twenty-four hundred miles from the Atlantic Ocean to the Ural Mountains.[6] Its greatest width is about twelve hundred miles between the Barents and Caspian Seas. Its narrowest width is about one hundred and twenty-five miles in the Low Countries.

The Great European Plain simultaneously tips in two directions. It tips *up* from the Atlantic Ocean to the Ural Mountains. Its average west-to-east gradient is twenty-six inches per mile. It tips *down* from the Alps to the North Sea (south-to-north direction). Most of the major rivers of the Great European Plain flow northward. For eons, humans have followed these rivers to settle Northern Europe. The geography of the major rivers of the Great European Plain creates a series of natural breaks for people migrating across the Great European Plain. These natural breaks divide the traverse of the Great European Plain into six or seven easy stages. The Great European Plain is a windy, dry sea of grasses except for the area between the Rhine and the Oder Rivers where impenetrable, forested hills dominate the landscape.[6]

The Rhine River flows seven hundred and sixty-six miles from glaciers in the Alps to the shallow depths of the North Sea near Rotterdam. Geographers divide the Rhine River into four sections—the High Rhine River (confined to the Alps), the Upper Rhine River (from Basel northward to Bingen), the Middle Rhine River (from Bingen to Bonn), and the Lower Rhine River (from Bonn to the Hook of Holland).

Cerf Berr spent most of his life in the region west of the Upper Rhine River. The Upper Rhine River receives many tributaries including the Ill River, which cleverly invests Strasbourg. The Quai Finkwiller outside of Cerf Berr's home in Strasbourg was an arm of the Ill River. The Ill River runs the length of Alsace, from its source in the Jura Mountains northward to its mouth on the Rhine River, which it reaches only after investing Strasbourg.

Alsace is a small French province, about one hundred miles long (south to north) by an average twenty miles wide (east to west). Its location is in the southernmost and westernmost part of the Rhine River Valley on France's northeastern flank. The natural physical boundaries of Alsace are the Rhine River in the east, the Vosges in the west, the Lauter River in the north, and the Jura Mountains in the south. Strasbourg is located in the northern half of Alsace.

Geographers divide Alsace into Lower and Upper Alsace. During the French Revolution, politicians divided Alsace into the Bas-Rhin Department (the Lower Rhine or Lower Alsace) and the Haut-Rhin Department (the Upper Rhine or Upper Alsace). The words upper and haut refer to the higher average altitude (closer to the Alps) of the so-designated region. The words lower and bas refer to their lower average altitude (farther from the Alps, closer to sea level at the Hook of Holland).

The Palatinate is the German region north of the Lauter River and west of the Rhine River. Baden-Württemberg and Hesse are German states east of the Rhine River, i.e., opposite the Palatinate. The Palatinate occupies the western side of the Rhine graben, north of Alsace. Mountains form part of the western aspect of the Palatinate; however, they are not as high as the Vosges of Alsace. The tallest mountain in the Palatinate is around twenty-eight hundred feet above sea level. The mountains of the Palatinate and the Vosges are the same upthrown shoulders of the downthrown Rhine graben.

Saarland is an obscurely-defined region of the Palatinate. Saarland shares its southern boundary with Lorraine Province, France. Lorraine and Alsace Provinces are contiguous along the western side of Alsace and the eastern side of Lorraine. Cerf Berr was born in Médelsheim, a rural village in the southeastern corner of Saarland. Médelsheim is one mile north of the boundary between Saarland and Lorraine.

Alsace forms a blunt point that pokes into Germany and Central Europe. Only the Rhine River separates France from Germany, and Western Europe from Central Europe. Paris is about two hundred and forty miles due west of Strasbourg.

During Cerf Berr's lifetime, Alsace was unlike any other part of France because of its unique geography and history. Most Alsatians spoke German, an Alsatian dialect, or Yiddish, and they could not fathom French. They initially shared the national enthusiasm for the French Revolution of 1789. However, they retained a strong sense of their peculiar local identity, which differed from that of Parisians and other French people who resided in the interior of France. For example, most Alsatians, including Cerf Berr, sympathized with the plight of King Louis XVI (1754–1793, ruled 1774–1791) during the French Revolution and applauded the adoption of the French Constitution of 1791, which created a constitutional monarchy. However, most Alsatians, including Cerf Berr, worried when the French Revolution took a radical turn in 1792. Historian Norman Hampson noted:

> The impact of the Revolution on this idiosyncratic society was both complex and difficult for men from the "interior" to appreciate. Alsace could not respond like the rest of the country to the new conception of France as an integrated national community. To the majority of the rural population, isolated

by the linguistic barrier, the Revolution was an essentially alien movement.[7]

Alsatian society was also distinctive because of its Ashkenazi population, which was the largest Jewish population in France during the eighteenth century. Before the French Revolution, France had four Jewish population centers:

- the Ashkenazim in the three provinces of Alsace, Lorraine, and the Three Bishoprics (i.e., Metz);
- the Sephardim in southwestern France (Bordeaux, Saint Esprit-les-Bayonne, and several smaller towns);
- the four Sephardi communities in the papal possessions of Avignon and Comtat Venaissin; and
- a mixed community of Ashkenazi and Sephardi Jews in Paris.[8]

The Sephardim, with whom Cerf Berr invariably clashed, immigrated to France from the Iberian Peninsula after expulsion by the Spanish Catholic King Ferdinand II of Aragon (1452–1516) and Queen Isabella I of Castille (1451–1504) during the fifteenth-century Spanish Inquisition (1492–1501). The word Sephardim derived from the Hebrew word for Spain. The Sephardi Jews rapidly assimilated into the mainstream of French society to become prosperous international traders. They received royal letters patent in the early eighteenth century that openly acknowledged their Jewish faith (for many years, they had pretended to be Christians) and granted them the rights of subjects of the French King and the Kingdom of France.

Letters patent were communications written on parchment, marked with the French King's seal and countersigned by the French King's Secretary of State. They were called patent (after the Latin word patere, meaning, to open) because they were delivered open (i.e., not in an envelope or folded).

About forty thousand Jews (Ashkenazim plus Sephardim) lived in France on the eve of the French Revolution. Of these forty thousand Jews, the Ashkenazim in Alsace comprised over seventy percent, or about twenty-eight thousand individuals, while the Sephardim comprised about twenty percent, or about eight thousand individuals.[9–10] In 1789, the total population of France was about twenty-eight million individuals.[11] Thus, in 1789, Jews made up a tiny percentage (about one-tenth of a percent) of the total French population. The French Protestants, the other significant minority in France, made up about two percent (about six hundred thousand individuals) of the population. French Catholics comprised more than ninety-seven percent (over twenty-seven million individuals) of the total population of France.[12]

In 1784, the total population of Alsace was around six hundred and twenty-four thousand individuals, according to a royal census in Alsace ordered by King Louis XVI. Of these six hundred and twenty-four thousand people, almost twenty thousand were Ashkenazim. Thus, in 1784, the Ashkenazim comprised slightly more than three percent of the population of Alsace, although this is almost certainly an underestimate.[13]

Most people living in Alsace and in Southern France personally knew Jews. However, in the rest of France, people could pass their entire lives without ever meeting a Jew. Their information about Jews came from printed materials and by word of mouth. Cerf Berr of Médelsheim relentlessly exposed the plight of the impoverished Ashkenazim to French Kings Louis XV (1710–1774; ruled 1715–1774) and Louis XVI, as well as to the National Assembly during the French Revolution.

In 1784, the Ashkenazim in Alsace lived in one hundred and eighty-two small and rural towns scattered throughout the province. These one hundred and eighty-two towns belonged to at least sixty-one different owners, including King Louis XVI, Roman Catholic authorities, municipal authorities, and nobles of the Holy Roman Empire.[9] Historian Zosa Szajkowski assembled a long list of the owners of Alsatian towns and cities in 1784 that permitted residence by Ashkenazim. Examples from this list follow:

* * * * * * * * *

Ownership of Alsatian Towns and Cities in which
Ashkenazim Were Permitted to Dwell (1784)

- King Louis XVI owned nine towns and cities, which were home to more than thirteen hundred Ashkenazim;
- The City of Colmar owned one city (itself), which was home to twenty-eight Ashkenazim;
- The City of Colmar and the Imperial Bailiff of Kayserberg together owned three towns and cities, which were home to about nine hundred Ashkenazim;
- The Prince Bishop of Strasbourg owned sixteen towns and cities, which were home to about fifteen hundred Ashkenazim;
- The Abbey of Neubourg owned two towns, which were home to eighty-one Ashkenazim;
- The Landgrave of Hesse-Darmstadt owned twenty-one towns and cities, which were home to about nineteen hundred Ashkenazim;
- The Prince of Hohenlohe owned six towns, which were home to about three hundred and fifty Ashkenazim;
- The Prince of Rohan-Soubise owned six towns, which were home to about six hundred Ashkenazim; and
- The Prince of Nassau-Saarbrücken owned one town, which was home to six Ashkenazim.[9]

* * * * * * * * *

In summary, during the eighteenth century, Cerf Berr of Médelsheim lived in Alsace Province, which was situated between the Rhine River and the Vosges of the Rhine River Valley, also known as the Rhine graben, in Northeastern France. The Ashkenazim and Sephardim comprised the majority and minority populations of Jews in France. The Ashkenazim and Sephardim together comprised a miniscule minority population in France. The Ashkenazim in France mostly lived in the three French provinces of Alsace, Lorraine, and the Three Bishoprics. In 1784, the Ashkenazim in Alsace were scattered across one hundred and eighty-two, privately-owned, small and rural towns of the province.

Chapter One Notes:

1. J. H. Illies: "The Rhine graben rift system-plate tectonics and transform faulting." *Surveys in Geophysics*. Volume 1, Number 1, 1972, pp. 27–60.

2. J. H. Illies: "An intercontinental belt of the world rift system." *Tectonophysics*, Volume 8, Issue 1, July 1969, pp. 5–29.

3. James E. Wilson: *Terroir: The Role of Geology, Climate, and Culture in the Making of French Wines*. Berkeley, California: University of California Press, 1998, pp. 82–107.

4. Jérôme Lambert, Thierry Winter, Thomas J.B. Dewez, and Philippe Sabourault: "New hypotheses on the maximum damage area of the 1356 Basel earthquake (Switzerland)." *Quaternary Science Reviews*, February 2005, Volume 24, Issues 3–4, pp. 381–399.

5. C. E. Perrin: "A lost identity: Philippe Frederic, Baron de Dietrich (1748–1793)." *Isis*, December 1982, Volume 73, Number 4, pp. 545–551.

6. Norman Davies: *Europe: a History*. New York City, New York: Oxford University Press, 1996, pp. 51–52.

7. Norman Hampson: *Saint-Just*. Oxford, England, United Kingdom: Basil Blackwell, 1991, pp. 140–141.

8. Zosa Szajkowski: "Relations among Sephardim, Ashkenazim, and Avignonese Jews in France from the 16th to the 20th centuries." In *Jews and the French Revolutions of 1789, 1830 and 1848*. New York City, New York: Ktav Publishing House, 1970, p. 235.

9. Zosa Szajkowski: "The demographic aspects of Jewish emancipation in France during the French Revolution." In *Jews and the French Revolutions of 1789, 1830 and 1848*. New York City, New York: Ktav Publishing House, 1970, pp. 45–74.

10. Zosa Szajkowski: "The growth of the Jewish population in France." In *Jews and the French Revolutions of 1789, 1830 and 1848*. New York City, New York: Ktav Publishing House, 1970, pp. 75–80.

11. Peter M. Jones: *Reform and Revolution in France: the Politics of Transition, 1774–1791*. Cambridge, England, United Kingdom: Cambridge University Press, 1995, p. 13.

12. Rémi Fabre: *Les Protestants en France depuis 1789*. Paris, France: La Découverte, 1999, p. 6.

13. The data collected during the Jewish census of 1784 is available in *Denombrement des Juifs d'Alsace, 1784*. Strasbourg, Alsace, France: Cercle de Généalogie Juive, Editions du Cédrat, no date. The book is available for purchase at http://www.genealoj.org/New/ENtexte/page06.php; accessed December 1, 2011. See also Simon Schwarzfuchs: "Alsace and Southern Germany: the creation of a border." In *Jewish Emancipation Reconsidered*. Michael Brenner, Vicki Caron, and Uri R. Kaufmann (eds.). London, England, United Kingdom: Leo Baeck Institute, 2003, p. 9.

CHAPTER TWO:

Cerf Berr's Jewish Heritage, 63 BC–AD 1726

———◆———

Cerf Berr of Médelsheim belonged to the ethno-religious group known as the Jews, Hebrews, or Israelites, whose roots are complex. The English word Jew derived from the Latin word Judaeus, which itself derived from the Hebrew word yehudi. The word yehudi derived from the proper name Yehuda, or Judah. Judah was the name of one of the twelve sons of Jacob. Judah was also the head of one of the Twelve Tribes of Israel. Judah's mother Leah named him Yehuda to "praise God for giving birth to so many sons" (Genesis 29:35).

During the first century BC, the Romans assigned the word Judaea to the Hebrew province centered on Jerusalem. The word Hebrew derived from the name of the original language (Hebrew) spoken by the Jews. In the first century AD, the Jews used the name Israel on their coins in conscious rejection of the Roman-assigned name Judaea.[1] The word Ashkenazim refers to the Yiddish-speaking group of Jews who first settled around 1000 AD on the banks of the Rhine and Moselle Rivers of Western Europe in the area designated by them as Loter.[2]

The following overview of the Jewish heritage of Cerf Berr of Médelsheim comprises five sections: the Roman era (63 BC–AD 476), the European Early Middle Ages (476–1000), the European High Middle Ages (1000–1300), the European Late Middle Ages (1300–1500), and the European Early Modern Period (1500–1726). Histories of the long Jewish experience before 63 BC are available elsewhere.[3]

The Roman Era, 63 BC–AD 476

On a Saturday during Sabbath in June 63 BC, a Roman Republic military commander named Gnaeus Pompeius Magnus (106–48 BC, henceforth, Pompey) conquered the Hebrew-speaking people of the Kingdom of Judaea by defeating the Hebrew Hasmonean dynast named King Aristobulus II (ruled 66–63 BC). The Roman soldiers entered the court of the Jewish Temple in Jerusalem through a breach they had blasted in the wall surrounding the court during a prolonged siege. They first killed the Jewish high priests as they stood sacrificing before the altar and then slaughtered around twelve thousand Judaeans who were attending Sabbath services. Pompey entered the sanctuary of the Jewish Temple to satisfy his curiosity about the much-rumored nature of Judaean worship. He found simplicity and no images. The Jewish religion prohibited visible representation of the Godhead. Pompey left untouched the sanctuary treasure of two thousand talents of sacred money. However, his entry into the sanctuary symbolically ended Jewish sovereignty and subjected Judaea to the rule of the Romans.[4]

Pompey executed the most determined of his Judaean prisoners of war, razed the walls of Jerusalem, placed Judaea in the category of conquered provinces, levied a tax on the people of Jerusalem, and transported King Aristobulus II, his daughters, and many learned and skilled Judaeans across the Mediterranean Sea to Rome on the west side of the Italian Peninsula. The Judaean captives joined a group of Jewish merchants already living as free men in Rome.[4]

In 26 AD, Praetorian Prefect Lucius Aelius Sejanus (20 BC–AD 31, henceforth, Sejanus) gained control of the entire state mechanism in Rome when Roman Emperor Tiberius (42 BC–AD 37, ruled 14 AD–37) withdrew to the Island of Capri off the coast of Naples, Italy. Sejanus dispatched Pontius Pilate (ruled 26–36 AD) to Judaea to succeed Valerius Gratus (ruled 15–26 AD) as the fifth prefect to govern Judaea since its conquest by Pompey in 63 BC.

Around 30 AD, the Galilean Jew named Jesus traveled to Judaea where he disturbed the Passover celebration in the Jewish Temple in

Jerusalem. Temple guards arrested and led him not before the great Synhedrion (Sanhedrin), but before twenty-three members of a smaller Court of Justice presided over by Joseph Caiaphas, a Roman-appointed high priest. Because Jesus answered questions in a certain way, the Jewish Court of Justice declared him guilty of blasphemy. Pontius Pilate then tried Jesus, who answered his questions in a certain way that led to a sentence of execution. Pontius Pilate alone had the power to enforce the verdict of execution. Roman soldiers treated Jesus according to Roman penal laws, which included scourging and crucifixion in Golgotha, the place of skulls. Jesus of Nazareth had twelve disciples while he was alive and preaching. After his crucifixion, the twelve disciples became the twelve apostles who proclaimed Jesus the risen lord Christ and the long-awaited Jewish Messiah. The apostles spread the gospel of Jesus to peoples living around the Mediterranean Basin.

From around 68 to 100 AD, four avowed Christians named Matthew, Mark, Luke, and John wrote separate narratives describing the life, teachings, crucifixion, and resurrection of Jesus. These narratives were included in the canonical Christian New Testament.[5]

In Jerusalem in 66 AD, a Jewish sect called the Zealots attempted to drive the Romans from Judaea through armed guerilla-type warfare. Roman Emperor Vespasian (9 AD–79; ruled 69–79) sent his eldest son, Titus Flavius Vespansianus (39–81, ruled 79–81), to subdue the Zealots. In 70, Titus finally won a prolonged siege of Jerusalem. The exhausted Romans took the rich spoils of the sanctuary of the Jewish Temple before roundly torching the Temple to the ground. They then depopulated Judaea by butchering, banishing, or selling the Hebrews.

In 132, a Judaean named Simon Bar-Cochba led another deadly revolt against the Romans, which required direct intervention by Roman Emperor Hadrian (76–138, ruled 117–138, henceforth, Hadrian). After three years of fighting, Hadrian's Army crushed the revolutionaries, razed the Temple Mount, and began construction of a new Greek-styled pagan city called Aelia Capitolina on the northern edge of Jerusalem. Hadrian forbade Jews from entering Aelia Capitolina. On the razed

Temple Mount, he built a column in his own honor and a temple to honor Jupiter, the Roman God of War.

Hadrian was so angry with the recalcitrant Judeans that he prohibited circumcision, keeping the Sabbath, marriages on Wednesday, attendance at religious schools, and other Jewish rites and customs. His persecution of the Jews was so severe that Jewish Christians sought political and religious recognition as a body separate from the Jews. Historian Heinrich Graetz wrote:

> Two teachers of the Church, Quadratus and Aristides, are said to have handed to Hadrian a petition in which they demonstrated that Christianity had no connection with Judaism. From this time dates the unity and identity of most of the Jewish-Christian and Gentile-Christian sects. The Jewish Christians gave up the Jewish laws, which they had hitherto kept, in a greater or less degree, adopting the dogmatic precepts of Christianity as they had been developed under Gentile-Christian views, and as proof of their sincere convictions, they for the first time placed an uncircumcised bishop at the head of the community. From the time of Hadrian, all connection between Jews and Christians ceased, and they no longer occupied the position of two hostile bodies belonging to the same house, but they became two entirely distinct bodies.[6]

Amid the tumult in Judaea in 135, Judah I, also known as Judah the Prince, was born. Around 189, fifty-four-old Judah I completed the compilation of Jewish oral law in a sacred text called the Mishna. Compilation of the Mishna had begun two generations earlier. Judah "endeavored to observe a certain systematic order in dealing with the various traditional laws relating to the prayers, to benedictions, taxes on agricultural produce, the Sabbath, festivals and fasts, marriage customs, vows and Nazarites, civil and criminal jurisdiction, the system of sacrifices, levitical purity, and many other points," said Heinrich Graetz.

The Mishna was a sacred text above and beyond the Hebrew Bible, or Torah. The Torah consists of the Law of God as revealed to Moses. The Torah comprises Genesis, Exodus, Leviticus, Numbers, and Deuteronomy of the Hebrew Bible. Other names for the Torah are the Books of Moses, the Pentateuch, and the Christian Old Testament.

The Mishna contains certain laws that Jews transmitted orally from one generation to the next over many centuries. "The constantly changing conditions of life required new regulations, and some sort of an organization must have been in operation from the times of Ezra on to make the Law effective in the life of the community, to preserve it, and to widen its scope," noted historian Hermann L. Strack.[7]

Why was the compilation of the Mishna completed in 189 AD, instead of, say, 100 AD or 300 AD? Hermann L. Strack advanced the theory that the "Jews were led to codify and write down in a definitive form certain oral law handed down over the centuries, with a view, in part at least, to the New Testament canon then in process of formation."[7]

The Mishna contains no laws pertaining to Christians, said Heinrich Graetz, suggesting that the "danger with which Judaism had been threatened by the Jewish Christians, since the destruction of the Temple until the Bar-Cochba War, had already been averted, and that danger was now no longer to be dreaded." On the other hand, the Mishna contains numerous laws directed against paganism and interaction with pagans, or Gentiles. The pagans were non-Abrahamic (i.e., not Jews, not Christians), Greco-Roman polytheistic believers. Paganism still suffused Palestine, and paganism's love of images of idols deeply offended the Jews. Mishnaic laws on this subject included prohibiting Jews from receiving medical care during any illness by pagans, selling ornaments or other objects for the use of idols to the pagans, or renting houses to them in Palestine, because pagans would desecrate the premises through introduction of images of idols.[8]

The Roman Emperor Caracalla (188–217, ruled 198–217) celebrated his Syrian roots. His father, Roman Emperor Septimius

15

Severus (145–211, ruled 193–211) and his mother, Julia Somna (or Martha) were Syrian natives. Caracella wore Syrian clothes, which were similar to Judaean clothes. In 211, Emperor Caracalla issued his famous Constitutio Antoniniana Edict, which extended citizenship to every inhabitant of the Roman Empire, including all Jews. The purpose of the Constitutio Antoniniana Edict was to augment the tax base of the Roman Empire, increase the number of men eligible to serve in the Roman Army, and abolish distinctions among the diverse peoples of the Roman Empire.[9]

The Constitutio Antoniniana Edict in 211 was the last edict to enfranchise Jews in Europe until September 27, 1791 when the French National Assembly passed into law the political emancipation of all Jews in France. In other words, Jews in Europe lived as a minority population outside the various prevailing political orders for almost sixteen hundred years.

In 313, Roman Emperor Constantine I (the Great, 272–337, ruled 306–337, henceforth, Constantine I), who worshipped pagan gods, decreed in Milan an Edict of Toleration that acknowledged throughout the Roman Empire the validity of all religions, including Christianity. The Edict of Toleration of 313 followed the horrendous persecution of the Christians in the Roman Empire that occurred between the ministry of Jesus and the Edict of Milan. During his life, Constantine I increasingly leaned toward Christianity to which he ultimately converted shortly before his death in 337. However, his devotion to Christianity increased in direct proportion to his contempt for Judaism, which he stigmatized as a profligate, godless sect (feralis, nefaria secta).[10] On October 18, 315, Constantine I prohibited Jews from proselytizing Christians as follows:

> We wish to make it known to the [Jews] and their elders and their patriarchs that if, after the enactment of this law, any one of them dares to attack with stones or some other manifestation of anger another who has fled their dangerous sect and attached himself to the worship of God [Christianity],

he must speedily be given to the flames and burnt together with all his accomplices. Moreover, if any one of the population should join their abominable sect and attend their meetings, he will bear with them the deserved penalties.[11]

In 325, Constantine I convened the Council of Nicaea to deal with the Arian heresy concerning the nature of the relationship of the persons of the Trinity. Members of the Council of Nicaea also discussed the common practice among many Christian churches in the East, especially the dioceses led by Antioch, of celebrating Easter on the same day that the Jews celebrated Passover. According to this approach, Easter sometimes fell on a day other than Sunday. However, Sunday was the day that Jesus arose from the dead (his resurrection). Constantine I believed that the celebration of the Easter event should occur on Sunday, always. In the west (e.g., Rome), Christians celebrated Easter on the Sunday after the full moon following the spring (vernal) equinox. In 325, Constantine I decreed the latter approach appropriate for all Christendom, as documented in a letter he wrote to the Council of Nicaea. In this letter, he also hurled calumny at the Jews.

* * * * * * * * *

Excerpt from a Letter by Roman Emperor Constantine I about the Timing of the Easter Celebration, 325 AD

At this meeting [at Nicaea], the question concerning the most holy day of Easter was discussed, and it was resolved by the united judgment of all present, that this feast ought to be kept by all and in every place on one and the same day [Sunday]. For what can be more becoming or honorable to us than that this feast from which we date our hopes of immortality should be observed unfailingly by all alike, according to one ascertained order and arrangement?

And first of all, it appeared an unworthy thing that in

the celebration of this most holy feast we should follow the practice of the Jews, who have impiously defiled their hands with enormous sin, and are, therefore, deservedly afflicted with blindness of soul [for refusing to accept Jesus as the long-awaited Jewish Messiah]. For we have it in our power, if we abandon their custom, to prolong the due observance of this ordinance to future ages, by a truer order, which we have preserved from the very day of the Passion until the present time.

Let us have nothing in common with the detestable Jewish crowd; for we have received from our Savior a different way. A course at once legitimate and honorable lies open to our most holy religion. Beloved brethren, let us with one consent adopt this course, and withdraw ourselves from all participation in their [the Jews'] baseness. For their boast is absurd indeed, that it is not in our power without instruction from them to observe these things.[11]

* * * * * * * *

During the fourth century, some Jews left the Italian Peninsula for Gaul and the Iberian Peninsula to escape the Jewish persecution of Constantine I and his son Constantius II (317–361; ruled 337–361). During the fourth century, Gaul consisted of present-day France, Luxembourg, Belgium, most of Switzerland, part of Italy, and parts of the Netherlands and Germany on the left (west) bank of the Rhine River.[12] The Gallo-Roman Jewish immigrants from the Italian Peninsula initially settled in about thirty-five localities along Gaul's Mediterranean coast and in Gaul's interior river valleys carved by the Rhône, Saône, and Rhine Rivers.

In 355, Roman Emperor Constantius II appointed Julian (331/332–363, ruled 361–363, known as the "Apostate" or the "Philosopher"; henceforth, Julian) as Caesar of the western provinces of the Roman Empire. Julian made the only serious attempt to hinder the anti-Jewish persecution that accompanied Christianization of the Roman Empire. Julian was a pagan, but he encouraged freedom of religion for all Roman citizens. As a friend of the Jews, he abolished the special taxes they paid to the Roman government and encouraged the rebuilding of Jerusalem, including the Jewish Temple (the project never got underway). Julian also became famous for crushing the Alamanni warriors in Gaul in 357 at the Battle of Argentoratum, the future site of Strasbourg.

On August 24, 410, the Visigoths, led by King Alaric I (circa 370–410, ruled 395–410), sacked Rome, which prompted many Romans to question their conversion from paganism to Christianity. Around 415, Augustine (354–430), a North African Christian scholar, wrote *The City of God* for at least two reasons that pertain to the sacking of Rome. First, Augustine wanted to console Roman Christians that their rejection of their traditional pagan gods had not caused the sacking of Rome by King Alaric I. Second, he sought to persuade Roman Christians that Christianity was the true religion among competing philosophies and religions. Augustine was trying to stem a movement among new Christians to return to their pagan system of beliefs.

Augustine proclaimed in *The City of God* some new thoughts about the Jews, which led to his call for Christians to preserve the Jews as a minority group in the expanding realm of Christendom. He appeared to have little concern or contact with the Jews of his day. However, the history of the Jews, which he avidly and respectfully studied in the Christian Old Testament, struck him as very important, and he felt driven to fuse Jewish history to the Christian faith.

Augustine's study of the Torah convinced him, "All that Moses wrote is of Christ—that is, it pertains completely to Christ—whether insofar as it foretells of him in figures or objects, deeds, and speech, or insofar as it extols his grace and glory."[15] Augustine believed, "All of the contents of the Old Testament were historically true (in the case of narrative) and/or valid (in the case of prophecy and precepts), and this accuracy underlay the truth of their prefigurative significance." Thus, the Old and the New Testaments, the Jews and the Christians, were irrevocably bound together. If one destroyed the Old Testament, one invalidated the message of the New Testament, because the latter is the fulfillment of the former. In fact, Augustine emphatically declared that Christians had a responsibility to *preserve* the Jewish people whose special covenant with God brought the Torah and its anticipatory Christian message into being.

However, continued Augustine, Christians were always superior to Jews, because Jews, by their obstinacy and flaws, especially their rejection of Jesus as the Messiah, had fallen into disfavor with God. What should Christians do about the Jews in their midst? Augustine said, "The Jews survive as living testimony to the antiquity of the Christian promise, while their enslavement and dispersion confirm that the church has displaced them." In other words, *The City of God* "interprets the divine prophecy of Jewish survival as a mandate for the faithful: Slay them not, that is, ensure their survival and that of the Old Testament observance; and scatter them guaranteeing that the conditions of their survival demonstrate the gravity of their error and the reality of their punishment."[15]

In his own words, Augustine wrote in *The City of God* the following about the status of the Jews in Christendom:

> Yet the Jews who slew Him [Jesus], and chose not to believe in Him…having been vanquished rather pathetically by the Romans, completely deprived of their kingdom (where foreigners were already ruling over them), and scattered throughout the world (so that they are not lacking anywhere), are testimony for us [Christians] through their own scriptures [Torah] that we [Christians] have not contrived the prophecies concerning Christ…Hence, when they do not believe our scriptures, their own, which they read blindly, are thus fulfilled in them… For we realize that on account of this testimony, which they unwillingly provide for us by having and by preserving these books [Torah], they are scattered among all the nations, wherever the church of Christ extends itself…For there is a prophecy in the Psalms (which they [Jews] still read) concerning this, where

it is written…: "Slay them not, lest at any time they forget your law; scatter them in your might." God thus demonstrated to the church the grace of his mercy upon his enemies the Jews, because, as the Apostle says, "Their offense is the salvation of the Gentiles." Therefore, he did not kill them—that is, he did not make them cease living as Jews, although conquered and oppressed by the Romans—lest, having forgotten the law of God, they not be able to provide testimony on our behalf [Christians] in this matter of our present concern. Thus it was inadequate for him to say, "Slay them not, lest at any time they forget your law," without adding "scatter them." For if they were not everywhere, but solely in their own land with this testimony of the scriptures, the church, which is everywhere, could surely not have them among all the nations as witnesses to the prophecies given previously regarding Christ.[15–16]

Augustine's message about the Jews in *The City of God* resounded through the centuries. It provided Christians in Augustine's own day with a theological rationale to boost their self-esteem in relation to the Jews in their midst. At the same time, Augustine's message forbade Christians from harming the Jews in their midst. Augustine strengthened his admonition to his fellow Christians by attributing his unique Jewish message to the design and will of God.

In 425, the earliest confirmed Jewish settlement bustled in Arles, Gaul, north of Augustine's home in Hippo (Annaba, Algeria), which was about five hundred miles to the south, across the Mediterranean Sea. Today, Arles is about twenty miles inland from the mouth of the Rhône River on the southern coast of France. In 425, Emperor Valentinian III (419–455, ruled 425–455), whose mother was Regent, addressed to the Royal Praetor of Gaul and to Patroclus, Archbishop of Arles (412–426), "a decree, enjoining them to forbid Jews and heathens to take up the career of arms, to enter the magistracy, or to possess Christian slaves. These restrictions, however, were not carried out, or, at any rate, did not last long; for some years later the bishopric of Arles was occupied by Hilary [circa 401–449, ruled 429–449], who cherished the most kindly feelings toward Jews in general, and especially toward those of Arles."[13] Meanwhile, Jewish merchants reliably supplied the Roman legions traveling up the Rhône River Valley of Gaul with wheat, wine, arms, straw, hay, oats, horses, and clothing.[14]

In 438 and 534, Roman Emperors Theodosius II (401–450, ruled 408–450) and Justinian I (483–565, ruled 527–565) published two legal corpora—the Latin *Codex Theodosianus* (438) and the Latin and Greek *Justinian Code* (534), respectively. These legal corpora contained all previous anti-Jewish decrees, beginning with those first issued by Constantine I, and influenced all subsequent Christian and Muslim legislation concerning the Jews. "The second-class status of the citizenship of the Jews as crystallized in the *Justinian Code* was thus entrenched in the medieval world, and under the influence of the Church, the disabilities imposed on [Jews] received religious sanction and relegated them to even lower levels," averred historian Jacob Rader Marcus.[12]

Recall that some Jews had moved to Gaul and the Iberian Peninsula to escape the persecutory laws of the Christianized Roman Empire and to seek economic opportunity. Initially, these Jews experienced little discrimination in Gaul and the Iberian Peninsula by Roman Christians, because the latter established themselves on the frontier of Christendom with difficulty. Heinrich Graetz said:

> The invasions of the barbarians [the Goths, an ancient Teutonic people] had completely changed the social order existing in [Gaul and Iberia]. Roman institutions, both political and ecclesiastical, were nearly effaced, and the polity of the empires established by heathen or half-Christianized nations was not built [on] Church law. It was a long while before [the Church] gained a firm footing in the west of Europe, and the Jews who had settled there enjoyed undisturbed peace until the victorious Church gained the upper hand.[17]

Heinrich Graetz noted that the first Jews to settle in the Rhine River Valley along the Upper Rhine River were women prisoner-wives of Roman soldiers who had been under the command of Titus when they razed the Jewish Temple in Jerusalem in 70 AD. "The children thus begotten of Jewish and Germanic parents were brought up by their mothers in the Jewish faith…It is these children who are said to have been the founders of the first Jewish communities between Worms and Mayence [Mainz]," that is, along the twenty-five-mile stretch on the west side of the Upper Rhine River. "It is certain that a Jewish congregation existed in the Roman colony, the City of Cologne [Lower Rhine River], long before Christianity had been raised to power by Constantine" in 315–320, declared Heinrich Graetz.[17]

As Roman citizens of Gaul, the earliest Gallo-Roman Jews enjoyed freedom of worship and access to public office. Gallo-Roman Jews "practiced trades that did not distinguish them from other Roman citizens, such as agriculture and wine-growing," noted historian Esther Benbassa. "Nor did they limit their activities to commerce alone. They dressed as the rest of the population dressed, bore arms, and spoke the local language; even in the synagogue, Hebrew was not the only language used for rituals. Their ancestral names—biblical, Roman, and Gallo-Roman—did not differentiate them from other inhabitants."[14]

In 476, the Western Roman Empire ended when Gothic General Flavius Odoacer (433–493, ruled 476–493), the first non-Roman to rule all Italy, deposed Romulus Augustus (circa 460–circa 500, ruled 475–476). Many historians cite the fall of Rome in 476 as the starting point of the Early Middle Ages (476–1000).

The European Early Middle Ages, 476–1000

In 496, Remigius (also known as Remi, circa 437–533), Bishop of Reims (the city was founded circa 80 BC), baptized the pagan King Clovis (circa 466–511, his real name was Hludovicus). Clovis became the first king of all the Franks following his victory over the Alamanni people at Tolbiac, a city in ancient Gaul near present-day Cologne. Clotilde (475–545), the devout Christian wife of Clovis, insisted on his baptism following the victory over the Alamanni people at Tolbiac. He agreed. The baptism of Clovis forged the alliance between the monarchy and the Church and conferred on the Frankish King a sacred character. King Clovis gave Bischheim, a small village north of present-day Strasbourg, to Bishop Remigius as a gift following the baptism. In 530, the testament of Remigius is the first historical mention of the Village of Bischheim, Alsace.[18]

Around 505, Babylonian rabbis in south-central Mesopotamia (present-day Iraq) completed compilation of the Gemara, another sacred text that attempted to clarify the meaning of laws articulated in the Mishna, previously described. Recall that Judah the Prince oversaw completion of the compilation of the Mishna around 189. "The Gemara developed orally for some three hundred years following the redaction of the Mishna," explained historian Aryeh Kaplan. "Finally, when [the Gemara interpretations of Mishnaic laws] came into danger of being forgotten and lost, Rav Ashi [352–427], together with his school in Babylonia, undertook to collect all these discussions and set them in order." The Jewish sacred text, the Talmud, contains the Mishna and the Gemara.[17]

From 450 to 751, the Frankish Merovingian dynasts ruled Gaul. They showed little hostility towards Jews living in Gaul. One reason for the good will between the Jews and Christians at both the elite and the popular level was a shared conception of God, averred historian Gavin I. Langmuir. He wrote:

> The conception of god [by the Frankish Christians] closely resembled that of the Jews. Unlike later Christians, [the Frankish Christians] paid little attention to Trinitarian divisions of the divinity and did not focus emotionally on the humanity and suffering of Christ. "Christ was…made almost the sole representative of the Holy Trinity" and their image of Christ was rather that of the God of the Old Testament than that of Jesus in the New. Like the Jews, they thought of

themselves as the people of God, their religiosity was highly ritualistic, and they resonated to the bellicosity of the Old Testament. Since there was little to disturb their belief that they and the Jews worshipped the same god, they felt little strain in tolerating Jews.[19]

In 591 and in 598, Pope Gregory I (540–604, ruled 590–604) established the Church's official status for the Jews in Europe. Many later Popes emulated Pope Gregory I's dictates concerning the Jews in Christendom. Two examples of Pope Gregory I's dictates were prohibition of the forcible baptism of Jews and prohibition of the desecration of synagogues. The following two excerpts are examples of his writings about the Jews:

1.   [Forcible baptism] should have no profitable effect; or there will ensue further (God forbid) the loss of the very souls which we wish to save. For, when any one is brought to the font of baptism, not by the sweetness of preaching but by compulsion, he returns to his former superstition, and dies the worse from having been born again. Let, therefore, your Fraternity stir up such men [Jews] by frequent preaching, to the end that through the sweetness of their teacher they may desire the more to change their old life...

2.   Moreover, let books or ornaments that have been carried off [from a desecrated synagogue] be in like manner sought for. And, if any have been openly taken away, we desire them also to be restored without any question. For, as there ought to be no license for them to do anything in their synagogues beyond what is decreed by law, so neither damage nor any cost ought to be brought upon them contrary to justice and equity.[20]

In 732, Charles Martel (686–741), a strong military leader employed by the Christian Frankish kings of the Merovingian dynasty, defeated the Muslim Umayyad Caliphate (circa 661–750) Army as it advanced northward to Poitiers, France. This defeat (in retrospect) was the crucial halting point in the dramatic Islamic advance into Europe.[21]

The Merovingian dynastic victory over the Muslim Umayyad Caliphate Army resulted in the acquisition by entrepreneurial Jews of many Muslim-controlled commerce supply lines, which linked the Far East and Gaul. The merchant Jews exported from Gaul "slaves, furs, and silk manufactures to Italy, Spain, and the Levant, and imported to Gaul spices, balsam, garum, dates, brocades, and precious metals. The crossroads of this luxury trade were located in the Meuse [River region in Northwestern France] and at Narbonne [in Southeastern France on the coast of the Mediterranean Sea]," said Esther Benbassa.[22]

In 752, the pro-Jewish Carolingian dynast Pepin the Short (circa 714–768, ruled 752–768), the son of Charles Martel, deposed the last Merovingian dynast. The son of Pepin the Short was Charlemagne (circa 742–814, ruled 768–814). Pepin the Short, Charlemagne, and other Carolingian dynasts nurtured economic relationships with Jewish merchants, particularly the Radanites (Rhadanites), who found markets for Frankish goods and imported foreign luxury goods into the Carolingian Frankish Kingdom. The Radanites' home base was probably in the Rhône Valley, according to historian Bernard S. Bachrach.[23] In 870, Persian postmaster and geographer Ibn Khordadbeh (circa 820–912) described the Radanites in *The Book of Roads and Kingdoms* as follows:

These merchants [Radanites] speak Arabic, Persian, Roman, the language of the Franks, Andalusians and Slavs. They journey from west to east, from east to west, partly on land, partly by sea. They transport from the west eunuchs, female and male slaves, silk, castor, marten and other furs, and swords. They take ship in the land of the Franks, on the Western Sea, and steer for Farama. There they load their goods on the backs of camels and go by land to Kolzum in five days' journey, over a distance of twenty-five parasangs. They embark in the East Sea and sail from Kozum to el-Jar and Jeddah; then they go to Sind, India, and China. On their return they carry back musk, aloes, camphor, cinnamon, and other products of the Eastern countries to Kolzum, and bring them to Farama, where they again embark on the Western Sea. Some make sail for Constantinople, to sell their goods to the Romans; others go to the palace of the King of the Franks [Charlemagne in Aachen] to place their goods.

Sometimes these Jewish merchants prefer to carry their goods for the land of the Franks in the Western Sea, making for Antioch [at the mouth of the Orontes River]: then they go by land to al-Jabia, where they arrive after three days' march. There they embark on the Euphrates for Baghdad, and then sail down the Tigris to al-Obolla. From al-Obolla they sail for Oman, Sind, Hind, and China. All this is connected one with another. These different journeys can also be made by land. The merchants that start from Spain to France go to Sous al-Akza, and then to Tangiers, whence they march to Karouan and the capital of Egypt. Thence they go to al-Ramla, visit Damascus, al-Kufa, Baghdad, and Basrah, cross Ahwaz, Fars, Kirman, Sind, Hind, and arrive at China. Sometimes they likewise take the route behind Rome, and, passing through the country of the Slavs, arrive at Khamlif, the capital of the Khazars. They embark on the Jorjan Sea, arrive at Balkh, betake themselves from there across the Oxus, and continue their journey toward the Yourts of the Toghozghor, and from there to China.[24]

Charlemagne employed Isaac the Jew as a royal diplomat to the Baghdad Court of the fifth and most famous Abbasid Caliph, Harun-al-Rashid (766–809). Caliph Harun-al-Rashid presided over the Arab Empire at its peak.

The Carolingian Frankish dynasts employed Jews for the settlement and garrisoning of frontier towns and for service in the military. During the Early Middle Ages in the Kingdom of the Franks, "the Jews carried on agriculture, trade, and commerce without restraint; they navigated the seas and rivers in their own ships," practiced medicine, bore the appellations that were common in the country, such as Armentarius, Gozolas, Priscus, or Siderius, and sometimes intermarried with Christians.[25]

Charlemagne was succeeded by Louis the Pious (778–840, ruled as King of the Franks 814–840), the only surviving son by his wife Hildegard (758–783). Charlemagne's grandsons fought a bitter civil war after the death of Louis the Pious. In 842, the Oaths of Strasbourg united the quarreling grandsons, Louis the German (died 876) and his half-brother, Charles the Bald (died 877). The Oaths of Strasbourg also united their respective Eastern and Western Frankish Kingdoms. In 962, Otto I (912–973), a descendant of Louis the German, became the first Holy Roman Emperor to rule the nascent Holy Roman Empire. In 993, the Strasbourg Episcopal See joined the Holy Roman Empire.

The European High Middle Ages, 1000–1300

At the beginning of the High Middle Ages, Jews living along the Rhine and Moselle Rivers called themselves Ashkenazim. The origin of the word Ashkenazim is the Hebrew word Ashkenaz. Ashkenaz was the son of Gomer, who himself was the grandson of Japheth and the great-grandson of Noah. Recall that Noah's three sons were Ham, the ancestor of the southern (Hamitic) peoples; Shem, the ancestor of the middle (Semitic) peoples; and Japheth, the ancestor of the northern peoples (Japhetic Eurasia), according to chapter ten in the Book of Genesis of the Hebrew Bible or Old Testament.[26]

The Ashkenazim believed that they were descended from Ashkenaz. The historical Ashkenazim are believed to represent a northern branch of Indo-Germanic tribes, who themselves probably were related to the Scythians and the Cimmerians.[27] In the 600s and 700s BC, the Cimmerians lived north of the Caucasus mountains and the Black Sea, according to Greek historian Herodotus (484–425 BC). Additional source materials from the Assyrians say that the Cimmerians lived near Urartu, an advanced civilization centered on Lake Van, now in Turkey.

Lake Van is about one hundred and ten miles southwest of Mount Ararat (maximum elevation about seventeen thousand feet above sea level).

The word Ashkenaz, in addition to referring to a branch of Noah's descendent families, meant Germany during the High Middle Ages. Ashkenaz included portions of present-day France and Germany along the course of the Rhine River and its tributaries. The Ashkenazi culture stretched from Prague in the east to Metz in the west, noted historian Jay R. Berkovitz.[28] Unifying elements of Ashkenazi culture were a "national language (Yiddish); religion (Judaism); textual tradition; material culture (architecture, dress, foodways, routes of trade and migration); systems of education, social welfare, and dispute adjudication; politics and ideology; national literature; and high and popular culture," said historians David Neal Miller and Neil G. Jacobs.[28] The Ashkenazim defined themselves as distinct both from the other emerging European peoples and cultures with which they co-existed and from other subgroups of Jews, such as the Sephardim.

Yiddish, the language of the Ashkenazim, is a fusion of German dialects with Hebrew, Aramaic, and Slavic languages, according to linguist Max Weinreich. Yiddish first developed around 1000 AD on the banks of the Rhine and Moselle Rivers in the area designated as Loter by the Ashkenazim who dwelled there.[3] The most important localities in Loter and its vicinity were Cologne, Mainz, Worms, Speyer, Metz, and Regensburg (Ratisbon).

Around 1000, Ashkenazim increasingly moved to the safer, walled Rhenish cities, such as Mainz and Worms, where they built houses and businesses in their own quarter of the city called the Jewish ghetto. For example, the Jewish quarter of medieval Worms was in the southeast corner of the city.[29] In Mainz, Talmudist scholar Gershom ben Judah (circa 960–1028) founded a yeshiva, or Talmudic school, which attracted Ashkenazi students from throughout Ashkenaz (from Metz to Prague).

Medieval Jews who lived in the walled cities along the Rhine River competed economically with the cities' Christian populations, which led to problems. In 1012, hostilities erupted between Christians and Jews in the City of Mainz, which resulted in expulsion of the Ashkenazim. This expulsion occurred during the rule of Henry II (972–1024), then King of Germany (ruled 1002–1024) and later Holy Roman Emperor (ruled 1014–1024). In 1012, the Archbishop of Mainz was Erkanbald (ruled 1011–1021).

The medieval Rhenish Jews sometimes became involved in political conflicts, such as the Investiture Controversy between the Popes and the Holy Roman Emperors during the eleventh and twelfth centuries. For example, in 1073, the Ashkenazim of Worms offered refuge to the twenty-three-year-old future Holy Roman Emperor Henry IV (1050–1106, ruled 1084–1105). On January 18, 1074, Henry IV rewarded the Jews and other citizens of the City of Worms for their fidelity to him by exempting them from customs duties in the royal-customs ports of Frankfurt, Boppard, Dortmund, and Goslar.[29]

In 1084, Rüdiger Huzmann, Bishop of Speyer (ruled 1073–1090), issued a charter that invited Jews expelled from the City of Mainz to move to the City of Speyer, stating that their presence would greatly enhance the reputation of his city. Bishop Rüdiger Huzmann settled the Jews in a walled area next to the cathedral for their protection and allowed them to employ Christian servants, own fields and vineyards, and carry weapons.

In 1090, Holy Roman Emperor Henry IV affirmed Bishop Rüdiger Huzmann's pro-Jewish charter. In the City of Worms, Holy Roman Emperor Henry IV permitted Jews to "own houses, gardens, and above all vineyards, to employ Christians in their homes and at work, and to trade in wine, dye, and medicine. The granting of these rights established a lasting alliance between the Jews and [Holy Roman Emperor Henry IV] that became a salient feature of local memory in Worms." Holy Roman Emperor Henry IV said that he based his pro-Jewish charter on ones issued by Frankish King Louis the Pious, but he went "beyond these traditions and gave the Jews not only comprehensive protection but also jurisdiction over internal disputes."[29]

For example, Holy Roman Emperor Henry IV granted the

Ashkenazim the privileges of free commerce and exemption from taxation and designated them as "subjects of his treasury." He placed them under his immediate protection, so that neither royal nor episcopal functionaries could exercise any jurisdiction over them. Their only authority was the so-called Bishop of the Jews, who they themselves appointed with approval from Holy Roman Emperor Henry IV. Note here that the state had not enfranchised the Jews as citizens of the Holy Roman Empire. On April 6, 1157 and again in 1236, Holy Roman Emperors Frederick I Barbarossa (1122–1190, ruled 1155–1190) and Frederick II (1194–1250, ruled 1220–1250), respectively, renewed the pro-Jewish privileges, including a measure of community autonomy, first decreed by Holy Roman Emperor Henry IV.[29]

On November 27, 1095, the last day of a ten-day synod of ecclesiastics and laymen at the Second Council of Clermont in France (the first Council of Clermont was in 535 AD), Pope Urban II (circa 1035–1099; ruled 1088–1099) preached the First Crusade (1096–1099) against the rampaging Seljuq Turks. The Seljuq Turks had become fully Muslim in the tenth century AD. Pope Urban II called for European Christians to attack the Muslim Seljuq Turks because the latter had encroached on Palestine. However, the Muslim Seljuq Turks had taken Palestine *not* from Christians, but from Arab Muslims in 1073, twenty-two years earlier. The Arab Muslims themselves had owned Palestine for more than four hundred years when the Muslim Seljuk Turks arrived on the scene.

The real reason that Pope Urban II preached the First Crusade was the request for help voiced by Byzantine Emperor Alexios I Komnenos (1056–1118, ruled 1081–1118). The Byzantine Emperor and the Pope did not usually get along. However, in 1090 and again in 1095 during the Council of Piacenza, the Byzantine Emperor had taken conciliatory measures toward the Pope. The Muslim Seljuq Turks had already overrun most of Asia Minor (present-day Turkey) and were now threatening Constantinople and the Balkans. Byzantine Emperor Komnenos needed military help to oppose the advance of the Seljuq Turks.

The Ashkenazim of the Rhine River Valley, rather than the Muslims of Southwest Asia, became the first victims of the Christian Crusaders raised by Pope Urban II. Peter the Hermit (died 1115), a priest of Amiens (France), led one of the first Crusader Armies from France. In 1096, on the first day of Passover, he and his fellow Christian soldiers arrived in the bustling and prosperous City of Trier (Treves) on the Moselle River in the Palatinate, north of Saarland.[29] Historical sources vary on what happened after Peter the Hermit and his Crusader Army reached Trier.

One source claimed that the Christian Crusaders attempted to force baptism on the Ashkenazim of Trier. When the Ashkenazim refused to submit to baptism, the Christian Crusaders destroyed the former's Torah scrolls. The Ashkenazim of Trier "undertook penitence and charity, and fasted six weeks from day to day [during the daytime hours], from Passover to Shavuot." Trier's Archbishop Egelbert (ruled 1079–1101), who was a friend of Holy Roman Emperor Henry IV and therefore a friend of the Ashkenazim, nevertheless supposedly grew frustrated with what he perceived as their intransigence in refusing baptism. Acts of Jewish martyrdom (i.e., Jewish suicides) occurred. Christian Crusaders apparently murdered two Jews who urinated on a crucifix presented to them in front of the gate to Bishop Egelbert's palace, according to one historian.[30]

A second source claimed that in 1096, the burghers of the City of Trier, not the Christian Crusaders, persecuted the Trier Jews as follows:

> On April 10, 1096, the first day of Passover, Peter the Hermit appeared before the gates of Trier armed with a letter from the Jewish communities of France to their co-religionists in Germany, requesting that they provide provisions for Peter and his Crusaders for their expedition to the Holy Land. The Jewish community responded to the letter, and Peter and his followers went on their way. Sometime later, the burghers of the city rose against the Jews; they discovered the community's Torah scrolls, which had been placed in a

building for safekeeping, and desecrated them. In panic the Jews fled to the palace of Archbishop Egelbert; somehow they rescued their desecrated [Torah] scrolls and took them along. [Archbishop Egelbert] did his best to protect them, and the Jews hoped to remain under his protection until the imminent return of [Holy Roman] Emperor Henry IV to Germany. A number of Jews were murdered and others committed suicide; [Archbishop Egelbert] and his retinue were themselves attacked for shielding the Jews. Under increasing pressure from a mob outside the palace, the archbishop prevailed upon the remaining Jews to convert, including their leader, Rabbi Micah, who was converted by [Archbishop Egelbert] himself. One year later, however, with the return of [Holy Roman] Emperor Henry IV to Germany, all of them were permitted to return to Judaism.[30]

German Count Emicho and his group of Christian Crusaders from Leiningen (a city owned by Count Emicho's family in the Palatinate) committed the worst massacres of Ashkenazim in Rhenish cities during the First Crusade, as noted by historian Shlomo Eidelberg:

An attack at Speyer resulted in the slaying of twelve Jews who refused to convert to Christianity; the rest were saved by the local bishop. In mid-May [1096], [Count] Emicho's men attacked the Jewish community at Worms, where they slaughtered five hundred Jews who were under the bishop's special protection. Emicho's arrival in Mainz was greeted by anti-Jewish riots within the barred gates of the city. In the course of these outbursts a Christian was killed, thus further enraging the populace and provoking defiance of Ruthard, Archbishop of Mainz. Disobeying [Archbishop Ruthard's] orders, Emicho's allies within the city opened the gates to a massive attack in which about one thousand Jews were slain.[31]

Solomon bar Samson, the major historian of the First Crusade, documented the slaughter of Jews in the City of Mainz by Christian Crusaders between May 25 and May 29, 1096 as follows:

It was on the third of Siwan...at noon [Tuesday, May 27, 1096], that Emico [*sic*] the wicked, the enemy of the Jews, came up with his whole army against the [Mainz] city gate, and the citizens opened it up for him. Then the enemies of the Lord [the Christian Crusaders] said to each other, "Look! They [residents of Mainz] have opened up the gate for us. Now let us avenge the blood of 'the hanged one' [Jesus]." The children of the holy covenant [Jews] who were there, martyrs who feared the Most High, although they saw the great multitude, as numerous as the sand on the shore of the sea, still clung to their Creator. Then young and old [Jews] donned their armor and girded on their weapons, and at their head was Rabbi Kalonymus ben Meshullam, the chief of the community. Yet because of the many troubles and the fasts which they had observed, they had no strength to stand up against the enemy. [When the Mainz Ashkenazim heard about the approaching mobs, they fasted, as in Trier, believing that this behavior had the power to mitigate impending evils.] Then came the gangs and bands, sweeping through like a flood, until [the City of Mainz] was filled from end to end.

The foe Emico proclaimed in the hearing of the community that the enemy [Jews] be driven from the city and be put to flight. Panic was great in the town. Each Jew in the inner court of the bishop girded on his weapons, and all moved towards the palace gate to fight the Crusaders and the citizens. They fought each other up to the very gate, but the sins of the Jews brought it about that the enemy overcame them and took the gate. [The enemy then moved to the inner courtyard where many Jews had taken refuge.] As soon as the enemy came into the courtyard, they found some of the very pious there with our brilliant master, Isaac ben Moses. He stretched out his neck, and his head they cut off first. [To avoid slaughter by the enemy,] [t]he women there girded their loins with strength and slew their sons and their daughters and then themselves. Many men, too, plucked up courage and killed their wives, their sons, their infants.[32]

After Mainz, Emicho's Crusaders headed to the City of Cologne to massacre more Jews. However, Christian residents of Cologne hid most of the Jews, and the Christian Crusaders simply burned the synagogue and moved on. Emicho headed east for Jerusalem, but some of his Christian Army traveled upstream in the Moselle River Valley to purge more Jews. In the City of Metz, the Christian Crusaders killed twenty-two Jews and then moved to Neuss, Wevelinghofen, Eller, and Xanten, where they murdered other Jews before returning to their homes in the Palatinate or catching up with Christian Crusader Armies.[32]

Why did Christian Crusaders attack the Ashkenazim during the First Crusade? Historian Jeremy Cohen suggested that Judaism, like Islam, threatened Christian supremacy:

The First Crusade, in its confrontation with the Muslim world, induced many Christians to associate Jews and Muslims, projecting the characteristics of one group onto the other and incorporating both groups into a larger genus of infidels who, by their existence and in their beliefs, challenged the supremacy of Christianity. No one, to be sure, posited complete equivalence between Jew and Muslim...Nonetheless, parallels between the two groups in matters of law and theology certainly made sense, and the tendency to classify them together proved irreversible.[33]

On December 1, 1145, following the fall to the Turks of the County of Edessa, the first Crusader state established in what is today Turkey,

Pope Eugene III (died 1153, ruled 1145–1153) asked French King Louis VII (1120–1180, ruled 1131–1180) of the Capetian dynasty to organize and lead a Second Crusade. King Louis VII was unable to persuade his vassals to accompany him on a Second Crusade, so he requested the assistance of French Cistercian Abbot Bernard of Clairvaux (1090–1153). Bernard of Clairvaux was the most powerful monk in Western Christendom.[34] Pope Eugene III himself was a Cistercian monk, who had joined the Cistercian order in 1138 under the influence of Bernard of Clairvaux. Pope Eugene III was the first Cistercian monk to become a Pope.

In March 1146, Abbot Bernard of Clairvaux drummed up support for the Second Crusade during a speech in Vézelay, France. He then travelled to Burgundy, Lorraine, and Flanders to persuade other French subjects to join King Louis VII on the Second Crusade.

During Abbot Bernard's travels in the Rhine River Valley, he learned from the Cologne and Mainz Archbishops that a certain Cistercian monk named Radulf was preaching anti-Jewish sentiments to induce rioting against the Ashkenazim. "Radulf's demotic anti-Semitism was expressed in a simple argument," said historian Christopher Tyerman. He continued:

> In summoning men to take the cross to fight the Muslims abroad, [Radulf] drew the same parallel that had been drawn in 1096 [the First Crusade], as a Jewish eyewitness recalled: "Avenge the crucified one [Jesus] upon his enemies [the Jews] who stand before you; then go to war against the Muslims," or, as Otto of Freising put it: "the Jews whose homes were scattered throughout the [Rhineland] cities and towns should be slain as foes of the Christian religion."[35]

Abbot Bernard located, recalled, and condemned Radulf for causing the spilling of Jewish blood. Abbot Bernard referenced Psalm 59:11 and Augustine's *The City of God* to explain to the crowds that God obliged Christians to preserve, not kill, Jews in their midst.[35] Abbot Bernard's sermons had their intended effect. A grateful rabbi thanked Abbot Bernard for subduing the mobs, as follows:

> Radulf…, the priest of idolatry, arose against the nation of God [the Jews] to destroy, slay, and annihilate them just as wicked Haman had attempted to do. [Haman is the main antagonist in the Book of Esther in the Hebrew Bible; Queen Esther, herself a Jewess, foiled Haman's plot to kill all the Jews in Persia.] [Radulf] set forth from France and traveled across the entire land of Germany…to seek out and contaminate the Christians with the horizontal-vertical sign [i.e., a cross]… Wherever he went, he spoke evil of the Jews of the land and incited the snake and the dogs against us…The lord heard our outcry, and he turned to us and had pity upon us. In his great mercy and grace, he sent a decent priest, one honored and respected by all the clergy in France, named Abbot Bernard, of Clairvaux in France, to deal with this evil person [Radulf]. Bernard…said to them: "It is good to go against the Ishmaelites [Muslims]. But whosoever touches a [Jew] to take his life is like one who harms Jesus himself […] for in the book of Psalms it is written of them, 'Slay them not, lest my people forget.'" All the Gentiles regarded this priest as one of their saints…When our enemies heard his words, many of them ceased plotting to kill us…Were it not for the mercy of our creator in sending the aforementioned abbot and his later epistles, no remnant or vestige would have remained of Israel. Blessed by the redeemer and savior, blessed be his name.[35]

Between 1145 and 1149, the years of the Second Crusade, Ashkenazi casualties abated in part because of Abbot Bernard's timely words and actions. However, during this time, two anti-Jewish myths forcefully emerged—the charge of ritual murder ("blood libel") and the charge of desecrating the Host. The first myth says that Jews slay a Christian child to obtain its blood to make matzos (unleavened bread) for

Passover. The charge against followers of a minority religion of using human flesh and blood for ritual purposes goes far back in history, noted historian Maurice Friedberg. For example, the Christian writer Tertullian (circa 160–circa 225) of Carthage (North Africa) noted, "We [Christians] are said to be the most criminal of men, on the score of our sacramental baby-killing, and the baby-eating that goes with it." Tertullian cited the "glory" of a pagan Roman magistrate "who had brought to light some Christian who had eaten up to date a hundred babies."[36]

The second myth states that Jews seek to desecrate the Eucharist wafer, or Host, which Christians believe is the Body of Jesus. The supposed point of Jews' desecration of the Host is to torment and destroy the Body of Jesus a second time; the first time was during the crucifixion at Golgotha. Many variations of the two myths exist.

Around 1150, anti-Jewish Benedictine Abbot Peter the Venerable (circa 1092–1156) of the Abbey of Cluny in France first accused the Ashkenazim of substituting the Talmud for the Torah and for blaspheming against Christianity in the Talmud.[36] Abbot Peter launched the anti-Talmud movement in Europe, which reached its apogee in the following century.

Despite the growing climate of anti-Judaism in medieval Europe, many Ashkenazim prospered, said Rabbi Benjamin of Tudela, who made his fantastic journey from Spain to China and back again between 1160 and 1173. An excerpt from Rabbi Tudela's report of his trip follows below.

* * * * * * * *

Rabbi Tudela on the Ashkenazim, circa 1170

It is twenty days' journey [from Tudela] to Verdun, which is the commencement of Alamannia [Germany], a land of mountains and hills. All the [Ashkenazi] congregations of Alamannia are situated on the great River Rhine, from the City of Cologne, which is the principal town of the [Holy Roman] Empire, to the City of Regensburg, a distance of fifteen days' journey at the other extremity of Alamannia, otherwise called Ashkenaz. And the following are the cities in the land of Alamannia which have Hebrew congregations: Metz, Treves [Trier] on the River Moselle, Coblenz, Andernach, Bonn, Cologne, Bingen, Munster, Worms.

All Israel is dispersed in every land, and he who does not further the gathering of Israel will not meet with happiness nor live with Israel. When the Lord will remember us in our exile, and raise the horn of his anointed, then everyone will say, "I will lead the Jews and I will gather them." As for the towns which have been mentioned, they contain scholars and communities that love their brethren, and speak peace to those that are near and afar, and when a wayfarer comes they rejoice, and make a feast for him, and say, "Rejoice, brethren, for the help of the Lord comes in the twinkling of an eye." If we were not afraid that the appointed time has not yet arrived nor been reached, we would have gathered together, but we dare not do so until the time for song has arrived, and the voice of the turtle-dove (is heard in the land), when the messengers will come and say continually, "The Lord be exalted." Meanwhile they send missives one to the other, saying, "Be ye strong in the law of Moses, and do ye mourners for Zion and ye mourners for Jerusalem entreat the Lord, and may the supplication of those that wear the garments of mourning be received through their merits."

In addition to the several cities which we have mentioned there are besides Strassburg [sic], Wurzburg, Mantern, Bamberg, Freising, and Regensburg at the extremity of the Empire. In these cities there are many Israelites, wise men and rich…The kingdom of France, which is Zarfath, extends from the town of Auxerre unto Paris, the great city—a journey of six days. The city belongs to King Louis [Louis VII]. It is situated on the River Seine. Scholars are there, unequalled in the whole world, who study the Law day and night. They are charitable and hospitable to all travelers, and are as brothers and friends unto all their brethren the Jews. May God, the Blessed One, have mercy upon us and upon them![37]

* * * * * * * * *

In 1179, fourteen-year-old Philip II Augustus (1165–1223, ruled 1180–1223) succeeded King Louis VII, who was senile. Philip II Augustus was the last King of the Franks (ruled 1180–1190) and the first King of France (ruled 1190–1221). In 1182, King Philip II Augustus replenished his flagging treasury by stripping the Jews of their assets and expelling them from Paris and other lands held by the Crown. The income produced by the royal manors had been unable to pay for the expenditures made by the Crown.

Monk Rigord described the reaction of King Philip II Augustus to the Ashkenazim living in his royal demesne:

> [The Ashkenazim] grew so rich that they claimed as their own almost half of the whole city [Paris], and had Christians in their houses as menservants and maidservants, who were open backsliders from the faith of Jesus Christ, and *judaized* [emphasis in original] with the Jews. And this was contrary to the decree of God and the law of the Church. And whereas the Lord had said by the mouth of Moses in Deuteronomy (23:20–21), "Thou shalt not lend upon usury to thy brother," but "to a stranger," the Jews in their wickedness understood by "stranger" every Christian, and they took from the Christians their money at usury. And so heavily burdened in this [v]ise were citizens and soldiers and peasants in the suburbs, and in the various towns and villages that many of them were constrained to part with their possessions. Others were bound under oath in houses of the Jews in Paris, held as if captives in

prison. The most Christian King Philip heard of these things, and compassion was stirred within him.[38-39]

In 1198, King Philip II Augustus readmitted the Jews to his lands, but cleverly regulated their banking business to divert profits to the royal treasury through a variety of taxes and duties.[38]

In 1199, Pope Innocent III (1160/61–1216, ruled 1198–1216) issued a papal bull titled "Constitution for the Jews" in response to a plea from the Jews for protection from their adversaries, which now included King Philip II Augustus. Pope Innocent III cited Psalm 59 and Augustine's *The City of God* as the reasons why Christians should tolerate Jews in their midst.

* * * * * * * * *

Constitution for the Jews, 1199
by Pope Innocent III

Although in many ways the disbelief of the Jews must be reproved, since nevertheless through them our own faith is truly proved, they must not be oppressed grievously by the faithful as the prophet says: "Do not slay them, lest these be forgetful of Thy Law," [Psalm 59] as if he were saying more openly: "Do not wipe out the Jews completely, lest perhaps Christians might be able to forget Thy Law, which the former, although not understanding it, present in their books to those who do understand it."

Just as, therefore, there ought not to be license for the Jews to presume to go beyond what is permitted them by law in their synagogues, so in those which have been conceded to them, they ought to suffer no prejudice. These men, therefore, since they wish rather to go on in their own hardness than to know the revelations of the prophets and the mysteries of the Law, and to come to a knowledge of the Christian faith, still, since they beseech the help of Our defense, We, out of the meekness proper to Christian piety, and keeping in the footprints of Our predecessors of happy memory, the Roman Pontiffs Calixtus [II; in 1120, he issued the first papal bull intended to protect Jews who suffered during the First Crusade], Eugene, Alexander [III], Clement, and Celestine [III, ruled 1191–1198], admit their petition, and We grant them the buckler of Our protection.

For we make the law that no Christian compel them, unwilling or refusing, by violence to come to baptism. But if any one of them should spontaneously, and for the sake of faith, fly to the Christians, once his choice has become evident, let him be made a Christian without any calumny. Indeed, he is not considered to possess the true faith of Christianity who is recognized to have come to Christian baptism, not spontaneously, but unwillingly.

Too, no Christian ought to presume, apart from the juridical sentence of the territorial power, wickedly to injure their persons, or with violence to take away their property, or to change the good customs which they have had until now in whatever region they inhabit.

Besides, in the celebration of their own festivals, no one ought to disturb them in any way, with clubs or stones, nor ought any one try to require from them or to extort from them services they do not owe, except for those they have been accustomed from times past to perform.

In addition to these, We decree, blocking the wickedness and avarice of evil men, that no one ought to dare to mutilate or diminish a Jewish cemetery, nor, in order to get money, to exhume bodies once they have been buried.

If anyone, however shall attempt, the tenor of this decree once known, to go against it—may this be far from happening!—let him be punished by the vengeance of excommunication, unless he correct his presumption by making equivalent satisfaction.

We desire, however, that only those be fortified by the guard of this protection who shall have presumed no plotting for the subversion of the Christian faith.

Given at the Lateran, by the hand of Raynaldus, Archbishop of Acerenza, acting for the Chancellor, on the 17th day before the Kalends of October, in the second indiction, and the 1199th year of the Incarnation of the Lord, and in the second year of the pontificate of the Lord Pope, Innocent III.[40]

* * * * * * * * *

During the reign of French King Philip II Augustus, some Jews moved to Alsace, which belonged to a host of princes of the Holy Roman Empire. From the late 1100s to the early 1300s, a Jewish community flourished in Strasbourg on Rue des Juifs (Street of the Jews), which was a short segment of the old Roman east-west road that ran through the city. The Jews established a Jewish cemetery outside the city; the date of the oldest known epitaph is 1213.[41]

Around 1201, the burghers of Strasbourg negotiated a treaty with the allies of Philip of Swabia (1177–1208), King of Germany and a rival of Holy Roman Emperor Otto IV (1175–1218, ruled 1208–1218). Through Philip of Swabia, the burghers of Strasbourg established a City Council made up of twelve members (consiliarii et rectores) and a city seal. King Philip of Swabia had led a devastating siege on Strasbourg in the previous years, laying the city to waste, because Strasbourg Bishop Konrad II von Huhnenburg (1190–1202) supported Holy Roman Emperor Otto IV, not Philip of Swabia, King of Germany. The new twelve-member Strasbourg City Council with its new city seal in hand signified that Strasbourg was now a Free City of the Holy Roman Empire.[42]

In the early thirteenth century, allegorical sculptures of Ecclesia, representing the Church and Christianity, and Synagoga, representing the Synagogue and Judaism, began to show up on the exterior of churches. For example, around 1220, pairs of statues were set into the exterior stone of the Chartres Cathedral in Chartres (about fifty miles southwest of Paris) and the Cathedral of Notre Dame of Paris. Around 1250, similar twin statues were set into the exterior stone of Strasbourg Cathedral on either side of the double-doored, double-arched south transept portal. Ecclesia on the left side of the portal stands erect in a beautiful draped gown, holding in her right hand a staff topped with a large cross and in her left hand a chalice holding the blood of the slain Jesus. Sad Synagoga on the right side of the portal stands with downcast head and blindfolded eyes preventing her from seeing the truth of the New Testament. In the crook of her right arm is a thrice-broken staff, representing the Hebrew Bible. The Tablets of Law are slipping out of the fingers of her left hand. The material of her dress is thin and her head is unadorned. The statues depict the triumph of the Church over the Synagogue and the superiority of Christianity over Judaism.[42] The twin statues adorned many cathedrals in France and Germany; their purpose was to influence the attitudes and behavior of Christians and Jews toward one another.

In 1228, the anti-Talmud movement earlier begun by Benedictine Abbot Peter the Venerable took a toxic turn when Nicholas Donin (dates of life unknown), a native of New Rochelle, France, denounced the Jews to troops volunteering for the Sixth Crusade (1228–1229) in Anjou, Poitou, and Aquitaine, France. Three years earlier, in 1225, Rabbi Yechiel of Paris (died 1286), a Talmudic scholar and head of the Talmudic School of Paris, excommunicated Nicholas Donin from the Jewish community for attempting to de-legitimize the Talmud. Nicholas Donin sought revenge against the Jews by agitating among the Christian Crusaders. "The volunteers [for the Crusade] were in an ugly mood, and needed little pretext to renew the pogroms that had accompanied every Crusade for more than a century," noted historian Allan Temko. "Homes and synagogues were burned, Torahs were torn to pieces. Then came a demand for mass conversion. Some five hundred Jews submitted and were baptized. Three thousand others perished, some in indescribable pain. The Crusaders had hit upon the idea of trampling men, women, and children with their war horses."[39]

Jews appealed for help from Pope Gregory IX (circa 1145–1241, ruled 1227–1241), who ordered French King Louis IX (Saint Louis, 1214–1270, ruled 1226–1270) and French prelates to protect the Jews. However, by the time Pope Gregory IX acted, the lynching mood had subsided. Many Jewish communities across the French interior lay in ruins.

Nicholas Donin continued his destructive tirade against the Jews. In 1236, he converted to Christianity and became a tonsured monk with the Franciscan mendicant order in Paris.[39,44–45] In 1238, Friar Donin went to Rome specifically to meet with Pope Gregory IX to present accusations against the Talmud and recommend its eradication as a mass of blasphemies. "He added that the Talmud alone kept the Jews in error, that the rabbis valued it more highly than the [Hebrew] Bible, and that without it the Jews would have been converted [to Christianity] long in the past. The last point in itself was enough to convince Gregory that an investigation, at least, was necessary." Allan Temko continued:

> Nevertheless, the Pope was taken totally by surprise. In countless previous attacks on the Jews, the Talmud had never before been called into question. Until [Friar] Donin's denunciation, [the Jews] had been considered only as defenders of the Old Testament, not as blasphemers of the New. What then, after centuries of Christian indifference to the Talmud, had given Donin's charges their special effectivness?[39]

Alan Temko answered:

> At the center of the situation lay the classic source of bigotry: ignorance. Not one Gentile in ten thousand had the faintest idea of the contents of the Talmud; not one in a million had an understanding of its ambiguities. An unprincipled apostate like [Friar Nicholas] Donin could easily take passages from context, and twist their meanings. But beyond ignorance of the Talmud, Christians had a distorted conception of the Jews

themselves. Rabble-rousers everywhere, like [French Priest] Foulque de Neuilly [died 1201], the organizer of the Fourth Crusade, had created a popular image of a monster. The Jew was vilified ingeniously. He was charged with ritual murder, with subterranean orgies of blood drinking, with desecration of scared objects that the clergy had left in his pawn. He was simultaneously reproached for poverty and for the practice of usury, both of which Christians had forced upon him. He was accused of being ugly, of being small in stature…Underlying all these emotional sources of Christian resentment was a hard new code of Church law. The Lateran Council of 1215 had gone further than the oppressive Council of 1179, and formulated a complete pariah status for the Jew. It initiated the marked costume and other crude indignities, which were to torment the Jew until the French Revolution.[39]

In 1236, Holy Roman Emperor Frederick II, the descendant of the pro-Jewish Holy Roman Emperor Henry IV, renewed the promise to protect Jews, but in return for an annual payment. The Strasbourg Ashkenazim paid two hundred marks annually to the imperial treasury; however, Holy Roman Emperor Frederick II later reduced this exorbitant sum to sixty marks annually.[43]

On June 9, 1239, Pope Gregory IX issued an encyclical that furthered the agenda of Nicholas Donin against the Jews. He gave to Nicholas Donin a letter to give to William of Auvergne, Bishop of Paris (1180/90–1249, ruled 1228–1249). The Pope's letter contained instructions that Bishop William was in turn to transmit to the Kings and Archbishops of France, England, Spain, and Portugal. Historian Saadia Eisenberg continued:

The papal directive commanded that all the books of the Jews were to be confiscated on the first Sabbath of Lent in the following year (March 3, 1240) while Jews attended their synagogue services, and then be transferred to the mendicant friars for safekeeping. On June 20, [1240], [Pope Gregory IX] instructed [Bishop] William and the Dominican and Franciscan priors to examine the books. Any texts containing doctrinal error were to be burned.[45]

Pope Gregory IX directed his plan to examine and likely burn Jewish books, not from Rome, but from the Episcopal Palace of Paris. Pope Gregory IX could count on William of Auvergne to conduct the investigation of the Talmud with thoroughness and energy. "If it ended in a fiasco, [Bishop William] would absorb any embarrassment rather than [Pope Gregory IX], who was publicly committed to protect Jewish freedom of religion. The [Paris] Bishop was also in an excellent position to influence King Louis [IX], whose palace stood a few hundred yards from the [Notre Dame de Paris] cathedral, at the opposite end of the Île de la Cité."[39]

King Louis IX was the only monarch to comply with this extraordinary papal order that invoked the entire judicial apparatus of church and state against the Jews in France. In a symbolic gesture, King Louis IX gave the Ashkenazim the opportunity to defend their Talmud and themselves in a bizarre public forum chaired by his elderly mother, Queen Blanche of Castille (1188–1252). Queen Blanche had acted as Regent twice during the reign of her son.

On June 25–26, 1240, Rabbi Yehiel of Paris and Friar Nicholas Donin confronted one another in a public forum in front of Queen Blanche and her ladies-in-waiting. Queen Blanche had denied the request of Rabbi Yechiel, who earlier had excommunicated Nicholas Donin, to move the "inquest" to Rome. After the hearing, Queen Blanche ruled that the Talmud was indeed heretical. The ad hoc court ordered the burning of all confiscated Talmuds. In 1242, thousands of Talmuds taken from Jewish homes, synagogues, and yeshivas across France burned on a pyre in Paris, as thousands of onlookers gawked at the fiery scene.[45] Saadia Eisenberg wrote:

The loss of books and resulting disruption of study among Jews contributed to the decline of the Jewish [Talmudic] schools in Northern France. Equally demoralizing for northern French Jewry was the vision of the Talmud, a symbol of Jewish history, accomplishment, tradition, values, and religion, going up in flames. From a long-range point of view, Jews in Christian lands were now put in the position of having to respond to challenges to Talmudic law, ideology, and literature proffered by antagonistic Christians.[45]

On May 15, 1248 in Paris, Papal Legate Odo of Tusculum again attacked the Talmud, decrying it for "its innumerable errors, abuses, blasphemies, and nefarious attacks on Christianity…Within a generation, these attacks on the Talmud had aroused increasing antipathy and intolerance for the Jews themselves," declared historian Irven M. Resnick. What were the alleged errors in the Talmud identified by thirteenth-century Christian elites?

Friar Nicholas Donin offered five categories of errors in the Talmud:

1. The exaggerated importance the Talmud had taken among the Jews; that it was more highly regarded than the Hebrew Bible.
2. Blasphemies against Jesus Christ.
3. Blasphemies against God the Father and against morality.
4. Blasphemies against Christians. The Talmud allegedly prescribes that the "best of the goyim" should be put to death.
5. Errors, Stupidities, Absurdities contained in the Talmud.[39]

Five specific examples of Talmud errors follow. First, a certain passage in the Talmud allegedly called Jesus Christ "that man…perpetually burning in boiling excrement." Saadia Eisenberg explained:

The implication of Jesus suffering in boiling excrement is that this is his ultimate end after being consumed by the faithful in Eucharistic form [i.e., the wafer, the Host]. After consuming the Host, the wafer travels through the body, eventually becoming excrement and being disposed of as waste…The twelfth century [was already witnessing] an underlying crisis of faith in the doctrine of transubstantiation. That a Jew should follow the same line of questioning resulting in a mockery of a Christian mystery was unconscionable.[46]

A second example of an error, according to Nicholas Donin, was that the Talmud allegedly called Mary, the mother of Jesus, an adulterer. This accusation was particularly damaging in the mid-thirteenth century when the Cult of Mary was popular. A third example was the Talmud's alleged partiality towards Jews in cases of criminal law, i.e., a Jew who murdered a "goy" was exempt from liability; however, if a Jew murdered another Jew, he was liable. A fourth example was the Talmud's alleged partiality against Christians in monetary practices: "one may steal, rob, or trick a 'goy' [out of his money]." A fifth example was the Talmud's alleged exhortation to Jews not to do business with Christians during Christian holiday seasons lest the Jew cause the Christian 'to go and thank his idolatry.'"[46]

The anti-Talmud movement affected the intellectual life of the once-flourishing Ashkenazi Talmudic community in France. "Medieval European Jews recognized and accepted that they were living as variably-welcome guests in a 'land that was not theirs' (Genesis 15:13), to which they claimed no rights of belong, nor an ultimate future," noted Saadia Eisenberg.[45]

Ashkenazi leaders repeatedly appealed to the papacy about the disparagement of the Talmud by Christian elites, explaining that without the Talmud, Jews could not properly understand or fulfill the precepts of the Hebrew Bible. Indeed, in 1240, Rabbi Yechiel defended the Talmud as a necessary means for explaining the Hebrew Bible. He cited numerous cases where the Bible contradicted itself, e.g., the

Bible says, "For I spoke to you from the heavens," while another verse states, "God descended upon Mount Sinai." Which was true? Did God speak to Moses from the sky or did God descend upon Mount Sinai to speak with Moses? "Both Christian and Jewish Bible scholars, then, could benefit from post-biblical literature to explain and resolve these contradictions." Rabbi Yechiel added that the divine nature of the Talmud was a core Jewish belief.

> [Rabbi Yechiel] made a case for the universal need for organization, commentary, and limits beyond those set by the biblical text. For [the Talmud] is a commentary to the Pentateuch and an explanation of the commandments…and if not for the Talmud a person would not be able to study a single commandment…the commandment of the Sabbath is written in five different places in Scripture, here a bit and there a bit. Before one studies one of the verses he will forget the next, and this [is the case for] many commandments. But through the Talmud commentary [the commandments] cling together and it is easy to study them.[47]

Christians who learned about the alleged inflammatory content of the Talmud soon viewed Jews as hostile and intransigent enemies of the Christian faith. Some Christians believed that Jews were "so venomous" that they would "take every opportunity to commit murder on unsuspecting and defenseless Christians, particularly young Christian boys [i.e., the ritual murder myth]."[47-48]

How did devout Ashkenazim respond to the Christian attack on the Talmud? Jewish morale declined and apostasy (conversion to Christianity) increased. Saadia Eisenberg explained:

> A stable and prosperous Christian society coupled with increasingly frequent anti-Jewish measures—heightened missionary activities, burgher violence, and expulsions—led to a decline in Jewish morale. Perhaps suggestive of a decline

in morale, by the latter half of the thirteenth century, Jewish conversion to Christianity seems to have increased…Numerous scholars have studied the challenges of survival confronting Jewish communities in medieval Ashkenaz. Often these studies examine voluntary martyrdom, usually highlighting the scenario of forced conversion on pain of death, ignoring or according only minimal attention to issues of doubt, skepticism, or the convert from conviction. Jews who accepted conversion at sword-point, in terror for their lives, posed a serious challenge to Jewish morale. Moreover, not all Jews converted under duress, and it was a particularly terrible blow to the Jewish community when a combination of Christian argument and Jewish misery convinced educated young men to reject their faith.[49]

Even as many ecclesiastics were denigrating the Jews and their Talmud, the economic life of Europe, in which Jews were essential participants, continued apace. In 1254, authorities in the Cities of Strasbourg, Mainz, Cologne, Worms, Speyer, Strasbourg, and Basel founded the Confederation of the Cities of the Rhine in part to stymie German barons who built castles along the Rhine River to levy tolls on watercraft floating by. The Rhine River between Mainz and Bonn had the greatest concentration of castles to collect tolls present in any river valley in the Holy Roman Empire. Thirty structures existed to collect tolls between Mainz and Cologne. In 1272, Rudolf I, King of the Romans (1218–1291, ruled 1273–1291), finally crushed the power of the toll-charging barons by destroying the castles of Rheinstein, Reichsenstein, Sooneck, and Rheineck.[50]

In 1255, the Confederation of the Cities of the Rhine standardized a legal interest rate for loans at thirteen and one-third percent per annum.[43,50] Although the interest rate of thirteen and one-third percent per annum was high, creditors advanced most of the loans with the expectation that the money was lent for the short term. Both Christian and Jewish creditors were supposed to adhere to these interest rates.

The Catholic Church officially prohibited Christians from practicing usury, even though the practice occurred widely throughout France, even where Jews did not live. "France presented the picture of a state, where loans on interest were officially forbidden by the Church, but where the government openly practiced a similar policy of credit, the laws regulated such credit operations, the judiciary bodies recognized these regulations, and the Church itself granted loans," noted Zosa Szajkowski.[51] However, the quality of Jewish and Christian money lending differed, observed historian Salo W. Baron. He wrote:

> While Christians as a rule lent hundreds of florins or more over terms of a year or longer and demanded expensive pledges like jewelry or other precious objects, Jews for the most part served the broader masses of the population with short-term loans of a few florins, accepted any kind of second-hand clothing or household goods as pawns, and permitted the borrowers to repay the loans at any time. Hence [argued the Jews], Jews ought to be allowed to charge a higher rate of interest for such costly transactions. Moreover, [the Jewish lenders] pointed out:
>
>> We are tolerated only by the grace of Christians, and as human beings must make a living. Yet we are not allowed to learn and exercise any craft under whatever name; nor are we admitted to any office of dignity; and we are precluded from the purchase of fields, vineyards, mills, and other landed possessions of any kind...We are allowed only to trade in open shops and to lend money on "Jewish interest." In addition, everyone knows that our assets are very small and that if a Jew were to lend a total of one hundred florins or so at a low rate of interest he would hardly be able to maintain his own person, not to speak of a wife and

children. It is also a matter of common knowledge that Jews must contribute [to the government].[52]

On November 18, 1262, Richard of Cornwall (1209–1272, ruled 1257–1272), King of Germany, confirmed the privileges of Strasbourg as a self-governing Imperial City of the Holy Roman Empire. King Richard of Cornwall made this decision to free Strasbourg from the Episcopal See after the Strasbourg burghers defeated the unpopular Bishop Walter of Geroldseck (ruled 1260–1263) in a battle on the field of Hausberg. The new bishop, Henry of Geroldseck (a cousin of Walter, ruled 1263–1273), guaranteed the rights and the customs of the Strasbourg residents, allowed them to contract alliances at their discretion, and gave the Strasbourg City Council the quality of an appellate court for the cities and villages of the bishopric. However, as bishop, he retained the right to appoint his clergy and the administrative leader of the city. In addition, the administrative leader would continue to appoint the tax assessors and the director of tolls.[53] In other words, the Church continued to wield power in the City of Strasbourg, despite the supposed emancipation of the city by King Richard of Cornwall.

The newly independent City of Strasbourg, which needed revenue for its treasury, began to charge Strasbourg Jews for protection services. The Jews struggled under the weight of the combined protection taxes levied by the Holy Roman Emperor, the Strasbourg Bishop, and now the City of Strasbourg. However, the Strasbourg Jews paid the taxes because through them they were guaranteed the right to dwell in safety inside the walled City of Strasbourg. Up to the mid-1300s, "Strasbourg practically remained the city of refuge for the Jews in Alsace. As its commerce and industry developed, the imperial free city adjusted its relations with the Jews in a manner that, though onerous, was at least endurable." The Jews "could not acquire real estate; [however], they were not compelled to submit their actions at law to any judges other than the mayor—a privilege that assured them a measure of protection [against adversaries]."[41]

On September 8, 1264, around six hundred and fifty miles

east of Strasbourg, the Duke of Greater Poland, Boleslaus the Pious (1224/1227–1279), issued to the Polish Ashkenazim the famous Charter of Jewish Liberties, also called the Statute of Kalisz. This document comprised forty-six brief chapters that granted exclusive jurisdiction over Jewish matters to Jewish courts, established a separate tribunal for criminal matters involving Christians and Jews, and granted protections to Jews, particularly from Christian adversaries. Note that the Jews were not subjects of Duke Boleslaus the Pious; rather they lived as semi-autonomous communities geographically within, but politically outside, the political structure of Greater Poland.

The Ashkenazim of Poland of this era feared the Christians as much as the Christians feared the Ashkenazim. For example, Chapter Two of the Statute of Kalisz reads, "Furthermore, if any Christian shall sue a Jew, asserting that he has pawned securities with him, and the Jew denies it, then if the Christian refuses to accept the simple word of the Jew, the Jew by taking oath must be free of the Christian." Chapter Seventeen reads, "Any Jew may freely and securely walk or ride without any let or hindrance from city to city and province to province in our realm, in accordance with the law of secure liberty in all our cities or provinces without let or hindrance on the part of their subjects [... and he...] shall pay customary tolls just as Christians do, and nothing otherwise." Chapter Twenty-two reads, "If any of the Christians rashly and presumptuously jeers at their synagogues, such a Christian shall be required to pay and must pay to our palatine their guardian two talents of pepper as punishment."[54]

French King Louis IX contrasted with Polish Duke Boleslaus the Pious by ordering all Jews in his Kingdom of France to sew the rouella (little wheel) on the front of their clothes to identify them as Jews to the Christian majority. French Jews wore the rouella for the next five hundred years. Thus, as the Christians in Western Europe moved toward the Renaissance (fourteenth through seventeenth centuries), the Jews plunged into a Dark Age. They would have "little but tragedy until the French Revolution," opined Allan Temko.[39]

The European Late Middle Ages, 1300–1500

The Late Middle Ages (1300–1500) were an unpleasant time for the Ashkenazim in Alsace. Powerful Christian artisan and merchant guilds tightly controlled their organizations for two reasons: to maintain monopolies on goods and services and to exclude Ashkenazi competitors.[55] In Strasbourg, these guilds excluded Jews from profitable craft and commercial professions, while ignoring less profitable trades, such as businesses associated with livestock (horses and cattle). Many Jews found work in livestock businesses; however, livestock businesses could not support all Jewish families.

Restriction on Jewish participation in the marketplace by Christians was the root cause of Ashkenazi misery and poverty in Alsace. The following memorandum written by a lawyer in 1717 on behalf of his Jewish clients explains the history of the circumstances of the Impoverished Ashkenazim in Alsace.

* * * * * * * * *

Memorandum on behalf of the Jews Established in Alsace, 1717

> Should [the rights of Jewish merchants] be limited, the King and the seigniors [nobles] might lose the large incomes paid by Jews in taxes on imported salt, coins, etc. [The monarchy held a royal monopoly on salt and levied a per capita charge on pre-assessed and obligatory consumption; Jewish importers paid that tax to the King]. Should the King's State Council allow it, the Jews would like to join the various businesses and guilds, which were then closed to them. The Jews are ready to respect the statutes of these guilds, if only their religious principles will not suffer from it (e.g., respect of the Sabbath); this would also greatly aid in combating illegal operations in commerce and credit. Not speculation, but the Jewish nature of economizing, allows [Jews] to sell goods cheaper than do

Christian merchants. For eighty years, Alsace has been a battlefield and Jews can do much for the province. In fact, with few exceptions, there are no Christian merchants. If there were no Jews, the noblemen and the peasants would have to travel to a far city in order to sell their crops, or to buy their wares. The travel expenses would eat up the greatest part of the profit from the crops and without the Jewish competition, the Strasbourg merchants will enforce a monopoly of high prices. As a result, the province will be ruined. The trade in old, worn-out goods is unknown in Alsace [Jews were allowed to do this]. Credit operations, too, are limited, because debtors can repay the loans mostly with their crops and by law Jews are not allowed to profit from such form of repayment. Horse and cattle traders are busy mostly in wartime. And thus, the Jews conclude, limitation of their trading in cattle, old goods, and money, will force them out of business altogether. The Jews declare further that they will not ask for new privileges, but for an Act of the King's State Council which should clearly acknowledge the existing privileges, so that the Jews might be unafraid of the many caprices of their adversaries. In order not to lose the help of the seigniors in this conflict the Jews declare that they do not want to abolish the seigniors' privileges over Jews; they do not seek the King's direct protection, which would deprive the seigniors of their income from the Jews [the seigniors charged the Jews taxes for protection]. The State Council can even specify that the existing seigniors' rights will not be abolished. Should the King's Council refuse them protection, the wealthiest Jews will be forced to leave for other countries willing to grant them more protection; only poor Jews will remain in Alsace. As for usury, the Jews state that the victim of usurious practices can ask the protection of the legal authorities, instead of making general, unspecified accusations against [all] Jews. Jews themselves will gladly combat usury.[56]

Some Ashkenazim in Alsace shrewdly "secure[d] relief from the existing severe restraints on their trade and industry by aiming at a greater turnover at less profit per unit. In this way, they made many lower-priced articles available to the masses for the first time." Jews also aggrieved their burgher competitors through clever practices, such as "securing business ahead of Christians by awaiting the arrival of visitors to the city in the inns."[52] In these ways, some Jews could largely survive despite the onerous industrial restrictions placed on them.

However, an increasing number of Jews turned to lending money at interest to support their families. Their money lending enterprises supplied the badly needed credit required by Strasbourg as it developed into an economic force in the 1300s.[51]

In 1306, Strasbourg received a second large influx of Ashkenazim from France (recall that the first large influx was under French King Philip II Augustus in 1180) when French King Philip IV (the Fair, 1268–1314, ruled 1285–1314) banished the Jews from his royal lands and seized their property. Some French Jews expelled by King Philip IV sought refuge in Savoy in Southeastern France, especially in the cities of Chambéry, Yenne, Seissel, Aiguebelle, Chillon, Chatel, and Montmélian.

In 1315, King Louis X (1289–1316, ruled France 1314–1316) authorized return of the Jews to France. However, in 1324, King Charles IV (1294–1328, ruled 1322–1328) again expelled the Jews from France. No French king ever overturned the Jewish expulsion decree of King Charles IV between its issue in 1324 and the French Revolution. Hence, the decree forbidding Jews from living anywhere in France was the law of the land for four hundred and sixty-seven years, ending only with the emancipation of all the Jews in France on September 27, 1791.

In 1332, ecclesiastics elected Bishop Berthold II of Bucheck (ruled 1328–1353) to the Strasbourg Episcopal See. Following his election, his creditors demanded eighteen thousand marks of silver to repay the ecclesiastics who voted for him against his rival Gebhart of Freiburg.

Bishop Berthold II of Bucheck raised the money by taxing the Jews of Strasbourg and other residents of his new diocese.

In 1332, an unexpected revolution erupted among a group of burghers of Strasbourg who opposed Strasbourg's nobility-dominated government. The nobles who served in the city government, said the burghers, had forgotten the humiliation of their defeat on the field of Hausberg in 1262. For seventy years, the nobles had failed to include burghers in the ranks of the city government. In addition, the nobles habitually failed to pay their debts, which required burghers to hire lawyers to obtain payment.

On May 20, 1332, a group of nobles was celebrating in the Hotel Ochsenstein in Strasbourg when a brawl erupted between the Zorn and the Mullenheim families. The brawl spilled into the streets necessitating intervention by Strasbourg authorities. People died during the fracas.

During the night following the mêlée, the Strasbourg burghers sent a deputation to meet with Strasbourg Magistrate Jean Sicke and the Strasbourg Council of the Senate. The Strasbourg burghers told Magistrate Jean Sicke that they were concerned about the ongoing struggle between the noble families and demanded that he relinquish the seal of the city and its banners and keys to a committee of the burghers until the struggle between the families of nobles ended. Strasbourg Magistrate Jean Sicke and the Strasbourg Council of the Senate acceded to the demands of the burghers.

The burghers then held an election to replace the noble members of the previous Strasbourg City Council. The burghers instructed each guild to name an assessor to designate a burgher Ammeister as head of the new Strasbourg City Council. The new government employed strong measures to maintain public order. For example, it kept the gates of the city closed and monitored the noble families in their neighborhoods. On August 12, 1332, the new Strasbourg City Government exiled many nobles, including former Magistrate Jean Sicke who had illegally mingled with the combatants. The new government even razed Jean Sicke's house. True to its anti-Jewish guild roots, the new Strasbourg City

Government clamped down on the Strasbourg Jews, who had previously received a measure of protection from the nobles, by prohibiting their ownership of houses, fields, and vineyards.

In 1336, a noble from Franconia in Northern Bavaria said an angel told him to lead a gang into Alsace to pillage and murder Ashkenazim. This anti-social behavior recurred in 1338–1339 when a former innkeeper (or butcher) named John Zimberlin (also known as King Armleder for the leather he wrapped around his arms) led a band of Judenschläger (Jewbeaters) to pillage and murder Jews in the Alsatian towns of Thann, Rouffach, and Ensisheim. Residents of the City of Colmar protected Jews who fled there for safety. King Armleder then besieged Colmar while devastating the surrounding countryside. Colmar citizens asked for help from Holy Roman Emperor Louis IV (1282–1347, ruled 1314–1347), who dispatched his Imperial Army to Alsace. However, by the time the Imperial Army arrived in Colmar, King Armleder and his gang had fled from the Holy Roman Empire across the border (west) into France.[57]

The Imperial Army eventually left Colmar. King Armleder and his gang reappeared. On May 17, 1338, a group of Christian Alsatian leaders (nobles, prelates, and burghers) formed an alliance to pursue King Armleder. The group included Albert, Count of Hohenberg; Berthold II of Bucheck, Bishop of Strasbourg; Abbot Murbach of the Benedictine Abbey Murbach (at the foot of Grand Ballon in the Vosges); the Lord of Rappoldstein (near Ribeauville); and magistrates representing the Cities of Strasbourg, Haguenau, Sélestat, Obernai, Rosheim, Mulhouse, Breisach, and Neubourg.[57] However, King Armleder and his followers were elusive. In 1339, Knight Rudolph of Andlau granted amnesty to King Armleder and his followers in return for ten years of peace toward the Jews in Alsace. Attacks abated.

During the ten-year armistice with King Armleder, the Ashkenazim in Alsace paid dearly for their continued protection. Strasbourg Jews paid the highest tax of all the Jewish communities in the Holy Roman Empire because of their need for protection from adversaries, such as King Armleder. A document dated 1338 noted that Strasbourg's

Ammeister Berthold Schwarber and the Strasbourg City Council gave a certificate of protection (Schutzbrief) to sixteen Jewish families, which was valid for five years and cost one thousand and seventy-two marks. Of these one thousand and seventy-two marks, one thousand were payable to Strasbourg authorities, sixty to Holy Roman Emperor Louis IV, and twelve to Strasbourg Bishop Berthold II of Bucheck. The Schutzbrief also permitted the sixteen Jewish families to engage in money lending. "The rate on loans [was] fixed for them at five or six percent per week, or at forty-three percent per annum."[41]

In 1348, an infectious disease epidemic called the Black Plague swept Europe, reaching Strasbourg early in 1349. Europeans did not know what caused epidemics, because the discovery of bacteria was at least five hundred years in the future. (The cause of the Black Plague was the Yersinia pestis bacteria, carried by fleas that transmit it to humans via rodents.) Epidemics during the Middle Ages were common. However, the Black Plague of 1348–1351 was one of the most devastating in human history, taking the lives of around twenty-five million European people. The plague seemed to appear everywhere at once, for example, "in Savoie [Savoy], in Venice, in Calabria, in Toulouse, in Bern, in Zurich, and in Zofingen."[58]

A persuasive fiction quickly developed and spread to explain the origin of the Black Plague. The fiction involved Jews. The perpetrators of the fiction accused Jewish leaders in Toledo (Spain) of initiating a plot to poison the drinking water wells and cisterns used by Christians in France, Switzerland, and Italy, to cause their deaths. The alleged chief conspirator was Rabbi Peyret of Savoy. Savoy was especially prominent in the Black Death tragedy. Recall that in 1306, King Philip IV (the Fair) had expelled Jews from France. Rabbi Peyret was one of the Jews who had fled France to settle in Savoy in southeastern France. The rumor said that Rabbi Peyret sought revenge against King Philip IV by dispatching poisoners from his home in Chambéry, Savoy to poison the wells of France, Switzerland, and Italy.

In 1348, fourteen-year-old Amadeus VI, Count of Savoy (1334–1383, ruled 1343–1383), wrote to his fellow nobles in the Rhine River

Valley about the arrest and confession under torture of a number of Jews in Geneva, who also had incriminated other Jews. The young Amadeus VI was under the control of Regents Louis II of Vaud and Amadeus III of Geneva. News of the confessions of the Jews in Geneva raced from one town to another in Switzerland and then north through the cities of the Rhine River Valley.[59] A typical description of a confession provided by a Jew named Agimet of Geneva follows:

* * * * * * * * *

Confession of Agimet of Geneva, Châtel, October 10, 1348

The year of our Lord 1348.

On Friday, the 10th of the month of October, at Châtel, in the castle thereof, there occurred the judicial inquiry which was made by order of the court of the illustrious Prince, our lord, Amadeus, Count of Savoy, and his subjects against the Jews of both sexes who were there imprisoned, each one separately. This was done after public rumor had become current and a strong clamor had arisen—because of the poison put by them into the wells, springs, and other things which the Christians use—demanding that they die, that they are able to be found guilty and, therefore, that they should be punished. Hence this their confession made in the presence of a great many trustworthy persons.

Agimet the Jew, who lived at Geneva and was arrested at Châtel, was there put to the torture a little and then he was released from it. And after a long time, having been subjected again to torture a little, he confessed in the presence of a great many trustworthy persons, who are later mentioned. To begin with it is clear that at the Lent just passed Pultus Clesis de Ranz had sent this very Jew to Venice to buy silks and other things for him. When this came to the notice of Rabbi Peyret, a Jew of Chambéry who was a teacher of their law, he sent for this Agimet, for whom he had searched, and when he had come before him he said: "We have been informed that you are going to Venice to buy silk and other wares. Here I am giving you a little package of half a span in size which contains some prepared poison and venom in a thin, sewed leather-bag. Distribute it among the wells, cisterns, and springs about Venice and the other places to which you go, in order to poison the people who use the water of the aforesaid wells that will have been poisoned by you, namely, the wells in which the poison will have been placed."

Agimet took this package full of poison and carried it with him to Venice, and when he came there he threw and scattered a portion of it into the well or cistern of fresh water which was there near the German House, in order to poison the people who use the water of that cistern. And he says that this is the only cistern of sweet water in the city. He also says that the mentioned Rabbi Peyret promised to give him whatever he wanted for his troubles in this business. Of his own accord Agimet confessed further that after this had been done he left at once in order that he should not be captured by the citizens or others, and that he went personally to Calabria and Apulia and threw the above mentioned poison into many wells. He confesses also that he put some of this same poison in the well of the streets of the City of Ballet...Asked if any of the Jews of those places were guilty in the above-mentioned matter, he answered that he did not know. And now by all that which is contained in the five books of Moses and the scroll of the Jews, he declared that this was true, and that he was in no wise lying, no matter what might happen to him. [Note: The books of Moses and the scroll of the Jews are identical.][59]

* * * * * * * *

Some Christians physically assaulted the Jews because of their alleged poisoning of the wells, as described below:

> Jews were massacred at Chambéry, Chillon, Chatel, Yenne, Saint-Genis, Aiguebelle, and Montmélian. In the last-mentioned town, the Jews were imprisoned, and while they were awaiting judgment, the populace invaded the prison and massacred them, with the exception of eleven persons who were later burned alive in an old barn filled with inflammable materials. A document relating to that persecution has preserved the names of the victims of Aiguebelle. These were Beneyton, Saul, the Jewess Joyon, Lyonetus, Soninus, Vimandus, Bonnsuper, Samuel, Mouxa, Beneyton, Coen, Helist, Jacob and his son Bonionus, Parvus Samuel, Abraham, Benyon, Sansoninus, Samuel, and Magister Benedictus.[59]

In September 1348, the well-educated Pope Clement VI (1291–1352, ruled 1342–1352) tried to stop the murderous behavior of many Christians by issuing an urgent papal bull that exonerated Jews as the cause of the epidemic. He explained that Jews were dying at the same rate as Christians and that where Jews were not living, Christians were still dying at the same rate as everywhere else. Pope Clement VI offered refuge to Jews in his papal state.[58]

On November 15, 1348, Rudolph of Oron, Bailiff of Lausanne [Switzerland], wrote a letter to the Strasbourg authorities in which he declared that certain Jews of Lausanne confessed to poisoning all the drinking wells in the Rhine River Valley by order of, and in collusion with, their co-religionists in Italy. They supposedly did so to avenge the cruelties of King Armleder, the Alsatian assassin. The poison, said Rudolph of Oron, killed Christians while sparing Jews.[59]

In December 1348, the Obernai City Council (Obernai is about fourteen miles southwest of Strasbourg) tortured five Jews who admitted (under torture) to participating in the crime of poisoning wells in the Rhine River Valley. On December 29, 1348, the Colmar

City Council, which formerly had protected Jews during the King Armleder episode, announced that a certain Hegmann, one of the Jews under city protection, had (under torture) accused Jacob, the cantor of the Strasbourg Synagogue, of having sent poison to him (Hegmann), which he (Hegmann) then dumped in Colmar's wells. The Colmar City Council added that one of Jacob's cousins, a woman named Bela, had similarly poisoned the wells of Ammerschweier, an Alsatian town five miles west of Colmar. Strasbourg Ammeister Peter Schwarber ignored this missive from the Obernai City Council and continued to protect the Jewish residents of Strasbourg.[41,59]

On Sunday, February 8, 1349, Berthold II of Bucheck, Bishop of Strasbourg, met with various nobles and municipal authorities of the Cities of Strasbourg, Freiburg, and Basel to rule on the fate of the Ashkenazim (i.e., Jacob and Bela) charged with the crime of poisoning the wells of Strasbourg. The committee ruled all of the Jews of Strasbourg guilty of poisoning the wells and sentenced all of them to death, against the advice of Strasbourg Ammeister Peter Schwarber.

Strasbourg Ammeister Schwarber refused to implement the sentence passed by the group led by the Bishop of Strasbourg, maintaining that to blame the Jews for poisoning wells was nonsense. The chief crime of the Jews, he continued, was their wealth, which caused envy. Furthermore, an unknown number of Christians in Strasbourg were indebted to the Jews. Conveniently, extermination of the Strasbourg Jews would nullify these debts. This was the real reason for charging the Jews in Strasbourg with the crime of poisoning the wells, said Ammeister Schwarber. Bishop Berthold II of Bucheck was the most adamant of the Jews' accusers, suggesting a level of indebtedness to Jewish creditors that he did not reveal.[58]

Strasbourg Ammeister Schwarber had two assistants, Conrad of Winterthur zum Engel and Gosse Sturm, who knew the Jews of Strasbourg well and testified that the Jews were incapable of poisoning the wells.[58] Ammeister Schwarber reminded the accusatory committee about the security guarantees owed the Jews by the City of Strasbourg. Nevertheless, the majority of the committee ruled against Ammeister

Peter Schwarber and condemned the Jews of Strasbourg to execution by burning at the stake.

From Sunday, February 8, 1349 to Saturday, February 14, 1349, the Strasbourg guilds distributed arms to their members and established a command center in Hotel Gurtlerhof on Rue du Dôme. On Tuesday, February 10, 1349, a mob deposed Ammeister Peter Schwarber, Conrad of Winterthur zum Engel, and Gosse Sturm, and took possession of the seal, banners, and keys of the City of Strasbourg. On Wednesday, February 11, 1349, the mob leaders appointed a new Strasbourg City Council. Butcher Johannes Betschold became the new Strasbourg Ammeister. Nicolas of Bulach and Gosso Engelbrecht became his two assistants. The new officers swore themselves into office, invalidated former Ammeister Peter Schwarber's rights of the bourgeoisie, and divided his fortune among themselves and his children. Peter Schwarber moved to Benfeld, Alsace where he lived for the rest of his life. The new Ammeister Johannes Betschold excluded Peter Schwarber's two assistants from the Strasbourg City Council for ten years.[59]

On Saturday, February 14, 1349 (Saint Valentine's Day), the Strasbourg mob led by Ammeister Betschold overran the Jewish quarter on Rue des Juifs, dragged around two thousand Jews to a pyre in the Jewish cemetery outside of town, burned several hundred Jews alive, forcibly baptized others, and expelled the rest from Strasbourg. Some Jews fled to nearby Bischheim. Strasbourg Bishop Berthold II of Bucheck and members of the new Strasbourg City Council destroyed evidence of the loans owed by Christians to Jewish creditors. In addition, the Strasbourg City Council and Bishop Berthold II of Bucheck divided among themselves the property of the eradicated Jews of Strasbourg.

When Holy Roman Emperor Charles IV (not to be confused with French King Charles IV) heard about the atrocities committed by some Strasbourg Christian residents against all the Strasbourg Jews, he threatened retaliation against the city. However, similar Jewish massacres were occurring across Alsace, including in the Cities of Benfeld, Sélestat, Molsheim, Lauterbourg, Obernai, Wissembourg,

Colmar, and Mulhouse. Furthermore, attacks on Jews spread through Ashkenaz in the spring and summer of 1349. On September 12, 1349, Holy Roman Emperor Charles IV officially pardoned the Strasbourg mob for their egregious behavior on Saint Valentine's Day. The city had suffered enough from the plague, he said, which had decimated the city's population.

Ashkenazim in many other Rhine River Valley cities also suffered in pogroms conducted by some crazed Christians. By 1351, Jewish adversaries had decimated sixty major (e.g., Frankfurt-am-Main, Mainz, and Cologne) and one hundred and fifty smaller Ashkenazi communities in over three hundred and fifty separate massacres, noted historian Robert Gottfried.[60]

After the Strasbourg massacre of February 14, 1349, the Strasbourg City Council voted to forbid the entry of Jews into Strasbourg for one hundred years. However, in 1369, the Strasbourg City Council again admitted Jews according to an ordinance (Judenordnung) dated May 14, 1375, which refers to the presence of a dozen Jewish families. In 1383, a second ordinance mandated that Jews receive the same treatment and protection as other Strasbourg citizens. A short time later, the Count of Öttinger recommended admission to Strasbourg for sixteen Jewish families from the Cities of Ulm, Bretten, Breisach, Wesel, and Mosheim. In 1384, the Strasbourg Ammeister appointed Ashkenazi Maître Gutleben as physician and paid him a salary of three hundred crowns (about three hundred and sixty dollars) per annum.[41] Thus, a small but affluent community of Jews continued to live in Strasbourg even after the Saint Valentine's Day Massacre.

Ashkenazim in the Rhine River Valley also continued to loan money to Christians. For example, by 1385, Robert I, Count Palatine of the Rhine (1309–1390, ruled 1356–1390), had acquired debt to the Jews of Strasbourg for the sum of fifteen thousand four hundred florins (about seventy-seven hundred dollars). In 1385, the Confederation of the Cities of the Rhine met in the City of Speyer to consider the question of Jewish wealth and usury. On February 6, 1386, Wenceslaus (also spelled Winceslaus), the debauched, alcoholic King of the Romans (1361–1419, ruled 1376–1400), ordered Strasbourg authorities to enforce sumptuary laws against the Jews in matters of dress. King Wenceslaus also required the Jews in Strasbourg to resume wearing yellow shoes and sugar-loaf hats.

In 1387, the Strasbourg Mayor assessed the Jews in Strasbourg twenty thousand florins (about ten thousand dollars). In 1387, the Jews were a source of considerable revenue to Strasbourg's treasury. For example, the twenty Jewish families of Strasbourg paid an annual tax of more than seven hundred florins (around three hundred and sixty-five dollars) and the richest one among them, "der ryche Sigmund," paid around two hundred florins (around one hundred dollars).[41]

In 1387, delegates of the Confederation of the Cities of the Rhine again met in the City of Speyer and adopted resolutions inimical to the Ashkenazim. "On the demand of the delegates from Strasburg [sic] it was resolved that neither male nor female Christians be allowed to act as domestic servants or wet-nurses in Jewish families, under penalty of being branded on the forehead." During 1387, "King Wenceslaus placed under the ban all Jews of Colmar, Schlettstadt (Sélestat), and Haguenau who refused to pay the taxes he demanded for their protection, and even included three imperial cities that had retained for themselves such Jewish contributions." In June 1387, a Jew of Italian or French origin named Mamelot der Morschele, der Walch, entered Strasbourg Cathedral. For entering Strasbourg Cathedral, the verger beat, expelled, and threatened Mamelot der Morschele, der Walch with drowning if he should ever reenter the City of Strasbourg.[41] A verger is an individual who takes care of the interior of a church and acts as an attendant during ceremonies.

In autumn of 1387, people accused Lauwelin, a weaver of Bischheim of offering his child to the Jews of Strasbourg for a ritual sacrifice, a crime to which he apparently confessed, under torture. His accusers put out his eyes as punishment.[41]

In early 1388, the Strasbourg authorities again expelled all Jews from Strasbourg and confiscated their real estate. However, some Jews had business concerns in Strasbourg and Strasbourg authorities permitted them to re-enter the city for a charge, called the Jewish body tax (péage corporel in French, or Juden-Leibzoll in Yiddish). When a Jew approached a city gate, a municipal worker interrogated, searched, and followed him all day. Any Jew who stayed overnight paid double the body tax. Soon Jews were forbidden even from staying overnight in Strasbourg. They had to leave at dusk.[41] Each evening, the keeper of Strasbourg Cathedral sounded the Kraeuselhorn (Grusselhorn) to order all Jews to leave the city. The law was strictly enforced for the next four hundred years.

In 1392, King Wenceslaus annulled all the claims of the Jews against their debtors in the City of Colmar. In 1394, French King Charles VI (1368–1422, ruled 1380–1422) confirmed the law of his ancestor King Charles IV and expelled Jews who had reentered France. This law, as noted above, remained in effect until the French Revolution, even though "wars had changed France's borders and small Jewish communities formed or were acquired in four locations of France, including Alsace."[61] In 1397, another story of poisoned wells circulated in Upper Alsace through a certain Jew of Ribeauville, whose confessions implicated fresh victims.[41]

In 1399, the electors of Holy Roman Empire finally deposed the indolent King Wenceslaus for selling the rights of the Holy Roman Empire in Italy and Germany. He replied, "We are overjoyed to be delivered from the burden of the [Holy Roman Empire]." However, he became miffed when the imperial cities, such as Strasbourg, began to send to him "some butts of their best wine."[61]

By the late 1300s and early 1400s, most of the Ashkenazim in Alsace had followed the Great European Plain eastward and the European rivers northward. At least some of these Ashkenazim reached Poland. Absolute rulers in Western Europe, such as French Kings Philip II Augustus, Philip IV, Charles IV, and Charles VI, persecuted the Ashkenazim, but "the debating and voting body of senators and representatives" of the Polish parliament "never likely ordered such persecutions," noted historian Iwo Cyprian Pogonowski.[62]

By the end of the 1400s, the Ashkenazim in Poland numbered

between ten thousand and thirty thousand; by the mid-1550s, between one hundred and fifty thousand and two hundred thousand; and by the end of the 1600s, seven hundred and fifty thousand, which represented fifty to seventy-five percent of the world's Jewry. The rapid increase in the numbers of Polish Ashkenazim was the result of "a deliberate [anti-Jewish] policy carried out throughout the fragmented German Empire," averred Iwo Cyprian Pogonowski.[63]

Economically, Poland's rich farmlands and forests gave her a lucrative role as the main supplier of food and natural products to Western Europe.[63] Ashkenazi managers operated large estates owned by Polish nobles and distributed Polish goods in international markets. "Jews were acceptable to the noble citizens of Poland as safe middlemen who had no political claims because of the reigning Christian feudal social order, and because of the Jewish self-perception of being outsiders, rooted in their theology of exile," declared Iwo Cyprian Pogonowski. "The Jews were more efficient, paid better than others, and therefore they were accepted into this unique alliance with the landowners." [64]

The European Early Modern Period: 1500–1726

During the 1500s, only a small number of Jews remained in the Rhine River Valley, probably working in the international networks of Jewish merchants. This small group of Jews witnessed the explosive Protestant Reformation (1517–1648), which divided the previously monolithic Christians into two feuding camps. Martin Luther (1483–1546), the German priest who challenged the Pope over charging people money to erase God's punishment for sin, usually receives credit for triggering the Protestant Reformation. Martin Luther initially turned to the Ashkenazim to support his new interpretation of the Bible and his rejection of papal claims. Historian Paul Johnson described the subsequent mercurial relationship of Martin Luther with the Ashkenazim:

In his 1523 pamphlet, *Das Jesus Christus ein geborener Jude sei*, [Martin Luther] argued that there was now no reason at all why [the Jews] should not embrace Christ, and foolishly looked forward to a voluntary mass conversion. When the Jews retorted that the Talmud conveyed an even better understanding of the Bible than his own, and reciprocated the invitation to convert, Luther first attacked them in 1526 for their obstinacy and then in 1543 turned on them in fury. His pamphlet *Von den Juden und ihren Lugen* (*On the Jews and their Lies*), published in Wittenberg, may be termed the first work of modern anti-Semitism…"First," he urged, "their synagogues should be set on fire, and whatever is left should be buried in dirt so that no one may ever be able to see a stone or cinder of it."[65]

In 1565, Sephardi Rabbi Joseph ben Ephraim Caro (1488–1575) made interpretation of Jewish law available once again to European Jews in the legal code he wrote, titled *Shulkhan Arukh*. The burning of the Talmud in Paris in 1242 and the persecution of Jews in Western Europe during the High Middle Ages had hampered communication among European Jews. The geographically isolated pockets of European Jews needed a simple and universal handbook explaining Jewish law, and Joseph Caro's *Shulkhan Arukh* filled that need. The *Shulkhan Arukh* was the first Jewish code of law to list the differing customs of the Sephardi and Ashkenazi Jewry, which was one reason for its universal acceptance. The book comprised four volumes devoted to laws of prayer and holidays; laws governing charity, Torah study, and the Jewish dietary laws; laws concerning Jewish marriage and divorce; and Jewish civil law, which included laws governing lending money at interest.[66]

Martin Luther progressed from vitriolic verbal abuse against the Jews to forcing their expulsion from Saxony in 1537. In 1543, he tried unsuccessfully to persuade the Elector to expel the Jews from Brandenburg. His followers sacked the Berlin Synagogue in 1572 and in 1573 succeeded in banning Jews from the entire country. Reformer John Calvin (1509–1564) was more kindly disposed to the Jews, partly because he tended to agree with them on lending money at interest. Nevertheless, some Calvinists expelled Jews, including the staunch Calvinist Frederic III of Simmern, Elector Palatine (1515–1576).[65]

The deep enmity of Martin Luther for the Jews drove the latter into the arms of the Roman Catholic Holy Roman Emperor Charles V (1500–1558, ruled 1519–1556), even though he did not particularly like Jews. Emperor Charles V valued the tax payments from the Jews and honored his commitment to protect them against their enemies. At the Diets of Augsburg (1530), Speyer (1544), and Regensburg (1546), he prevented their expulsion from the Holy Roman Empire. The Catholic bishops also found the Jews useful as allies against the Protestant burghers, even if they were not prepared to admit it in public.[65]

Alsatian Ashkenazim Josel ben Gershon of Rosheim (circa 1480–1554), also known as the "commander of Jewry in the Holy Roman Empire of the German Nation," denounced Martin Luther as a ruffian and referred to Holy Roman Emperor Charles V as an angel of the Lord. Josel ben Gershon led his co-religionists in prayers for the success of the Imperial Army of Holy Roman Emperor Charles V. They also supplied the Imperial Army with money and provisions, "thus setting a new and important Jewish survival-pattern," wrote Paul Johnson.[65,67]

Overall, the Ashkenazim probably benefited from the Protestant Reformation because Christians could no longer aspire to a single-faith society, declared historian Mary C. Boys. The Protestant Reformation ended the "exposed isolation of the Jews as the only nonconformist group [and] the debates of reformers, taken up in a new way during the Enlightenment, helped to open up consideration of religious tolerance, freedom of conscience, and the separation of church and state."[68]

The deadly Thirty Years' War erupted in 1618, causing some Ashkenazim to return to the Rhine River Valley to supply needed military goods and services to the armies fighting there. "At the time, military rule superseded civil authority everywhere; and both the chiefs of the various factions and those of the army availed themselves of the keen commercial instinct of the Jews to equip their cavalry and to replenish their commissariats. To the soldiers they were indispensable as agents for the disposal of pillage."[41] Many of the Ashkenazim who returned to the Rhine River Valley during the Thirty Years' War chose to live in the Strasbourg Diocese, the county of Hanau-Lichtenberg, on the estate of the lords of Ribeaupierre, and in the City of Haguenau. Most of them avoided living in major cities because of their ancestors' horrific experiences during the Crusades and the Black Plague.[41]

The unprecedented size of armies during the Thirty Years' War necessitated an increase in logistical support, noted historian Martin van Creveld, because armies could not live off the land for very long, as they had done with variable success in the past. For example, in 1631/1632, Protestant King Gustavus Adolphus of Sweden (1594–1632, ruled 1617–1632), Commander of his cherished Swedish Protestant Army, and Albrecht Wenzel Eusebius von Wallenstein (1583–1634), Supreme Commander of the Holy Roman Empire Armies, each led armies comprised of more than one hundred thousand soldiers.[69]

In 1643, King Louis XIV (1638–1715, ruled 1643–1715) proudly ascended the throne of France. His nickname was Sun King. He ruled for seventy-two years. In 1648, the Peace Treaties of Westphalia ended the Thirty Years' War. Notably, Austria ceded her possessions in Alsace to France. The war severely depopulated and lay waste to much of the Rhine River Valley. The region was ripe for repopulation by many immigrant groups, including the Ashkenazim.

In 1648–1649, Ukrainian Cossack Bohdan Chmielnicki (1595–1657) led a brutal peasant uprising against the Poles and the Ashkenazim in Eastern Europe. "The Greek Orthodox Cossacks, semi-military bands [that] had been settled in the country north of the Black Sea, were mistreated by their Roman Catholic Polish lords. The Ukrainian peasants, also Greek Orthodox, bitterly resented the Jewish stewards of the larger estates because of the heavy taxation demanded by the Jews to satisfy the Jews' spendthrift Polish masters."[70]

The Chmielnicki Revolt (1648–1649) sought to free the Ukraine from Polish and Jewish domination. It decimated the large Polish Jewish communities and sent many Jews fleeing westward, including to the depopulated areas of the Rhine River Valley. "Now these regions were crying out for new settlers, who would help to reconstitute the population of recently depopulated cities and villages and would revitalize the sagging economies of the region," noted historian Simon Schwarzfuchs. He continued, "[D]uring this period all governing powers in Alsace were interested in stimulating immigration to the province [to] rehabilitate its shattered economy. In addition to Jewish immigrants, many Catholic and, more surprisingly, many Protestant immigrants found their way to Alsace as well."[71]

In 1678/1679, the Treaties of Peace of Nimjegen awarded King Louis XIV the Duchy of Lorraine, which strengthened France's northern perimeter. On September 27, 1681, King Louis XIV rudely annexed the City of Strasbourg, which had remained neutral during the Thirty Years' War and had been a self-governing city since 1262, as described above. Strasbourg was valued for its strategic position on France's eastern perimeter. From 1682 to 1685, King Louis XIV's famous military engineer, Sébastien Le Prestre of Vauban (1633–1707), strengthened the fortifications of Strasbourg by building a pentagonal Citadel armed with five bastions.[72]

During the early 1680s, King Louis XIV further pursued his quest to create an impregnable perimeter for his French Kingdom. He sent emissary Charles Colbert de Croissy (1625–1696) to work with the Parliament of Metz to investigate alleged "usurpations" of lands by France's northern neighbors. These neighbors had based their own interpretations of what land belonged to them according to the Peace Treaties of Westphalia in 1648. Charles Colbert de Croissy had served formerly as the King's Intendant in Alsace, where he had studied old documents to determine the legal status of the cities in "that confused area."[73]

The Parliament of Metz assigned thirteen members to serve as a special Metz Chamber of Réunions, whose task was to incorporate into France the lands near the Three Bishoprics (Metz, Toul, and Verdun) that King Louis XIV could claim, based on *his* interpretation of earlier peace treaties. Historian Andrew Lossky noted, "The usual procedure was to determine which lands had owed allegiance of any sort to the fiefs of towns ceded to France. Once such dependence was ascertained, sometimes in the remote past, troops were sent to establish Louis's sovereignty in the area in question."[73]

In this way, between 1679 and 1682, King Louis XIV acquired parts of Saarland—the small, geographically folded, mineral- and ore-rich (iron ore and coal) region situated north of Lorraine, south of the Palatinate, east of Luxembourg, and west of the Duchy of Zweibrücken. The French province of Saarland existed from 1682 to 1814.

The Metz Chamber of Réunions adjudged King Louis XIV owner of the Duchy of Zweibrücken (in French, the Duchy of Deux Ponts), which was contiguous with the eastern border of the French Province of Saarland. However, King Louis XIV declined to exercise his perceived right to the Duchy of Zweibrücken because it was the home of the Swedish Royal Family ever since the accession of King Charles X in 1654, and the Swedish Royal Family was a French ally.[73]

King Louis XIV's creation of the French Province of Saarland allowed Saar iron manufacturing concerns to begin recovery from the ruination caused by the Thirty Years' War. For example, in 1635, Spanish troops had leveled the famous ironworks in Neunkirchen, the second largest city (after Saarbrücken) in Saarland.[74]

On September 25, 1657, King Louis XIV officially placed the Ashkenazim in Alsace under his protection. He awarded them the same rights accorded them by the Holy Roman Emperors and the same privileges received by the Ashkenazim of Metz who, one hundred years earlier, had come under the protection of the French Crown.[75] King Louis XIV divided Ashkenazim in Alsace into five cantons:

1. the lands of the Diocese of Strasbourg,

2. the King's lands in Lower Alsace,

3. the King's lands in Upper Alsace,

4. nobles' lands in Lower Alsace, and

5. the lands of the County of Hanau-Lichtenberg in Lower Alsace, whose capital was Bouxwiller.[76]

In 1660, King Louis XIV was too late to save Raphael Levy, a Jewish visitor in Metz, who was burned at the stake by some Christian citizens for allegedly committing a ritual murder of a three-year-old Christian child. "Curiously, this trial was not brought to Louis XIV's attention by the Jewish elders in Metz until after the defendant had been executed and they themselves had been fined," noted Salo W. Baron. "When the king reproached [the Jewish elders] for their delay, which had prevented his saving Levy's life, they offered the rather lame excuse that they had not felt entitled to appeal to the French Crown in behalf of a stranger to their community."[77]

On January 13, 1683, a Jewish couple in Bordeaux committed "an act of sacrilege" (not further described), which King Louis XIV learned about from Monsieur of Ris, his Bordeaux Intendant. King Louis XIV wanted to expel "all the Jews" from France, but knew that almost all commerce was "in the hands of these people," and so such a measure would be dangerous for the French Kingdom, noted historian Roland E. Mousnier.[78]

In 1689, Strasbourg Intendant Jacques of the Grange conducted a census of the Jewish Nation (Nation Juive) of Alsace. He identified five hundred and twenty-five Jewish families, or about twenty-six hundred Jews. Of the five hundred and twenty-five Jewish families, three hundred and ninety-one families lived in Lower (north) Alsace versus one hundred and thirty-four families in Upper (south) Alsace. The number of Jews living in cities was insignificant.[41]

In 1697, the Intendant of Alsace deemed the Jews of Metz indispensable, because "[t]hey smuggled horses from Germany, which the cavalry badly needed. They also furnished supplies for the French Army. They sold goods more cheaply than the Christians did. They delivered their goods more quickly. It was in the interests of the state to retain them as a 'singularité,' an element sui generis, neither subjects nor aliens," wrote Roland E. Mousnier.[78]

In 1726, Cerf Berr was born in Médelsheim in a region of Saarland owned by nobility associated with the Holy Roman Empire.

In summary, in 63 BC, the Romans conquered the Jewish descendants of Noah's son Shem in Palestine, according to the Book of Genesis in the Hebrew Bible, also known as the Christian Old Testament. Some of these Jews migrated to Rome and then to Gaul and the Iberian Peninsula to escape mounting persecution by Christianized Roman Emperors. About 1000 AD, a group of Jews who considered themselves descendants of Ashkenaz (a descendant of Noah's son Japheth), settled in the Rhine River Valley in Europe. Christian Crusaders during the High Middle Ages pillaged and killed Jews and Muslims equally as the enemies of Christianity. Anti-Jewish persecution during the Black Death in Europe sent Jews fleeing elsewhere until conditions in the late 1600s caused Jews to again move west. Some of them gambled on a return to the Rhine River Valley, which the Thirty Years' War had devastated. Some dynasts protected Jews, while others persecuted them. Cerf Berr was born in 1726 into a vortex of anti-Jewish bias and unparalleled economic opportunity.

Chapter Two Notes:

1. Norman Solomon: *The Talmud*. London, England, United Kingdom: Penguin, 2009, pp. li–lii.

2. Max Weinreich: *History of the Yiddish Language*, Volume 1. Chicago, Illinois: University of Chicago, 2008, p. 1. See also Simon Schwarzfuchs: "Alsace and Southern Germany: the creation of a border." In *Jewish Emancipation Reconsidered*. Michael Brenner, Vicki Caron, and Uri R. Kaufmann (eds.). London, England, United Kingdom: Leo Baeck Institute, 2003, pp. 11–12; and Kirsten A. Fudeman: *Vernacular Voices: Language and Identity in Medieval French Jewish Communities*. Philadelphia, Pennsylvania: University of Pennsylvania Press, 2010.

3. William W. Hallo, David B. Ruderman, Michael Stanklawski (eds.): *Heritage: Civilization and the Jews: Source Reader*. Westport, Connecticut: Praeger, 1984; Salo Wittmayer Baron: *Social and Religious History of the Jews*. Eighteen volumes. Philadelphia, Pennsylvania: Columbia University Press and the Jewish Publication Society of America, 1952–1983; Heinrich Graetz: *History of the Jews*. Six volumes. Philadelphia, Pennsylvania: Jewish Publication

Society of America, 1893; *Encyclopaedia Judaica*. Sixteen volumes and supplements. Jerusalem, Israel: Keter Publishing House, circa 1972; Hayim Ben Sasson (ed.): *A History of the Jewish People*. London, England, United Kingdom: Weidenfeld and Nicolson, 1976; Louis Finkelstein: *The Jews: their History, Culture, and Religion*. New York City, New York: Schocken Books, 1970; and Paul Johnson: *A History of the Jews*. New York City, New York: Harper and Row, 1987.

4. Heinrich Graetz: *History of the Jews*. Philadelphia, Pennsylvania: Jewish Publication Society of America, 1893, Volume 2, pp. 66–68. Historian Josephus (37 AD–circa 100) wrote, "Of the Jews there fell twelve thousand, but of the Romans very few…and no small enormities were committed about the Temple itself, which, in former ages, had been inaccessible, and seen by none; for Pompey went into it, and not a few of those that were with him also, and saw all that which it was unlawful for any other men to see but only for the high priests. There were in that temple the golden table, the holy candlestick, and the pouring vessels, and a great quantity of spices; and besides these there were among the treasures two thousand talents of sacred money: yet did Pompey touch nothing of all this, on account of his regard to religion; and in this point also he acted in a manner that was worthy of his virtue. The next day he gave order to those that had the charge of the Temple to cleanse it, and to bring what offerings the law required to God; and restored the high priesthood to Hyrcanus, both because he had been useful to him in other respects, and because he hindered the Jews in the country from giving Aristobulus any assistance in his war against him." Source: Flavius Josephus: *The Antiquities of the Jews*. Translated by William Whiston, Book 14, Chapter 4. Blacksburg, Virginia: Unabridged Books, 2011. Also available at http://www.gutenberg.org/ebooks/2848; accessed December 23, 2011.

5. Raymond E. Brown: *An Introduction to the New Testament*. New York City, New York: Doubleday, 1997.

6. Heinrich Graetz: *History of the Jews*. Philadelphia, Pennsylvania: Jewish Publication Society of America, 1893, Volume 2, pp. 431–432.

7. Hermann L. Strack: *Introduction to the Talmud and Midrash*. New York City, New York: Meridian Books, 1959, pp. 9, 12–13.

8. Heinrich Graetz: *History of the Jews*. Philadelphia, Pennsylvania: Jewish Publication Society of America, 1893, Volume 2, pp. 476–479.

9. Ibid, pp. 468–469.

10. Ibid, pp. 562–563.

11. Jacob Rader Marcus: "Christianity objects to the Sabbath and to the Jewish dating of Easter." In *The Jew in the Medieval World: a Source Book: 315–1791*. Cincinnati, Ohio: Hebrew Union College Press, 1999, pp. 3–4, 115–119. The entire letter of Roman Emperor Constantine I to the Council of Nicaea is available in Eusebius: *Life of Constantine*. Book III, Chapters xvii–xx. Oxford, England, United Kingdom: Oxford University Press, 1999.

12. Julius Caesar: *The Conquest of Gaul*. New York City, New York: Penguin Classics, 1983, p. 28.

13. Richard Gottheil, S. Kahn, Isaac Broydé. "Arles." *Jewish Encyclopedia*, 1906. Available at http://www.jewishencyclopedia.com/articles/1784-arles; accessed January 10, 2012. For more on Arles, see Thomas Scott Holmes: *The Origin and Development of the Christian Church: Being the Birkbeck Lectures for 1907 and 1908 in Trinity College, Cambridge*. London, England, United Kingdom: Macmillan and Company, 1911, pp. 362–363.

14. Esther Benbassa: *The Jews of France: a History from Antiquity to the Present*. Princeton, New Jersey: Princeton University Press, 2001, pp. 3–4.

15. Jeremy Cohen: *Living Letters of the Law*. Berkeley, California: University of California Press, 1999, pp. 32–33; and Paul Johnson: *A History of the Jews*. New York City, New York: Harper & Row, 1988, p. 165.

16. Augustine of Hippo: *The City of God*. New York City, New York: Penguin Classics, 2003. Book 18, Chapter 46; and Psalm 59:11, Hebrew Bible, or Christian Old Testament.

17. Heinrich Graetz: *History of the Jews*. Philadelphia, Pennsylvania: Jewish Publication Society of America, 1894, Volume 3, pp. 34–41; and Aryeh Kaplan: *Handbook of Jewish Thought*. Volume 1, Brooklyn, New York: Moznaim Publishing, 1990, Chapter 9, pp. 47–48.

18. For more information on King Clovis and Bishop Remi, see Gregory of Tours: *The History of the Franks*. Book II. New York City, New York: Penguin Classics, 1976, pp. 101–158; and Jean-Pierre Zeder: *Aspects de Bischheim au Fil des Siècles*. Volume 1, Strasbourg, France: Éditions Oberlin, 1982, p. 17. The actual testament of Bishop Remi that mentions Bischheim is available in French (translated from the Latin) on p. 18 of *Aspects de Bischheim au Fil des Siècles*.

19. Gavin I. Langmuir: "Intolerance and tolerance." In Tony Kushner and Nadia Valman: *Philosemitism, Antisemitism, and the Jews: Perspective from the Middle Ages to the Twentieth Century.* Aldershot, Hampshire, England, United Kingdom: Ashgate Publishing, 2004, p. 25.

20. Jacob Rader Marcus: "Pope Gregory the Great and the Jews 590–604." In *The Jew in the Medieval World: a Source Book: 315–1791.* Cincinnati, Ohio: Hebrew Union College Press, 1999, pp. 124–127.

21. Bernard S. Bachrach: *Early Medieval Jewish Policy in Western Europe.* Minneapolis, Minnesota: University of Minnesota Press, 1977, pp. 59–61; See also David Nicolle: *Poitiers AD 732: Charles Martel Turns the Islamic Tide.* Oxford, England, United Kingdom: Osprey Publishing, 2008.

22. Esther Benbassa: *The Jews of France: a History from Antiquity to the Present.* Princeton, New Jersey: Princeton University Press, 2001, p. 8. See also Louis I. Rabinowitz: *Jewish Merchant Adventures: a Study of the Radanites.* London, England, United Kingdom: Edward Goldston, 1948.

23. Bernard S. Bachrach: *Early Medieval Jewish Policy in Western Europe.* Minneapolis, Minnesota: University of Minnesota Press, 1977, pp. 66–83.

24. Louis I. Rabinowitz: *Jewish Merchant Adventures: a Study of the Radanites.* London, England, United Kingdom: Edward Goldston, 1948, pp. 9–10. See also Elkan Nathan Adler: *Jewish Travellers* [sic] *in the Middle Ages.* New York City, New York: Dover Publications, originally published in 1897, pp. 38–63.

25. Heinrich Graetz: *History of the Jews.* Philadelphia, Pennsylvania: Jewish Publication Society of America, 1894, Volume 3, pp. 34–41.

26. Chapter Ten of the Book of Genesis reads as follows:

1: These are the generations of the sons of Noah, Shem, Ham, and Japheth; sons were born to them after the flood.

2: The sons of Japheth: Gomer, Magog, Madai, Javan, Tubal, Meshech, and Tiras.

3: The sons of Gomer: Ash'kenaz, Riphath, and Togar'mah.
4: The sons of Javan: Eli'shah, Tarshish, Kittim, and Do'danim.

5: From these the coastland peoples spread. These are the sons of Japheth in their lands, each with his own language, by their families, in their nations.

6: The sons of Ham: Cush, Egypt, Put, and Canaan.

7: The sons of Cush: Seba, Hav'ilah, Sabtah, Ra'amah, and Sab'teca. The sons of Ra'amah: Sheba and Dedan.

8: Cush became the father of Nimrod; he was the first on earth to be a mighty man.

9: He was a mighty hunter before the LORD; therefore it is said, "Like Nimrod a mighty hunter before the LORD."

10: The beginning of his kingdom was Ba'bel, Erech, and Accad, all of them in the land of Shinar.

11: From that land he went into Assyria, and built Nin'eveh, Reho'both-Ir, Calah, and

12: Resen between Nin'eveh and Calah; that is the great city.

13: Egypt became the father of Ludim, An'amim, Leha'bim, Naph-tu'him,

14: Pathru'sim, Caslu'him (whence came the Philistines), and Caph'torim.

15: Canaan became the father of Sidon his first-born, and Heth,

16: and the Jeb'usites, the Amorites, the Gir'gashites,

17: the Hivites, the Arkites, the Sinites,

18: the Ar'vadites, the Zem'arites, and the Ha'mathites. Afterward the families of the Canaanites spread abroad.

19: And the territory of the Canaanites extended from Sidon, in the direction of Gerar, as far as Gaza, and in the direction of Sodom, Gomor'rah, Admah, and Zeboi'im, as far as Lasha.

20: These are the sons of Ham, by their families, their languages, their lands, and their nations.

21: To Shem also, the father of all the children of Eber, the elder brother of Japheth, children were born.

22: The sons of Shem: Elam, Asshur, Arpach'shad, Lud, and Aram.

23: The sons of Aram: Uz, Hul, Gether, and Mash.

24: Arpach'shad became the father of Shelah; and Shelah became the father of Eber.

25: To Eber were born two sons: the name of the one was Peleg, for in his days the earth was divided, and his brother's name was Joktan.

26: Joktan became the father of Almo'dad, Sheleph, Hazarma'veth, Jerah,

27: Hador'am, Uzal, Diklah,

28: Obal, Abim'a-el, Sheba,

29: Ophir, Hav'ilah, and Jobab; all these were the sons of Joktan.

30: The territory in which they lived extended from Mesha in the direction of Sephar to the hill country of the east.

31: These are the sons of Shem, by their families, their languages, their lands, and their nations.

32: These are the families of the sons of Noah, according to their genealogies, in their nations; and from these the nations spread abroad on the earth after the flood.

*Source: Book of Genesis, Holy Bible, Revised Standard Version. Oxford University Computing Service and University of Virginia Library, Charlottesville, Virginia. 1995: http://etext.virginia.edu/etcbin/toccer-new2?id=RsvGene.sgm&images=images/modeng&data=/texts/english/modeng/parsed&tag=public&part=all; accessed November 6, 2011.

27. Allen P. Ross: "The Table of Nations in Genesis 10—its content." *Bibliotheca Sacra*, Volume 138, 1980, pp. 22–34. Available at http://faculty.gordon.edu/hu/bi/Ted_Hildebrandt/OTeSources/01-Genesis/Text/Articles-Books/Ross-TableNations-BSac.pdf; accessed November 4, 2011.

28. Jay R. Berkovitz: *Rites and Passages: the Beginnings of Modern Jewish Culture in France, 1650–1860*. Philadelphia, Pennsylvania: University of Pennsylvania Press, 2004, p. 62; David Neal Miller and Neil G. Jacobs: "Ashkenaz." Available at http://www.brooklyn.net/classes/y241/ashkenaz.html; accessed February 28, 2012; and Neil G. Jacobs: *Yiddish: a Linguistic Introduction*. New York City, New York: Cambridge University Press, 2005, p. 4.

29. Nils Roemer: *German City, Jewish Memory: the Story of Worms*. Lebanon, New Hampshire: University Press of New England, 2010, p. 12–13; Heinrich Fichtenau: *Living in the Tenth Century: Mentalities and Social Orders*. Translated from the German by Patrick J. Geary. Chicago, Illinois: University of Chicago, 1991, p. 9; and Gotthard Deutsch, Abraham Lewinsky, Joseph Jacobs, and Schulim Ochser: "Worms." *Jewish Encyclopedia*, 1906. Available at http://www.jewishencyclopedia.com/articles/15013-worms; accessed January 10, 2012.

30. First point of view: Elliott Horowitz: "The Jews and the cross in the Middle Ages." In Tony Kushner and Nadia Valman: *Philosemitism, Antisemitism, and the Jews: Perspective from the Middle Ages to the Twentieth Century*. Aldershot, Hampshire, England, United Kingdom: Ashgate Publishing, 2004, pp. 123–125. Second point of view: Alexander Shapiro and Mordechai Ansbacher: "Trier." *Jewish Virtual Library*. Available at http://www.jewishvirtuallibrary.org/jsource/judaica/ejud_0002_0020_0_20041.html; accessed January 10, 2012.

31. Shlomo Eidelberg: *The Jews and the Crusaders: the Hebrew Chronicles of the First and Second Crusades*. Jersey City, New Jersey: Ktav Publishing, 1996, pp. 3–5.

32. Jacob Rader Marcus: "The Crusaders in Mayence, May 27, 1096." In *The Jew in the Medieval World: a Source Book: 315–1791*. Cincinnati, Ohio: Hebrew Union College Press, 1999, pp. 128–134. See also I. S. Robinson: *Henry IV of Germany, 1056–1106*. Cambridge, England, United Kingdom: Cambridge University Press, 1999.

33. Jeremy Cohen: *Living Letters of the Law: Ideas of the Jews in Medieval Christianity*. Berkeley, California: University of California Press, 1999, pp. 219–220.

34. Shlomo Eidelberg: *The Jews and the Crusaders: the Hebrew Chronicles of the First and Second Crusades*. Jersey City, New Jersey: Ktav Publishing, 1996, pp. 7–8.

35. Jeremy Cohen: *Living Letters of the Law*. Berkeley, California: University of California Press, 1999, p. 221; and Christopher Tyerman: *God's War: a New History of the Crusades*. London, England, United Kingdom: Penguin Books, 2007, pp. 282–283.

36. Irven M. Resnick: "Albert the Great on the Talmud and the Jews." In Tony Kushner and Nadia Valman: *Philosemitism, Antisemitism, and the Jews: Perspective from the Middle Ages to the Twentieth Century*. Aldershot, Hampshire, England, United Kingdom: Ashgate Publishing, 2004, pp. 133–137. The source of the Tertullian quote is Sholom Aleichem: *The Bloody Hoax*. Translated by Aliza Shevrin. Bloomington, Indiana: Indiana University Press, 1991, p. xi.

37. Benjamin of Tudela: *The Itinerary of Benjamin of Tudela: Travels in the Middle Ages*. Cold Spring, New York: Nightingale Resources, 1983. Available at http://depts.washington.edu/silkroad/texts/tudela.html#itinerary_1; accessed November 6, 2011; and Elkan Nathan Adler: *Jewish Travellers in the Middle Ages*. New York City, New York: Dover Publications, originally published in 1897.

38. Jacob Rader Marcus: "The expulsion of the Jews from France, 1182." In *The Jew in the Medieval World: a Source Book: 315–1791*. Cincinnati, Ohio: Hebrew Union College Press, 1999, pp. 27–30.

39. Allan Temko: "The burning of the Talmud in Paris." *Commentary Magazine*, May 1954. The article is available at http://www.commentarymagazine.com/article/the-burning-of-the-talmud-in-parisdate-1242/; accessed December 20, 2011. See also Israel Abrahams: *Jewish Life in the Middle Ages*. Philadelphia, Pennsylvania: Jewish Publication Society of America, 1993; Leonard B. Glick: *Abraham's Heirs: Jews and Christians in Medieval Europe*. Syracuse, New York: Syracuse University Press, 1998; and Judah M. Rosenthal: "The Talmud on trial: the disputation at Paris in the year 1240." *Jewish Quarterly*, Volume 47, Number 1, July, 1956.

40. "Innocent III: Constitution for the Jews (1199)." *Internet Medieval Sourcebook*. Fordham University. Available at http://www.fordham.edu/halsall/source/in3-constjews.asp; accessed November 6, 2011.

41. "Strasbourg: (Bas-Rhin département, Alsace region)." *Jewish Cemetery Project*. Available at http://www.iajgsjewishcemeteryproject.org/france/strasbourg-bas-rhin-departement-alsace-region-region.html; accessed November 6, 2011. See also Robert Weyl: "Les juif d'Alsace et les droits de l'homme." 1984. Available at http://judaisme.sdv.fr/histoire/historiq/droitsh/drh1.htm; accessed November 6, 2011; and Toni L. Kamins: "The virtual Jewish history tour, Strasbourg." *Jewish Virtual Library*. Available at http://www.jewishvirtuallibrary.org/jsource/vjw/Strasbourg.html; accessed November 6, 2011.

42. Nina Rowe: *The Jew, the Cathedral, and the Medieval City: Synagoga and Ecclesia in the Thirteenth Century*. Cambridge, England, United Kingdom: Cambridge University Press, 2011, pp. 3, 226.

43. Max Warschawski: "Histoire des Juifs de Strasbourg." Available at http://judaisme.sdv.fr/histoire/villes/strasbrg/hist/index.htm; accessed November 6, 2011; and Zosa Szajkowski: "The Jewish aspect of credit and usury." In *Jews and the French Revolutions of 1789, 1830 and 1848*. New York City, New York: Ktav Publishing House, 1970, pp. 152–162.

44. See Jeremy Cohen: *The Friars and the Jews: the Evolution of Medieval Anti-Judaism*. Ithaca, New York: Cornell University Press, 1982.

45. Saadia R. Eisenberg: *Reading Medieval Religious Disputation: the 1240 "Debate" between Rabbi Yehiel of Paris and Friar Nicholas Donin*. University of Michigan Dissertation, 2008. Available at http://deepblue.lib.umich.edu/handle/2027.42/60741; accessed December 17, 2011.

46. Ibid, pp. 48–56.

47. Ibid, pp. 44–45.

48. See Cecil Roth (ed.): *The Ritual Murder Libel and the Jews*. London, England, United Kingdom: Woburn Press, 1935.

49. Saadia R. Eisenberg: *Reading Medieval Religious Disputation: the 1240 "Debate" between Rabbi Yehiel of Paris and Friar Nicholas Donin*. University of Michigan Dissertation, 2008, pp. 72–73. Available at http://deepblue.lib.umich.edu/handle/2027.42/60741; accessed December 17, 2011.

50. J. E. Kaufmann and H. W. Kaufmann: *The Medieval Fortress: Castles, Forts, and Walled Cities of the Middle Ages*. Cambridge, Massachusetts: Da Capo Press, 2004, p. 237.

51. Zosa Szajkowski: "The Jewish aspect of credit and usury." In *Jews and the French Revolutions of 1789, 1830 and 1848*. New York City, New York: Ktav Publishing House, 1970, pp. 152–162.

52. Salo Wittmayer Baron: *A Social and Religious History of the Jews*. Volume 14. Philadelphia, Pennsylvania: Columbia University Press and the Jewish Publication Society of America, 1969, pp. 243–245.

53. Louis Spach: *Histoire de la Basse Alsace de la Ville de Strasbourg*. Strasbourg, France: Berger-Levrault, 1858, pp. 88–91.

54. Iwo Cyprian Pogonowski: *Jews in Poland*. New York City, New York: Hippocrene Books, 1993, pp. 45, 49, 50, and 65. The unabridged text (translated into English) of the 1264 Statute of Kalisz and subsequent ratifications by Polish kings is available on pp. 39–58.

55. Bernard Vogler: *L'Alsace, une Histoire*. Strasbourg, France: Oberlin, 1990, pp. 70–71.

56. Zosa Szajkowski: *Franco-Judaica: an Analytical Bibliography of Books, Pamphlets, Decrees, Briefs and Other Printed Documents Pertaining to the Jews in France 1500–1788*. New York City, New York: American Academy for Jewish Research, 1962, pp. 4–5, Note #48: "Memoire pour les Juifs établis en Alsace." Note that the publication date for this memorandum was 1717; however, Christian guildsmen felt the same way about their Jewish competitors both in the 1300s and in the 1700s.

57. "Armleder persecutions." *Jewish Encyclopedia*. New York City, New York: Funk and Wagnalls, 1906. Available at http://d31lnalg6cshkc.cloudfront.net/EH2H12HU.jpg; accessed November 4, 2010. See also Élie Scheid: *Histoire des Juifs d'Alsace*. Paris, France: Durlacher Armand, 1887.

58. Robert Weyl: "Les juif d'Alsace et les droits de l'homme." 1984. Available at http://judaisme.sdv.fr/histoire/historiq/droitsh/drh1.htm; accessed November 6, 2011. See also Max Warschawski: "History of the Jews in Strasbourg." Available at http://judaisme.sdv.fr/histoire/villes/strasbrg/hist/hist2.htm; accessed November 6, 2011.

59. Jacob Rader Marcus: "The Black Death and the Jews." In *The Jew in the Medieval World: a Source Book: 315–1791*. Cincinnati, Ohio: Hebrew Union College Press, 2000, pp. 49–53. Available

at http://www.fordham.edu/halsall/jewish/1348-jewsblackdeath.
html; accessed November 4, 2011. See also Joseph Jacobs and Isaac
Broydé: "Savoy." *Jewish Encyclopedia*, 1906. Available at http://
www.jewishencyclopedia.com/articles/13237-savoy; accessed
January 12, 2012; Lazare Landau: "Le massacre de la Saint-
Valentin." Available at http://judaisme.sdv.fr/histoire/historiq/stval/
stval.htm; accessed November 6, 2011; and Eugene L. Cox: *The
Green Count of Savoy*. Princeton, New Jersey: Princeton University
Press, 1967.

60. Robert S. Gottfried: *The Black Death: Natural and Human Disaster
in Medieval Europe*. New York City, New York: Free Press, 1983, pp.
73–74.

61. Esther Benbassa: *The Jews of France: a History from Antiquity to the
Present*. Princeton, New Jersey: Princeton University Press, 2001,
p. 23; and Michael Goldfarb: *Emancipation*. New York City, New
York: Simon & Schuster, 2009, p. 5. The information about King
Wenceslaus is from William Russell: *The History of Modern Europe*.
Volume 2. Philadelphia, Pennsylvania: Robert Carr, 1802, p. 18.

62. Iwo Cyprian Pogonowski: *Jews in Poland*. New York City, New York:
Hippocrene Books, 1993, pp. 64–65.

63. Ibid, p. 16.

64. Ibid, p. 70.

65. Paul Johnson: *A History of the Jews*. New York City, New York: Harper
Perennial, 1988, pp. 241–242.

66. Joseph Telushkin: "The Shulkhan Arukh." In *Jewish Literacy*.
New York City, New York: William Morrow and Company, 1991;
available at http://www.jewishvirtuallibrary.org/jsource/Judaism/
shulkhan_arukh.html; and Shira Schoenberg: "Joseph ben Ephraim
Caro (1488–1575)." *Jewish Virtual Library*. Available at http://www.
jewishvirtuallibrary.org/jsource/biography/Caro.html; accessed
December 3, 2011.

67. Selma Stern: *Josel of Rosheim*. Philadelphia, Pennsylvania: Jewish
Publication Society of America, 1965; and "Joseph (Joselmann) Ben
Gershon of Rosheim." *Jewish Virtual Library*. Available at http://www.
jewishvirtuallibrary.org/jsource/judaica/ejud_0002_0011_0_10295.
html; accessed December 4, 2011.

68. Mary C. Boys: *Has God Only One Blessing? Judaism as a Source of Christian Self-Understanding.* Mahwah, New Jersey: Paulist Press, 2000, p. 70.

69. Martin van Creveld: *Supplying War: Logistics from Wallenstein to Patton.* Cambridge, England, United Kingdom: Cambridge University Press, 2004. p. 5.

70. Jacob Rader Marcus: "The Cossack revolt and the fall of Nemirov, June 10, 1648." In *The Jew in the Medieval World: a Source Book: 315–1791.* Cincinnati, Ohio: Hebrew Union College Press, 2000, pp. 513–517.

71. Simon Schwarzfuchs: "Alsace and Southern Germany: the creation of a border." In *Jewish Emancipation Reconsidered.* Michael Brenner, Vicki Caron, and Uri R. Kaufmann (eds.). London, England, United Kingdom: Leo Baeck Institute, 2003, pp. 5–17.

72. Jean-Denis G. G. Lepage: *Vauban and the French Military under Louis XIV.* Jefferson, North Carolina: McFarland, 2009, pp. 183–184.

73. Andrew Lossky: *Louis XIV and the French Monarchy.* New Brunswick, New Jersey: Rutgers University Press, 1994, pp. 169–171.

74. The history of the ironworks at Neunkirchen, Saarland is available in an article titled "History of the Neunkirchen Plant" available at http://www.saarstahl.com/geschichte_neunkirchen.html?L=1; accessed November 10, 2011.

75. Moses Ginsburger: *Cerf-Berr et son Epoque.* Société d'Histoire des Juifs d'Alsace-Lorraine: Guebwiller, Alsace, France: J. Dreyfus, 1908, p. 6. Available at http://gallica.bnf.fr/ark:/12148/bpt6k5427849p/f8.image; accessed November 3, 2011.

76. Max Warschawski: "Hirtz de Médelsheim dit Cerf Berr, représentent de la 'nation juive' d'Alsace." Available at http://judaisme.sdv.fr/perso/cerfberr/index.htm; accessed November 12, 2011.

77. Salo Wittmayer Baron: *Social and Religious History of the Jews*: Volume 15. Philadelphia, Pennsylvania: Columbia University Press and the Jewish Publication Society of America, 1973, p. 116.

78. Roland E. Mousnier: *The Institutions of France under the Absolute Monarchy, 1598–1789.* Translated from the French by Brian Pearce. Chicago, Illinois: University of Chicago Press, 1979, pp. 415–416.

CHAPTER THREE:

Cerf Berr's Alsace Gamble, 1726–1763

By the later 1600s and the early 1700s, Ashkenazim were again living in Alsace, the Palatinate, and Saarland on the west side of the Rhine River. At least three main reasons existed for the Ashkenazi reappearance in large numbers in the Rhine River Valley. First, the Treaties of Westphalia in 1648 ended the Thirty Years' War in these areas, which needed immigrant settlers to rebuild the shattered economies. Second, the Chmielnicki Revolt, in part against the Ashkenazim in Poland, sent many Jews fleeing westward across the Great European Plain to find new places to dwell in safety.

Third, King Louis XIV annexed part of Saarland on which he built Fort Saarlouis (built between 1680 and 1683) to protect his interests and to defend against encroachment on France from adversaries to the north of Saarland. The presence of Fort Saarlouis and French troops meant security for the Ashkenazim in Saarland.

Ashkenazim Settle in Alsace, France

The Ashkenazim who reappeared in Alsace in the later 1600s and early 1700s settled in five townships, according to historian Max Warschawski. The five townships were:

- the lands of the Diocese of Strasbourg (Lower Alsace) owned by the Catholic Church,

- the lands of Lower Alsace owned by the King of France,

- the lands of Upper Alsace owned by the King of France,

- the lands of various ennobled landowners of Lower Alsace, and

- the lands owned by the Counts of Hanau-Lichtenberg (Lower Alsace).[1]

Of these five regions, the lands of Hanau-Lichtenberg attracted most Ashkenazim. In 1725, a census of Jews living in the lands of Hanau-Lichtenberg identified one hundred and fifty-seven families and nine widows. Thirty-one Jewish families and five Jewish widows lived in Bouxwiller, the capital of Hanau-Lichtenberg.[2]

The Ashkenazim communities in Alsace continued their long tradition of semi-autonomy from the political units in which they resided. Historian Paula Hyman described the semi-autonomous Ashkenazi communities as follows:

Because of their [population] size and their unbroken connection with the Central European Ashkenazi tradition, the Jews in Alsace and Lorraine maintained institutionally diversified communities. With its synagogue or place of prayer, its mikveh (ritual bath), school, cemetery, and court, the Jewish community provided fully for the religious needs of its members, saw to their education, assumed responsibility for the resident poor, and adjudicated civil cases between Jewish litigants. Since taxes were imposed upon corporate groups rather than on individuals, the various Jewish communities were responsible for paying to the appropriate authorities the numerous charges to which the Jews were subjected. For the authorities, of course, this was the primary function of the Jewish communities, followed by maintaining order among the Jewish population. As late as 1768, for example, the Jewish community of Metz issued sumptuary legislation to limit public displays of luxury.[3]

The semi-autonomous communities of the Ashkenazim in Alsace were not democratic. "Voting privileges depended upon gender, marital status, and wealth; in general, prosperous married men selected the communal leadership. The wealthiest laymen, an oligarchy of Jewish notables, led the community," serving as its Préposés (leaders). "Usually merchants, bankers, or industrialists on a grand scale, [Préposés] exerted the most influence with both local and national authorities because of their contributions to the economy. They also bore the bulk of the communal tax burden. Sophisticated and somewhat acculturated, they often had international commercial contacts and access to French governmental representatives."[3]

Recall that beginning in 1388, Strasbourg authorities levied a body tax on all Jews who entered the city for the day. As early as 1698, the Strasbourg authorities began to farm the Jewish body tax, meaning that a tax farmer paid an annual lump sum to the Strasbourg authorities and recouped his money from the authorities of the semi-autonomous Ashkenazi communities. An effective tax farmer could make his living from the difference between the money he paid to the Strasbourg authorities and the money he recouped from the Ashkenazi Préposés.

In 1698, the price of the Strasbourg Jewish body-tax lease was one thousand livres. The livre was the currency of France until 1795. Established by Charlemagne, one livre was the equivalent of a pound of silver. One livre equaled twenty French sous or two hundred and forty French deniers. Sometimes the word pound replaced the word livre. Under the tax farming system, all Jews who wished to enter Strasbourg for the day did so without incurring a charge at the point and time of entry. In theory, the Ashkenazi Préposés collected money from the members of the semi-autonomous Ashkenazi communities to reimburse the farmer of the Jewish body tax.[4] However, as noted above by Paula Hyman, the Ashkenazi Préposés usually bore the bulk of the communal tax burden.

Taxes and tolls were rife in France before the French Revolution of 1789. Various authorities in France levied taxes on horses, cattle, and merchandise passing through various lands. For example, during the early seventeenth century, almost fifty-seven hundred separate tolls existed in France.[5] However, Strasbourg authorities and the French King were unique in charging a human body toll tax on Jews to enter the City of Strasbourg and Lower Alsace, respectively. "The body tax in effect treated a man as an animal," hissed historian David Feuerwerker.[6]

In the early eighteenth century, the King of France appointed by letters patent two official rabbis, called Patent Rabbis, to oversee the Jewish Rabbinical Courts in Lower and Upper Alsace. This reality was one reason why the Ashkenazi communities in Alsace were *semi*-autonomous and not autonomous. The Patent Rabbi for Lower Alsace worked in Haguenau and the one for Upper Alsace in Ribeauvillé.[1] The Patent Rabbis were the only rabbis recognized by the King of France and other authorities external to the semi-autonomous Jewish communities in Alsace. However, some Jewish communities elected their own sous (under) rabbis, who existed in addition to the Patent Rabbis. In the 1740s, there were thirteen known sous-rabbis in Lower Alsace and nine in Upper Alsace.[2]

In the early 1700s, most of the Ashkenazim in Alsace worked as peddlers, who traveled from place to place selling small goods, and livestock merchants, who sold horses, cattle, and forage, including hay, straw, oats, green vegetables, and grains. Alsatian laws prohibited the entry of Ashkenazim into trades such as tanning, weaving, tailoring, fishing, selling wine, milling, and farming. However, a few Ashkenazi families acquired large fortunes by supplying the huge number of horses and amounts of forage required by the French Armies garrisoned in Alsace and Lorraine. The Ashkenazi military purveyors became the most important people in their Ashkenazim communities, lent large sums of money, and functioned as bankers and Ashkenazi Préposés.

For example, one such Ashkenazi Alsatian military purveyor was

Moses Blien of Mutzig (1700–1762, also spelled Belin, Blin, Blien, Blein, and Ballin). He was also an early Ashkenazi General Préposé in Alsace and a tax farmer for the Strasbourg Jewish body tax. He belonged to the same generation as Cerf Berr's father. Moses Blien's own father was Aron Blien, who was born in Bühl, Rastatt in Baden, about sixteen miles northeast of Strasbourg. Aron Blien probably belonged to the Ballin family of Worms.[6] Moses Blien married Malka Gombricht (1705–1772) of Obernai, Alsace, who was herself a daughter of Obernai banker Samuel Ephraim Gombricht (1680–1756). Moses and Malka Blien had seven daughters and two sons, all but one of whom were born in Mutzig, Alsace.

Moses Blien supplied the French Army garrisoned in Strasbourg with necessities ordered by King Louis XV's sequential Secretaries of War. During his professional life, Moses Blien worked closely with the following Secretaries of War under King Louis XV:

* * * * * * * *

French Secretaries (Ministers) of War, 1718–1757

- Claude Le Blanc (served 1718–1723);
- François Victor Le Tonnelier of Breteuil (1723–1726);
- Nicolas Prosper Bauyn of Angervilliers (served 1728–1740);
- François Victor Le Tonnelier of Breteuil (1741–1743, second term); and
- Marc-Pierre of Voyer of Paulmy, Count of Argenson (1743–1757)

* * * * * * * *

The French Secretary of War's competence covered many matters. These matters included "the standing army, the militia, coastal defense, the École Militaire [military school], the Invalides [home and hospital for aged and unwell soldiers], the *haras* or royal stud farms, and the Maréchaussée" (the constabulary, which was the ancestor of the gendarmerie—that is, military personnel charged with police activities). In addition, the Secretary of War "was charged with the collection of the taillon or supplementary taille [types of taxes], and with the administration of the frontier provinces and generalities." These frontier provinces were Alsace, the Three Bishoprics (Metz, Toul, and Verdun), Le Barrois, Artois, Flandre, Hainault, Franche-Comté, Roussillon, Dauphiné, and Sedan with its dependencies.[7] The French Secretaries of War understood the struggles of the Ashkenazim in Alsace Provinces.

On May 15, 1743, Secretary of War Marc-Pierre of Voyer of Paulmy, Count of Argenson (1696–1764; henceforth, Marc-Pierre Argenson), permitted Moses Blien and his Ashkenazi business partners to reside temporarily overnight in Strasbourg to oversee military provisioning operations during the War of the Austrian Succession (1740–1748). This exception to the otherwise strict Strasbourg laws prohibiting overnight habitation by Ashkenazim later served as the precedent for Cerf Berr's quest to live in Strasbourg.[8]

In 1745, Moses Blien of Mutzig first farmed the Strasbourg Jewish body tax for the 1745–1754 term. In 1746, he became one of three Ashkenazi General Préposés of Alsace. The other two Ashkenazi General Préposés were Jacob Baruch Weyl (1695–1775) of Obernai and Aaron (Aron) Mayer (Meyer) of Mutzig.

Ashkenazim Settle in Saarland and the Palatinate, Holy Roman Empire

During the later 1600s and early 1700s, some Ashkenazim immigrated to the Saarland and the Palatinate, which were a part of the Holy Roman Empire. Recall that these lands still lay wasted from the devastation wrought by the Thirty Years' War. Certain noble families owned large pieces of land and whole towns and cities in Saarland and the Palatinate. For example, Karl Kaspar Franz, Count of Leyen (1655–1739, ruled

1705–1739), owned the Village of Médelsheim in southeastern Saarland. The von der Leyen dynasty also owned territories in southwestern Palatinate.[9] Médelsheim had a vibrant Ashkenazi community during the late 1600s and early 1700s.

In 1725, Dov Baer Naftali Berr Médelsheim (1700–1778?[10]) established himself in the Village of Médelsheim, Saarland.[1] Médelsheim was conveniently located around fifteen to thirty miles from Herr Berr's businesses in Saarbrücken to the west and the Rhine River Valley to the east of Médelsheim. His eldest daughter (Rebecca?) was born in 1723 in Ottersheim (Palatinate), about seven miles west of the Rhine River.[1] His wife, whose name may have been Guelché, died in 1767.[10]

In 1726 in Médelsheim, Dov and Guelché (?) Berr welcomed their first son, Cerf Berr. "Cerf" in French means "stag" (a large buck or male deer) and was a name given to many first-born sons of the time. Cerf Berr's other name was Hirtz (Hertz, Herz, Hirz, Hirtz) Berr (Ber, Beer, Baer). He usually signed his name Cerf Berr of Médelsheim but also used the names Hirtz of Bischheim and Hirtz of Médelsheim. Cerf Berr had a second sister named Esther Berr (1743–1793) and three brothers, Marchand Kaufmann Menaché Seligman Berr (1730–1778), Mayer Moyses (Moses) Berr (1740–1774), and Seligmann Berr (1742–1779).[6,10–11]

As a youngster, Cerf Berr was exposed to a traditional Talmudic education for young Ashkenazi boys, although the length and quality of this education in Médelsheim is unknown. The nature of a traditional Talmudic education remained virtually unchanged from the High Middle Ages to at least the time of the French Revolution. A boy's Talmudic education began when he was five years old or later if he was weak or sickly. Historian Israel Abrahams described a boy's initiation to his Talmudic education as follows:

> The ceremony of initiation was performed partly in a school and partly in the synagogue, and the favorite occasion was the Feast of Pentecost [or Feast of Weeks, which celebrates the

giving of the Torah at Mount Sinai and the harvesting of the first fruits of the season, in May or June]. Early in the morning the boy was dressed in new clothes, and three cakes of fine flour and honey were baked for him by a young maiden. Three eggs were boiled, and apples and other fruit were gathered in profusion. Then the child was taken in the arms of the Rabbi or another learned friend first to the school and then to the synagogue, or vice versa. The child was placed on the reading-dais before the Scroll, from which the Ten Commandments were read as the lesson of the day. In the school, he received his first lesson in reading Hebrew. On a slate were smeared in honey some of the letters of the Hebrew alphabet, or simple texts, such as "Moses commanded us a law, an inheritance for the assembly of Jacob" (Deuteronomy 33:4); and the child lisped the letters as he ate the honey, the cakes, and the other delicacies, that the words of the Law might be sweet in his lips. The child was then handed over to the arms of his mother, who had stood by during this delightful scene.[12]

Israel Abrahams noted, "Elementary schools existed in every Jewish community, but were not all supported by public funds…The father was rightly thought by some to be disqualified from teaching his own children, but he was bound to pay a teacher for them." Israel Abrahams continued:

The hours of instruction were long, and in winter the children went to school one or two hours before daylight. Sometimes the signal for school was the jingling of the silver bells which fringed the mantles of the Scrolls of the Law. The boys continued at their lessons until the time for morning prayer, when their teacher took them to synagogue, or had a private service in his own house. The children then went home for a hasty breakfast, after which lessons were resumed until eleven o'clock, when there was a break for the midday meal, all the pupils re-assembling exactly at twelve. There was another very short interval between two and three o'clock, and work was continued until the time for evening prayer, after which the children returned home. Night preparation [homework] was encouraged in the Jewish homes...

The boys were first taught Hebrew reading, beginning with the alphabet, which absorbed a month. The teacher used a small wooden pointer, called in France a tendeur, with which he indicated the letters. When the letters were known, the vowel signs were taken, to which another month was devoted, and lastly the pupil learnt the combination of consonants and vowels into syllables. Three months apparently sufficed for this difficult step. In the fourth month the reading of the Pentateuch was started with the Book of Leviticus. During the second three months the boy read a portion of the weekly lesson in Hebrew. The following six months were used in translating the weekly lessons into the vernacular [Yiddish]. By that time the boy was six years old. Books were naturally, scarce, but the teacher took a tablet or slate and wrote on it three or four verses, or even whole chapters, and this served as the week's lesson. The words were then rubbed off and a fresh section written on the same slate.

In his next year's course the boy was taught the Aramaic version of the Pentateuch, which he translated into the vernacular; the next two years were devoted to the [seventeen] prophetical books [e.g., Isaiah, Jeremiah, Lamentations, Ezekiel, Daniel, Hosea and Jonah) and the hagiographa [the third part of the Hebrew Bible canon (the other two were the Law and the Prophets); it includes Job, Proverbs, and Psalms]. At the age of ten, the boy began the Mishna, and by the age of thirteen he had read a selection of the most important of the smaller tractates of the Talmud. Those who were destined to qualify as professional students devoted the next seven years to the greater tractates of the Talmud.[12]

All Jews felt the "charm of a beautiful handwriting," noted Israel Abrahams. Beautiful handwriting was an "index of the writer's worth." The following poem, written by Joseph Ezobi, a late thirteenth-century poet of Perpignan (France) to his son, demonstrates this appreciation of beautiful handwriting:

> And like thy father sing in tunefulness;
> Hark though, a barren soul is profitless.
> Purge well thy soul, no stain therein to leave,
> Remove its grosser parts in virtue's sieve.
> When thou a letter sendest to thy friend,
> Is it neatly written? Nay? 'twill sure offend;
> For in his penmanship man stands revealed—
> Purest intent by chastest style is sealed.
> Be heedful then when thou dost pen thy songs;
> To lofty strains a goodly hand belongs.[12]

Cerf Berr of Médelsheim had beautiful handwriting. He also had a great love of books. The Talmudic education inculcated a love of books, as Judah Ibn Tibbon (1120–after 1190) noted:

> Avoid bad society, but make your books your companions. Let your bookcases and shelves be your gardens and your pleasure grounds. Pluck the fruit that grows therein, gather the roses, the spices, and the myrrh. If your soul be satiate and weary, change from garden to garden, from furrow to furrow, from sight to sight. Then will your desire renew itself, and your soul be satisfied with delight.[13]

The Talmudic teachers instructed boys to "use only books which are beautifully written, on good paper, and well and handsomely bound." The teachers admonished their students, "Read in a pretty well-furnished room, let your eye rest on beautiful objects so that you may love your work. Beauty must be everywhere, in your books and in your house." "The wealthy must honor the Law, says the Talmud; let them do this by paying for beautiful copies of the Scriptures. Use eye and ear; read aloud, do not work in silent poring."[12]

Advanced pupils proceeded from the elementary Talmudic schools to yeshivas. They lived together in the house of the head of the yeshiva or in a special nearby building.

In 1735, while nine-year-old Cerf Berr may have been studying the Mishna in Médelsheim, seventeen-year-old William Henry (1718–1768), Count of Nassau-Saarbrücken (ruled 1741–1768, henceforth, Count William Henry), for whom Cerf Berr would one day work, inherited the County of Nassau-Saarbrücken in Saarland.[14] Count William Henry was a member of the House of Nassau, whose origins dated to the 1100s. He was raised a Calvinist (Protestant).

In the early 1740s, Count William Henry moved from his birthplace in Usingen, Hesse to the City of Saarbrücken, the capital of the County of Nassau-Saarbrücken. The two cities were about one hundred miles apart. Saarbrücken was mostly in ruins when Count William Henry first arrived there. The armies of the Thirty Years' War had decimated the city and no one yet had undertaken to rebuild it. Count William Henry dedicated his life to rebuilding Saarbrücken. He ordered construction of a new Saarbrücken castle after clearing the ruins of the remains of the seventeenth-century castle. Castles had stood on the site since 999 AD when the castle was known as Castellum Sarabrucca.

Count William Henry also ordered construction of other important buildings in the City of Saarbrücken, including the Basilica of Saint John (built from 1754 to 1758) and the Ludwig Protestant Church (1762–1775). Architect Friedrich Joachim (1694–1787) designed these and many other Baroque-style buildings in Saarbrücken. Count William Henry admired the Baroque style, which he first encountered at age twenty-one during a grand tour to Paris and Versailles in 1739. Count William Henry maintained cordial relations with King Louis XV, his giant dynast neighbor to the south.[14]

In 1740, Count William Henry led his own regiment of grenadiers in the War of the Austrian Succession.[15] In 1742, he sold his regiment to Louis VIII, Landgrave of Hesse-Darmstadt (1691–1768, ruled 1739–1768)[16], while the two nobles were in Frankfurt to witness the coronation of Holy Roman Emperor Charles VII (1697–1745, ruled 1742–1745). Cerf Berr would become a close friend of Louis VIII, Landgrave of Hesse-Darmstadt. Count William Henry again led his own troops during the Seven Years' War (1754–1763)[17], which was the conflict in which Cerf Berr cut his teeth as an army purveyor to the French Army in Alsace.

By 1749, thirty-one-year-old Count William Henry had incurred a heavy debt load because of the combined cost of his building projects in Saarbrücken and maintaining his mistresses and his regiment of grenadiers. He needed money to continue his ambitious projects and life style and turned to a Saarland consortium of Ashkenazim to whom he sold the lease on his three iron forges at Geislautern, Fischbach and Scheidt. In 1749, the consortium of Ashkenazi leaseholders and industry managers were Dov Berr of Médelsheim (Cerf Berr's father), Franz Didier, Jean-Clément Quien, and Solomon Alexander.[6] The iron forges were located in three valleys rich in coal and iron ore and covered with thick forests in Saarland. Count William Henry owned these three valleys, whose names were the Sulz, Fischbach and Scheidterbach River Valleys. These three valleys converge onto the northern aspect of the City of Saarbrücken.[18]

On November 4, 1750, Moses Blien of Mutzig (previously mentioned) became one of the leaseholders for Count William Henry's iron forges in the County of Nassau-Saarbrücken. On that day, records show that the Count amended the lease contract for the three iron mills by replacing Jean-Clément Quien with Moses Blien of Mutzig.[6] The same year (1750), Moses Blien alone leased the iron forges of Jägersfreude. Count William Henry leased his industry works only to financially strong groups for a good price. The lease farmers then had to manage carefully the operations of the industry works to maximize their own profit. The consortium of Ashkenazi industrialists pleased the Count as judged by his renewal of the leases to them.

Cerf Berr Moves from Saarland to Alsace

Around 1748, twenty-two-year-old Cerf Berr moved from his birthplace in Médelsheim, Saarland to Bischheim, Alsace, about forty-three miles to the southeast.[19] On September 3, 1748, he married Ytele Judith (Jüdel, Juttel) Weill (Weyl) (1730–1783), daughter of Abraham Weill (Weyl) of Bischheim.[10] In 1748, twenty-two-year-old Cerf Berr and eighteen-year-old Jüdel Berr welcomed their first child, a daughter named Rebecca.

In 1748, Bischheim was about a half-day's horse ride north of Strasbourg. Anti-Jewish laws, dating from the late fourteenth century, as described above, prohibited Cerf Berr from residing in Strasbourg. Cerf Berr wanted to live in Strasbourg. Recall that Remigius, Bishop of Reims, in 496 AD received the Village of Bischheim as a gift from Frankish King Clovis. Around 1100, the Bishopric of Strasbourg annexed Bischheim. In 1411, the Catholic Church sold the village to the Boecklin of Boecklinsau family of Alsace. When Cerf Berr moved to Bischheim, the Boecklin of Boecklinsau family still owned the Village of Bischheim.

The first mention of Jews in Bischheim was in 1636 when Rabbi Aberlin of Bischheim pronounced a funeral oration for Ascher Levy of Richshoffen. However, Jews probably earlier had settled in Bischheim in the wake of the Saint Valentine's Day Massacre in Strasbourg on February 14, 1349.[20]

The French Crown classified newcomer Cerf Berr of Médelsheim as a foreigner (étranger). As an Ashkenazim, he belonged to a semi-autonomous religious community, as described above. In other words, Cerf Berr was not a subject of the French King even though he lived in Alsace, which was part of the French Kingdom.

Various French authorities levied at least five types of taxes on Cerf Berr and other Ashkenazim living in Alsace. The first tax was a Jewish body tax levied by the French Crown on Ashkenazim whenever they entered or left Lower Alsace. The second tax was the one-time permission tax owed to the Boecklin of Boecklinsau family, owners of the Village of Bischheim. The third tax was the annual residence tax paid by Jews to the Boecklin Boecklinsau family to live in Bischheim. The amount of annual residence tax paid to the Boecklinsau family by Cerf Berr is unknown. However, in 1744, each family of Jews in the City of Rosheim paid twenty livres per year to that town's owners. The Intendant of Alsace reformed the tax in 1744 so that the Jews in the City of Rosheim had to pay an additional tax of two hundred and fifty-five livres "for the relief of the Christian population." The Jewish families of Rosheim each paid a portion of this additional tax, explained historian Robert Weyl.[21]

The fourth tax paid by Cerf Berr upon moving to Bischheim was a protection tax levied by the French King on all Jews living in the Kingdom of France. Thus, even though Cerf Berr was not a subject of the French King, he still paid a mandatory protection tax to the French King. The fifth tax was the reviled Jewish body tax levied by the Strasbourg authorities on all Jews without distinction who entered the City of Strasbourg for the day. Beyond these five main taxes, some Ashkenazim in Alsace paid various other taxes, including taxes for the right to peddle, obtain water, market iron, graze livestock, and slaughter animals for meat according to ritual.[22]

Around 1720, the Jews of Bischheim built a synagogue to replace the only place of worship located in a private home. In 1726, the Sovereign Council of Alsace (the French King's Court in Alsace) ordered the destruction of the synagogue, according to historian Louis Schlaefli.[22] Thus, when Cerf Berr arrived in Bischheim, no synagogue existed. As a pious and observant Ashkenazim, he created a place for prayer in his home.

The Ashkenazi population of Bischheim increased over time, according to Louis Schlaefli as follows:

1689—no Jewish families;
1716—two families,
1720—twenty-three families,
1723—twenty-five families, and

1784—fifty-three families (two hundred and fifty-six individuals).[22]

The Ashkenazi population of Alsace also increased over time, according to Simon Schwarzfuchs, as follows:

1716—about six thousand individuals,
1732—eighty-three hundred individuals,
1744—ten thousand five hundred individuals; and
1754—thirteen thousand individuals.[23]

In November 1751, twenty-five-year-old Cerf Berr of Médelsheim joined a partnership with five other Ashkenazim to purchase the lease for operating the Saarland iron mills owned by Count William Henry. Cerf Berr's partners were his father, Dov Berr of Médelsheim, Moses Blien, and three brothers of the Alexander family—Seligman, Solomon, and Samuel, according to historian Pascal Faustini.[6]

In 1754, forty-five-year-old Lehmann Netter of Rosheim (1709–1792) replaced fifty-four-year-old Moses Blien as General Préposé of the Jewish Nation in Alsace. Moses Blien sold his property in Mutzig and retired to Metz after a short stay in Paris.[6] The executive board of the Jewish Nation of Alsace (Nation Juive) now consisted of three General Préposés—Aaron Mayer of Mutzig, Jacob Baruch Weyl of Obernai, and Lehmann Netter of Rosheim.[21]

In 1756, King Louis XV's controller-general of finance, in response to complaints from some Alsatian Christians about the Ashkenazim, asked Governor Marshal de Coigny of Alsace for information about the trade carried on by the Jews. King Louis XV's Intendants were unanimous in replying that the Jews "should not be banned from the fairs and markets, for they kept prices low, whereas they brought about an expansion of trade."[24]

In 1756, the Seven Years' War erupted between France and England over their possessions in North America and in the West Indies. Protestant Prussia sided with Protestant England, and Roman

Catholic France with Roman Catholic Austria. The latter alliance ended a previous rivalry that had endured for about two hundred and fifty years. France and Austria together defeated Prussia; however, the price of victory was France's loss of Belgium.[25] Some historians believe that the Seven Years' War was a mere continuation of the War of the Austrian Succession and that the various peace treaties concluded at the end of the latter war were little more than an armistice.[26]

During the Seven Years' War, the French Secretary of War was responsible for the conduct of the war and administration of Alsace Province, as described above. Cerf Berr, during the early part of his career as an entrepreneur in the military purveying business, did business with the following Secretaries of War:

* * * * * * * *

French Secretaries (Ministers) of War, 1750–1775

- Marc-Pierre of Voyer of Paulmy, Count of Argenson (served 1743–1757);
- Marc-René of Voyer of Paulmy of Argenson (1757–1758);
- Charles Louis Auguste Fouquet, Duke of Belle-Isle (1758–1761);
- Étienne-François, Count of Stainville, Duke of Choiseul (1761–1770);
- Louis François, Marquis of Monteynard (1771–1774);
- Emmanuel-Armand of Vignerot of the Plessis of Richelieu, Duke of Aiguillon (1774); and
- Louis Nicolas Victor of Félix of Ollières, Count of Muy (1774–1775);

* * * * * * * *

In 1756, the French Secretary of War was Marc-Pierre Argenson. Recall that he was the royal official who had written the letter to the Strasbourg authorities on behalf of Moses Blien and his partners to permit their temporary overnight stay in Strasbourg. However, in 1757, Madame de Pompadour (1721–1764), the mistress of King Louis XV, used her influence to exile Marc-Pierre Argenson to his country seat (Ormes).

In 1757, Cerf and Jüdel Berr had their second child, a daughter named Minette, in Bischheim. In 1758, Cerf and Jüdel Berr had their third child and first son, Max, also known as Mardoche or Marx Nathanail (1758–1817; henceforth, Max). Max was born in Bischheim.

On September 29, 1758, Count William Henry signed a lease with a consortium of industrialists consisting of Cerf Berr and his three brothers (Cerf Berr had continued his Saarland businesses with Count William Henry, even after moving to Bischheim). The term of the lease was for twelve years, from 1758 to 1770. This lease meant a steady income of unknown amount for Cerf Berr if he and his brothers efficiently operated the iron works. The iron works in Nassau-Saarbrücken were "Geislauterner Eisen-Schmelz-Hammer and Huttenwerk..., die Fischbacher Schmelz, den Plathinenhammer und Meyer, und den Scheider Hammer mit dem Hammer Meyer."[11] Cerf Berr's three co-signatories listed on the lease were Marchand "Beer" of Saargemünd (Sarreguemines), Lorraine; Mayer Beer of Bischheim, Alsace; and Seligmann Beer of Rosheim, Alsace. In 1768, Count William Henry died at age fifty years after a stroke.[26]

In 1760, the Boecklin of Boecklinsau family officially authorized Ashkenazim to live in Bischheim, even though Jews had been living there since the Boecklin of Boecklinsau family purchased the town in 1411. The new authorization permitted the Boecklin of Boecklinsau family to collect a tax on the proceeds of the multiple businesses run by the Ashkenazim who lived in Bischheim. This famous Dorfordnung (village order or rule) of 1760 required the Bischheim Mayor to supervise the signing of all contracts between the Ashkenazim and Christian artisans and peasants living in Bischheim. The Bischheim Mayor said his presence was necessary to protect the Ashkenazim and the Christians, but his real reason was to collect the taxes on the transactions, averred historian Jean-Pierre Zeder.[20]

In 1761, the Secretary of War of France was Étienne-François, Count of Stainville, Duke of Choiseul (1719–1785; henceforth, the Duke of Choiseul). The Duke of Choiseul first met Cerf Berr during the Seven Years' War. The Duke of Choiseul liked and helped Cerf Berr for many years.[1,28] Born in Lorraine, the Duke of Choiseul served as French Ambassador to the Court of Vienna, then as French Secretary for Foreign Affairs (1758–1761), and finally as French Secretary of War (1761–1770). When the Duke of Choiseul became Secretary of War, he found the French Army in organizational tatters. For example, the Ministry of War comprised eight bureaus that defied logic, as follows:

- Provisions, discipline, and military correspondence (the most important bureau);
- Nominations, vacancies, decorations, and pensions;
- Troop movements, particularly marches;
- Pay, pensions, gratifications, and brevets (a brevet was a commission promoting a military officer in rank without an increase in pay);
- Details of officers' salaries and infractions of military justice;
- Expedition of royal orders and arrest (stoppages or cancellations);
- Artillery, fortifications, Maréchaussée, food, and forage; and
- Militia, hospitals, uniforms, and "bed, wood, and candle"— the three facilities accorded to troops in winter quarters.[7]

The Duke of Choiseul reorganized the French War Ministry, which, in 1771, comprised seven bureaus as follows:

- Gratifications, pensions, commissions, and leaves;

- Routes, troop movements, remounts (horses), and militia;
- Artillery, fortifications, engineers;
- Official correspondence;
- Clothing and equipment;
- Archives; and
- Subsistence.[7]

A major figure in supplying the French Armies was the French Army Intendant, whose role was second only to that of the French Army Commander. The Army Intendant was responsible for "supply, subsistence, finance, military police, transport, and hospital service." He "brought the army into existence, supervising the marshaling of its elements; the Commander arrived only after the army was formed and ready for operations." Many war commissaries, who generally were highly paid nobles, aided the Army Intendant. A war commissary received between two hundred and fifty and eight hundred livres per month and generous rations of bread and forage for livestock, compared to the French Army Intendant, who received one thousand livres per month and fifty rations of bread and thirty of forage.[29]

The Army Intendant supervised the system of requisition used in occupied territories, negotiated contracts for the French Army's needs, managed fiscal matters, and supervised corporations that supplied goods. Examples of these corporations were the bread company (called the munitionnaire); the meat supplier, the forage (fourrage) régie (more below); and the various private contractors, such as Moses Blien and Cerf Berr of Médelsheim. The French Army Intendant "bore a royal commission, and though he was nominally subordinate to the Commander, he had the right of direct correspondence with Versailles. His opinion carried much weight in the conduct of the campaign, and he could in fact exercise a veto over proposed campaigns," noted historian Lee Kennett.[27]

During the Seven Years' War, the munitionnaires (bread suppliers) fed the French Armies, which numbered around two hundred and eighty thousand men. The munitionnaires employed thousands of workers and great numbers of wagons and horses. For example, during the Seven Year's War, the munitionnaires used twenty-three thousand horses to move the bread-making capability (e.g., bricks to build the numerous bread ovens) alongside the French Armies. The annual budget of the munitionnaires was around twenty million livres. Munitionnaires maximized use of the resources available in Alsace and other French border provinces to minimize the cost of transporting grain and flour to the battlegrounds in Central Europe.[30]

While the munitionnaires fed the French Armies, various categories of army purveyors provided other supplies. For example, the meat suppliers provided a quarter pound of meat each day to every soldier in the French Army of the Lower Rhine.

The task of supplying forage for the military horses was so herculean and fraught with risk that most army purveyors avoided competing for the contract. In response to the state of scarcity of forage for the livestock, the French Crown created the forage régie, a government corporation that was supposed to supply the French Army horses with a ration of twelve pounds of hay and two-thirds of a bucket of oats per horse per day.[31]

In 1759, the French Armies in Soissons, Flanders, Champagne, Metz, Alsace, and Hainaut required four million rations of horse forage to carry the French Armies through six months of winter quarters.[31] "A field force of sixty thousand men could contain forty thousand horses, who could consume one thousand tons of green fodder daily," said historian John A. Lynn.[32] "A French soldier required only a pound and a half of bread to sustain him each day, but his horse consumed twenty pounds of dried fodder or fifty pounds of fresh green grass cut from the fields in addition to oats."

When normal means of purchasing army provisions failed, which was a recurrent problem, the French Field Commander ordered the French Army Intendant into the open market to obtain supplies. The French Secretary of War in Versailles disapproved of this approach of meeting need, because the cost of supplies increased. For example, a ration of forage in the French government-run requisition system (forage régie) cost sixteen sous (just under one livre) compared with a ration of forage from an independent contractor, who might charge twenty-one to twenty-five sous (just over one livre). Sheer necessity led the French Army Intendant "to ignore the injunctions of Versailles, and constant use was made of the [open market]," explained Lee Kennett. [30]

Alsatian Jewish entrepreneurs, including Cerf Berr, dominated the horse fodder military business during the Seven Years' War. This reality offended some Christian observers. For example, on April 18, 1758, Louis, Count of Clermont (1709–1771), Commander of the Army of the Lower Rhine, wrote the following to Secretary of War Charles Louis Auguste Fouquet, Duke of Belle-Isle (predecessor of the Duke of Choiseul): "The Jews who handle this enterprise [army provisioning] have as good a reputation as Jews can have." Commander Clermont was also Abbot of the Roman Catholic Abbey Saint Germain-des-Prés in Paris. He obtained papal dispensation to embark on a military career, but retained his military command for only six months. [33]

French King Louis XV was adamant against conducting battles of the Seven Years' War on French soil and pushed his armies as far as possible eastward into Central Europe to wreak their destruction there. However, this approach complicated supplying the French Armies. Lee Kennett observed:

> The [French Army in Central Europe] was drawing much of its needs from a distance of several hundred miles with a very unsatisfactory transportation system [during] the winter months…The large number of [French] effectives in Germany— as many as two hundred thousand—required tremendous amounts of provisions and matériel of all kinds. In addition, for every two soldiers, a non-combatant existed who likewise had to be maintained. The lavish rations of food and forage accorded to the general officers placed further demands on the supply system…According to the calculations of Audouin, an army of one hundred thousand men consumed two hundred

thousand pounds of flour each day. The seventy-five thousand horses used in Germany required during the winter months a total of [almost nine million] forage rations—some seventy thousand tons of hay and four million bushels of oats.[31]

The French Army supply system was supposedly chaotic compared with the supply systems of the Prussian and Austrian Armies, whose officers claimed that they better appreciated the importance of supplying the war. During the Seven Years' War, France was the only major belligerent to still use the private contracting approach (private army purveyors) to supply the war instead of establishing a government commissariat, except for the forage régie, which rarely worked.

Why did the French Crown still use the private contracting system? As the Seven Years' War progressed, France fell deeper into debt, as described elsewhere.[34] The private contracting system enabled the French government to buy goods on credit by compensating the private contractors, such as Moses Blien and Cerf Berr, "lavishly but gradually." The French Crown also required that army purveyor entrepreneurs accept a large amount of government paper, whose value fluctuated. "The munitionnaires…accepted thirty-nine million livres in this manner, taking a loss of from thirty to sixty percent," noted Lee Kennett. In 1763, the government still owed the munitionnaires company more than fifteen and one-half million livres. One observer quipped, "The entrepreneurial system was one of 'usury lending to necessity.'"[35]

In 1760 and 1762, Cerf Berr and Jüdel welcomed their fourth and fifth children, two sons named Lippman (also known as Hippolite, 1760–1827; his name is also spelled Lipman, Liepman, Lepman, and Lipmann) and Baruch (also spelled Barac, 1762–1824).

The Seven Years' War was a decisive event in the history of France. On February 10, 1763, all parties to the war—Britain, France, and Spain with Portugal in agreement—signed the Peace of Paris, which humiliated France. France ceded Canada and control of India to England. Lee Kennett summarized the long-range impact of the Seven Years' War on the history of France:

The nation entered into the [Seven Years' War] without enthusiasm, fought without distinction, and emerged from it without victory. The long struggle perceptibly weakened the ties, which had bound the people of France to the dynasty for a thousand years, and in its course, it took the country far down the road, which led to the cataclysm of 1789 [bankruptcy and the French Revolution]. The strain of war revealed as never before the serious shortcomings of the royal government; to compound the damage, the military defeats, the financial crises, and the political instability occurred precisely at a time of great intellectual ferment [emergence of the philosophes]."[36]

France suffered from her participation in the Seven Years' War. However, Cerf Berr benefited from the war, because army contracting could be a lucrative, sustainable business, especially if conducted in an honest and reliable manner. Ashkenazi army purveyors, including Cerf Berr, "invested the money they earned supplying provisions into the import and export of a wide range of commodities, in banking and commercial paper, and even in tax farming," noted historian Arthur Hertzberg.[37]

In summary, in 1726, Cerf Berr of Médelsheim was born in an Ashkenazi community in the Village of Médelsheim, Saarland, Holy Roman Empire. He was exposed to a traditional Talmudic education. He started his career in industrial management by joining a consortium of businessmen who purchased leases to manage the iron work industries in the County of Nassau-Saarbrücken, Saarland. In 1748, Cerf Berr moved to Bischheim, Alsace, France and married Jüdel Weill of Bischheim with whom he had two daughters and three sons in Bischheim between 1748 and 1762. A Strasbourg anti-Jewish law dating to 1388 prohibited Cerf Berr from living in Strasbourg. He wanted to live in Strasbourg. In 1754, Moses Blien, an army purveyor, tax farmer, Alsatian Ashkenazi General Préposé, and business partner of Cerf Berr, retired to the City of Metz, thereby opening business opportunities for Cerf Berr in Lower

Alsace. During the Seven Years' War, Cerf Berr built up his business and reputation with the French Secretaries of War as a trustworthy purveyor of forage to the French Army garrisoned in Strasbourg. The French Secretaries of War also functioned as the French King's administrators of Alsace Province.

Chapter Three Notes:

1. Max Warschawski: "Hirtz de Médelsheim dit Cerf Berr, représentant de la 'Nation Juive' d'Alsace, 1726–1793." *Judaisme d'Alsace et de Lorraine*. Available at http://judaisme.sdv.fr/perso/cerfberr/index.htm; accessed November 12, 2001.

2. "Bouxwiller: Bas-Rhin department, Alsace region." International Jewish Cemetery Project, International Association of Jewish Genealogical Societies. Available at http://www. iajgsjewishcemeteryproject.org/france/bouxwiller-bas-rhin-departement-alsace-region.html; accessed January 14, 2012.

3. Paula Hyman: *The Jews of Modern France*. Berkeley, California: University of California Press, 1998, pp. 10–11. For more information on Ashkenazi Préposés and Parnassim, see Arthur Hertzberg: *The French Enlightenment and the Jews*. New York City, New York: Columbia University Press, 1968, pp. 319–322; Zosa Szajkowski: "Discussion on Jewish autonomy during the old regime." In *Jews and the French Revolutions of 1789, 1830 and 1848*. New York City, New York: Ktav Publishing House, 1970, p. 655, Note #148; and Cyrus Adler and Gotthard Deutsch: "Parnas." *Jewish Encyclopedia*, 1906, available at http://www.jewishencyclopedia.com/articles/11915-parnas; accessed December 7, 2011.

4. David Feuerwerker: *L'Emancipation des Juifs en France*. Paris, France: Albin Michel, 1976, pp. 8–9.

5. David Feuerwerker: "The abolition of body taxes in France." *Annales Économies, Sociétés, Civilisations*, 1962, Volume 17, Number 5. Available in English (translator: Mitchell Abidor) at http://www. marxists.org/history/france/annales/1962/body-taxes.htm; accessed January 16, 2012.

6. Pascal Faustini: "Entrepreneurs juifs en Sarre dans la second moitié du XVIIIe siècle: Éléments généalogiques concernant les familles

Alexander, Blien, et Beer." Available at http://judaisme.sdv.fr/histoire/historiq/fer/fer.htm; accessed November 6, 2011.

7. Lee Kennett: *The French Armies in the Seven Years' War*. Durham, North Carolina: Duke University Press, 1967, pp. 10–11.

8. Zosa Szajkowski: "The Jewish problem in Alsace, Metz, and Lorraine on the eve of the Revolution." In *Jews and the French Revolutions of 1789, 1830 and 1848*. New York City, New York: Ktav Publishing House, 1970, pp. 304–305. See also Yves Combeau: *Le Comte d'Argenson, 1696–1764: Ministre de King Louis XV*. Paris, France: Mémoires et Documents de L'École nationale des chartes, 1999.

9. See Martin Klewitz: *Das Saarland*. Berlin, Germany: Deutscher Kunstverlag, 1982. A historical map of the holdings of the Leyen dynasty is available at http://www.hoeckmann.de/deutschland/saar-karte.htm; accessed November 8, 2011. A historical map of Saarland is available at http://en.wikipedia.org/wiki/File:Historical_map_of_the_Saarland_1793.gif; accessed November 11, 2011.

10. Pierre Delaunay: "Hirsch Hirtz Cerf Naftali Berr Cerf Berr of Médelsheim." Available at http://gw3.geneanet.org/delaunaypierre?lang=en&p=hirsch+hirtz+cerf+naftaly+le+grand+cerf+berr&n=berr+cerf+berr+Médelsheim; accessed January 20, 2012. Zosa Szajkowski noted that the birth and death dates of Cerf Berr's father were 1670 and 1762, respectively. Source: Zosa Szajkowski: "The Alsatian debts." In *Jews and the French Revolutions of 1789, 1830, and 1848*. New York City, New York: Ktav Publishing House, 1970, p. 703, Note #274.

11. Albert Marx: *Die Geschichte der Juden im Saarland vom Ancient Regime bis zum Zweiten Weltkrieg*. Saarbrücken, Germany: Verlag "Die Mitte," 1992, pp. 41–42; and Rosanne and Daniel N. Leeson: *Index de Memoire Juive en Alsace: Contrats de Mariage au XVIIIème Siecle par A. A. Fraenckel*. Volume I, Bas-Rhin. Strasbourg, Alsace, France: Cercle de Généalogie Juive, Editions du Cédrat, 1997, pp. 5–6. The *Index de Memoire Juive en Alsace* is available for purchase at http://www.genealoj.org/New/ENtexte/page06.php; accessed December 1, 2011.

12. Israel Abrahams: *Jewish Life in the Middle Ages*. Philadelphia, Pennsylvania: Jewish Publication Society of America, 1896, pp. 348–355; Jacob Rader Marcus: "Jewish Education about 1180–1680." In *The Jew in the Medieval World: a Source Book: 315–1791*. Cincinnati, Ohio: Hebrew Union College Press, 1999, pp. 428–437; and Moses Ginsburger: "Talmud Tora: Étude de la Loi" in "Une Fondation de

Cerf Berr." Available at http://judaisme.sdv.fr/synagog/basrhin/a-f/
bischhei.htm; accessed November 11, 2011.

13. Joseph Ezobi's "Silver Bowl." Translated by D. I. Friedmann. *Jewish
Quarterly Review*, Volume 8. Also reproduced in Israel Abrahams:
Jewish Life in the Middle Ages. Philadelphia, Pennsylvania: Jewish
Publication Society of America, 1896, p. 354.

14. For more information on William Henry, Count of Nassau-
Saarbrücken, see Winfried Dotzauer: "Fürst Wilhelm Heinrich von
Nassau Saarbrücken." In Richard van Dülmen and Richard Klimmt:
Saarländische Geschichte. Eine Anthologie. St. Ingbert/Röhrig, 1995,
pp. 87–94.

15. See Reed Browning: *The War of the Austrian Succession*. New York
City, New York: St. Martin's Press, 1993.

16. Recall that the Landgrave of Hesse-Darmstadt owned twenty-one
Alsatian communities in which almost nineteen hundred Jews
lived. Source: Zosa Szajkowski: "The demographic aspects of Jewish
emancipation in France during the French Revolution." In *Jews and
the French Revolutions of 1789, 1830 and 1848*. New York City, New
York: Ktav Publishing House, 1970, pp. 45–74.

17. See Franz A. J. Szabo: *Seven Years War in Europe, 1756–1763.*
Edinburgh, Scotland: Pearson Education, 2008.

18. For information on iron manufacture from iron ore, see Richard
Hayman: *Ironmaking: the History and Archaeology of the Iron Industry.*
Stroud, Gloucestershire, England, United Kingdom: History Press,
2011.

19. Charles Friedemann: "Bischheim." Available at http://judaisme.sdv.fr/
synagog/basrhin/a-f/bischhei.htm; accessed November 11, 2011.

20. Jean-Pierre Zeder: *Aspects de Bischheim au Fil des Siècles.* Volume 1,
Strasbourg, France: Éditions Oberlin, 1982, pp. 81–86; and Louis
Schlaefli: "Biesheim," 1997, available at http://judaisme.sdv.fr//
synagog/hautrhin/a-f/biesheim.htm; accessed November 11, 2011. See
also "Juifs de Bischheim et Strasbourg." *Ville de Bischheim*. Available
at http://www.ville-bischheim.fr/culture/le-musee-juif/juifs-de-
bischheim-et-strasbourg; accessed January 18, 2012.

21. Robert Weyl: "Les Juifs à Rosheim." In *Saisons d'Alsace*, Number 66,
1978. Available at http://judaisme.sdv.fr/synagog/basrhin/r-z/rosheim.
htm; accessed January 11, 2012.

22. Zosa Szajkowski: *Franco-Judaica: an Analytical Bibliography of Books, Pamphlets, Decrees, Briefs and Other Printed Documents Pertaining to the Jews in France 1500–1788*. New York City, New York: American Academy for Jewish Research, 1962, pp. xii, xv.

23. Simon Schwarzfuchs: "Alsace and Southern Germany: the creation of a border." In *Jewish Emancipation Reconsidered*. Michael Brenner, Vicki Caron, and Uri R. Kaufmann (eds.). London, England, United Kingdom: Leo Baeck Institute, 2003, p. 9.

24. Roland E. Mousnier: *The Institutions of France under the Absolute Monarchy, 1598–1789*. Translated from the French by Brian Pearce. Chicago, Illinois: University of Chicago Press, 1979, p. 416.

25. Moses Ginsburger: *Cerf-Berr et son Époque*. Société d'Histoire des Juifs d'Alsace-Lorraine. Guebwiller, Alsace, France: J. Dreyfus, 1908, p. 5. Available at http://gallica.bnf.fr/ark:/12148/bpt6k5427849p/f8.image; accessed November 3, 2011.

26. Frank A. J. Szabo: *The Seven Years War in Europe: 1756–1763*. Edinburgh, Scotland: Pearson Education, 2008, p. 2.

27. "Schloßkirche Saarbrücken. Die Bestattung des Fürsten Wilhelm Heinrich von Nassau-Saarbrücken." Available at http://www.zeitensprung.de/intwil.html; accessed January 17, 2012.

28. Arthur Hertzberg: *The French Enlightenment and the Jews*. New York City, New York: Columbia University Press, 1968, p. 60.

29. For more information on the Duke of Choiseul, see Roger Henry Soltau: *The Duke de Choiseul: The Lothian Essay*. Oxford, England, United Kingdom: B. H. Blackwell, 1908.

30. Lee Kennett: *The French Armies in the Seven Years' War*. Durham, North Carolina: Duke University Press, 1967, pp. 99–103.

31. Ibid, pp. 32–33.

32. John A. Lynn: *The Wars of Louis XIV, 1667–1714*. Harlow, England, United Kingdom: Pearson Education, 1999, pp. 53–54.

33. Lee Kennett: *The French Armies in the Seven Years' War*. Durham, North Carolina: Duke University Press, 1967, p.16.

34. See James C. Riley: *The Seven Years War and the Old Regime in France: the Economic and Financial Toll*. Princeton, New Jersey: Princeton University Press, 1986.

35. Lee Kennett: *The French Armies in the Seven Years' War*. Durham, North Carolina: Duke University Press, 1967, pp. 111–112.

36. Ibid, p. ix.

37. Arthur Hertzberg: *The French Enlightenment and the Jews*. New York City, New York: Columbia University Press, 1968, pp. 123–124.

CHAPTER FOUR:

Cerf Berr Besieges Strasbourg, 1763–1784

On February 10, 1763, representatives of the governments of France, Britain, and Spain signed the Treaty of Paris, which officially ended the Seven Years' War. Thirty-seven-year-old Cerf Berr of Médelsheim was living in Bischheim, Alsace with his thirty-three-year-old wife Jüdel and their five young healthy children—Rebecca, Minette, Max, Lippman, and Baruch. Cerf Berr supported his family through his iron industries lease with Count William Henry in Saarland and his French Army military forage supply business in Alsace and Lorraine. Since his immigration to Bischheim in 1750, Cerf Berr had established himself as a notable in Alsace. His co-religionists and government authorities respected him for his prodigious energy, hard work and honesty.

In 1763, Cerf Berr obtained the position of tax farmer for the Jewish body-tax lease sold by the Strasbourg authorities to a private person or group. Recall that from 1745 to 1754, Moses Blien had farmed the Strasbourg Jewish body tax. When Moses Blien retired to Metz in 1754, a consortium of four Ashkenazim jointly purchased and farmed the Jewish body-tax lease until 1763 when Cerf Berr purchased the lease.

As tax farmer, Cerf Berr paid an annual lump sum of money—forty-two hundred livres per year from 1763 to 1781—for the Jewish body-tax lease. This lump sum was supposed to cover the cost of admission for all Ashkenazim entering Strasbourg during the year. This practice meant that individual Jews entering Strasbourg for the day were not required to pay a usage fee *at the time of entry* through one of the city's five gates. Rather, Jewish families paid annual taxes assessed by their community Préposé, who theoretically assessed each family a fair amount of money to cover their Strasbourg usage fees.

The Strasbourg Jewish body-tax farmer was supposed to recoup from his co-religionists at least the amount of money he paid in a lump sum to the City of Strasbourg each year. People who farmed taxes for a livelihood counted on recovering more money than they paid for the lease. However, tax farmers for the Jewish body tax usually failed to recoup the amount of money that they paid for the lease because of the widespread poverty of the Ashkenazim in Alsace. The tax farmer then had three choices. He could make up the difference from his personal funds, borrow money to make up the difference, or try to drive down the price for the lease sold by the Strasbourg authorities. Cerf Berr farmed the Strasbourg Jewish body-tax lease from 1763 to 1783.[1–3]

In 1764 in Bischheim, Cerf and Jüdel Berr welcomed their third daughter and sixth child. They named her Fradel, but she later called herself Fachon, which sounded more French, which was important to her.

In 1765 in Bischheim, twenty-two-year-old Esther Berr (Cerf Berr's sister) married twenty-year-old Joseph David Sinzheim (also spelled Sintzheim, Zinsheim, Zinsheimer; henceforth, David Sinzheim) (1745–1812). David Sinzheim's father, Isaac (Yitzhak) Sinzheim was the Treves (Trier) Rabbi in Palatinate, where David was born and raised. In 1762, Isaac Sinzheim moved to Niedernai (Alsace) to replace Joseph ben Menahem Mendel Steinhardt (circa 1720–1776) as Patent Rabbi of Lower Alsace. Rabbi Joseph Steinhardt moved to the rabbinate of Fürth, Bavaria, where he officiated until his death.

Ashkenazi rabbis commonly moved without problem from one Ashkenazi community to another throughout Ashkenaz. For example, King Louis XVI issued letters patent to Isaac Sinzheim to serve as Patent Rabbi of Lower Alsace and Rabbinical Court President even though Isaac Sinzheim was not a native-born Frenchman. Isaac

Sinzheim died five years after his appointment as Patent Rabbi of Lower Alsace.

Isaac Sinzheim's daughter (David's sister), Gittel (born circa 1740) married Selig Avzieri Auerbach (circa 1726–1767), who was a sous-rabbi of Bouxwiller. Selig Auerbach died the same year that his father-in-law died (1762). The son of Selig and Gittel Auerbach was Abraham Auerbach, who later married Gittelé Sinzheim, daughter of Esther and David Sinzheim.

David Sinzheim received his Talmudic education from his father and later studied under Metz Rabbi Shmuel Hillman-Halpern. Esther and David Sinzheim settled near Cerf and Jüdel Berr in Bischheim, where they lived for the next twenty-eight years. The dowry provided by Esther Berr enabled David Sinzheim to devote his time entirely to study of the Talmud and to write his major work in Hebrew titled *Yad David*. In his author's introduction, David Sinzheim stated that his purpose for writing *Yad David* was to complete the work of two earlier Talmudic scholars: Hayyim Benveniste (1603–1673), who wrote *Keneset ha-Gedolah*, and Aaron Alfandari (1690–1774), who wrote *Yad Aharon*. Completing their works, according to David Sinzheim, involved providing additional source references and comments scattered in other works. David Sinzheim claimed to have added comments from no less than three hundred works. He made known the places in the Talmud and the commentaries where there were difficulties and provided resolutions for those problems. In 1799, David Sinzheim finally published *Yad David*. In his remarks, he recounted the difficulties that beset the Jewish community during the French Revolution, when government authorities closed yeshivas and burned sifrei kodesh (holy books).[4] David Sinzheim would become an extremely important Ashkenazim leader during the reign of Napoleon Bonaparte (1767–1821, ruled 1804–1814/1815). The point here is that he spent a quarter century of his adult life under the influence of his adored brother-in-law, Cerf Berr of Médelsheim.

Cerf Berr Moves to Strasbourg

In 1766 in Bischheim, forty-year-old Cerf Berr and thirty-six-year-old Jüdel Berr welcomed their fourth daughter and fourth son (fraternal twins?). They named them Jeanette (1766–1829) and Théodore (1766–1832). Cerf Berr now was the sole provider for, and protector of, his wife and eight children—Rebecca, Minette, Max, Lippman, Baruch, Fradel, Jeanette, and Théodore.

In 1767, gangs of robbers infested Alsace, recalling the horrific days of 1338 to 1339 when King Armleder and his assassins roamed the Alsatian countryside in search of Jews to rob and butcher. The brigands alarmed Cerf Berr. The Boecklin of Boecklinsau family, who owned Bischheim, did not provide protection services for town residents. Cerf Berr paid an annual protection tax to French King Louis XV, but the latter lived in Paris and his royal soldiers lived in the garrison in Strasbourg, miles away. Robbers targeted the homes of wealthy Jews, such as Cerf Berr. The robbers struck at night under cover of darkness. During the winter months, nights were longer and provided the best opportunity for a successful attack. Thus, August 5, 1767, Cerf Berr approached the Strasbourg authorities for permission to rent a Strasbourg house large enough for his family for the winter of 1767 to 1768. His memorandum in the original French read as follows:

* * * * * * * *

Mémoire du sieur Cerf Berr, du 5 août 1767.

Sur des représentations faites à MM. les magistrats de Strasbourg par ledit Cerf Berr, que des bandes nombreuses de brigands infestent le pays, qu'ils en veulent surtout aux juifs, et qu'ils sont surtout à craindre pendant l'hiver, où la longueur des nuits leur en donneront encore plus de facilité: ledit Cerf Berr supplie de lui permiettre de se réfugier avec sa famille et ses meilleurs effets dans la ville pendant l'hiver, en y louant une maison bourgeoise, se soummettant de ne faire aucun commerce contraire aux statuts, et conservant sa maison a Bischheim pour y retourner après l'hiver, et après que le calme contre les voleurs sers rétabli: il espère que la grâce qui'il demande lui sera accordée.[5-6]

* * * * * * * *

In English, the memorandum read:

* * * * * * * *

Memorandum of Mr. Cerf Berr, August 5, 1767

On representations made to the magistrates of Strasbourg, Cerf Berr said that numerous bands of robbers infested the countryside and that they especially targeted Jews. The robbers were a special concern during the winter because the prolonged length of the nights facilitated more robberies. Cerf Berr asked to be able to take refuge with his family and effects in the City of Strasbourg during the winter, renting a house there while promising not to conduct any trade there that was contrary to the laws. Meanwhile, he would keep his house in Bischheim and return to it after winter when the thieves had gone and peace was restored. He hoped that the magistrates would grant his request.

* * * * * * * *

Cerf Berr further explained to the Strasbourg authorities that he was a military purveyor for King Louis XV and often possessed large sums of royal money, which he felt was no longer safe in his house in Bischheim because of the robbers. Unmoved, the Strasbourg authorities dallied. In December 1767, four months after Cerf Berr sent his petition to them, he still had received no reply. Finally, the authorities declined his petition, stating that if Cerf Berr lived in Strasbourg, he would attract Jewish beggars, which would increase thefts in the city.[6-7]

Frustrated, but tenacious, Cerf Berr turned to his friend and protector, Secretary of War and Alsace Administrator, the Duke of Choiseul. The Duke of Choiseul wrote two letters to the Strasbourg authorities on behalf of Cerf Berr.[7] He sent the letters on December 24, 1767 and on January 22, 1768, The letter dated January 22, 1768 read as follows:

* * * * * * * * *

Lettre de duc de Choiseul à Strasbourg, 22 janvier 1768.

Versailles, le 22 janvier 1768.

Vous avouerai qu'après avoir examiné les considérations que vous opposez la demande du juif Cerfbeer, je ne vois rien qui les fonde. De ce que les gens de sa nation ne doivent avoir ni bureaux ni comptoirs à Strasbourg, il ne s'ensuit nullement que vous ne puissiez permettre à ce juif d'y demeurer durant la saison de l'hiver; toute exception aux règles en est communément regardée comme la confirmation, parce qu'elle en renferme la reconnaissance et l'aveu. Mais elle est si légère dans le cas actuel, qu'à peine peut-elle faire la moindre sensation; car il ne s'agit point ici de tolérer un domicile constant de Cerfbeer, mais *une demeure* momentanée, que le seul motif de l'humanité devrait faire accorder. D'ailleurs, vous êtes à portée de prendre les précautions nécessaires pour prévenir ou réprimer tout abus de sa part, et je suis persuadé que ces réflexions vous porteront à penser que la permission, dont il a besoin, ne soutire point de difficultés réelles.

« *Signé:* Le DUC DE CHOISEUL[5]

* * * * * * * *

In English, the letter read:

* * * * * * * *

Letter of the Duke of Choiseul to Strasbourg, January 22, 1768.

> You confess that after reviewing the considerations, you oppose
> the request of the Jew Cerf Berr. I see nothing to substantiate
> your opposition [to Cerf Berr]. You say that people of his nation
> [Nation Juive] should have no offices in Strasbourg, but it does
> not follow that you cannot allow a Jew to live there during the
> winter season. Cerf Berr does not request a permanent home,
> only a temporary home, and for humanity's sake you should
> allow him to have that. Besides, you are in a position to take
> necessary precautions to prevent any abuse on his part. I am
> confident that you will give the permission that he needs.

> Signed: the Duke of Choiseul

* * * * * * * *

The Duke of Choiseul also reminded the Strasbourg authorities they
had previously accorded the temporary right of residence to certain Jews
who had special value to the French Crown and thus merited exceptional
treatment. He was referring to Secretary of War Marc-Pierre Argenson
who, on May 15, 1743, had compelled the Strasbourg authorities to
permit overnight residence in Strasbourg for army purveyor Moses
Blien and his partners during the War of the Austrian Succession.[8] The
letter from the Duke of Choiseul to the Strasbourg authorities resulted
in permission for Cerf Berr and his family to live in Strasbourg during
the winter months of 1768.

In January 1768, Cerf Berr, his family, and his servants (at least sixty people, according to historian Moses Ginsburger[7]) moved into the large, black-and-white, timber-framed Hotel Ribeaupierre at number nine Quai Finkwiller in Strasbourg.[9] The Hotel Ribeaupierre comprised at least four buildings, which surrounded an interior quadrangular courtyard, according to historian Thierry Hatt.[9] Christian IV (1722–1775, ruled 1735–1775), Duke of Deux Ponts (in German, Zweibrücken; in English, Two Bridges), owned Hotel Ribeaupierre in 1768. Deux Ponts was a city and a duchy located in the Palatinate, about eight or nine miles northeast of Médelsheim, the birthplace of Cerf Berr.[9]

When winter ended in 1768, Cerf Berr moved his wife, nine children (his youngest child, a daughter named Eve, was born sometime in 1768), and servants back to Bischheim. The robbers had left the countryside near Bischheim, and Cerf Berr and his family dwelled there safely for the next two years.

Beginning around 1770, the financial situation of the Ashkenazim in Alsace began to deteriorate, noted Robert Weyl. Even powerful families, such as the one headed by Jacob Baruch Weyl, one of the three Ashkenazi General Préposés, carried substantial debt. For example, when eighty-year-old Jacob Baruch Weyl died in 1775, he left a debt of around eighty-one thousand livres. Only the fortune of Cerf Berr grew.[10]

In 1770, the Ashkenazi General Préposés of Alsace wrote to the Alsace Intendant that the dearth of jobs available to Jews was impoverishing most of them. The destitute Jews could not pay the taxes owed to the French Crown. The General Préposés complained that they themselves had already advanced considerable sums from their own savings to address the difference between what their co-religionists could afford to pay in taxes and what the French Crown asked the Ashkenazi semi-autonomous communities to pay. The Ashkenazi General Préposés of Alsace sought and received permission from the Alsace Intendant to seek a loan of fifteen thousand livres from Christian bankers to cover the amount of taxes owed by the Ashkenazim in Alsace to the French Crown.[10] The loan temporarily averted the crisis.

In the early 1770s, Cerf Berr replaced Jacob Baruch Weyl as

the third General Préposé to govern the body of Alsatian Ashkenazi leaders (Préposés) now known as the Council of the Alsatian Jewish Communities (Nation Juive), noted historian Jay R. Berkovitz.[11] Aaron Mayer of Mutzig and Lehmann Netter of Rosheim were the other two Ashkenazi General Préposés in Alsace. The Ashkenazim in Alsace did not appoint or elect the three General Préposés, according to Max Warschawski; rather, the three General Préposés assigned themselves to this role.[11] Most of the individual Ashkenazi communities in Alsace had a community-level Préposé, who participated in the provincial governance structure led by the three General Préposés.

During the winter of 1770/1771, famine struck Strasbourg. François, Baron of Antigny (died 1822), a Royal Lender (designated by the French Crown) in Strasbourg, invited Cerf Berr to purchase one thousand bags of German wheat on behalf of the Strasbourg government authorities.[12] Cerf Berr agreed. To do so, he again moved his family and servants to Hotel Ribeaupierre in Strasbourg for the winter of 1770/1771. He was under royal protection to supply wheat to the city's population.

Cerf Berr ordered wheat from his German suppliers in Mainz. Many versions exist of what happened next. One version said that the wheat merchant in Mainz dispatched the wheat, which was supposed to arrive in Strasbourg in early 1771. However, even before the grain arrived, Strasbourg authorities complained that the grain was of poor quality and would require sifting and purification before it could be deemed usable. The Strasbourg authorities threatened Cerf Berr, telling him if good wheat did not arrive within eight days, he needed to purchase good wheat with his own money. Cerf Berr apparently went to Mainz to assess the grain situation. While he was in Mainz, one hundred and twenty-five sacks of clean, usable wheat arrived in Strasbourg, which contradicted the earlier complaint issued by the Strasbourg authorities. Cerf Berr used his own money to purchase eight hundred and forty-two more bags of clean, usable wheat in Mainz. All of the wheat finally arrived in Strasbourg. It was good wheat. However, Cerf Berr said he lost about four thousand livres of his own money during the various transactions.[7]

On January 16, 1771, at about the same time he was purchasing wheat for the residents of Strasbourg, Cerf Berr secretly and illegally purchased Hotel Ribeaupierre. The purchase occurred in the following way, according to historian Abbé Joseph Lémann.[9]

On December 31, 1770, Christian IV, Duke of Deux Ponts (mentioned above), consented to sell Hotel Ribeaupierre to Charles-Joseph, Chevalier (Knight) of la Touche. Charles-Joseph, Chevalier of la Touche, was also a lieutenant general in the French Army of King Louis XV, a former French Ambassador to the Court of Vienna, a resident of Strasbourg, and a friend of Cerf Berr.

On January 16, 1771, a royal notary of Strasbourg witnessed the sale of Hotel Ribeaupierre for thirty-three thousand livres by the Duke of Deux Ponts (represented by his staff members, Jean-David Papelier and Casimir-Henry Radius) to the Chevalier of la Touche. The same day, the Chevalier of la Touche sold Hotel Ribeaupierre to Cerf Berr for an undisclosed sum. The Chevalier of la Touche met Cerf Berr in Colmar, Upper Alsace, where a second notary deposed the transaction. The purchase remained a secret between the Chevalier of la Touche and Cerf Berr for the duration of the knight's life. The two notarized letters of sale for the hotel are available elsewhere.[9] Did Christian IV, Duke of Deux Ponts, know about the sale of Hotel Ribeaupierre to Cerf Berr? Abbé Joseph Lémann wrote, "probably," because Cerf Berr was the Duke Christian IV's personal advisor of commerce.[8]

When winter 1771 ended, Cerf Berr and his family again trudged back to Bischheim. The loss of four thousand livres during the 1770/1771 winter wheat transaction bothered Cerf Berr; however, the requirement to leave Strasbourg after winter upset him more. Moving back and forth between Bischheim and Strasbourg was inconvenient and unjust, he opined, especially since living in Strasbourg was desirable both for his army supply business and his family's safety and well-being.

On June 5, 1771, Cerf Berr wrote a letter to the Baron of Antigny in which he politely shared his Strasbourg wheat woes, his loss of four thousand livres, and the necessity to leave Strasbourg at the end of the winter because he had no permit to reside there during the summer.

Cerf Berr gently, without expectations, queried the Baron of Antigny about his possibly approaching the appropriate royal minister about Cerf Berr's wish to reside in Strasbourg during the summer, in addition to during the winter. Cerf Berr's letter to the Baron of Antigny is available elsewhere.[12] The Baron of Antigny forwarded Cerf Berr's request to the Secretary of War in Versailles.[12]

On November 5, 1771, the Secretary of War, Louis François, Marquis of Monteynard, who succeeded the Duke of Choiseul, wrote a letter on behalf of Cerf Berr to Strasbourg Royal Praetor, Maréchal of Contades (1704–1795). In his letter Secretary of War Monteynard requested that Royal Praetor Contades permit Cerf Berr and his family to live in Strasbourg during the winter *and* during the summer, that is, *all year long*. Cerf Berr, he added, was under royal protection. Secretary Monteynard's letter to Royal Praetor Contades in Strasbourg read as follows:

* * * * * * * *

Lettre de M. le marquis de Monteynard à M. le Prêteur Royal de Strasbourg, 5 november 1771.

Le juif Cerfbeer [*sic*] a déjà obtenu, Monsieur, la permission de résider pendant l'hiver à Strasbourg, où sa présence est également nécessaire durant l'été; le Roi ne juge pas que la différence des saisons doive obliger ce particulier de changer de domicile, et son intention est qu'il demeure dans la ville pendant toute l'année; c'est ce dont je vous prie de vouloir bien prévenir le Magistrat.
Je suis. etc.[5]

* * * * * * * *

In English, the letter read:

* * * * * * * *

Letter of the Marquis of Monteynard to the Royal
Praetor of Strasbourg, November 5, 1771.

Sir, the Jew Cerf Berr has already obtained permission to reside
in Strasbourg in the winter; his presence also is necessary in the
summer. [King Louis XV] does not consider that the change of
seasons should require the individual to change his domicile,
and it is [King Louis XV's] intention that [Cerf Berr] live in
the city throughout the year; this is what I ask you to bring
before the [Strasbourg] magistrate.

* * * * * * * *

On November 12, 1771, Royal Praetor Contades delivered the letter
from Secretary of War Monteynard to the Strasbourg authorities, who
reluctantly responded on November 20, 1771, as follows:

* * * * * * * *

Lettre à marquis de Monteynard, 20 november 1771.

20 novembre 1771

Monseigneur,

Quoique ce juif, par le placet qu'il avait adressé en 1767 à M.
le duc de Choiseul, et par la requête qu'il nous avait présentée,
se fût engagé lui-même à ne demeurer dans cette ville que
pendant l'hiver, nous n'avions pas pensé à l'inquiéter, même
pendant les temps d'été; nous l'inquiéterons encore moins,
Monsieur, depuis vos ordres; nous osons cependant espérer
que cette exception en faveur du juif Cerfbeer ne tirera pas

à conséquence pour la prolongation de sa demeure au delà
du terme de son entreprise des fournitures pour le service du
Roi.

Nous sommes, etc.[5]

* * * * * * * * *

The letter from the Strasbourg authorities (above) said that in 1767,
the Duke of Choiseul had asked the Strasbourg authorities to permit
Cerf Berr and his family to live in Strasbourg during the winter, and
that the Strasbourg authorities had not thought about his living in
Strasbourg also during the summer. Adding summer to his temporary
permit, as King Louis XV was now requesting, did not worry them.
However, they trusted that this exception to the Jew Cerf Berr's residing
in Strasbourg would not extend beyond the term of his position as a
supplier to the French Army of King Louis XV.

On November 20, 1771, the Strasbourg authorities notified Cerf
Berr that they had not meant to upset him, although he had promised
to stay in the City of Strasbourg only during the winter and now he was
asking to live in the city year-round. The authorities stressed to Cerf
Berr that other Jews should *not* now also expect to live in Strasbourg. In
addition, they told Cerf Berr he was welcome in the city only as long as
he was in the service of King Louis XV and under his royal protection.
Furthermore, Cerf Berr was subject to all Strasbourg laws, which the
Strasbourg police would enforce. The authorities cautioned Cerf Berr
against trying to open a place for Jewish worship in Strasbourg. If Cerf
Berr or his family needed to pray, they were to go to Bischheim ("s'il
veut prier, il n'a qu'à aller à Bischheim").[12–13] In late 1771, Cerf Berr
moved his family and entourage into Hotel Ribeaupierre, which he
secretly owned.

During the eighteenth century, many Christians in Alsace
increasingly complained about what they perceived as usurious rates of
interest charged by Ashkenazim moneylenders. Most of the Christian

debtors and most of their Ashkenazim creditors were equally poor. However, the Christian peasants were the majority, and they almost universally believed that the Talmud allowed, and even compelled, Jews to charge usurious rates of interest on loans granted to Christians.[14]

Many, but not all, of the charges of usury against Ashkenazi creditors made by Alsatian Christian debtors were unfounded. The charges of usury and Christian debtors' refusal to repay loans upset the Ashkenazi creditors because they had few other ways of earning a living. When Ashkenazi creditors sought redress in the local courts, local Christian seigniorial judges employed by ennobled Christian landowners usually ruled in favor of the Christian debtors.

In December 1771, the Ashkenazi General Préposés of Alsace first petitioned the Sovereign Council of Alsace (the French Crown's Court in Alsace Province) to assign royal judges appointed by the French Crown, rather than local seigniorial judges hired by ennobled landowners, to hear cases of usury allegedly committed by the Ashkenazim in Alsace. Many seigniorial judges were ignorant at best and blatantly anti-Jewish at worst, noted Zosa Szajkowski. Indeed, some of the judges in the Sovereign Council of Alsace were anti-Jewish. For example, Nicolas III of Corberon and François Henri of Boug, both First Presidents of the Sovereign Council of Alsace, "made derogatory remarks in their collections of ordinances about Jews in general and about their legal status in particular. François Henri of Boug stated that Jews were permitted by their religion to practice usury at the expense of Christians, that Rabbis made of this practice an art, and that Jews' right of residence should be influenced by the fact that they were condemned to remain wanderers without a fixed country."[14]

In 1772 and 1773, certain local judges deliberately sought cases of usury to force Christian debtors to bring their Jewish creditors to justice, said Zosa Szajkowski. The Ashkenazi General Préposés wanted to combat true usury as much as Christians did; however, the Ashkenazi General Préposés opposed false accusations of usury. During the early 1770s, the Ashkenazi General Préposés grew increasingly troubled by the antics of François-Joseph-Antoine of Hell (1731–1794, henceforth,

François Hell), the Landser Bailiff, Landser Judge, and an anti-Jewish zealot. The Countess of Sénozan, Périgord, of Miramond and of Veyne, who owned the Village of Landser in Upper Alsace, employed François Hell as Landser Bailiff and Judge.

The Ashkenazi General Préposés hired Attorney Christian H. P. Simon to plead their case for royally appointed judges before the Sovereign Council of Alsace. H. P. Simon based his clients' request for royally appointed judges on "article 202 of the ordinance of Blois [France] of 1254 AD. This ordinance declared that usury was a criminal offence [that] could be punished by confiscation of property or deportation; that only royal judges could pass such severe sentences; and that the privileges of local seigniorial judges were mostly limited to watching over the safety of people's properties and over social welfare."[14]

In addition, H. P. Simon declared that the lawyers who drew up the ordinances of 1311, 1312, and 1576 AD, which curbed usury, intended the regulations for royal judges only, and that the Paris Parliaments of March 11, 1623 and March 18, 1625 published their decisions in the same spirit. The local seigniorial judges of Alsace, said H. P. Simon on behalf of the Ashkenazi General Préposés, lacked culture and a spirit of justice. Furthermore, the seigniorial judges were brutal and incapable of objectivity in passing sentences. The Ashkenazi General Préposés approved of sentencing true Jewish usurers, but they begged the Sovereign Council of Alsace to permit only royally appointed judges to do so, using the framework of general French law.

On December 17, 1771, the Sovereign Council of Alsace rejected the request of H. P. Simon on behalf of his clients, the Ashkenazim of Alsace.[14] However, the Ashkenazi General Préposés persisted in their efforts to bring about this reform in the justice system in Alsace.

In 1773, sixteen-year-old Minette Berr, Cerf Berr's second-oldest daughter, married nineteen-year-old Wolff (Wolf) Lévy, who was born in Bonn.[15-16] They lived in the Hotel Ribeaupierre from 1773 to 1777 as part of Cerf Berr's extended family. In 1777, Minette and Wolff Lévy had their first child, a son named Marx.

On December 16, 1773, residents in the British Colony of

Massachusetts dumped tea in the Boston Harbor in a historic event known as the Boston Tea Party. The Boston residents did so to register their displeasure with the British Parliament's Tea Act of 1773, which taxed the people of the British Colonies in North America without first obtaining their agreement to taxation.

In 1774, twenty-six-year-old Rebecca Berr, Cerf Berr's oldest daughter, married twenty-six-year-old Samuel Seligmann Alexandre (henceforth, Seligmann Alexandre), who was born in Bouxwiller. Rebecca and Seligmann Alexandre lived in Hotel Ribeaupierre from 1774 to 1777. Between 1772 and 1776, they had three daughters named Judela, Gelché, and Ettellé.[16]

In early May 1774, sixty-four-year-old King Louis XV, for whom Cerf Berr had worked devotedly for more than ten years, became acutely ill with a virulent form of smallpox.[17] The French Crown invited the Ashkenazi General Préposés of Alsace to ask for the Ashkenazim of Alsace to pray for the recovery of King Louis XV. The Ashkenazi General Préposés dispatched a circular to all Ashkenazi communities to pray for the recovery of King Louis XV and to gather alms for the poor. On May 10, 1774, despite the prayers and alms of his people, King Louis XV died. Twenty-one-year-old King Louis XVI reluctantly ascended the throne.[18]

King Louis XVI Naturalizes Cerf Berr, 1775

In early 1775, forty-nine-year-old Cerf Berr wrote a letter to King Louis XVI in Versailles to thank him for the privilege of serving under his predecessor, King Louis XV, as a royal purveyor to the French Army. Cerf Berr was not the only Ashkenazi notable to write such a letter to newly anointed French Kings or their Intendants. When a French King or an Intendant died, Ashkenazi feared possible anti-Jewish reactions from Christian adversaries. Moreover, a new French King or a new Intendant could rescind previously issued letters patent by writing new ones that overrode the older ones. Thus, most Ashkenazi notables tried to secure as quickly as possible the renewal of privileges granted them by the previous ruler, even though the renewals usually cost large sums of money.

Cerf Berr's letter to King Louis XVI listed the many ways in which Cerf Berr had shown his patriotism toward France. Yet, he said, even though he was born in France (Cerf Berr insisted that France owned Médelsheim when he was born there), he could not enjoy all the benefits of being a subject of King Louis XVI. Cerf Berr explained to King Louis XVI that his large Ashkenazi family desired nothing more than to remain in France and to be useful. His heart grieved that one day he would leave his family without support since he was unable to own property to pass on to them. Cerf Berr said that he had the good fortune that King Louis XV had deemed him worthy of royal protection, and he hoped that King Louis XVI would extend his interest to him and his (Cerf Berr's) children. He closed his letter by saying that he prayed that King Louis XVI would grant him permission to acquire real estate in France, which he could then leave to his (Cerf Berr's) descendants.[19]

In March 1775, King Louis XVI responded to Cerf Berr by awarding him letters patent of naturalization, reproduced below:

* * * * * * * * *

King Louis XVI's Lettres Patent à Cerf Berr, mars 1775

Louis, par la grâce de Dieu, roi de France et de Navarre…
Voulant donner au sieur Cerf Beer un témoignage particulier de la satisfaction, que Nous avons des services qu'il a rendus et qu'il continue de Nous render, *avec autant de zèle et d'intelligence que de désintéressement et de probité* [emphasis in original]. A ces causes et de notre grâce spéciale, Nous avons accordé et accordions audit Cerf Berr, à ses enfants nés ou à naître en légitime mariage, les mêmes droits, facultés, exemptions, avantages et privilèges, dont jouissent nos sujets naturels

ou naturalisés. En conséquence permettons audit Cerf Berr d'acquérir par achat, donation, legs, succession, ou autrement, tenir et posséder dans notre royaume tous biens, meubles et immeubles de quelque nature qu'ils puissant être,...

Donné à Versailles, l'an de grâce 1775, au mois de Mars. Signé: Louis.[19]

* * * * * * * *

The letter in English read:

* * * * * * * *

King Louis XVI's Letters Patent to Cerf Berr, March 1775

Louis, by the grace of God, King of France and Navarre,... desires to give thanks to Mr. Cerf Berr for the services he has rendered and continues to render to us, with *zeal and an intelligence that reflects his selflessness and integrity* [emphasis in original]. Because of his service and our special thanks, we grant to Cerf Berr's children, born and unborn in lawful marriage, the same rights, liberties, exemptions, benefits and privileges enjoyed by our natural and naturalized subjects. We also allow Cerf Berr to acquire by purchase, gift, bequest, inheritance or otherwise, and hold and possess any property in the Kingdom of France and personal property of any kind... Given at Versailles, the year of 1775, the month of March.

Signed: Louis.

On April 5, 1775, the Parliaments of Paris and Nancy (Lorraine), as well as the Sovereign Council of Alsace, duly recognized and registered King Louis XVI's letters patent of naturalization for Cerf Berr of Médelsheim. This registration process by the Parliaments validated and activated the naturalization of Cerf Berr. Theoretically, Cerf Berr could now reside in *any* city and purchase and hold property *anywhere* in the Kingdom of France. However, when Cerf Berr attempted to legalize his Strasbourg residence with the Strasbourg authorities, they adamantly refused to recognize King Louis XVI's letters patent of naturalization for Cerf Berr.[8]

Cerf Berr was not the only Ashkenazi notable to receive letters patent of naturalization from a French King and then experience trouble with acceptance of the letters patent by local authorities. In 1769, King Louis XV presented letters patent of naturalization to the Ashkenazi military purveyor and banker Liefman Calmer (1711–1784) (born Moses Eliezer Lippman ben Kalonymus in Hanover). In 1774, Liefman Calmer purchased the Barony of Picquigny in Northern France, thus making him the Baron of Picquigny and the Viscount of Amiens. The property cost one million five hundred thousand livres. "One of the rights that pertained to the property was that of conferring two ecclesiastical benefices, subject to investiture by the Bishop of Amiens. The Bishop of Amiens refused to confirm Calmer's appointments on the grounds that a Jew had no right to nominate priests to any office."[20] A second prelate, Abbè Charles Louis Richard, who was a French Dominican priest, native of Lorraine, and hovering bystander, ripped Liefman Calmer for his arrogance, writing the following vituperative slur:

> A Jew is a born and sworn enemy of all Christians. It is a principle of his faith to regard them [Christians] as blasphemers and idolaters who should be put to death, and whom he should harm as much as he can without endangering himself. The Christians in turn regard Jews as the God-killing executioners

of Jesus Christ, the man-God, whom Christians adore and accept as their Messiah, their supreme head, their immortal Savior.[20]

Abbè Charles Louis Richard also wrote, "The Church, as the bride of Christ, must reject 'ministers at its altars whom a descendant of the killers of Christ is presuming to appoint to them.'"[20] Abbè Charles Louis Richard also had choice invective for the eighteenth-century philosophes.

In 1775, Cerf Berr and his two fellow General Préposés of the Council of the Alsatian Jewish Communities (Nation Juive) borrowed twenty-four thousand livres to fund the Council's activities. The majority of this money covered travel expenses, the preparation of memoranda, and fees for consultations (e.g., attorney fees), said Zosa Szajkowski.[10,21]

In 1775, Cerf Berr, possibly emboldened by his letters patent of naturalization granted by King Louis XVI and understandably angry about the Strasbourg authorities' refusal to acknowledge them, requested a downward adjustment in the price of the Jewish body-tax lease that he farmed. He had two complaints about the price of the lease. First, he believed that he, his family, and his employees deserved exemption from the Strasbourg Jewish body tax because they lived in Strasbourg and should not have to pay to re-enter the city each time they left it. According to statistics collected by the Strasbourg authorities, the number of Cerf Berr's family and employees was one hundred and fifty-two individuals. These individuals collectively generated forty-four hundred livres per year to cover their fees for entering Strasbourg.[22]

Cerf Berr's own documents, dated 1773 to 1775, stated that he employed one hundred and nineteen people. Of these one hundred and nineteen people, sixty-three resided in or near Bischheim, twenty-three in other parts of Alsace, sixteen in Lorraine, five in Metz, nine in other parts of the Metz province, and three in the Comté de Bourgogne. In 1775, of these one hundred and nineteen people, thirty-five men and thirty-five women lived with Cerf Berr in Hotel Ribeaupierre.[22] The

Strasbourg authorities refused Cerf Berr's request to forgo the assessment of eighteen hundred pounds per year to cover Strasbourg entry fees just for his family and employees.[23]

Cerf Berr's second complaint about the price of the Strasbourg lease for the Jewish body tax was that between 1769 and 1775, he personally lost eight thousand livres in farming the lease.[2] Cerf Berr offered to purchase the lease for thirty-six hundred livres per year, instead of the forty-two hundred livres per year he had been paying since 1763. The Strasbourg authorities eventually yielded to Cerf Berr's request by reducing the price of the lease to thirty-six hundred livres per year beginning in 1775 (this price level remained in place until 1781). Even as Cerf Berr haggled for a lower body tax lease price, more Jews than ever were entering the City of Strasbourg. The Strasbourg authorities were aware of this upward trend and in 1780 began to carefully count the number of Jews entering the city.

Thus, beginning in 1775, Cerf Berr of Médelsheim and the Strasbourg authorities became staunch adversaries for at least two reasons. First, the Strasbourg authorities refused to acknowledge King Louis XVI's March 1775 letters patent of naturalization for Cerf Berr, which granted him the legal right to reside in the City of Strasbourg. Second, the Strasbourg authorities refused to waive the Strasbourg Jewish body tax for Cerf Berr, his family, and his employees. The bitter dispute between the two sides raged for sixteen years, until the emancipation of the Ashkenazi Jews on September 27, 1791. The Strasbourg authorities initially believed that they could crush Cerf Berr, because they had many important friends associated with the French Crown and the Sovereign Council of Alsace, as well as many attorneys, judges, and residents of Alsace who promised aid in "fighting the arrogance of a Jew."[24]

However, Cerf Berr enjoyed the support of King Louis XVI and his Secretaries of War. From 1775 to 1791, the French Secretaries of War were:

* * * * * * * *

ecretaries (Ministers) of War, 1775–1791

s, Count of Saint-Germain (1775–1777);

Marie Léonor of Saint-Mauris of Montbarrey
(1, ,);

- Philippe Henri, Marquis of Ségur (1780–1787);
- Louis Charles Auguste le Tonnelier, Baron of Breteuil, Baron of Preuilly (1787);
- Louis-Marie-Athanase of Loménie, Count of Brienne (1787–1788);
- Louis Pierre of Chastenet, Puységur (1788–1789);
- Victor François of Broglie, Second Duke of Broglie (1789);
- Jean-Frédéric of La Tour of the Pin Gouvernet (1789–1790); and
- Louis Lebègue Duportail (1790–1791).

* * * * * * * *

King Louis XVI depended on Cerf Berr in no small part for the military defense of Northeastern France, because the French Army depended on horses for movement and horses needed food. The French Crown's following decision shows the importance of Cerf Berr to the French Army, noted Zosa Szajkowski. On May 31, 1776, King Louis XVI's Secretary of War, Claude Louis, Count of Saint-Germain, reorganized the military to abolish the old system of contracting exclusively with private individuals. Instead, the French Crown created administrative supply councils in each French Army regiment. The provinces of Northeastern France were included in this new army supply system. To retain the services of Cerf Berr in Alsace, Lorraine, the Three Bishoprics, and Franche-Comté, King Louis XVI appointed Cerf

Berr as his General Director of Military Forage (Directeur Général des Fourrages Militaries).[19,25]

Cerf Berr, happy over his royal appointment yet stung by his treatment by the Strasbourg authorities, vowed to work the rest of his life to abolish the oppressive exceptional laws directed against the Ashkenazim in Alsace for the previous four hundred years. Cerf Berr's quest to abolish the exceptional laws against his fellow Ashkenazim would be his tour de force during his lifetime and would lead to the political emancipation of the Ashkenazim in France.

In December 1775, Benjamin Franklin (1706–1790), a sixty-nine-year-old American colonist in Philadelphia, met there with a representative of King Louis XVI and came away from this meeting "with the impression that France would be willing to support, at least secretly, the American rebellion."[26] However, any decision of the French Crown to become involved in the American Revolution against the British Crown was fraught with risk for at least two reasons. First, King Louis XVI would be supporting revolutionaries who were casting off a hereditary monarch. Might the American anti-monarchy movement spread to King Louis XVI's own people?

Second, France was in financial shambles and could not afford to support the American colonists' rebellion against Britain.[26] King Louis XVI had inherited the debts of King Louis XV, who himself had inherited the debts of King Louis XIV and had multiplied them during the disastrous Seven Years' War. In addition, King Louis XVI's own family members were profligate spenders, the nobles and the Catholic Church paid minimal amounts to the royal treasury, and the heavily taxed peasantry resisted all attempts to raise taxes. King Louis XVI now faced the additional request to support the American colonists, which would cost untold millions of livres. He pondered the idea.

On July 4, 1776, the Continental Congress in Philadelphia ratified the Declaration of Independence, which announced both the union of the Thirteen American Colonies and the American Colonies' independence from the British Crown. In December 1776, seventy-year-year-old Benjamin Franklin sailed to France to serve as American Commissioner to France for the next ten years.

In 1776, King Louis XVI's Controller-general, Anne-Robert-Jacques Turgot, Baron of Laune Turgot (1727–1781, served 1774–1776), retired from his position after trying and failing both to impose taxes on the tight-fisted clergy and nobility and to abolish the expensive and rife privileges among the same two groups. Jacques Turgot's replacement was Geneva banker, Protestant, and grain speculator, Jacques Necker (1732–1804), who served his first ministry with King Louis XVI from 1776 to 1781.[27]

On July 21, 1777 in Strasbourg, Cerf Berr decided to reduce the concentration of family members living in Hotel Ribeaupierre and sought permission from the Strasbourg authorities to rent two houses to accommodate his sons-in-law, Wolff Lévy and Seligmann Alexandre, and their growing families. The Strasbourg authorities approved his request to rent two houses on Rue des Serruriers in Strasbourg.[28]

In 1777, Cerf Berr, who theoretically could purchase land legally anywhere in France, bid four hundred thousand livres and eight livres per acre in annual rent for three thousand acres of forestland north of the City of Haguenau, about fifteen miles north of Strasbourg. Cerf Berr dreamed of converting the property into arable land to grow grain, hay, straw, and vegetables to supply the French Armies in Northeastern France. In addition, he was trying to develop agricultural colonies where his co-religionists could farm for their livelihood, rather than lending money (even though Jewish exceptional laws forbade Jews from all agricultural pursuits).[29]

Cerf Berr was not successful in purchasing the Haguenau property. However, he and his younger colleague, Berr Isaac Berr of Nancy (1744–1828), founded agricultural colonies elsewhere in Northeastern France where they employed their co-religionists in farming. Unfortunately, little is known about these colonies, said Zosa Szajkowski.[30]

Berr Isaac Berr was the son of Isaac Berr (circa 1695–1754), a Polish Ashkenazim born in Frankfurt am Main. In 1753, Stanislaw Leszczyński (1677–1766), King of the Polish-Lithuanian Commonwealth and

Duke of Lorraine, appointed Isaac Berr as Syndic of the Ashkenazim of Lorraine. Berr Isaac Berr was eighteen years younger than Cerf Berr. In 1783, he worked for a time as general cashier in Nancy for Cerf Berr's Nancy storehouses (more below).

Berr Isaac Berr received a privileged education, especially in Hebrew and rabbinical literature from Rabbi Jacob Perle of Nancy. Berr Isaac Berr owned an estate named Turique west of Nancy. Thus, he signed his name Berr Isaac Berr of Turique. Berr Isaac Berr became a wealthy tobacco manufacturer, married Merlé Miriam Mathilde Goudchaux (1745–1802), fathered ten children, and worked closely with Cerf Berr in Paris during the first two years of the French Revolution.[31]

In 1777, King Louis XVI's Intendant in Alsace formerly assented to the three General Préposés—Cerf Berr, Aaron Meyer of Mutzig, and Lehmann Netter of Rosheim—as leaders of the Council of the Alsatian Jewish Communities (Nation Juive).[10] The three men had been functioning as Ashkenazi General Préposés since the early 1770s.

On February 6, 1778 in Versailles, representatives of the American Colonies and France signed a military alliance treaty against Britain. The Treaty of Alliance, negotiated by Benjamin Franklin and other Americans, required that neither France nor the American Colonies agree to a separate peace with Britain, and that American independence be a condition of any future peace agreement. In addition to the Treaty of Alliance, France and the American Colonies signed the Treaty of Amity and Commerce to promote trade and commercial ties.[32] King Louis XVI had decided that revenge on Britain, France's eternal foe, and the opportunity to expand France's trade were worth lending monetary and military support to the American Colonies. His decision was fraught with risk.

On March 20, 1778 in Versailles, King Louis XVI invited Benjamin Franklin to sign the two treaties mentioned above. Wigless Benjamin Franklin wore his usual brown suit and spectacles and carried no sword. One observer took him for a "big farmer." At the mid-afternoon supper, he stood next to twenty-three-year-old Queen Marie Antoinette as she played at the gambling tables. "Alone among the throng at Versailles, she seemed to have little appreciation for [Benjamin Franklin] who, she had been told, had once been a 'printer's foreman.' As she noted dismissively, a man of that background would never have been able to rise so high in Europe," wrote historian Walter Isaacson.[33]

In 1778 and 1779, Jacques Necker, King Louis XVI's finance minister, conducted a bold experiment. In two royal administrative districts (Berry and Haute-Guyenne), he shifted responsibility for broad areas of provincial administration from the French Crown's Intendants to elected Provincial Assemblies comprised of property owners. The purpose of the new Provincial Assemblies was to provide the public with a means of expressing its collective opinion. In addition, Jacques Necker hoped that the Provincial Assemblies would be the means through which the French Crown could overhaul and reform the failing financial system of the Kingdom of France.[34]

On March 12, 1778 in Strasbourg, Cerf Berr requested two new houses for his two sons-in-law and their families. The first houses he had rented for them not worked out for unknown reasons. The Strasbourg authorities approved a house for the Alexandre family behind Saint-Louis Roman Catholic Church and a house for the Wolff Lévy family in a house on Rue Sainte-Elisabeth in Strasbourg.[35]

In 1778, the three General Préposés of the Council of the Alsatian Jewish Communities (Nation Juive) borrowed between forty thousand and fifty thousand livres to pay for the Council's growing expenses. Zosa Szajkowski said that the Council of the Alsatian Jewish Communities possibly took out other loans of which history has lost track.[10,21]

In 1779, thirty-seven-year-old Seligmann Berr of Rosheim, Cerf Berr's youngest brother and the son-in-law of Lehmann Netter (one of the three General Préposés of Alsace), died suddenly during a stay in Paris. In 1762, Seligmann Berr had married Mariam Netter. Beginning in 1769, he farmed the revenues of the City of Rosheim. He and Mariam had nine children. Jewish law appointed Cerf Berr as guardian of his brother's minor children, manager of his brother's estate, and provider of the dowries for his deceased brother's daughters. Seligmann Berr of

Rosheim received burial in the Jewish La Villette Cemetery in Paris, according to Robert Weyl.[10]

Case of the Counterfeit Receipts of Alsace, 1777–1779

Near the end of 1777, an unusual situation erupted in Alsace that "endangered the entire economy of the French province, brought about the economic ruin of the Jews, threatened their very existence, and even influenced the struggle for the Jewish emancipation during the Revolution of 1789," declared Zosa Szajkowski. The misery of the Alsatian Christian peasants was so great that when criminals tantalized them with the chance to avoid payment of their debts to Jewish creditors by illegal means, they readily seized the opportunity to do so.[31]

Jewish history is replete with conflicts between Jewish creditors and their Christian debtors. However, the case of the counterfeit receipts in Alsace was unique in character, scope, and implications for the economies of Alsace and even France. In the years 1777 and 1778, a mass of counterfeit receipts signed in Hebrew characters flooded Alsace, especially Upper Alsace. Ashkenazim in Alsace rarely signed documents using Latin letters. Ashkenazi creditors purportedly issued these signed receipts to their Christian debtors to show partial or full payment of owed money.[31] However, the receipts were counterfeit.

An example of the type of fraud that many Alsatian Christian debtors attempted to perpetrate on their Ashkenazi creditors involved Benjamin (an Ashkenazi Jew) who in 1771 granted a loan to two Alsatian Christian peasants named Henri Mouches and Jean George Oberlin. Eight years later, the debtors still had not repaid their loan. However, in 1779, Henri Mouches and Jean George Oberlin (the debtors) declared that they had already repaid part of the loan and were able to prove it with a receipt.

Benjamin (the creditor) did not recognize the receipt as genuine. Nevertheless, Henri Mouches and Jean George Oberlin obtained a petition through a notary in the City of Haguenau. The petition requested that Benjamin meet them at a fixed hour in the notary's office where they would pay him the remainder of the debt. Benjamin knew that the receipt was counterfeit. He had only one legal recourse if he wanted to avoid the trap, which was to refrain from going to the notary's office and instead to reply in writing to the debtor's request. In this way, the conflict would move into the jurisdiction of the local court, most likely run by a local seigneurial (non-royally appointed) judge. This approach involved risk and expense but was the only way for Benjamin to stand a chance to call in the full amount of his loan.[31]

The case of the counterfeit receipts was actually a well-organized operation among many Alsatian Christian debtors to avoid repayment of debts they owed to their Ashkenazi creditors. Upon hearing of the scandal, King Louis XVI and his "judicial administration in Alsace, the Sovereign Council, were compelled to strive for legally liquidating the affair of the false receipts in some manner and as soon as possible. Had this not been the state of affairs in Alsace, the Jews would have lost all their possessions at the very beginning of the case."[31]

Why did poor Alsatian farmers borrow money from poor Ashkenazim in Alsace? The province of Alsace lacked capital. Peasant pawnshops, which existed throughout France to sell seed to peasants on five percent interest, did not even exist in Alsace. The peasants instead visited local creditors to obtain the cash they needed to purchase seed, plows, draft animals, and even taxes to pay to the French Crown. Zosa Szajkowski continued:

> For a creditor, the peasant was a poor risk and consequently creditors frequently charged usurious rates of interest. The Alsatian historian Goetzmann cited a memorandum of the Intendant d'Angervilliers (1716) who wrote that in difficult times, such as in times of war, etc., peasants could obtain loans from Jews in order to pay taxes, to buy cattle and seed. Of course, the Jews charged a high rate of interest, but in such emergency cases even usurious rates of interest were better than

a complete ruin. Even the Alsatian anti-Jewish leader [François] Hell wrote in 1779 that the peasants could obtain loans only from Jews. This does not prove that only Jews practiced honest or usurious credit operations…But the Jewish creditor was the most easily accessible, the most willing to grant loans on conditions the peasant could meet. The Jewish creditor came himself to the village, or he could be reached easily through a mediator, the Jewish horse- or cattle-dealer, or the peddler. The [non-Jewish] creditor was more of a city-element; the peasant was forced to lose much of his valuable time in order to reach him, and moreover, he was forced to incur expenses to do so. The peasant was trusted more by a Jewish than a [non-Jewish] creditor because the Jews came more often in close contact with peasants and were familiar with their condition. But most important of all—the Jew was forced to grant loans because this was his main source of income, as he was shut off from all honest trades.[36]

On July 11, 1778, the Sovereign Council of Alsace assumed management of the case of the counterfeit receipts by creating a First Chamber, which became a sort of Court of Accounts. The First Chamber appointed Royal Commissioners who spread out across Alsace to deal with all the incidents of alleged counterfeit receipts issued by Christian debtors to Jewish creditors.

In August 1778, anti-Jewish riots erupted across Alsace, forcing many Jews out of their homes to save their lives. On September 2, 1778, the Abbot of Raze in Upper Saône, Franche-Comté wrote to the Bishop of Basel that in Upper Alsace, particularly around Thann, Durmenach, and Hagenthal, unidentified people were planning to assassinate the Jews while they gathered in their synagogues during the Day of Atonement (Yom Kippur) on the evenings of both September 30, 1778 and October 1, 1778.

Communication to the Jews about this plot precluded the disaster. Someone then distributed in Alsace an anonymous one-page leaflet that told the story of the crucifixion of Jesus by the Jews and declared that Judaism allowed the deception of Christians. In 1779, someone distributed another anonymous writing, this time a book, which compiled anti-Jewish accusations dating back centuries. These publications fueled the charged anti-Jewish atmosphere and emboldened debtors to continue their fraud.

Monsieur Kraus was the busiest Royal Commissioner of the First Chamber of the Sovereign Council of Alsace. On October 16, 1780, he reached the Chateau of Blotzheim (between Landser and Basel), which was his base of operations in the Sundgau region of Upper Alsace. The Sundgau was the center of the case of the counterfeit receipts. Some five hundred and eighty-six separate debtor-creditor files awaited Royal Commissioner Kraus on his first day of work. He processed these files and fourteen hundred more files before he completed his work for the First Chamber. Most of the debtors abandoned the falsified receipts fraud when Royal Commissioner Kraus granted them long terms for repayment of their debts, often up to fifteen years. Jewish creditors gasped.

Eventually the First Chamber identified and prosecuted a number of perpetrators of the case of the counterfeit receipts. The First Chamber began as a civil court. However, on November 6, 1778, King Louis XVI issued letters patent that extended the right of the First Chamber to judge criminal cases. The First Chamber identified a cabal of thirty-two people involved in counterfeiting and distributing the fraudulent receipts. Two of the thirty-two people were Jews—Joseph Lévy of Leymen (Upper Alsace) and Marx David of Zinswiller (Lower Alsace). The cabal of thirty-two people received harsh sentences, including death by hanging (three people), galleys for life (five), and galleys for ten to fifteen years (three). In addition, authorities branded the convicts with a hot iron on their shoulders to identify them as counterfeiters.

The First Chamber identified other perpetrators. The most important—the mastermind of the case of the counterfeit receipts—was Judge François Hell of Landser. Historian Heinrich Graetz described François Hell:

A lawyer, not without brains and literary culture, named Hell, belonging to a poor family and ardently wishing for a high position, being acquainted with the devices of the Jewish usurers, actually learned the Hebrew language, to be able to levy black mail on them without fear of discovery. He sent threatening letters in Hebrew, saying that [Ashkenazim] would inevitably be accused of usury and deception, if they did not supply him with a stated sum of money. This worthless lawyer afterwards became district judge to several Alsatian noblemen [and a noblewoman], and thus the Jews were given wholly into his power. Those who did not satisfy his continually increasing demands were accused, ill-treated, and condemned.[37]

Zosa Szajkowski described François Hell this way:

Hell came from a fifteenth-century Frankfurt family. He was born on June 11, 1731, in Hirsingue (Upper Alsace). At the start of the falsified receipts affair, Hell was the Bailiff of Landser…Hell himself was indebted to many creditors. He probably also had Jewish creditors, and if this was so, this fact greatly influenced his relationship to the Jews. Hell was greatly indebted because of not only his many financial speculations and his chase for riches, but also because of his squandering and his part in many obscure transactions. He married the daughter of a rich Dauphiné [a province in southeastern France] man named Savoye only for her money. He warned his wife that he would divorce her if her father would refuse him money. On February 17, 1787, Hell's father-in-law wrote in a letter to his daughter that Hell squandered about forty thousand pounds of the king's treasury. Hell asked his father-in-law to give him thirty thousand pounds in order to repay the royal money before the embezzlement would be discovered, but Savoye did not have so much money, so Hell deserted his wife.[38]

When authorities discovered the central role played by François Hell in the case of the counterfeit receipts, he "became afraid and promised the Prince of Montbarrey [Secretary of War] that, if he were only freed, he would never again concern himself with the Jewish question." François Hell admitted authorship of the venomous work against the Jews distributed in 1779, which he had titled, "Observations of an Alsatian upon the Present Quarrels of the Jews in Alsace." In that work, he had "collected all the slanderous accusations against Jews from ancient times, in order to present a repulsive picture of them, and expose them to hatred and extermination."[37]

François Hell had many allies, including some members of the Roman Catholic clergy, "who silenced the scruples of conscientious debtors and assured them that robbing the Jews was a righteous act."[37] Thus, François Hell avoided a criminal trial. However, the Sovereign Council of Alsace considered him dangerous and on June 10, 1780 ordered him to leave Alsace for a forced residence in Valence in the province of Dauphiné, where his wife's family resided. François Hell spent three years in prison awaiting his sentence and in exile, but eventually found his way back to Alsace where many Christians welcomed him home as a hero.[39]

The problem with trying cases of usury in local, non-royal courts in Alsace persisted despite attempts by the Ashkenazi General Préposés to lobby the Sovereign Council of Alsace to try cases of usury only in royal courts, as noted above. Jews were not the only ones who distrusted the local courts. In 1780, as resolution of the case of the counterfeit receipts was winding down, "non-Jewish official administrative circles prepared a project to create a royal court in the seigniory of Belfort (Upper Alsace). The authors of the project stated that Alsace was the province with the least number of royal courts, especially courts of the medium class between the Sovereign Council of Alsace and the local seigniorial judges. The Sovereign Council of Alsace occupied itself with what it considered minor suits and both parties of lawsuits were frequently ruined."[40]

In 1779, the Société des Philantropes, a private Strasbourg club for men, sponsored an essay contest on the subject of ameliorating the plight of the Ashkenazim in Alsace. Twenty-nine-year-old Jean of Turckheim (1749–1828, henceforth, Jean Turckheim) and his brother Bernard of Turckheim, sons of a Lutheran banker in Strasbourg, founded the Société des Philantropes in the late 1770s. The importance of this club and its essay contest to the present book was the entry by a highly motivated, twenty-eight-year-old French Catholic priest named Henri Grégoire (1750–1831). He came from the Village of Emberménil, Lorraine and sought close friendships in the club. Henri Grégoire later admitted that the information in the contest's call for entries first stimulated his interest in the plight of the Ashkenazim in Alsace.

Historian Alyssa Goldstein Sepinwall explained why writing contests appealed to Henri Grégoire and other young men in France during the eighteenth century:

> Entering the contest offered the young cleric a chance not only to gain the respect of fellow members, but also to attract acclaim from people far beyond, since essay contests were a promising springboard to a career in letters for ambitious young men in the late eighteenth century. Indeed, by the late 1770s, Henri Grégoire was a regular entrant in essay contests.[41]

How did Jean Turckheim and the other Christian members of the Société des Philantropes view the Ashkenazim in Alsace? Many of the club members personally witnessed the anti-Jewish violence associated with the case of the counterfeit receipts. However, "[f]or the most part, the contest program adopted the point of view of anti-Jewish peasants," averred Alyssa Goldstein Sepinwall. "It framed the problem as one of helping [the peasants] escape the scourge of Jewish usury rather than of rescuing Jews from prejudice and oppression. It suggested the Jews, through religious pride and cruel business practices, bore the responsibility for their outcast status." Jewish usury, said the members of the Société des Philantropes, "posed terrible dangers for the social, economic and moral order of the French countryside."[41] Jean Turckheim especially worried about Jews' fecundity and warned that the Jewish population in Alsace might triple within a century. However, members of the Société des Philantropes admitted they owed the Jews more humane treatment to help them out of their oppressed condition. The club members announced their hope that society would find ways to lift up the Jews while protecting the peasants.

Henri Grégoire's essay for the Société des Philantropes' contest in 1779 does not survive. However, the club's idea of usurious Jews taking advantage of helpless peasants resurfaced in a later essay written by Henri Grégoire in 1785 in Metz, and this essay does survive.

Cerf Berr Turns to Moses Mendelssohn, 1780

The case of the counterfeit receipts was a watershed in the history of the Jews in France because of the cascade of important events that it triggered. In 1780, Cerf Berr, still fighting the Strasbourg authorities over his right to live legally in Strasbourg, turned to his friend Moses Mendelssohn (1729–1786) to seek help in responding to the case of the counterfeit receipts. Moses Mendelssohn was a respected Ashkenazi philosopher, who fathered the eighteenth-century Jewish Enlightenment (Haskalah). This movement charted a new way forward for the Ashkenazim, away from Talmudism.[42]

Moses Mendelssohn was born in Dessau and lived in Berlin, some four hundred miles northeast of Strasbourg. Cerf Berr, a devout Talmudic Jew, nevertheless asked Moses Mendelssohn for help in composing a memorandum for submission to King Louis XVI's Council of State. In the memorandum, Cerf Berr wanted to relate the unbearable conditions under which Alsatian Jews lived and to plead for help from King Louis XVI to suppress (i.e., abolish) Jewish exceptional laws, beginning with the humiliating Jewish body tax required for Jews to enter the City of Strasbourg for the day.

Moses Mendelssohn supported Cerf Berr's idea of writing a

memorandum to King Louis XVI, but suggested that its impact would be much greater if it came from the heart and pen of a Christian essayist. Moses Mendelssohn recommended to Cerf Berr the twenty-nine-year-old German civil servant Christian William Dohm (1751–1820). Interestingly, Christian William Dohm belonged to the Société des Philantropes of Strasbourg, although he was not present when Henri Grégoire read his essay in 1779, according to Alyssa Goldstein Sepinwall.

Cerf Berr agreed to hire Christian William Dohm to write the essay because Moses Mendelssohn recommended him and because Cerf Berr had no one else to whom he could turn. Cerf Berr was a pragmatist who understood that "the road to influencing the French Enlightenment regarding Jews ran through Berlin," said historian Robert Badinter.[42–43]

In 1780, Christian William Dohm completed the treatise for Cerf Berr. Its title was "Concerning the Amelioration of the Civil Status of the Jews." In 1780, Cerf Berr forwarded a copy of the treatise to King Louis XVI's Council of State.[44]

What did Christian William Dohm's treatise say about the plight of the Ashkenazim? Christian William Dohm argued from the Enlightenment premises of universal natural rights and religious toleration, which attributed the cause of the degraded condition of Jews to the negative environmental conditions under which they had long been forced (by Christians) to live. He believed that Jews required access to agricultural and artisan trades, which would serve to counteract the effects of their overconcentration in the spheres of commerce and finance. Christian William Dohm strongly supported the right of Jews to continue to exercise (semi-) communal authority even while living in the Kingdom of France.[44]

Heinrich Graetz elaborated on the themes of Christian William Dohm's essay as follows:

> Dohm suggested a plan whereby the amelioration of the condition of the Jews might be facilitated, and his proposals

formed a program for the future. In the first place, [the Jews] were to receive equal rights with all other subjects [of King Louis XVI]. In particular, liberty of occupation and in procuring a livelihood should be conceded them, so that, by wise precautions, they would be drawn away from petty trading and usury, and be attracted to handicrafts, agriculture, arts, and sciences, all without compulsion. The moral elevation was to be promoted by the foundation of good schools of their own, or by the admission of their youth into Christian schools, and by the elevation of adults in the Jewish Houses of Prayer.[45]

On April 5, 1781, Cerf Berr, who had appointed himself Grand Préposé of the Ashkenazim in Alsace (but not of the Jews in Lorraine and the Three Bishoprics), laid out a plan for the assimilation of the Ashkenazim of Alsace in a letter to King Louis XVI's Keeper of the Seals (Garde des Sceaux), Armand Thomas Hue of Miromesnil (1723–1796, served 1774–1787). In this letter, Cerf Berr proposed that France assimilate the Ashkenazim in Alsace in the same way that France had assimilated the Sephardim of Bordeaux. The Jews of Bordeaux "are like other subjects of the King," said Cerf Berr, who continued:

> [The conduct of the Jews of Bordeaux] is in no way objectionable; in a word, they are happy. And those of Alsace can assure [King Louis XVI] that things will be the same for them if they receive from the king's bounty and the beneficence…an honest and assured establishment. They have the means to assist in the good of the state and will have even more in order to encourage the precious memory of a benefit for which they will never cease to be grateful.[46]

In 1781, Cerf Berr also produced a "Memorandum for the Jewish Nation Established in Alsace; on its Current State and the Need to

Remedy It," in which he denounced the Jewish body tax "as humiliating as it is contrary to nature's wishes." Cerf Berr continued:

> It is easy to understand how exorbitant and unjust this toll is, since this city [Strasbourg], being the capital of the province, is the center of commerce; and it is unheard of to make subjects pay so high a tax who go there to purchase the most necessary of things, like comestibles, cloth for garments, or to consult their affairs or their health.[46]

In 1781, the Jewish community of Bischheim built a wooden synagogue.[47]

On May 19, 1781, two years before the end of the American Revolutionary War, Jacques Necker resigned as Controller-general for King Louis XVI. He resigned because he was frustrated and unable to persuade the nobility and clergy to implement the financial reforms needed to save the French Kingdom from bankruptcy.[48]

In the summer of 1781, Christian William Dohm published a larger work on the Jews, which dealt not only with the current condition of the French Jews, but also with the condition of the Jews in different stages of their history. It included his treatise, "Concerning the Amelioration of the Civil Status of the Jews." The first German-language edition of his book immediately sold out. Cerf Berr suggested that Christian William Dohm translate his book into French. Christian William Dohm concurred and chose Swiss scholar and mathematician Bernoulli to translate his book.

In 1781, the Council of the Alsatian Jewish Communities, led by the three General Préposés, again asked the Sovereign Council of Alsace to replace seigniorial judges with royal judges in cases of alleged usury involving Alsatian Jews. The Sovereign Council again turned down the request of the Council of the Alsatian Jewish Communities.[14]

Lawyer fees were costly in the ongoing struggle over the qualifications of judges in Alsace. From November 1781 to September 1787, the budget of the Council of the Alsatian Jewish Communities was almost thirty-three thousand livres. The largest part, almost seventeen thousand livres, went for travel expenses, the preparation of memoranda, and fees for consultations.[21]

On September 14, 1781, the Strasbourg authorities brought up for renewal their Jewish body-tax franchise, which Cerf Berr had held for eighteen years. From 1763 to 1775, Cerf Berr had paid forty-two hundred livres per year for the lease. However, between 1775 and 1781, he paid only thirty-six hundred livres per year for the lease.[2] Recall that in 1775, some observers believed that many more Jews than ever before were entering Strasbourg, but the Strasbourg authorities lacked data to establish the actual rate. The Strasbourg authorities remedied the problem by collecting that data for the years 1780 and 1781. What did they learn?

In 1780, there were about twenty-eight thousand passages made by Jews through the three gates of Porte Blanche, Porte de Saverne, and Porte de Pierre into the City of Strasbourg. The total population of Jews in Alsace was almost four thousand families, or almost twenty thousand men, women, and children, according to data provided by David Feuerwerker.[2]

The Strasbourg authorities conducted a second census of Jewish passages into Strasbourg in 1781. Between January and July 1781, they counted more than twenty-thousand passages of Jews through all five gates to the city, including the Jewish and Wickhaussel gates.[2] The number for the first seven months of the year 1781 extrapolated to more than thirty-five thousand passages for the twelve months of 1781. One difference between the two censuses of 1780 and 1781 was that authorities counted Jewish entries during the year 1780 for three gates only and during the year 1781 for all five gates to the city.

The data showed that the use of Strasbourg by Jews was increasing over time. The majority of Jews entered through the Porte Blanche and Porte de Pierre, because these two city gates were closest to the big centers of Jewish population outside of the City of Strasbourg, especially the Village of Bischheim. The shortest and most direct road between Bischheim and Strasbourg ended at Porte de Pierre.[2]

Based on the Jewish entry data, the Strasbourg authorities reasoned that the Jewish body-tax lease was worth much more than the thirty-six hundred livres per year paid by Cerf Berr. Thus, in 1781, the Strasbourg authorities decided to auction the Jewish body-tax lease to the highest bidder instead of renewing it with Cerf Berr. The intent of the Strasbourg authorities was to maximize the revenue generated by the lease to plump the city's coffers.

The record of the actual auctioning of the Jewish body-tax lease still exists. It specified that the following men were present: Schoentzel; Isaac Lehmann, Jew of Bischheim, also known as Reb Leima; Gaillard; Durmeniger; Picquet; and Jean-Baptiste Leury. Cerf Berr was not at the auction. Reb Leima of the Lehmann family of Bischheim bid forty-eight hundred livres for the lease, which was twelve hundred more livres than what Cerf Berr had been paying. However, a Christian named Claude Joseph Picquet won the adjudication for a shocking bid of ten thousand livres per year.[49–50]

When Cerf Berr learned of the bid placed by Reb Leima, he became so furious over the latter's meddling in the franchise that he asked David Sinzheim (Cerf Berr's brother-in-law and the Cerfberr family rabbi) to excommunicate Reb Leima in Bischheim. The Berr and the Lehmann families of Bischheim were both wealthy, had their own sous-rabbis, and jostled for dominance.[51] Reb Leima quickly appealed to the Rabbinical Court in Niedernai, which overturned his excommunication by David Sinzheim. Cerf Berr submitted willingly to the Patent Rabbi's ruling and asked the pardon of Reb Leima. After this experience, Cerf Berr was determined more than ever to end the Jewish body tax.

In autumn 1781, soon after Claude Joseph Picquet won the adjudication for the Strasbourg Jewish body-tax lease, the new Secretary of War and Alsace Administrator, Philippe Henri, Marquis of Ségur (henceforth, Ségur), made known to the authorities of Strasbourg the following:

A regulation concerning the Jews in Alsace is about to appear and [King Louis XVI] wishes that, instead of proceeding to a new adjudication [of the Jewish body-tax lease], the magistrate order that the lease agreed upon with Cerf Berr, and which was going to expire, be prolonged indefinitely.[46]

The letter from Secretary of War Ségur was referencing the French Crown's work on a General Regulation concerning the Ashkenazim in Alsace. Recall that in April 1781, Cerf Berr had been working with the Keeper of the Seals and other ministers in the King's Council of State to find ways to assimilate the Ashkenazim in Alsace into the French Kingdom.

The surprised Strasbourg authorities complied with the request by Secretary of War Ségur to halt adjudication of the Jewish body-tax lease, but agreed only to suspend its definitive adjudication until 1783.

During 1781, France spent two hundred million livres on the American Revolutionary War. When Jacques Necker left his post on May 19, 1781, he gave to King Louis XVI a statement of the financial situation of the French Kingdom for the remainder of 1781. The statement suggested that King Louis XVI could anticipate a surplus of about sixty-four million livres in the royal treasury at the beginning of 1782.[48]

On January 2, 1782, Cerf Berr's attempts to suppress Jewish exceptional laws in Alsace received a boost when Holy Roman Emperor Joseph II (1741–1790, reigned 1764–1790), the older brother of French Queen Marie Antoinette, issued in both Vienna and Lower Austria a twenty-five-article Edict of Toleration that granted religious toleration for the Ashkenazim of the Holy Roman Empire. A year earlier (1781), Holy Roman Emperor Joseph II had issued a similar edict granting religious tolerance for Lutherans, Calvinists, and the Greek Orthodox residents of the Holy Roman Empire. The edict pertaining to the Jews of Austria allowed Jewish children to attend schools and universities and Jewish merchants to open factories. It also removed onerous restrictions, such as forcing Jews to wear gold stars and paying *a body tax to enter a city* [emphasis added]. Holy Roman Emperor Joseph II's Edict of Toleration of 1782 also abolished use of Yiddish and Hebrew by Jews and required them to use the national language of the country in which they lived.

On February 22, 1782, Cerf Berr sent a French translation of Holy Roman Emperor Joseph II's Edict of Toleration of 1782 to the French Crown's Keeper of the Seals, Armand Thomas Hue of Miromesnil. Cerf Berr drew Miromesnil's attention to Article Nineteen of the Edict of Toleration of 1782, which ordered the total suppression of the body tax in the Holy Roman Empire. King Louis XVI and his ministers took notice of Holy Roman Emperor Joseph II's Edicts of Toleration of both 1781 and 1782. However, the project to develop a General Regulation for the Ashkenazim of Alsace dragged on. Cerf Berr paced.

In spring 1782, Bernoulli finished his translation into French of *Ueber die Bürgerliche Verbesserung der Juden* by Christian William Dohm. Honoré Gabriel Riqueti, Count of Mirabeau (1749–1791, henceforth, Honoré Mirabeau), who later became a moderate leader during the French Revolution and who wrote his own book on the plight of the Jews, obtained authorization to publish Christian William Dohm's book in France. Honoré Mirabeau subsequently learned with horror that someone had burned all the copies of Christian William Dohm's book intended for a French audience.

During 1782, France spent *another* two hundred million livres to support the American Revolutionary War.[48]

In 1782, Max Berr, the oldest son of Cerf Berr, married Esther Bouf (1757–1821), who was born in La Haye, Pays-Bas, France. They had two sons and two daughters, whose names were Samson (1777–1826), Berr (1780–1824), Adélaïde (1781–1818), and Fleurette (Flore, 1782–1820). The four children of Max and Esther Berr were born in Hotel Ribeaupierre in the City of Strasbourg.

On January 20, 1783, the hostilities between the Americans and the British ended. On September 3, 1783, representatives of British King George III (1738–1820, ruled 1760–1820) and representatives of the United States of America signed the final Treaty of Versailles. The British lost the Thirteen American Colonies and France won a propaganda war against the British, which made up for France's demoralizing defeat in the Seven Years' War. However, France paid a huge price for this victory, because it incurred a staggering debt in helping the American colonists win the American War of Independence (1775–1783).

In 1783, Cerf Berr of Médelsheim became involved in a dispute with the Baron Jean of Dietrich (1719–1795, henceforth, Jean Dietrich), a wealthy Alsatian landowner and owner of the "Castle of the English Court," a famous residence in Bischheim sitting on a loop of land surrounded on three sides by the Ill River. Jean Dietrich was the father of Frederic Dietrich, the future mayor of Strasbourg. Cerf Berr applied for a license to extract gravel from the nearby Reid River. Cerf Berr claimed the rights of the bourgeoisie. On February 26, 1783, he lost his case against Jean Dietrich in court. The judgment said that Jean Dietrich's rank as a Baron of the Holy Roman Empire meant that he deserved more respect than Cerf Berr did, and that Cerf Berr and other Jews were not bourgeois (burghers), but only residents of Bischheim under the protection of the seigneurs of Bischheim.[20]

On July 12, 1783, the Strasbourg authorities asked Cerf Berr to produce a list of his employees, including family members, who lived in the City of Strasbourg and various provinces in France where he conducted business. On July 18, 1783, Max Berr wrote back to the Strasbourg authorities, explaining that he was working on the list with his father, who was in Paris, and would provide the list to the Strasbourg authorities as soon as his father sent it back to him. Max Berr also noted that he had visited the Chancellery in Strasbourg that day to tell the authorities this information in person, but no one was present in the office.[52]

On July 22, 1783, Cerf Berr, frustrated by the slow rate of progress on King Louis XVI's General Regulation for the Ashkenazim in Alsace, modified his approach. He turned his attention from the Keeper of the Seals to Secretary of War Ségur for help in obtaining some information, which he believed would help his case.[46] Secretary of War Ségur agreed to obtain the information and wrote to Bon Guy Doublet of Persan

(1730–1802), the French Crown's Master of Requests and Procurator General of the Bureau of Tolls. The desired information concerned the whether a Jewish body tax existed in other provinces of France.

Cerf Berr asked Bon Guy Doublet of Persan to find out "if it is true that the tolls in the regions of Lyon, Languedoc, and the Dauphiné were abolished without indemnification and without the substitution of other tolls, and if it's true that *Alsace is currently the sole province in which the body tax on Jews persists*" (emphasis added).[46] The phrase "without indemnification" suggests that the Strasbourg authorities already were demanding indemnification for the revenue they stood to lose from abolition of the Jewish body tax, and that Cerf Berr was aware of their demand.

On July 25, 1783, Bon Guy Doublet of Persan certified and communicated to Secretary of War Ségur the following information about whether a Jewish body tax existed in other parts of France:

> Where tax levels had been audited, the Commissioners took care to revise the articles having to do with the persons of Jews, *considering these fees contrary to humanity* [emphasis added]. This rule was adopted in the regions of Lyon, Languedoc, the Dauphiné and *all of France* [emphasis added]. These tolls were suppressed everywhere *without the substitution of other fees and without indemnification* [emphasis added].[46]

In other words, Alsace was the *only* place in all France that still charged Jews to enter both Strasbourg and Lower Alsace. Indeed, the French Crown itself levied the body tax on Jews entering Lower Alsace.

List of Cerf Berr's Employees, 1783

On July 25, 1783, Max Berr forwarded to the Strasbourg authorities the list of Cerf Berr's employees, including family members. Cerf Berr placed his employees in categories, based on where they lived, i.e., in the City of Strasbourg, in Alsace, in Lorraine, in the Three Bishoprics, and in Comté de Bourgogne.[52] Cerf Berr's list provides an extraordinary look at the complexity and scope of his royal military fodder supply business.

* * * * * * * *

List of Cerf Berr's Employees, Categorized by Place, in Cerf Berr's Own Words, 1783

Strasbourg:

- Cerf Berr;
- Max Berr, married son of Cerf Berr;
- Liepman [Lippman] Berr; married son of Cerf Berr;
- Baruch Berr; unmarried son of Cerf Berr;
- Théodore Berr; unmarried son of Cerf Berr;
- Seligmann Alexandre;
- Mayer Lazar;
- Wolff Lévy;
- Abraham Cahen, first clerk of Bischheim;
- Joseph Levy, first clerk;
- Raphael Marx, clerk;
- Simon Harbourg, clerk;
- Raphael Mayer Berr, clerk;
- Moyse Levy, clerk;

- Gottlieb Isaac, clerk;
- Heyem Wolff, clerk;
- Heyem Flersheim, clerk;
- Moyse Samuel, bureau boy;
- Five servants [no names provided];
- Joseph, children's tutor from Lingolsheim;
- Abraham Moyse, hotel manager of Bischheim;
- Samuel Jacob, coachman of Bischheim;
- Lyon Weyl, porter;
- Emanuel, (horse) groom;
- Wolff, domestic;
- Lyon, domestic;
- Simon, domestic;
- Jacob, domestic;
- Joseph, domestic;
- David, tutor;
- Zacarias, domestic for Max Berr;
- Five servants [no names provided];
- Michel Benjamin, clerk;
- Raphael Gugenheim, tutor;
- Löb, domestic;
- A son of Seligmann Alexandre [no name provided];
- N., tutor
- Moyse, domestic of Mayer Lazar.
- Four servants [no names provided];
- Abraham Sinzheim, clerk
- Emanuel, tutor;
- Scholem Amschel, domestic of Wolff Lévy; and
- Six servants [no names provided].

Alsace Province, but not in Strasbourg:

- Emanuel Weyl, buyer of Bischheim for the storehouses in Strasbourg;
- Isaac Salomon, buyer of Bischheim for the storehouses in Strasbourg;
- Gottlieb Cahen, buyer of Bischheim for the storehouses in Strasbourg;
- Lehmann Berr Weyl, buyer of Bischheim for the storehouses in Strasbourg;
- Isaac Hirschel of Carlruhe, buyer for the storehouses in Strasbourg;
- Löp Oppenheim of Hoffenheim, buyer for the storehouses in Strasbourg;
- Heyem Oppenheim of Hoffenheim, buyer for the storehouses in Strasbourg;
- Michel of Echtersheim, buyer for the storehouses in Strasbourg;
- Liepmann Nathan of Grombach, buyer for the storehouses in Strasbourg;
- Aron Samuel Simon of Landau, buyer for the storehouses in Landau;
- Elias Jonas of Obernheim, inspector of the province;
- Cerf Marchand Berr of Lauterbourg, buyer for the storehouses in Lauterbourg;
- Jacob Löb of Lauterbourg, buyer for the storehouses in Lauterbourg;
- Amschel Cahen of Weissembourg [Wissembourg], buyer for the storehouses in Weissembourg;
- Moyses Weyl of Valck, buyer for the storehouses in Haguenau;

- Alexander Samuel of Haguenau, buyer for the storehouses in Haguenau;

- Jacob Gumbrich of Obernheim, buyer for the storehouses in Schlettstadt;

- Michel Levy of Epfig, buyer for the storehouses in Schlettstadt;

- Baruch Levy of Epfig, buyer for the storehouses in Schlettstadt;

- Seligman Weil of Krusheim, buyer for the storehouses in Neuf-Brisach;

- Michel Sinsheim of Huningue, controller; and

- Samuel Manheimer of Uffholz, buyer for the storehouses in Huningue.

Lorraine Province:

- Mayer Marx of Nancy, director of operations in Nancy;

- Lehmann Mayer Marx of Nancy, assistant director of operations in Nancy;

- Isaac Lazar of Nancy, guard of the storehouses in Nancy;

- Berr Isaac Berr of Nancy, general cashier for the storehouses in Nancy;

- Isaac Wolff of Nancy, sub-general cashier of the storehouses in Nancy;

- Abraham Brisack of Lunéville, buyer for the storehouses in Nancy;

- Berel Moch of Bouxwiller, guard of the storehouses in Nancy;

- Lehmann Michel of Metz, buyer for the storehouses in Commercy;

- Baruch Berr of Sarguemines [also spelled Sarreguemines], controller for the storehouses in Sarguemines;

- Marx Isaac of Sarguemines, cashier for the storehouses in Sarguemines;
- Löb Levy of Boquenom, buyer for the storehouses in Sarguemines;
- Nathan Cahen of Boquenom, buyer for the storehouses in Sarguemines;
- Seligman Hess of Putelange, controller for the storehouses in St. Avold;
- Lazar Mayer of Epinal, buyer for the storehouses in Epinal;
- Mayer Marx of Epinal, controller for the storehouses in Epinal; and
- Mayer Levy of Metz, buyer for the storehouses in Epinal.

Three Bishoprics (Verdun, Metz, Toul):

- Aron Bloch, inspector;
- Cerf Alexander Cahen, buyer;
- Abraham Marchand Berr, clerk;
- Louis Mayer of Metz, controller;
- Moyses Liepman of Metz, controller for the storehouses in Metz;
- Salomon Cahen of Metz, buyer for the storehouses of Vic;
- Cerf Zacharias of Saarlouis, buyer for the storehouses in Saarlouis;
- Raphael Liepman of Saarlouis, guard for the storehouses in Saarlouis;
- Mayer Levy of Buttingen, buyer for the storehouses in Thionville;
- Löb Hanau of Sedan;
- Abraham Coblence of Metz, controller for the storehouses in Sedan;

- Marchand Aron of Phalsbourg, buyer for the storehouses in Phalsbourg;
- Lazar Aron of Phalsbourg, inspector for the storehouses in Phalsbourg; and
- Salomon Benedic Cahen of Phalsbourg, guard for the storehouses in St. Mihel.

Comté de Bourgogne:

- Moyses Cahen of Metz, inspector for the storehouses in Besançon;
- Baruch Levy of Epfig, buyer for the storehouses in Vesoul; and
- Lyon Gugenheim of Obernheim, buyer for the storehouses in Gray.[53]

* * * * * * * *

Suppression of the Strasbourg Jewish Body Tax, January 1784

On August 11, 1783, Secretary of War Ségur told Bon Guy Doublet of Persan (Master of Requests and Procurator General of the Bureau of Tolls) that the King's Council of State wanted to separate the Jewish body-tax issue from the General Regulation for the Ashkenazim in Alsace, and to rule separately on each. Secretary of War Ségur wrote, "In the projected General Regulation that will be established relating to the Jews, an article bearing the suppression of the body tax on the Jews in Alsace is foreseen. [King Louis XVI] leaves it to the commission, and *it [the Jewish body tax] will thus not be dealt with in the General Regulation* [emphasis added]."[46]

The decision of the King's Council of State to deal with the Jewish body tax separately from the General Regulation for the Ashkenazim in

Alsace prompted Cerf Berr to leap into action. On August 13, 1783, he sent a letter to the King's Council of State to request suppression of the Jewish body tax. In his letter, Cerf Berr gave four reasons for suppressing the Jewish body tax. First, local and regional governments throughout France had already suppressed the Jewish body tax, thus providing the precedent needed to suppress the body tax in Alsace and Strasbourg.

Second, levying a tax on a human being was contrary to human rights and to nature, and the act of its levying was both harsh and humiliating to Jews. Third, "Strasbourg capitulations and the public tariff" and its fees and revenues never foresaw such exorbitant tolls. Fourth, Strasbourg laws prohibited Christian residents from engaging in commerce with Jews who went to Strasbourg only to meet basic needs, to purchase clothing, and to consult on their affairs and health.[45]

Cerf Berr then analyzed the reasons why Claude Joseph Picquet purchased the Jewish body-tax lease from the City of Strasbourg for ten thousand livres. Cerf Berr posited two possibilities. First, Claude Joseph Picquet may have experienced an "error of appreciation." Second, Strasbourg authorities knew that eventually King Louis XVI would suppress the Jewish body tax. The Strasbourg authorities used Claude Joseph Picquet as a dupe (or an accomplice) to drive up the price of the lease to ten thousand livres, which the city could then use as the figure for its demand for indemnification when King Louis XVI suppressed the tax.[45]

In August 1783, King Louis XVI asked various local authorities in Alsace to review his decree on the suppression of the Jewish body tax. Only the Strasbourg authorities disputed the decree. They predictably demanded indemnification for ten thousand livres, the price of Claude Joseph Picquet's auction bid. In September 1783, the French Crown transformed the decree into letters patent to give the ruling more weight; however, the French Crown then delayed issue of the letters patent. Meanwhile, the Strasbourg authorities, as promised, planned to start Claude Joseph Picquet's contract on September 29, 1783. Cerf Berr worried.

King Louis XVI continued to move slowly. Suppression of the

Jewish body tax was not a foregone conclusion. Thus, from August 1783 to October 1783, Cerf Berr intensely lobbied King Louis XVI, his ministers, including the Procurator General of the Bureau of Tolls, and any other government official who would listen to him. Cerf Berr's lobbying efforts took him to Paris, Versailles, and even Fontainebleau. On October 30, 1783, while at Fontainebleau, Cerf Berr told King Louis XVI's ministers that he was worried that the Nation Juive in Alsace was in difficulty and that he needed to return there. He pleaded with them to "dispatch the edict [for suppression of the body tax] so that it could be signed as soon as possible [by King Louis XVI]."[47] Why was the ruling being delayed?

One big problem was holding up King Louis XVI's issue of the letters patent to suppress the Jewish body tax—the indemnification demanded by Strasbourg authorities for their anticipated loss of city revenue. Cerf Berr wanted to deal with the Strasbourg indemnification clause of the edict by offering a total annual sum of twenty-four hundred livres, *not* the ten thousand livres demanded by the Strasbourg authorities. David Feuerwerker wrote:

> A clear-sighted ambassador and alert negotiator, [Cerf Berr] insisted that in the final writing of the edict there be no question of an indemnification paid by the Jews for the suppression of the body tax, but only a tax that [France] would pay for the carrying out of commerce, in Strasbourg as elsewhere. Cerf Berr's influence was such that that he could even intervene in the very writing of the edict. His remarks were fully in accord with the project of the Procurator Doublet of Persan, as we find it laid out in the "Reason for the Decree" of August 20, 1783. Doublet of Persan says, without any ambiguity, that Strasbourg must be placed before a fait accompli. *Any possible subsidiary problems would be settled later. First the toll had to be suppressed; the indemnification could be settled afterwards* [emphasis added]. In a short letter dated Wednesday, November 19, 1783, the controller-general of finances [met with] Doublet of Persan

in order to settle with him, on the basis of his "Work," the abolition of the body tax. This session, the final step before the definitive solution to the problem, was scheduled for Wednesday, November 26, 1783.[46]

On November 3, 1783, the free-spending Charles Alexander, Viscount of Calonne (1734–1802, served 1783–1787; henceforth, Calonne) and foe of Jacques Necker, became King Louis XVI's Controller-general of Finances. Calonne's "fundamental conviction was that the grandeur, prestige, and the éclat of the throne was the only consideration," observed historian Robert D. Harris. He continued:

> A wealthy country could afford great expenditures by [King Louis XVI]. The miserly policy of [Jacques] Necker [he resigned as director of finances in 1781, as noted above] may have been suitable for a city-state like Geneva [the native city of Jacques Necker] but not for the greatest kingdom in the world. [Calonne believed that] the remedy for financial problems was for [King Louis XVI] to repudiate his debts, which after all, were held by creditors who were mostly Jews, Swiss, or Dutch Protestants, and similarly disreputable bourgeois people… [Calonne believed] that Necker's economy was totally unfit and unnecessary for France. As Intendant of Valencienne during Necker's first ministry, Calonne was among those Intendants who bitterly opposed Necker's plans to establish Provincial Assemblies, which were at the expense of the power of the Intendants in the generalities.[53]

In 1783, Jüdel Berr passed away in Strasbourg at age fifty-three years. She left behind Cerf Berr, their nine grown children, and many grandchildren.

In 1784, twenty-two-year-old Baruch Berr married nineteen-year-old Amélie Alexandre (daughter of Rebecca Berr [Baruch's sister] and Seligmann Alexandre [Baruch's brother-in-law]); both bride and groom were born in Bischheim. Also in 1784, twenty-year-old Fradel (Fachon) Berr (born in Bischheim) married thirty-year-old Löb Levy (born in Hanover).[16] As of 1784, five of Cerf Berr's nine children had married: Rebecca, Minette, Max, Baruch, and Fradel. Lippman, Jeanette, Théodore, and Eve remained single.

In January 1784, King Louis XVI finally issued his letters patent to suppress the Jewish body tax. On January 24, 1784, the Sovereign Council of Alsace transcribed King Louis XVI's ruling on the abolition of the body tax. The same day, Strasbourg authorities officially ended the body tax levied on Jews. On January 28, 1784, Cerf Berr proclaimed victory upon learning that King Louis XVI had finally issued the letters patent to suppress the Jewish body tax. "In a letter to Doublet of Persan, Cerf Berr announced that the City of Strasbourg recognized [King Louis XVI's] edict bearing the exemption from the body tax…The first step in the emancipation of the Jews had become a reality."[46]

On January 28, 1784, the Bischheim Ashkenazi community rejoiced over the suppression of the loathed Jewish body tax. It prayed for King Louis XVI at a special religious ceremony. In 1780, Abraham Auerbach (1763–1845) had married Gittelé Sinzheim, daughter of David and Esther Sinzheim. Abraham Auerbach composed a joyous ode in Hebrew on the history of the Jewish body tax and its abolition. He glorified Cerf Berr with enthusiastic expressions. On a 1784 plan of the Bischheim wooden synagogue, the place of honor to the right of the Holy Ark went to "the chtadlan, parnass, and manhig" (leader of Israel), Rabbi Hirtz Médelsheim.[54] These words—chtadlan, parnass, manhig, and rabbi—were the highest praise a Jewish community could bestow on one of its members.

In 1784, Ashkenazi writer Hirtz Wesel (1725–1805), a friend of Moses Mendelssohn, published an article that praised the suppression of the Jewish body tax to enter Strasbourg and Lower Alsace. He published it in the very first volume of *Meassef*, or *HaMe'assef* (1784–1797), which was the leading literary organ of the Jewish Enlightenment in Europe.[55–56] Cerf Berr, although a devout Talmudic Jew, generously supported the publication.

Did the Strasbourg authorities receive monetary indemnification for the loss of revenue from the suppression of the Jewish body tax? Cerf Berr's efforts to persuade King Louis XVI to distribute the indemnification cost across the Kingdom of France failed. David Feuerwerker wrote that the Council of the Alsatian Jewish Communities ended up paying the indemnification:

> On January 30, 1784, Cerf Berr submitted a proposal, as was requested by Controller-general Calonne, to pay forty-eight thousand livres for the suppression of the body tax. Why forty-eight thousand livres? This was the capital necessary for constituting an annuity of twenty-four hundred livres annually, the price of the lease [i.e., the Strasbourg authorities failed to get their ten thousand livres and furthermore received only twenty-four hundred livres per year, which was lower than the thirty-six hundred livres per year paid by Cerf Berr for many years]. Cerf Berr solicited the favor of being able to pay off this large amount in four payments. Contrary to legend, Cerf Berr received no profit from the toll; neither he nor his family lived off it. On the contrary, Cerf Berr had advanced one hundred and twenty thousand livres during the 1780s to the Jews in Alsace. In the name of the Jewish Nation, Cerf Berr asked that this payment be spread out so as not to weigh down the finances of the community. This sum of forty-eight thousand livres would thus be divided up among the whole of the Jewish Nation and a receipt was given to Cerf Berr in order to facilitate this division. By a Decree of Council of June 24, 1785, the indemnification of the City of Strasbourg for the suppression of the body tax was fixed at an annual and perpetual annuity of twenty-four hundred livres. This decree, in order to be executable, was confirmed by letters patent of January 25, 1786, sent to the Parliament of Metz on March 15, 1786, and registered there on March 30, 1786. Crolbois, agent

of the City of Strasbourg, in Paris then wrote to his principals: "The affair is thus finalized."[46,57–58]

In 1784, the Ashkenazi General Préposés again requested royal, rather than seigniorial, judges to try cases of alleged usury involving Jews in Alsace. The Sovereign Council of Alsace, for the third time, turned down their request.[14]

In summary, between 1763 and 1784, Cerf Berr moved year-round to Strasbourg, secretly purchased Hotel Ribeaupierre in Strasbourg to house his family, became a naturalized French citizen and royally appointed provider of fodder for the French military, compelled the historic suppression of the four hundred-year-old Jewish body tax, and buried his wife of thirty-six years.

Chapter Four Notes:

1. Roger Lévylier: *Notes et Documents sur la famille Cerf-Berr*. Volume I. Paris, France: Plon, 1902, p. 23.

2. David Feuerwerker: *L'Emancipation des Juifs en France*. Paris, France: Albin Michel, 1976, pp. 8–11.

3. A second source says that Cerf Berr first farmed the body tax in 1769, not 1763. See Arthur Hertzberg: *The French Enlightenment and the Jews*. New York City, New York: Columbia University Press, 1968, p. 124, Note #138.

4. "Yad David." Available at http://www.virtualjudaica.com/Item/6019/Yad_David; accessed February 4, 2012; and Max Warschawski: "David Sintzheim." In *"L'Almanach du KKL-Strasbourg 1749-1989."* Available at http://judaisme.sdv.fr/histoire/rabbins/sintzhei/sintzhei.htm; accessed February 4, 2012.

5. "Chapitre V: Les lettres patents de 1784 sont aussi le premier effort d'un gouvernement paternal qui veut avoir soin Israelites comme de ses autres enfants." *Livres-mystiques.com*. Available at http://livres-mystiques.com/partieTEXTES/Lemann/Israelites/1chap5&6.html; accessed January 18, 2012.

6. Abbé Joseph Lémann: *L'Entrée des Israélites dans La Société Francaise et Les États Chrétiens d'apres des Documents Nouveaux*. Paris, France: Librairie Victor Lecoffre, 1886, pp. 102–107.

7. Moses Ginsburger: *Cerf-Berr et son Époque*. Société d'Histoire des Juifs d'Alsace-Lorraine. Guebwiller, Alsace, France: J. Dreyfus, 1908, pp. 7–8.

8. Zosa Szajkowski: "The Jewish problem in Alsace, Metz, and Lorraine on the eve of the Revolution." In *Jews and the French Revolutions of 1789, 1830 and 1848*. New York City, New York: Ktav Publishing House, 1970, pp. 304–305. See also Yves Combeau: *Le Comte d'Argenson, 1696–1764: Ministre de King Louis XV*. Paris, France: Mémoires et Documents de l'École nationale des chartes, 1999.

9. Dewey A Browder: *Zweibrücken: Yesterday and Today*. Zweibrücken, Germany: Pfaelzischer Merkur, 1975. For more information on Hotel Ribeaupierre in Strasbourg, see "9 quai Finkwiller." *Archi-Strasbourg. org*. Available at http://www.archi-strasbourg.org/adresse-9_quai_finkwiller_finkwiller_centre_ville_strasbourg-2775.html?check=1&archiAffichage=adresseDetail&archiIdAdresse=2775&archiIdEvenementGroupeAdresse=6452#3; accessed March 2, 2012; and Thierry Hatt: "Cerf Baer un Juif revendiquant d'être 'citoyen' en 1789; localisation de son habitation a l'aide du plan de 1725." Contribution a l'exposition "Les Juifs a Strasbourg." December 2002. Available at http://thierry.hatt.gps.free.fr/01-site-acad-tous-pdf/cerf-baer-02.pdf; accessed March 11, 2012. The second source has excellent photographs of the layout of Cerf Berr's Hotel Ribeaupierre.

10. Robert Weyl: "Les Juifs à Rosheim." In *Saisons d'Alsace*, Number 66, 1978. Available at http://judaisme.sdv.fr/synagog/basrhin/r-z/rosheim.htm; accessed January 22, 2012; and Robert Weyl: "Chronique des juifs à Rosheim." In *Saisons d'Alsace*, Number 66, 1978. Available at http://judaisme.sdv.fr/synagog/basrhin/r-z/rosheim/chroniq.htm; accessed February 2, 2012.

11. Jay R. Berkovitz: *Rites and Passages: the Beginnings of Modern Jewish Culture in France, 1650–1860*. Philadelphia, Pennsylvania: University of Pennsylvania Press, 2004, p. 54. Max Warschawski: "Hirtz de Médelsheim." Note #2. Available at http://judaisme.sdv.fr/perso/Cerf Berr/index.htm; accessed November 13, 2011.

12. Moses Ginsburger: *Cerf-Berr et son Époque*. Société d'Histoire des Juifs d'Alsace-Lorraine. Guebwiller, Alsace, France: J. Dreyfus, 1908, pp. 9–12. The letter is available at http://judaisme.sdv.fr/perso/cerfberr/

epoque/epoque.htm. The entire work by Moses Ginsburger is available at http://gallica.bnf.fr/ark:/12148/bpt6k5427849p/f8.image; accessed November 3, 2011.

13. Max Warschawski: "Hirtz de Médelsheim." Available at http://judaisme.sdv.fr/perso/Cerf Berr/index.htm; accessed November 13, 2011.

14. Zosa Szajkowski: "The Jewish aspect of credit and usury." In *Jews and the French Revolutions of 1789, 1830, and 1848*. New York City, New York: Ktav Publishing House, 1970, pp. 194, 1999; and Zosa Szajkowski: *Franco-Judaica: an Analytical Bibliography of Books, Pamphlets, Decrees, Briefs and Other Printed Documents Pertaining to the Jews in France 1500–1788*. New York City, New York: American Academy for Jewish Research, 1962, pp. xiii, xv.

15. Rosanne and Daniel N. Leeson: *Index de Memoire Juive en Alsace: Contrats de Mariage au XVIIIème Siecle par A. A. Fraenckel*. Volume I, Bas-Rhin. Strasbourg, Alsace, France: Cercle de Généalogie Juive, Editions du Cédrat, 1997, p. 54. The book is available for purchase at http://www.genealoj.org/New/ENtexte/page06.php; accessed December 1, 2011.

16. Moses Ginsburger: *Cerf-Berr et son Époque*. Société d'Histoire des Juifs d'Alsace-Lorraine. Guebwiller, Alsace, France: J. Dreyfus, 1908, pp. 31–33. Available at http://gallica.bnf.fr/ark:/12148/bpt6k5427849p/f8.image; accessed November 3, 2011.

17. For more information on King Louis XV, see Oliver Bernier: *Louis the Beloved: the Life of King Louis XV*. New York City, New York: Doubleday, 1984; and François Bluche: *King Louis XV*. Paris, France: Editions Perrin, 2000.

18. For more information on King Louis XVI, see John Hardman: *King Louis XVI: the Silent King*. London, England, United Kingdom: Arnold Press, 2000; Munro Price: *The Road from Versailles: King Louis XVI, Marie Antoinette, and the Fall of the French Monarchy*. New York City, New York: St. Martin's Griffin, 2004; and Pierre Rétat: *Le Dernier Règne: Chronique de la France de King Louis XVI, 1774–1789*. Paris, France: Librairie Artheme Fayard, 1995.

19. Abbé Joseph Lémann: *L'Entrée des Israélites dans La Société Francaise et Les États Chrétiens d'apres des Documents Nouveaux*. Paris, France: Librairie Victor Lecoffre, 1886, pp. 99–101, 112; and Zosa Szajkowski: "The Jewish problem in Alsace, Metz, and Lorraine on the eve of the

Revolution of 1789." In *Jews and the French Revolutions of 1789, 1830 and 1848*. New York City, New York: Ktav Publishing House, 1970, p. 305, Note #12.

20. Arthur Hertzberg: *The French Enlightenment and the Jews*. New York City, New York: Columbia University Press, 1968, pp. 136, 250.

21. Zosa Szajkowski: "The Alsatian debts." In *Jews and the French Revolutions of 1789, 1830, and 1848*. New York City, New York: Ktav Publishing House, 1970, p. 700.

22. Zosa Szajkowski: "The Jewish problem in Alsace, Metz, and Lorraine on the eve of the Revolution." In *Jews and the French Revolutions of 1789, 1830 and 1848*. New York City, New York: Ktav Publishing House, 1970, p. 305, Note #13.

23. Ibid, pp. 313–314.

24. Ibid, p. 306.

25. Ibid, p. 304, Note #11.

26. Walter Isaacson: *Benjamin Franklin: an American Life*. New York City, New York: Simon & Schuster, 2004, p. 321.

27. See Robert D. Harris: *Necker and the Revolution of 1789*. Lanham, Maryland: University Press of America, 1986, pp. 1–30.

28. Archives de la ville de Strasbourg, requête ou soumission du 21 juin, 1777, signé Cerfbeer, en hébreu et avec paraphe, as noted by Abbé Joseph Lémann: *L'Entrée des Israélites dans La Société Francaise et Les États Chrétiens d'apres des Documents Nouveaux*. Paris, France: Librairie Victor Lecoffre, 1886.

29. Zosa Szajkowski: "Occupational problems of Jewish emancipation in France, 1789–1800." In *Jews and the French Revolutions of 1789, 1830 and 1848*. New York City, New York: Ktav Publishing House, 1970, p. 512, Note #45; and G. Huffel: *La Forêt Sainte de Haguenau en Alsace*. Nancy-Paris-Strasbourg: Berger-Levrault, 1920, pp. 85–86.

30. Zosa Szajkowski: "Occupational problems of Jewish emancipation in France, 1789–1800." In *Jews and the French Revolutions of 1789, 1830 and 1848*. New York City, New York: Ktav Publishing House, 1970, p. 520.

31. Zosa Szajkowski: "The case of the counterfeit receipts in Alsace, 1777–1789." In *Jews and the French Revolutions of 1789, 1830, and 1848*. New York City, New York: Ktav Publishing House, 1970, pp. 202–219. The information about Berr Isaac Berr of Turique is from

"Berr Isaac Berr of Turique." *Jewish Encyclopedia*, 1906. Available at http://www.jewishencyclopedia.com/articles/3158-berr-isaac-berr-of-turique; accessed January 12, 2012.

32. A copy of the 1778 Treaty of Alliance with France is available at the Library of Congress website at http://www.loc.gov/rr/program/bib/ourdocs/alliance.html; accessed January 19, 2012. See also Ronald Hoffman and Peter J. Albert: *Diplomacy and Revolution: the Franco-American Alliance of 1778*. Charlottesville, Virginia: University of Virginia Press, 1981.

33. Walter Isaacson: *Benjamin Franklin: an American Life*. New York City, New York: Simon & Schuster, 2004, pp. 347–348.

34. James Van Horn Melton: *The Rise of the Public in Enlightenment Europe*. Cambridge, United Kingdom: Cambridge University Press, 2001, pp. 59–61.

35. Abbé Joseph Lémann: *L'Entrée des Israélites dans La Société Francaise et Les États Chrétiens d'apres des Documents Nouveaux*. Paris, France: Librairie Victor Lecoffre, 1886, pp. 108–109.

36. Zosa Szajkowski: "The Jewish aspect of credit and usury." In *Jews and the French Revolutions of 1789, 1830, and 1848*. New York City, New York: Ktav Publishing House, 1970, p. 154.

37. Heinrich Graetz: *History of the Jews*. Volume V. Philadelphia, Pennsylvania: Jewish Publication Society of America, 1895, pp. 349–350.

38. Zosa Szajkowski: "The case of the counterfeit receipts in Alsace, 1777–1789." In *Jews and the French Revolutions of 1789, 1830, and 1848*. New York City, New York: Ktav Publishing House, 1970, pp. 195–196.

39. Ibid, p. 213.

40. Ibid, p. 196.

41. Alyssa Goldstein Sepinwall: "L'Abbé Grégoire and the Metz contest: the view from new documents." *Revue des Études Juives*, Volume 166, Numbers 1–2, 2007, pp. 243–258. For more information on Moses Mendelssohn, see Alexander Altmann: *Moses Mendelssohn: a Biographical Study*. Oxford, England, United Kingdom: Littman Library of Jewish Civilization, 1998. See also Jonathan I. Helfand: "The symbiotic relationship between French and Germany Jewry in the age of emancipation." *Leo Baeck Institute Yearbook, 1984,* Volume

29 Issue 1, pp. 331–350. Available at http://leobaeck.oxfordjournals. org/content/29/1/331.extract; accessed March 2, 2012.

42. Robert Badinter: *Free and Equal: Emancipating France's Jews 1789–1791*. Translated into English from the French by Adam Simms. Teaneck, New Jersey: Ben Yehuda Press, 2010, p. 7.

43. Christian William Dohm's "Concerning the Civil Amelioration of the Condition of Jews in History" is available at "German History in Documents and Images (1781)," Volume 2, *From Absolutism to Napoleon, 1648–1815* at http://germanhistorydocs.ghi-dc.org/sub_ document_s.cfm?document_id=3647; accessed November 27, 2010.

44. Frances Malino: *A Jew in the French Revolution: the Life of Zalkind Hourwitz*. Oxford, England, United Kingdom: Blackwell Publisher, 1996, p. 214, Note #46; and Robert Badinter: *Free and Equal: Emancipating France's Jews 1789–1791*. Translated into English from the French by Adam Simms. Teaneck, New Jersey: Ben Yehuda Press, 2010, pp. 68–72.

45. Heinrich Graetz: *History of the Jews*. Volume V. Philadelphia, Pennsylvania: Jewish Publication Society of America, 1895, p. 355.

46. David Feuerwerker: "The Abolition of Body Taxes in France." Translated into English by Mitchell Abidor. *Annales. Économies, Sociétés, Civilisations*, Volume 17, Number 5, 1962 (not paginated; use search option). Available at http://www.marxists.org/history/france/ annales/1962/body-taxes.htm; accessed November 17, 2011. David Feuerwerker also published an abridged version of "The Abolition of Body Taxes in France." In David Feuerwerker: *L'Emancipation des Juifs en France*. Paris, France: Albin Michel, 1976, pp. 3–48. See also David Feuerwerker: *L'Emancipation des Juifs en France*. Paris, France: Albin Michel, 1976, pp.12–15.

47. "Bischheim." Available at http://www.jewishvirtuallibrary.org/jsource/ judaica/ejud_0002_0003_0_03020.html; accessed February 4, 2012.

48. Robert D. Harris: *Necker and the Revolution of 1789*. Lanham, Maryland: University Press of America, 1986, p. 31.

49. Arthur Hertzberg: *The French Enlightenment and the Jews*. New York City, New York: Columbia University Press, 1968, p. 124, Note #138.

50. Moses Ginsburger: *Les Familles Lehmann et Cerf Berr*. Paris, France: Cerf in Versailles, 1910. Available at http://sammlungen.ub.uni-frankfurt.de/freimann/content/titleinfo/277414; accessed November 12, 2011.

51. Arthur Hertzberg: *The French Enlightenment and the Jews*. New York City, New York: Columbia University Press, 1968, p. 167.

52. Moses Ginsburger: *Cerf-Berr et son Époque*. Société d'Histoire des Juifs d'Alsace-Lorraine. Guebwiller, Alsace, France: J. Dreyfus, 1908, pp. 28–31. Available at http://gallica.bnf.fr/ark:/12148/bpt6k5427849p/f8.image; accessed November 3, 2011.

53. Robert. H. Harris: *Necker and the Revolution of 1789*. Lanham, Maryland: University Press of America, 1986, p. 46.

54. Max Warschawski: "Hirtz de Médelsheim." Available at http://judaisme.sdv.fr/perso/Cerf Berr/index.htm; accessed November 13, 2011. The map of the synagogue in 1784 is in Moses Ginsburger: *Histoire de la communauté israélite de Bischheim au Saum*. Strasbourg, Alsace, France: Etoile Alsace impression, 1997.

55. Moses Ginsburger: *Cerf-Berr et son Époque*. Société d'Histoire des Juifs d'Alsace-Lorraine. Guebwiller, Alsace, France: J. Dreyfus, 1908, pp. 17–18. Available at http://gallica.bnf.fr/ark:/12148/bpt6k5427849p/f8.image; accessed November 3, 2011.

56. Steven M. Lowenstein: *The Berlin Jewish Community: Enlightenment, Family, and Crisis, 1770–1830*. New York City, New York: Oxford University Press, 1994, p. 234, Note #50.

57. Arthur Hertzberg: *The French Enlightenment and the Jews*. New York City, New York: Columbia University Press, 1968, p. 319.

58. For a good discussion of Calonne's term as Controller-general in France, see Robert. H. Harris: *Necker and the Revolution of 1789*. Lanham, Maryland: University Press of America, 1986, chapter 2, pp. 31–73.

CHAPTER FIVE:

Cerf Berr: Grand Syndic of the French Ashkenazim, 1784–1788

———◆———

On July 10, 1784, King Louis XVI issued his long-awaited General Regulation for the Ashkenazim in Alsace. Armand Thomas Hue of Miromesnil, Keeper of the Seals, and other ministers had been working on the General Regulation for the Jews in Alsace since the case of the counterfeit receipt debacle in Alsace in the late 1770s.[1] King Louis XVI declared that he wanted to be a fair and just ruler. Thus, he had ordered his ministers to develop a Jewish General Regulation that both protected his Catholic subjects and improved the deplorable situation of the Alsatian Jewry.[2]

Below is the English translation of the memorandum that accompanied King Louis XVI's Alsatian Jewish General Regulation of July 10, 1784. The French original is available elsewhere.[3]

* * * * * * * *

Memorandum Accompanying King Louis XVI's
Alsatian Jewish General Regulation of July 19, 1784

Sire,

Most Jews settled in Alsace subsist only by usury and are therefore very harmful. They have successively become the creditors of a very large number of men in the class of the people [the peasants]. Certain men [the fraud perpetrators] gave the insidious advice to debtors [the peasants] to oppose the usurers [allegedly, the Jews] by producing false receipts. If the government administration had not stepped in to deal with these criminals, the debtors [the peasants] would have become insolvent. [Recall that the commissioners of the First Chamber of the Sovereign Council of Alsace had eased the burden of the debtors by allowing them up to fifteen years to repay their Jewish creditors]. It is also clear that the manner in which Jews exist in Alsace [allegedly by usury] has caused much inconvenience and use of time, and it must stop. To do so, Your Majesty has supported the leaders of the administration of the province of Alsace [the Secretary of War] to seek and identify the real causes of evil and to fix them.[4] That is what they have done!

Above all, the first goal is to safeguard the interests of the [Catholic] Christian subjects of the King [Protestant Christians were not considered subjects of the King]. At the same time that the King is protecting the interests of his Christian subjects, he eagerly proposes to pity the fate of the Jews, and to improve their sad and unbearable social situation. Here is how:

Jews are excluded from public employment and almost all kinds of commerce and industry. They cannot own or rent land. In general, all honest means of subsistence are prohibited. On the other hand, Jews are the object of public scorn and are degraded by body tolls that treat them like animals. *They have been deprived of all hope of becoming dignified because they have done nothing to merit dignity* [emphasis in original]. Reduced to such a life they speculate with their money, which is the only resource that they have left. All lawful means of subsisting have been taken away from them, so they resort to expedients more or less illegitimate and odious.

Of course, one does not want to overemphasize the

unfortunate social situation of the Jews. This letter is impartial. If, on the one hand, it says that the Jews are a *terrible nuisance* [emphasis in original] to Christians, on the other, it deplores that *all the honest means of subsistence* have been denied the Jews [emphasis in original].

To achieve the dual purpose—the protection of the interest of Christians and improvement of the situation of the Jews— the wisdom of King Louis XVI precedes each of the twenty-five articles that form the body of the [General Regulation in the form of] letters patent of [July 10] 1784. We exhibit below the twenty-five articles of the letters patent...[to] safeguard the interest of the Christian people and [to improve] the moral and social development of the Jews. Protecting and improving, is not that the great task of governing?[3]

* * * * * * * *

Several examples in English from King Louis XVI's original Alsatian Jewish General Regulation (Preamble, Articles I–VII) of July 10, 1784 follow below. The original French version of the Alsatian Jewish General Regulation of July 10, 1784 is available elsewhere.[5]

* * * * * * * *

King Louis XVI's General Regulation
concerning the Jews in Alsace, July 10, 1784

Preamble

Louis [XVI], by the grace of God, King of France and of Navarre: To all who see these letters patent, hello. We have reviewed the rules established relative to the Jews of our Alsace Province and, after weighing the advantages and disadvantages, we have found it necessary to make some changes, by which we propose, as far as we thought possible, to conciliate their interests with those of our [Catholic] subjects. To these causes and others that move us, compelled by the advice of our lawyer, our knowledge, and our royal authority, we want to please you with the following rules and orders of these letters patent, which we have signed with our own hand:

Article I

Jews have spread throughout Alsace Province, who, at the time of the publication of the present articles, have no fixed or known address, do not pay the protection tax to the King, do not pay the reception or living tax to the lords or to the cities, and do not contribute to the cost of communities. [These Jews] will be required in three months, counting from the day of this publication, to leave Alsace Province even if they offer to pay for such taxes and such contributions. Jews, who, after the expiration of the terms fixed by this article, are found in Alsace Province, will be prosecuted and punished as vagabonds and vagrants according to strict laws.

Article II

All lords, cities, and communities enjoying the right of lordship are explicitly prohibited in the future from admitting any foreign Jew until [this admission] has been otherwise ordered by us.

Article III

Foreign Jews who travel to Alsace for reasons of commerce or other affairs will be required to bring certificates or passports to be signed by the magistrate of the places where [the Jews] ordinarily stay. These certificates will contain their names, positions, and professions and will designate the places where they plan to stay and the time during which they propose to stay. The foreign Jews will present these certificates or passports to the magistrate of the first city in Alsace through which they pass. By virtue of these passports and visas, foreign Jews will be able to stay for three months in the places of Alsace that they have specified. They can extend their stay for six weeks, if the circumstances warrant and the magistrate gives permission. If a foreign Jew does not find a magistrate available, a judge may give the permission.

Article IV

All foreign Jews who do not meet the requirements of the preceding article will be arrested and punished as vagrants and vagabonds according to strict laws.

Article V

All rabbis and other Jews in the future are prohibited from facilitating stopping points, lodging, or feeding of [foreign] Jews. Likewise, we forbid all resident Jews in Alsace to provide resting benefits for any foreign Jews. All innkeepers, hotelkeepers, and other providers of shelter, if they have not reviewed the passports, which foreign Jews must have in their possession, prior to housing and receiving them, will be levied a fine of three hundred pounds for each infraction.

Article VI

We explicitly forbid in the future all Jews and Jewesses who are currently residents of Alsace to marry without our express permission, even outside the states of our dominion, on pain of immediate expulsion from Alsace.

Article VII

We accordingly forbid the rabbis to proceed with the celebration of marriage unless they have our permission, under penalty against those rabbis of a fine of three thousand pounds and expulsion for repeat offenders.[5]

* * * * * * * * *

There were seventeen additional articles in the Alsatian Jewish General Regulation of July 10, 1784. Zosa Szajkowski summarized what he believed were the most important points in the articles:

Jews without legally assigned residences were to leave Alsace within three months' time; foreign Jews were forbidden to reside in Alsace; Jews were allowed to own factories and cultivate the land, but not to employ Christian farm laborers; Jews were not allowed to purchase houses, except for their own use; the rights of the rabbis in charge of the juridical administration of the Jewish communities were restricted; Jews were required to request permission to marry; contracts between Jews and Christians had to be legalized in the presence of two officials, except contracts with bankers; interest on loans was to be paid by Christian debtors to Jewish creditors in cash, never in products; [and] the "More judaico" was introduced in law-courts.[6]

[The More judaico was an oath dating to the Middle Ages that Jews took by order of Christian courts in lawsuits with non-Jews. "Both the text of the oath and the symbolic ritual involved in taking it were intended to give it the explicit character of a self-imposed curse, entailing detailed punishment if it were falsely taken. The ceremony and symbolism were intended to strengthen and make vivid the curse as well as to stress the distrust of the Jew and the wish to humiliate him that were at the root of this special oath ritual."[7]]

Jews were still restricted to reside in small cities and villages, far from the large commercial centers; the order making it mandatory for a Jew to request permission to marry was new and inhuman...Prior to July 1784, jurisprudence on Jews of the Alsatian Sovereign Council allowed them to purchase real estate property, provided that the property be sold in the course of one year and that Christian buyers be favored. Article X of the new letters forbade Jewish real estate transactions. According to the memorandum, this was harmful not only to the Jews, but to the Christians as well, since the new letters [patent] practically abolished free competition in the real-estate field and thus enabled Christian traders to force high prices upon prospective buyers. In addition, Article XIV prohibiting simple I. O. U.'s would be costly to Christian debtors of small sums because of the high rates charged by the notaries.[6]

Arthur Hertzberg evaluated the Alsatian Jewish General Regulation of July 10, 1784 as follows:

This second letters patent [the first was abolition of the Jewish body tax in January 1784] was the most comprehensive decree about Jews ever issued by the French Crown. It was a retrograde act. The few increased opportunities that were now afforded were available only to the rich [e.g., Cerf Berr]; but the essence of the Jewish problem in Alsace was the poor masses, and their lot was now being made harder. Every liberalization in the decree was counter-balanced by a new and severe restriction. In the area of personal status, the question had often been litigated throughout the eighteenth century whether a nobleman or the authorities of a town could exclude a Jew at will, after having once admitted him. The new law agreed with the Jewish contention that such reception was irrevocable, except for a cause that could be proved in a court of law. On the other hand, all the Jews residing in Alsace were now forbidden to contract any marriage whatsoever without express royal permission, and any rabbi who performed such a marriage was subject to the most severe penalties. In effect, no new Jewish family could henceforth be started in Alsace until an older one ceased to exist.[8]

Arthur Hertzberg continued:

The traditional major Jewish pursuits in Alsace, the trade in cattle and grain and in money lending, were surrounded by new restrictions. Contracts for all such transactions would henceforth have to be executed either before a notary or before two Préposés of the Jewish community. Receipts and contracts must be signed in French or German, if possible. On the other hand, the few Jews in Alsace who had that kind of capital were now permitted to engage in banking and in every kind of large-scale business or commerce, subject to the restrictions, which usually governed such pursuits. They were also authorized to open factories, especially in textiles, as well as to establish works in iron, glass, and pottery on an equal basis with the king's Christian subjects [this provision certainly helped Cerf Berr and his wealthy co-religionist industrialists]…

The previously existing [General Préposés] were renamed Syndics, but their powers were kept intact. As previously, they were elected by the Jews themselves. It was their duty to assess their individual share of the royal impositions upon each of the Jews of the province and to collect the sums involved. The Préposés who were elected to lead each individual Jewish community were to supervise the collection of royal and local taxes in each town and were to exercise supervision over the internal affairs of the Jewish community. There was in these letters patent, however, more than a hint of a desire to lessen the cohesiveness of the Jewish community…Jews were forbidden to go to court except as individuals, unless they could clearly demonstrate that the case at issue involved them collectively.[8]

Historian Robert Badinter interpreted the Alsatian Jewish General Regulation of July 10, 1784 as follows:

According to the terms of the royal declaration, these letters patent were intended to reconcile "the interest of the Jews of our province of Alsace with those of our subjects." In fact, they were issued with one concern in mind: to end growing tensions in Alsace over usury practiced by Jews. The special commission had envisaged two principal means to accomplish this: providing the Jews with other ways to earn livelihoods, and limiting their number in the province. Therefore, the royal order lifted economic restrictions [that] weighed heavily upon the Jews. Henceforth they were able to lease land, vineyards and forests—but on the condition that they worked these themselves, without the aid of agricultural laborers, and without the ability to become owners. They were also permitted to establish factories, work mines, engage in wholesale and retail trade, and become bankers. These measures demonstrate the constant concern of the Intendants to harness competition provided by the Jews' entry into the marketplace as a way to stimulate economic activity in the provinces. At the same time, however, the authorities took rigorous steps against usury: all loans had to be negotiated in the presence of two witnesses, and documents regarding the terms of these loans could not be written in Hebrew. In order to prevent growth of the Jewish population in the province, Jews without a fixed domicile or who had not paid "protection" fees had to leave the kingdom. Finally, Jews had to obtain royal authorization to marry, based on approval provided by the Intendant.[9]

Robert Badinter noted the abject failure of the Alsatian Jewish General Regulation of July 10, 1784 to satisfy either the Ashkenazim of Alsace or their Christian adversaries. He wrote:

> The [Alsatian Jewish General Regulation] satisfied neither the Jews nor their enemies. The Jewish communities sent a memorandum to King Louis XVI's Council of State protesting the cruel restrictions and unjust conditions imposed on them that were not imposed on other Jewish communities in the [Kingdom], notably those of Metz, Nancy, and, especially, Bordeaux. Cerf Berr continued in vain to intervene and reiterate his protests. [Minister of Justice, Armand Thomas Hue of Miromesnil] remained indifferent. Nor did the Jews' enemies yield. In August 1786, a royal commissioner in Strasbourg wrote, "The city's magistracy views, as does all of the middle class, the legal entry of Jews as a plague destroying commerce, industry, and good order."[9]

The King's Alsatian Jewish General Regulation of July 10, 1784 ordered a royal census of the Ashkenazim in Alsace in preparation for expulsion of all those Jews who could not prove their legal right to live there. This census identified approximately four thousand Jewish families (about twenty thousand individuals) in Alsace.[10] This was "almost beyond doubt…an understatement," averred Arthur Hertzberg. He continued:

> The size of the Jewish population in Alsace in the years immediately before the [French] Revolution was more than four thousand families, meaning that the number of Jewish individuals in Alsace approached twenty-five thousand individuals. Quite apart from those not recorded, who were protected by the Alsatian Jews against the threat of expulsion, there must be added an unknown but noticeable number of the most miserable of all, Jews with no domicile whatsoever,

who wandered in the province with their families in search of alms or some temporary means of support.[8]

The French Crown noted the upward trend in the size of the Jewish population living in Alsace between 1732 and 1784:

1732: About seventeen hundred Jewish families (eighty-three hundred individuals)

1744: About twenty-one hundred Jewish families (more than ten thousand individuals)

1754: About twenty-five hundred Jewish families (about thirteen thousand individuals)

1780–1781: About thirty-six hundred Jewish families (more than eighteen thousand individuals)

1784: Almost four thousand Jewish families (about twenty thousand individuals)[10]

However, the *total* population of Alsace was also exploding during roughly this same time span, i.e., from two hundred and fifty-seven thousand individuals in 1697 to six hundred and twenty-four thousand individuals in 1784.[10] From 1732 to 1784, the Jewish *percentage* of the total population of Alsace remained steady at slightly more than three percent. In other words, the Jewish population was growing at about the same rate as the total population of Alsace. Nevertheless, a perception existed among Catholic Christians that too many Jews lived in Alsace. Hence, King Louis XVI issued his Alsatian Jewish General Regulation of July 10, 1784.

The royal census of 1784 showed that the Village of Bischheim, with its four hundred and seventy-three Ashkenazim, was the largest Jewish community in Alsace.[10] In 1774, the Jewish population in Bischheim had been only two hundred and ten individuals. In other words, in one decade, the Jewish population of Bischheim more than doubled in size.[11] However, in 1784, the Jews of Bischheim comprised about two and a half percent of the total Jewish population of Alsace, demonstrating the degree to which the Ashkenazim were scattered among one hundred and eighty-two communities in Alsace Province.

Cerf Berr and his fellow Ashkenazi Syndics engaged the services of Attorney Mirbeck, who also provided legal services to King Louis XVI's Council of State, to petition against the Alsatian Jewish General Regulation of July 10, 1784 as a whole. For example, in 1784, Monsieur Mirbeck declared, "Alsace is two centuries behind the other provinces of the French Kingdom. By persecuting the Jews, the people believe they are fulfilling the decrees of heaven."[12]

Despite King Louis XVI's Alsatian Jewish General Regulation of July 10, 1784, which banished transient Jews from Alsace, outsiders continued to live there.[13] Some transient Jews were undoubtedly relatives or employees of Ashkenazim who were permanent residents of Alsace.[13]

Death of the Chevalier of la Touche, 1784

In 1784, the enigmatic Chevalier of la Touche died. Recall that in January 1771, the Chevalier of la Touche purchased the Hotel Ribeaupierre in Strasbourg from Christian IV, Duke of Deux Ponts, and then sold it the same day to Cerf Berr of Médelsheim in Colmar, Upper Alsace. The Strasbourg authorities reviewed the knight's estate in 1784, learned that Cerf Berr *owned* Hotel Ribeaupierre, and promptly declared that his purchase and ownership of the hotel was invalid. They asserted that Cerf Berr was not a Christian and, as a Jew, lacked the right of citizenship or special permission to own *any* property in the City of Strasbourg.[14]

Cerf Berr retorted that his 1775 letters patent of naturalization from King Louis XVI permitted him to own property anywhere in France. However, Cerf Berr had purchased the Hotel Ribeaupierre in 1771, which was before he had received his naturalization papers from King Louis XVI. The Strasbourg authorities were beside themselves. They again declared Cerf Berr's letters patent of naturalization as invalid in the City of Strasbourg. Cerf Berr and the Strasbourg authorities now had a third issue to divide them. Recall that lawyers for each side in Versailles had been wrangling since 1775 over the Strasbourg authorities' refusal to acknowledge Cerf Berr's right as a naturalized citizen to live legally in Strasbourg. Now they quarreled over the right for Cerf Berr to own property in Strasbourg.

What did each side of the Cerf Berr/Strasbourg conflict allege? Cerf Berr's side accused Strasbourg authorities of 1) rebelling against the sovereignty of King Louis XVI, 2) selfishness, and 3) inhumanity.[15] In the first allegation, the Strasbourg authorities failed to honor King Louis XVI's letters patent of naturalization to an individual (Cerf Berr); was this not rebellion against the French King's sovereignty? Second, Strasbourg was the safest and most convenient place for Cerf Berr to run his army supply business for the royal troops in Alsace province. Why did the Strasbourg authorities insist on following their quaint custom of expelling Jews from the City of Strasbourg? This custom was selfish, narrow, and ceded the general interest of the French Kingdom to the specific interests of the narrow-minded authorities of a provincial city.

Third, Cerf Berr's side evoked the inhumanity of Strasbourg Christians dating back to 1349 when they burned Jews at the stake for an alleged crime (poisoning the city's wells), which was not susceptible to proof. Burning Jews at the stake was the height of absurdity, because the punishment was more criminal than the alleged crime! One could not deny that such an episode of fanaticism actually happened, because to do so would be to "slander fanaticism," which is the father of so many horrors attributable to execrable inhumanity. Furthermore, extant archival materials and the Strasbourg street named Brûlée (burned), so named for several centuries, proved that the story of burning the Jews at the stake was true. The point was, said Cerf Berr's side, Strasbourg authorities in 1349 never proved the authenticity of the charge of Jews' poisoning the wells, yet they forbade Jews from living in Strasbourg for the next four centuries! Strasbourg should unload the memory of this terrible execution of innocent Jews. Why, Cerf Berr's side asked the Strasbourg side, do you retaliate against Jews and continue this absurd, outrageous, and inhumane custom of excluding Jews from living in Strasbourg?

Cerf Berr personally turned to King Louis XVI to plead that his co-religionists were more worthy of receiving letters patent of naturalization than he was. Cerf Berr urged King Louis XVI not to naturalize Jews one at a time, because King Louis XVI had the power to use his strong hand to break all the bonds at once that held the Ashkenazim in their pitiful state of misfortune.[15]

The Strasbourg side of the conflict countered the first allegation made by Cerf Berr's side—Strasbourg's alleged disregard of the sovereignty of King Louis XVI —by saying that the Strasbourg authorities had too much respect for the King's wishes to oppose a grace (the King's letters patent of naturalization) that he had granted to Cerf Berr. In addition, the Strasbourg side did not dispute Cerf Berr's letters patent of naturalization or his permission to acquire real estate in the Kingdom of France. The Strasbourg side only wished to point out that Strasbourg itself had a law from time immemorial that required removal from the city all Jews who tried to settle there.[16] In other words, the Strasbourg side declared, Cerf Berr was free to buy real estate anywhere in the French Kingdom, but not in the City of Strasbourg.

The Strasbourg side countered Cerf Berr's second charge—that Strasbourg authorities were selfish—by reversing the charge. Cerf Berr was asking the French Crown to abrogate its own laws that forbade settlement of Jews since 1324 when French King Charles IV banished all Jews from France and French King Charles VI in 1394 validated the expulsion. Who then was selfish? The Strasbourg side hoped that the smooth politics of Cerf Berr would not persuade King Louis XVI to revoke the law barring Jews from settlement in France. Furthermore, the Strasbourg side predicted that Jews would pour into France if King Louis XVI revoked the exceptionally wise medieval Jewish expulsion law first issued by his predecessor King Charles IV. The Strasbourg side admonished King Louis XVI, "Let one Jew in and other Jews who provide services to the troops will ask for the same rights!" The Strasbourg side asked, "Is the French nation so lacking in smart men who can provide supplies to the military as Jews do without pay in advance?" Cerf Berr made an immense fortune providing the King's armies, the Strasbourg side continued. Must he incur a further reward? The authorities did not need to give in to Cerf Berr's insistence to remain in Strasbourg. If King Louis XVI permitted Cerf Berr to do so, the sovereign undermined the Constitution of Strasbourg and forgot the commitments he made to conserve the ancient rights of Strasbourg.[16]

The Strasbourg side responded to the third charge—inhumanity toward Jews—by telling the Jews to stop moaning about their misfortunes. When the Jewish Nation stopped violating the rights of humanity with its foul practice of usury, which ruined people who were imprudent enough to deal with the Jews, then the Jews could invoke humanity owed to all people. Until then, the Jews, most particularly Cerf Berr, should be silent. In addition, observed the Strasbourg side, few trials of usury occurred in Strasbourg. Was this not proof that Jews should not live in Strasbourg? Punishment of Jewish usury did not restore lost fortunes. Was it not wiser and more humane to exclude Jews before they committed their usurious crimes? The Sovereign Council of Alsace needed to rush to the aid of the people of Alsace after the Jews had incurred ten million livres of indebtedness from them (referring to the case of the counterfeit receipts). The Jewish usurers had reduced these poor peasants to such despair, that counterfeiters had hoodwinked them into obtaining false receipts! The disorder was so great that the Sovereign Council of Alsace had been obliged to grant extensions for repayment by debtors and to conduct a number of criminal trials against counterfeiters. The Strasbourg side exclaimed, "You want us to admit Jews to live in Strasbourg? Oh! No!"[16]

King Louis XVI and his ministers did not know what to do. The King's letters patent of naturalization clearly gave Cerf Berr the right to purchase land and live anywhere in the Kingdom of France, including in the City of Strasbourg. However, Strasbourg authorities refused to acknowledge Cerf Berr's right to live or to own land in the city because of its ancient municipal rights, based on its own Strasbourg Constitution. Eventually, King Louis XVI wrote down his views on the conflict: he hoped that a public law would leave no further pretext for the City of Strasbourg or any other city to treat adversely so essentially unhappy a nation as the Ashkenazim of Alsace. In addition, he hoped that individual letters patent of naturalization issued to individual Ashkenazim would be unnecessary because all Jews in France would one day become his loyal subjects.[17]

List of Cerf Berr's Family Members, 1784

On June 1, 1784, Cerf Berr married Hanna (Hana, Hannah, Anna, Hannle) Brühl (Brüll, Brill) (1748–1810). Hanna Brühl previously was married to Jacob Hirsch Regensburger, who was born in Fürth, Bavaria and died there in 1780.[18] Little else is known about Jacob Hirsch Regensburger. Hanna Brüll had three children with Jacob Hirsch Regensburger: a son named Jacob Sussmann (1770–1830), a daughter named Zardlé (born 1774), and another son named Wolff (1780–1855). All three children were born in Fürth, Bavaria.[18] In 1784, after her marriage to Cerf Berr, Hanna Brühl and her ten-year-old daughter Zardlé moved to Strasbourg.

Zardlé Regensburger changed her name to Sophie Ratisbonne (Ratisbon is the French name for Regensburg; Ratisbonne is the French feminine form of Ratisbon). Hanna Brühl's two sons moved to Strasbourg to live with Cerf Berr *after* completion of the royal census of Ashkenazim in Alsace as Cerf Berr did not list the two boys as members of his household in the 1784 royal census (see below). Around 1784, Hanna Brühl's fourteen-year-old son Jacob Sussmann Regensburger changed his name to Auguste Ratisbonne, and her four-year-old son Wolff Regensburger changed his name to Louis Ratisbonne.

In November 1784, Cerf Berr produced a list of his family members who lived in Strasbourg, probably as part of the Ashkenazi census of

1784 ordered by King Louis XVI.[18] The list is organized according to the four houses/households of Cerf Berr's extended family then living in Strasbourg, i.e., his own house and the houses of Max Berr, Seligmann Alexandre, and Wolff Lévy. The list provides a rare glimpse into the life of a wealthy eighteenth-century Ashkenazi extended family in Alsace.

* * * * * * * *

List of Cerf Berr's Family Members living in Strasbourg in 1784

I.   House of Cerf Berr [in Hotel Ribeaupierre]

- Cerf Berr, fifty-eight-years-old, born in Wittelsheim [*sic*], married for the second time for the past six months;
- Löb Levi, son-in-law, thirty-years-old, born in Hanover (Germany);
- Théodore Berr, son, eighteen-years-old, born in Strasbourg [*sic*];
- Hana, second wife of Cerf Berr, thirty-eight-years-old, born in Fürth;
- Fachon Berr, [daughter of Cerf Berr], spouse of Löb Levi, twenty-years-old, born in Strasbourg;
- Eve Berr, [daughter of Cerf Berr] fifteen-years-old, born in Strasbourg;
- Zaradlé, [stepdaughter of Cerf Berr], daughter of Hana, ten-years-old, born in Fürth;
- Sara, daughter of Meyer Berr [Cerf Berr's brother], niece of Cerf Berr, twelve-years-old, born in Bischheim;
- Reitz Seligmann Berr, niece of Cerf Berr, fifteen-years-old, born in Rosheim [daughter of the late Seligmann Berr, Cerf Berr's brother];

- Rabbi Joseph, forty-years-old, born in Trembach [Trimbach, Lower Alsace], domiciled in Lingolsheim [Lower Alsace];
- Simon Halle, secretary of the Nation Juive, seventy-years-old, born in Obernheim, his home;
- Heyman Wolf, secretary, twenty-three-years-old, born in Grieshaber [Germany], lodged in the city in the house of Pfeffinger;
- Moyse Lewi, thirty-years-old, born in Fürth;
- Gottlieb Isaac, controller, forty-eight-years-old, born in Küttolsheim [Lower Alsace];
- Joseph Lewi, clerk, thirty-years-old, born in Grumstatt, lodges in the city at Bruxberger's place;
- Simon Harbourger, clerk, twenty-eight-years-old, born in Grieshaber [Germany], lives in the city with Mr. Lichtenberger, retired official;
- Moyse Samuel, g. d. bur. [sic], twenty-four-years-old, born in Rosheim;
- Isaac, copyist, seventeen-years-old, born in Hagenthal;
- Lowel Weil, porter, fifty-six-years-old, born in Bischheim;
- Mendle, coachman, twenty-eight-years-old, born in Hattstatt;
- Joseph Gugenheim, twenty-years-old, born in Obernheim [no occupation listed];
- Sara Brisack, governess, sixty-years-old, born in Tränheim [Lower Alsace];
- Reyer, children's nurse, forty-years-old, born in Soultz;
- Männel, servant, forty-five-years-old, born in Walck; and
- Reysla, cook, fifty-years-old, born in Hattstatt.

II.   Family [House of Max Berr in Hotel Ribeaupierre]:

- Marx [Max] Berr, son of Cerf Berr, twenty-seven-years-old, born in Bischheim and married for two years;
- Samson, son of Max Berr, seven-years-old, born in Strasbourg;
- Beer [Berr], son of Max Berr, four-years-old, born in Strasbourg;
- Ester Bouf (!) [*sic*], wife of Max, twenty-seven-years-old, born in La Haye;
- Fleurette [daughter of Max Berr], three-years-old, born in Strasbourg;
- Selche, daughter of Marx [Marchand] Berr [Cerf Berr's brother], niece of Cerf Berr, fourteen-years-old, born in Sarguemines [Lorraine], boarder;
- Moyses, schoolmaster, twenty-six-years-old, born in Fürth;
- Zacharias, domestic, sixteen-years-old, born in Frauenberg;
- Guhatz, children's nurse, sixty-years-old, born in Schweinheim;
- Jugla, chambermaid, seventeen-years-old, born in Rosenheim;
- Jeras, servant, seventeen-years-old, born in Schweinheim; and
- Sara, cook, forty-four-years-old, born in Strasbourg.

III.   House of Seligmann Alexandre:

- Samuel Seligmann Alexandre, son-in-law of Cerf Berr, born in Bouxwiller, thirty-six-years-old, married ten years;
- Barac [Baruch] Berr, brother-in-law of Seligmann Alexandre and son of Cerf Berr, twenty-four-years-old, born in Bischheim, married for six months;

- Marx Alexandre, son of Seligmann Alexandre, fifteen-years-old, born in Bischheim;

- Beer Alexandre, son of Seligmann Alexandre, six-years-old, born in Strasbourg;

- Rebecca, wife of Seligmann Alexandre [oldest daughter of Cerf Berr], thirty-two-years-old, born in Bischheim;

- Melle, wife of Barac [Baruch] Berr, nineteen-years-old, born in Bischheim;

- Judela, daughter of Seligmann Alexandre, twelve-years-old, born in Strasbourg;

- Gelché, daughter of Seligmann Alexandre ten-years-old, born in Strasbourg;

- Ettellé, daughter of Seligmann Alexandre, eight-years-old, born in Strasbourg;

- Raphael Gugenheim, tutor, twenty-eight-years-old, born in Obernheim;

- Benjamin Cadet, secretary, twenty-two-years-old, born in Hügenbourg;

- Meyer Weil, clerk, sixteen-years-old, born in Bischheim;

- Löb, domestic, nineteen-years-old, born in Saarbourg;

- Keyla, chambermaid, fifteen-years-old, born in Niederenheim;

- Leya, children's nurse, forty-years-old, born in Niederenheim;

- Feyla, cook, twenty-four-years-old, born in Herlisheim; and

- Guttelé, servant, seventeen-years-old, born in Bischheim.

IV. House of Wolff Lévy:

- Wolff Lévy, son-in-law of Cerf Berr, thirty-years-old, born in Bonne, married twelve years;

- Marx Wolff, eight-years-old, son of Wolff Lévy, born in Strasbourg;

- Daniel, seven-years-old, son of Wolff Lévy, born in Strasbourg;

- Emanuel, six-years-old, son of Wolff Lévy, born in Strasbourg;

- Beer, four-years-old, son of Wolff Lévy, born in Strasbourg;

- Minette, wife of Wolff Lévy [second oldest daughter of Cerf Berr], twenty-seven-years-old, born in Bischheim;

- Brentelé, five-years-old, daughter of Wolff Lévy, born in Strasbourg;

- Rella, two-years-old, daughter of Wolff Lévy, born in Strasbourg;

- Rebecca, daughter of Mayer Berr [Cerf Berr's brother], niece of Cerf Berr, sixteen-years-old, born in Bischheim;

- Emanuel, tutor, twenty-four-years-old, born in Fürth;

- Nathan, domestic, twenty-two-years-old, born in Obernheim;

- Hanna, children's nurse, thirty-six-years-old, born in Mutzig;

- Mentele, children's nurse, twenty-four-years-old, born in Balbronn;

- Rechela, cook, twenty-four-years-old, born in Westhoffen; and

- Edel, servant, twenty-four-years-old, born in Bergheim.[18]

* * * * * * * *

In 1785/1786, Cerf Berr purchased the seigneury of Tomblaine near Nancy from the Count of Salles, who himself had purchased the property from the Beauvau Royal Family. Tomblaine is about seventy miles due west of Strasbourg. The estate was located on the east side of the Meurthe River, opposite the City of Nancy on the west side of the river. In 1785, Tomblaine consisted of twenty households. Cerf Berr built a structure (castle?) on his land and presided over his seigneury as Lord of Tomblaine.[19] The forest on the estate became known as the "Forest of the Jew."[20] In 1788, Cerf Berr established at least one factory in Tomblaine to manufacture wool, linen, cotton, and serge fabrics.[21] His two sons, Théodore and Baruch, ran the factory and employed many Ashkenazi workers.[22] Tomblaine remained in the Cerf Berr family until October 5, 1810, when Cerf Berr's sons, Lippman, Baruch, and Théodore, sold it.

On April 22, 1785, Cerf Berr purchased land in Paris on which he established a cemetery for Ashkenazim who died in Paris. The land was in Petit Vanves on the Route de Châtillon in Montrouge, a suburb in southwestern Paris. Why did he do this? Recall that in 1779, Seligmann Berr, Cerf Berr's youngest brother, had died unexpectedly in Paris. At that time, Liefman Calmer, the military purveyor and banker (previously mentioned) was working to establish a cemetery for burial of both Sephardim and Ashkenazim who died in Paris. This new joint cemetery was to replace an "undignified and semi-clandestine burial place that had been used for decades," noted Arthur Hertzberg.[21] However, the initiative failed. On March 7, 1780, the Sephardi Jews of Bordeaux sought and received a permit from the Paris authorities to establish their own cemetery in the Paris suburb of La Villette.

In 1781, the year after the Sephardim first established their cemetery in La Villette, they were "vexed" to find at least one Ashkenazi corpse buried in their Sephardim-only cemetery. Recall that Cerf Berr buried his brother, Seligmann Berr, in the La Villette cemetery.[21] On February 8, 1782, Cerf Berr approached the Sephardi leaders of Bordeaux to request permission to bury Ashkenazi decedents in the Sephardim-owned cemetery. On February 22, 1782, the Sephardi leaders refused Cerf Berr's request. Thus, on April 22, 1785, Cerf Berr personally purchased land for burial of Ashkenazim who died in Paris. He established the Ashkenazi cemetery on land in Petit Vanves on the Route of Châtillon in Montrouge on the southwestern outskirts of Paris, as noted above.[21]

In 1785, pro-Jewish Honoré Mirabeau traveled to Berlin to obtain a better understanding of the Jewish Enlightenment. Recall that in 1782, Honoré Mirabeau had tried to distribute in Paris the first French edition of Christian William Dohm's book, which contained the treatise, "Concerning the Amelioration of the Civil Status of the Jews," only to discover that someone had burned all the copies. Between 1785 and 1787, Honoré Mirabeau researched and wrote his own book about the Ashkenazim, which he titled *Sur Moses Mendelssohn, sur la Réforme Politique des Juifs* (*On Moses Mendelssohn, on Political Reform of the Jews*). Honoré Mirabeau published his book in London, not Paris, "far from the reach of his homeland's censors."[23]

In his book, Honoré Mirabeau argued that circumstances generated Jewish faults, not inherent defects in the Jewish character. He disliked the Talmudic teachings that guided the behaviors of pious Ashkenazi Jews, including Cerf Berr, but considered Judaism a moral faith and defended it against attacks. He concurred with Christian William Dohm's assertion that denial of basic human rights corrupted the Jews. Honoré Mirabeau "proposed that France's Jews be granted not only civil rights, but that they be allowed to maintain their religious customs and retain their [R]abbinical [C]ourts."[23] Cerf Berr concurred with Honoré Mirabeau's proposal to allow Ashkenazim to retain their religious customs and courts.

In August 1785, the local newspaper of the City of Metz, *Affiches des Trois-Évêchés et Lorraine*, published the questions for a biannual essay contest on science and society held by the Metz Royal Society of Sciences and Arts. Pierre-Louis Roederer, the attorney for the Metz Royal Society of Sciences and Arts, oversaw the essay contest. In 1785, the science question was, "Is there a way to make a better wine press?" The social question was, "Are there means to render the Jews happier and more useful in France?" ("Est-il des moyens de rendre les Juifs plus utiles et plus heureux en France?") Alyssa Goldstein Sepinwall described why this essay contest was a seminal event in French-Jewish history:

Historians have often told the story of the Metz contest in the following way: in the wake of a debate in the German states about the status of the Jews, and following the death of the esteemed Metz Rabbi Lion Asser [died 1785], Pierre-Louis Roederer and the members of the Royal Academy of Metz decided to import this discussion into France. Using a standard device of eighteenth-century academies, they held an essay contest to ask how the treatment of the Jews might be altered in light of Enlightenment ideas. The contest is seen as a landmark in French-Jewish history, a seminal event calling attention to the problems faced by Jews on the eve of the French Revolution and thus putting their fate on the national agenda.[24]

Historian Michael Goldfarb explained why he believed the academy chose the topic of Jews for the 1785 essay contest:

The Jews in Alsace, Lorraine, and Metz were the source of national anxiety about aliens infecting the French body politic. They were also regarded as a sample group on which to test the new philosophical theories about humanity and society that were part of the age: If all men are created equal, an enlightened thinker might ask, does that mean the Jews, with their strange clothes [and] odd language [Hebrew, Yiddish]… are our brothers as well?[24]

Two contestants in the Metz essay contest were Polish Ashkenazim Zalkind Hourwitz (1738–1812)[25], who was living illegally in Paris, and Abbè Henri Grégoire, mentioned earlier, who said he yearned for social justice for the Ashkenazim.[26]

On January 4, 1786, fifty-seven-year-old Moses Mendelssohn died in Berlin. Countless people revered him during and after his life. He helped many Ashkenazim leave their self-imposed Jewish ghettos and ghetto lifestyles to enter the secular mainstream of society. He translated the Hebrew Bible into German with a Hebrew commentary called *Biur*, campaigned for the emancipation of Jews with colleagues (including Cerf Berr), instructed Jews to form bonds with secular governments, tried to improve the relationship between Jews and Christians, argued for tolerance and humanity, and became the symbol of the Jewish Enlightenment.

On May 6, 1786, the Sovereign Council of Alsace voiced its intent to expel within one month all transient Ashkenazim from Alsace. However, the Sovereign Council of Alsace failed to write an edict to this effect.[27] More time passed.

On August 10, 1786 in Versailles, Controller-general Calonne, now in his third year of office, discovered the French Crown's looming financial meltdown. Calonne presented a plan of reform to King Louis XVI, which included revamping the tax system to eliminate the exemptions of the privileged classes (clergy and nobility). The most productive source of tax revenue for the French Crown was the land tax from which, however, the Roman Catholic Church, the largest landowner in France, was exempt. In addition, most landed nobles managed to avoid paying any land tax. Controller-general Calonne reasoned:

If the land tax could be levied uniformly on all lands, without exception, the burden need not be increased for those who already paid the tax in full measure [i.e., the peasants and artisans]. Such a reform could hardly be opposed by those privileged classes without revealing their utter egotism and lack of patriotism or concern for the well-being of the king and country.[28]

Controller-general Calonne wanted to submit his financial reforms to an Assembly of Notables handpicked by King Louis XVI. Calonne hoped that King Louis XVI would convene the Assembly of Notables no later than December 1786, because the Kingdom of France was tottering on the verge of bankruptcy. Robert D. Harris explained why Controller-general Calonne preferred convening an Assembly of Notables rather than taking his reform plan directly to the Parliament of Paris, which was the normal procedure for registering new royal edicts:

Calonne hoped by [convening an Assembly of Notables] to get the support of public opinion for his project. He knew the sovereign courts [e.g., Parliament of Paris] would resist the project or at least the fiscal parts of it. If he could take away the basis of popular support for the parliamentary side, [its] opposition would not be dangerous enough to prevent the implementation of the plan. Once the Assembly of Notables had approved the plan, [King Louis XVI] would send it to the twelve [Sovereign Parliaments of France] to be registered.[29]

King Louis XVI asked Controller-general Calonne why he wanted to convene an Assembly of Notables, instead of the Estates-General, as suggested by another advisor, Guillaume-Chrétien of Lamoignon of Malesherbes (1721–1794, henceforth, Malesherbes).[30] In 1775, Jacques Turgot had persuaded Malesherbes to join the staff of King Louis XVI. Malesherbes condemned the extravagant spending of the monarchy, telling King Louis XVI in a letter that the only way to provide relief for the government's fiscal deficit was to call for economies in the royal household and in government, and *to convene the Estates-General as proof of good faith with the people* [emphasis added].[30]

The Estates-General was a legislative assembly comprised of the different classes, or estates, of subjects of the King of France. Each of the three estates—clergy, nobility, and the people—had its own assembly in the tri-assembly Estates-General. Only the King of France could call into session and dismiss the Estates-General. The Estates-General had last met in 1614.[31]

Controller-general Calonne explained to King Louis XVI that he (Calonne) had opted for an Assembly of Notables because constituents of the three classes in the bailiwick assemblies *elected* their deputies to represent them in the Estates-General, whereas King Louis XVI would *appoint* the delegates to an Assembly of Notables. In addition, the notables would not bring cahiers de doléances, or lists of grievances, to present to the government, which the format for the Estates-General required them to do. Rather, the notables would come to listen to the proposals of King Louis XVI's ministers, specifically, Controller-general Calonne. "It is the King himself who determines the objects upon which [the notables] are to deliberate, and they cannot discuss other matters," chirped Calonne. The Assembly of Notables would be an advisory assembly, and it would finish its work quickly, in a month at most, predicted Calonne.[29] King Louis XVI pondered the idea.

In October 1786, at Fontainebleau (one of the French Crown's country homes and hunting preserves, southeast of Paris), Louis Joseph of Bourbon, Prince of Condé (1736–1818), a junior member of the House of Bourbon and later the émigré military leader of an army against France during the French Revolution, hosted a party in honor of Controller-general Calonne. "Calonne appeared radiant, ceaselessly untying the string of the purse from which favors poured forth. He had just purchased nine horses from Siberia as a gift for Monsieur the Dauphin [the heir apparent to the throne], and this greatly pleased" both Queen Marie Antoinette and King Louis XVI, remarked Robert D. Harris. In mid-November 1786, an English diplomat, who was at Fontainebleau with the Royal Family during the festivities, reported to the British government the expenditures incurred in moving the Royal Family back to Versailles:

> Their Majesties, the Dauphin, and the rest of the Royal Family are removed from Fontainebleau to Versailles. The Dauphin set out on Monday, the Queen on Tuesday, and the King on Wednesday. The expense attending these journeys of the Court is incredible. Your Lordship may have a faint idea of it from the number of Post Horses that have been employed in these last three days. The Duke of Polignac told me that he had given orders for two thousand one hundred and fifteen horses for this service on roads leading from Fontainebleau to Paris, which, considering the distance to either of those places is not equal to forty English miles, is prodigious. Besides this,

an adequate proportion of horses are ordered for the removal of the heavy baggage belonging to the Royal Family. How Monsieur de Calonne contrives to furnish means to answer such vast demands cannot be conceived, but he still enjoys great credit at court.[32]

In November 1786, advocates for the Alsatian peasants who still owed money to their Ashkenazi creditors after the case of the counterfeit receipts lobbied King Louis XVI to decree the debts invalid. King Louis XVI offered the suggestion that the peasant debtors pay their Jewish creditors only one-fifth of owed debts, which meant that Alsatian Jews would be dispossessed of four-fifths of their loans.[33]

Cerf Berr Retires from his Businesses, 1786

On October 9, 1786 in Bischheim, the aging sixty-year-old Cerf Berr started to retire from his businesses by establishing a philanthropic foundation in his name. He convened David Sinzheim, Seligmann Alexandre, R. Meir of Mutzig, Wolff Lévy, and Max, Baruch, and Lippman Berr to oversee the Cerf Berr Foundation in Bischheim. David Sinzheim headed the foundation.

Cerf Berr was a very wealthy man and could afford to fund a foundation with three purposes, which he carefully delineated. The first purpose of the foundation was to fund a yeshiva in Bischheim for the study of the Talmud. Cerf Berr wanted as many young Ashkenazim in Alsace as possible to have the opportunity to study the Talmud. In the past, only the sons of wealthy families could afford to study with the master Talmudists located in Germany and Metz. In the second half of the eighteenth century, three yeshivas were already open in Alsace—two in Lower Alsace (one in Bouxwiller and one in Ettendorf) and one in Upper Alsace (in Sierentz). Thus, Cerf Berr's yeshiva was the fourth one established in Alsace. Cerf Berr's founding of a school whose goal was to propagate the Talmudist-inspired way of Ashkenazi life underscored his cherished feelings for his orthodox Ashkenazi faith. He appointed David Sinzheim head of the Bischheim Talmudic yeshiva.

Cerf Berr seeded his foundation with one hundred and seventy-five thousand livres. He said that the capital must remain intact, while David Sinzheim was to use the interest on the capital to fund the yeshiva and the other two elements of Cerf Berr's Foundation. Cerf Berr allocated seven thousand livres per year to maintain three Talmudists in three houses located next to Cerf Berr's house in Bischheim. Two of the houses already existed and Cerf Berr built a third one to house the yeshiva. All three structures were to house Talmudists. Cerf Berr added many more instructions pertaining to the Talmudists. For example, he required that one of his descendants or a relative of his first wife Jüdel or his second wife Hanna who sought a position as a Talmudist in the Bischheim yeshiva could receive preference only on condition that he met in his person the moral and intellectual qualities to perform his duties.[34]

The second purpose of Cerf Berr's foundation was to provide dowries for girls whose fathers were without means. Cerf Berr's own father earlier had designated money for this same purpose, suggesting that Cerf Berr's father was also a man of means. Cerf Berr used the sum passed down by his father and added his own contribution to make a combined account, said Moses Ginsburger. Cerf Berr established many rules for the "Hakhnassat Kalla" (marriage of a girl), as described elsewhere.[34] For example, preference for providing dowries went to relatives of Cerf Berr, e.g., to his nieces produced by the marriage between his late brother Seligmann Berr and his brother's wife Mariam Netter. Recall that Seligmann Berr died in 1779 in Paris, leaving nine children. The girl who ultimately received the dowry money first had to prove her good conduct with a certificate filled out by the rabbi or the trustee in her place of residence. Elle ou son père avait à faire ses déclarations devant les membres de l'administration, qui devaient en dresser procès-verbal. She or her father had to make her statements to members of the directors of the Cerf Berr Foundation, who were to draw up reports, said Cerf Berr.[34]

The third purpose of Cerf Berr's foundation was to provide Cedaka or charity to the poor. Preference went to Cerf Berr's grandparents, because Cerf Berr's father had designated money for them. Again, Cerf Berr was perpetuating his own father's philanthropy. Since Cerf Berr's grandparents and their relatives were already dead, Cerf Berr indicated that the charity was to go to poor relatives of Cerf Berr's first and second wives. If there were not enough poor relatives of Cerf Berr's first and second wives, the money was to go for the purchase of shirts, shoes, pants, jackets, and vests to distribute to the needy.[34]

On December 20, 1786, Cerf Berr relinquished his banking affairs to his sons and sons-in-law and published a leaflet in which he gave notice to the public of this fact.[35] He continued to manage his military supply business, probably because it served as the legal basis for his continuing to reside in Strasbourg. Recall that he was in the midst of an ongoing lawsuit with the Strasbourg authorities who wanted to expel him and his family from the city.

In 1786, seventeen-year-old Eve Berr, Cerf Berr's youngest daughter and child, married David Speyer, a banker in Frankfurt on the Oder. Of Cerf Berr's nine children, Lippman, Jeanette, and Théodore Berr remained single.

King Louis XVI Convenes Assembly of Notables, 1787

On December 29, 1786, King Louis XVI announced to the public his intention to convene an Assembly of Notables. "His Majesty declares his intention," said the proclamation, "to convene an assembly composed of persons drawn from diverse conditions, who are the most qualified in their rank, in order to communicate to them his views concerning the welfare of his people, the order of his finances, and the reform of several abuses." The same day of the proclamation, King Louis XVI sent out letters under secret seal to one hundred and forty-four men. He instructed them to meet him at Versailles on January 29, 1788.[36]

On January 10, 1787, the Sovereign Council of Alsace confirmed

King Louis XVI's proposal to repudiate four-fifths of the amount of loans owed by Christian debtors to their Jewish creditors in Alsace. However, King Louis XVI and the Sovereign Council in Alsace reversed their decision after thinking through the possible consequences of such an act. Instead, the Sovereign Council of Alsace decreed that debtors could exercise a new right of term payments of their debts.[35]

In 1787, Cerf Berr sent a letter to the editors of the Jewish Enlightenment publication *Meassef* in which he objected to an earlier article published by the journal that rejected traditional views of François Hell as a Jew-hater.[41] The journal had become increasingly critical of traditional Talmudic Judaism. Its editors responded to Cerf Berr's outcry by publishing an article titled "Chikkur Hadin" to assuage orthodox Talmudic Jews who objected to the journal's growing radicalism.

On January 29, 1787, one hundred and forty-four notables, who comprised the Assembly of Notables, arrived on schedule in Versailles. However, they found that Controller-general Calonne was not prepared to open the Assembly of Notables, which peeved them, because most of them held responsible positions in the Kingdom of France and hardly had time to devote to a delay.

On February 22, 1787, the Assembly of Notables finally got underway. King Louis XVI presided while Controller-general Calonne presented the much-anticipated package of reforms. Controller-general Calonne explained that at the conclusion of the American Revolutionary War, the principal task of the French government was to put its finances on a sound basis, which meant liquidating the past by paying off all the debts associated with the American Revolutionary War. The idea was to put the expenditures of the government on a level with its income. However, the French government owed six hundred million livres, there was neither money nor credit, and the situation was desperate.[36] The solution, he opined, was to levy new land taxes!

The notables listened with interest. They were "well aware that Calonne had painted himself into a financial corner, and they were not disposed to help him find an easy escape," noted Robert D. Harris. He continued:

[The notables] knew [Calonne's] motive in summoning the Assembly was to make it possible for him to ignore the remonstrances of the sovereign courts [the Parliaments] to new loans or taxes. Therefore in deliberating upon the land tax proposal the notables asserted that they could not give their assent to a proportional tax that would levy permanently a percentage of the taxpayers' income...Therefore it would be necessary for the notables to see those financial statements that Calonne had sent to [King Louis XVI] in order to verify the deficit, and to see what specific sum was needed by the general tax subsidy.[36]

Controller-general Calonne complied with the request of the Assembly of Notables. The Assembly of Notables met five times in 1787: February 22–23, March 12, March 29, April 23, and May 25, 1787. After receiving and evaluating the financial statements, the notables announced the need for a regular institution to guarantee that a single individual (the King of France) could never again determine the fate of millions of Frenchmen. The notables demanded that King Louis XVI convene an Estates-General to carry out the reform.

King Louis XVI responded to this popular ultimatum by dismissing Calonne from his post as Controller-general. On May 3, 1787, King Louis XVI appointed Calonne's replacement, Étienne Charles of Loménie Brienne (1727–1794, henceforth, Loménie Brienne), Archbishop of Toulouse. Loménie Brienne was a special friend of Queen Marie Antoinette.

On May 25, 1787, Loménie Brienne dismissed the Assembly of Notables (on behalf of King Louis XVI) and began his stormy year as King Louis XVI's Finance Minister. In summary, the Assembly of Notables rejected most of Controller-general Calonne's reform program and demanded the convocation of the Estates-General. King Louis XVI began eating more, hunting more, and growing increasingly dependent on Queen Marie Antoinette.[37]

Malesherbes' Unfinished Work for Jews in France, 1787–1788

In 1787, as the Assembly of Notables was meeting in Versailles, King Louis XVI asked Malesherbes to restore some civil rights to the Protestants in France (i.e., the Huguenots, or French Calvinists). One hundred years earlier, in October 1685, King Louis XIV had issued the Edict of Fontainebleau, which had abrogated the rights of Protestants in France. Between 1774 and 1776, Malesherbes and Jacques Turgot together had tried, but failed, to rectify some of the misfortunes of the French Protestants, as described elsewhere.[38] Now King Louis XVI asked Malesherbes to try again to rectify some of the hardships experienced by the French Protestants. Malesherbes worked diligently to accomplish that end.

On November 28, 1787 in Versailles, King Louis XVI issued an Edict of Toleration pertaining to the French Protestants, which granted them a modest bill of civil and religious rights, including the right to authenticate their births, marriages, and deaths in their own special Protestant État-civil, or Registry. Why did Protestants seek the right to authenticate their births, marriages, and deaths in an État-civil? A royal edict of August 1, 1539, issued during the Protestant Reformation, first introduced the Royal État-civil into the Kingdom of France. *The French Crown allowed only Catholic clergy to enter only Catholic births, marriages, and deaths into the Royal État-civil.* The French Crown excluded Protestants, Jews, Muslims, Greek Orthodox, and other non-Catholics from registering their births, marriages, and deaths in the Royal État-civil. These religious groups could keep their own private registries, if they chose to do so, explained the French Crown.

The problem with this system was that the official registration of the birth, marriage, and death constituted recognition of the legal status of a person in France and in many cases even of his or her family, from the perspective of the French Crown. Because the Royal État-civil did not register the births, marriages, and deaths of non-Catholics, non-Catholics did not exist in a legal sense in France and therefore were not subjects of the French King. In other words, only Catholics legally existed in France and were subjects of the French King. Thus, the French Protestants considered their acquisition of the right to register their births, marriages, and deaths in a Royal État-civil as a stride forward in their fight for full emancipation.

In November 1787, King Louis XVI began a Royal État-civil specifically for the six hundred thousand Protestants in France. The preamble to the Edict of Toleration of November 28, 1787 summed up its miserly basic provisions:

> The Catholic religion…will alone enjoy in our realm the rights and honors of public worship; while our other, non-Catholic, subjects, deprived of all influence upon the order established in our states, declared in advance and forever incapable of forming a single body within our realm, and subject to the ordinary regulations for the observance of feast-days, will obtain from the law only what natural justice does not permit us to deny them, namely, the authentication of their births, marriages, and deaths.[39]

The term non-Catholic did not apply to Jews in France, as the Jews in France soon learned. Nevertheless, they were happy that at least recognition in France in the Royal État-civil no longer depended on being a Catholic.

In February 1788, King Louis XVI asked Malesherbes to begin study of the Jewish question. Malesherbes "never organized a formal commission [to study the Jewish status in France] but he did co-opt a number of men with some record of involvement in the Jews to advise him," said Arthur Herzberg.[41] Malesherbes conceded that King Louis XVI's Alsatian Ashkenazi General Regulation of July 10, 1784 had failed and that piecemeal tinkering of the General Regulation would not fix it. Rather, he believed a fundamental new policy was in order. His advisors included Nicolas-François Dupré of Saint-Maur (1732–1791), who had once been an Intendant in Bordeaux; Pierre-Louis of Lacretelle (1751–1824), who had once defended two Jews in Metz over admission to the Christian guilds[42]; and Pierre-Louis Roederer (1754–1835), attorney for the Metz Royal Society of Sciences and Art, who was still busily conducting the Metz essay contest mentioned earlier.

On April 15, 1788, two Bordeaux Sephardim, Lopes Dubec and Abraham Furtado (1756–1816), met with Malesherbes. They chose to emphasize the differences between the Sephardi Jews in France and the mostly poor Ashkenazi Jews in France. The Sephardim learned the following during their meeting with Malesherbes:

> [Malesherbes' goal was to develop] a single law that granted civil status to all the Jews of the realm. Jews were to be integrated into guilds according to their occupations, and they would be able to form associations, but only for religious purposes. The way in which Jewish communities had traditionally been organized and governed, by syndics and rabbis, amounted to a nation within the nation, and had to disappear. Moreover, if Jews wished to have the same status as other royal subjects, France's Jews could no longer demand to be treated differently on the basis of whether they were Portuguese or German.[40]

Malesherbes believed that the time was ripe to integrate the Jews in France. However, "the state would not sanction an imperium in imperio [nation within a nation] and would not accommodate anything different about the Jews, other than their religious faith."[40]

On May 8, 1788, the Sephardi Syndics in Bordeaux sent a letter to their two delegates in Paris, which read:

> You know too well the incompatibility of customs, habits and ways of life of other Jews with ours to not to make it known as you should…You can show that they alter [religious dogma] with many ridiculous ceremonies and rabbinic ideas, and they are in some ways so much enslaved to all sorts of superstitions or boycotts that these have reduced them further in our eyes

to the point that we never permit alliances with them through marriage.[40]

In the spring of 1788, Malesherbes interviewed Cerf Berr, Berr Isaac Berr[43], and several of their Ashkenazi associates. The ebullient Cerf Berr captured the attention of the cynical Malesherbes, who subsequently described the meeting with his friend Pierre-Louis Roederer. Malesherbes, who was Catholic, said, "Le roi ma dit qu'il me faisait juif, et voilà Cerf Berr qui veut me faire janseniste; il ne sait plus auqel entendre." The following interaction took place between Malesherbes and Cerf Berr:

> Cerf Berr, drawing distinctions between the religious practices of Alsatian Jews and the Sephardim of Bordeaux, insisted that the latter's observances were lax and exhausted the minister's [Malesherbes'] patience as he [Cerf Berr] provided examples. The following day, Malesherbes told Roederer: "The king told me he made me a Jew [to carry out this inquiry], and now Cerf Berr wants to make me a Jansenist," a reference to a puritanical strand in seventeenth-century French Catholic thought that had been denounced as heretical by the Church and suppressed by [King] Louis XIV.[44-45]

Cerf Berr pleaded with Malesherbes "for the broadest kind of economic equality" for *all* the Jews in France because that approach would be the only means of enabling the majority of Jews, who lived in Alsace, "to leave usury and become self-supporting in less dangerous and more normal occupations." Arthur Hertzberg commented:

> Cerf Berr and his several associates who had come to Paris in the spring of 1788 wanted rights for the Ashkenazim as large as those that the Sephardim had already attained. Despite the growing attacks on all sides of the organized Jewish community, and Malesherbes' own unfriendliness on this point, the leaders of the Ashkenazim kept insisting that the

> *communal autonomy of the Jews should be maintained and that
> the power of the [Syndics] within such a structure should even
> be strengthened* [emphasis added]. The leaders of the Jews of
> [Northeastern] France entered the Revolutionary era holding
> to this position; they were to surrender it with the greatest
> reluctance.[41]

In June 1788, Malesherbes completed his deliberations on the
status of the Jews in France. "Whether the inquiry might have led
[King Louis XVI] to issue a decree of Jewish emancipation and
what its terms might have been are ultimately unknowable since
the French Revolution began before Malesherbes could formulate
recommendations."[46] However, Malesherbes did write an advisory
opinion in 1788 on a separate question involving the Jews, which
shed some light on his thoughts about the Jews in France. Robert
Badinter wrote:

> Malesherbes revealed the fundamental outline of his thoughts
> about the Jews when in 1788 he wrote an advisory opinion
> addressed to [King Louis XVI's Council of State] regarding
> a question that had arisen when wealthy Jews purchased
> seigniorial estates: did Jews, by virtue of purchasing these
> properties, acquire the right to participate in Provincial
> Assemblies? He began by noting that the position of Jews in
> the Kingdom "is in many respects different from that of other
> non-Catholics"—namely Protestants. Then he observed that "a
> strong hatred exists within the hearts of most Christians against
> all of the Jewish Nation, hatred based on the memory of their
> ancestors' crime [the charge of deicide], and strengthened by
> the fact that Jews everywhere devote themselves to the kinds of
> trade that Christians regard as causing their ruin." Declaring
> this hostility to be deplorable, Malesherbes then shifted his
> focus to what he viewed as a crucial policy issue:

This nation [of Jews] has always remained a foreign nation in the midst of all nations: an imperium in imperio. And I believe it is their policy to remain apart from all citizens of the countries in which they live, despite the daily disagreements it creates among people. They have become, moreover a power independent of all others on earth and, in some instances, perhaps dangerous to those among whom they live, by virtue of the close relations among all Jews in the world. And he concluded: "I have not yet plumbed far enough into the depths of this matter to dare to say whether a nation thus constituted can become useful or whether it can only be a danger."[40]

Meanwhile, on May 3, 1788, Finance Minister Loménie Brienne developed and implemented an ambitious program to slash government expenditures and introduce multiple reforms to reduce the deficit. The reforms ranged from abolition of the French Army's supply system[47], to creating (on June 22, 1787) representative Provincial Assemblies in seventeen French Provinces beyond the original two established by Jacques Necker in 1778–1779. Finance Minister Brienne also devised a tier of Municipal Assemblies elected by a franchise based almost entirely on property rather than on juridical estate.

Jacques Necker and Loménie Brienne both viewed the Provincial Assemblies as "repositories of enlightened opinion whose support would enable the French Crown to circumvent the entrenched opposition of the [Sovereign Parliaments]," observed historian James Van Horn Melton. He continued:

Under Brienne's ministry the behavior of the Provincial Assemblies, which generally supported royal measures that the Parliaments had stubbornly opposed, seemed to bear out such hopes. In fact, however, the Provincial and Municipal Assemblies only hastened the process through which political initiative shifted from Crown and Parliaments alike to the nation at large. As the Provincial Assemblies began to circulate printed accounts of their deliberations, political and constitutional debate became increasingly national in scope. From the village to the provincial level, the assemblies had the effect of introducing ever-wider circles of society into the administration of the realm. In the process, they expanded the political consciousness of many who later gained election to the National Assembly.[48]

In 1787, François Hell, who had completed his court sentence for masterminding the case of the counterfeit receipts, savored his election to the newly created Provincial Assembly of Alsace. He also headed a special committee endorsed by the Intermediary Commission of Alsace located in Strasbourg to prepare a "Statute for the Alsatian Jews." In September 1788, François Hell's special committee resolved to call for the abolition of all the semi-autonomous Jewish communities in Alsace, according to Zosa Szajkoswki.[49]

From the perspective of the Ashkenazim, the Provincial Assembly of Alsace was extremely important as "nothing could be done without [its] consent in favor of the Jews, before the actual outbreak of the Revolution," noted Zosa Szajkowski. He continued:

The new liberal feelings toward the Jews failed to penetrate the Provincial Assemblies, whose views were traditionally anti-Semitic. For this reason, despite the liberal sentiments in France, nothing might have been done to better the Jews' status, and had the Revolution of 1789 not come, Jewish Emancipation might not have been realized until a much later date.[50]

In 1787, some of the original members of the Provincial Assembly of Alsace were François Hell, Charles of Broglie, J. A. Plieger, Joseph Schwendt, and Jean-François Reubell (also Rewbell, 1747–1807; henceforth, Reubell). This group of Alsatian men led the fervent, destructive fight to prevent the political emancipation of the Jews during the French Revolution.[50]

In July 1787, Finance Minister Loménie Brienne dutifully presented his plan for financial reform to the Parliament of Paris, hoping that the one hundred and forty-four members would oblige King Louis XVI by cooperatively registering the new royal laws without further ado. The various Parliaments of France, of which the Parliament of Paris was the oldest, largest, and most important, recorded all royal edicts and laws. The Parliaments also possessed the power to pass legislation within their own districts. The Parliament of Paris developed the habit of refusing to register royal legislation it opposed until the French King held a lit de justice or sent a lettre de cachet to force the obstreperous Parliament to record the edict or law and thus activate it.

The reforms of King Louis XVI, as articulated by Finance Minister Loménie Brienne, threatened the status quo for most French subjects. Even common soldiers, whose material condition the reforms improved, were "deeply offended by [the introduction of] some Prussian forms of discipline...that were alien to French ways, such as punishment by running the gauntlet and being struck by the flat of the sword of the entire unit."[51]

However, in the reform package submitted by Finance Minister Loménie Brienne, the Parliament of Paris was most suspicious of the additional tax revenue needed to reduce the French Kingdom's ruinous annual deficit. French Minister Loménie Brienne had already reduced expenditures by twenty million livres and said he was confident that King Louis XVI would make good on his promise to reduce regular expenditures by forty million more livres. However, the royal treasury would require additional tax revenue to erase the deficit, and this additional tax revenue would come from 1) a stamp tax and 2) a new land tax. The stamp tax would raise twenty million livres. Loménie Brienne did not elaborate on the amount the new land tax would raise. He also did not say how long the two new taxes would remain in place. He did say that as soon as the deficit had been eliminated, the stamp tax would be repealed, in any case, not later than January 1, 1798.[52]

The members of the Parliament of Paris voiced their concern and asked Finance Minister Loménie Brienne to provide them with the actual financial statements and pièces justificatives for the ameliorations, so that they could verify the need of the French Crown for additional tax revenue.[52] King Louis XVI angrily refused the request of the Parliament of Paris, saying that the Assembly of Notables had already reviewed and approved these financial statements.

On July 16, 1787, the members of the Parliament of Paris and the Court of Peers asserted that only the Estates-General could approve a tax that had no specified quantity or duration. What was the Court of Peers? The Peers of France comprised a group of the highest-ranking nobles in the Kingdom of France. Since the Middle Ages, they had acquired the right to sit in the general assemblies of the Parliament of Paris and to take part in the deliberations and voting of the assembly, as they wished. On July 16, 1787, the following Peers of France joined the Parliament of Paris: seven princes of the blood, who had served as heads of the seven bureaus of the Assembly of Notables; seven Church prelates; and twenty-seven lay peers.[52] A prince of the blood was a person who was legitimately descended in the male line from the monarch. During the Ancien Régime in France, the rank of prince of the blood was the highest held at court after the immediate family of the French King. The Court of Peers and the Parliament of Paris formally called upon King Louis XVI to convene the Estates-General to solve the French Kingdom's dire financial problems.

Finance Minister Loménie Brienne brushed aside the formal request of the Parliament of Paris and Court of Peers and instead presented the two combined bodies with King Louis XVI's edict pertaining to the new land tax, which taxed all landowners, without exemptions. The Parliament of Paris and the Court of Peers solemnly reviewed the documents. On July 30, 1787, they voted to reject King Louis XVI's package of reforms and reiterated their call for his convening the Estates-General for the consideration of approval of all new taxes of any kind in France.[52]

On August 6, 1787, King Louis XVI convened a lit de justice in Versailles. He formally set aside the decree of the Parliament of Paris and Court of Peers dated July 16, 1787 (i.e., to convene the Estates-General) and, in his presence, forced registration of the two tax measures (stamp and land taxes). "It was the hottest day of the summer, the hall was packed full, [King Louis XVI] dozed, and, according to one eye-witness, snored."[52] After the forced signing, the members of the Parliament of Paris and the Court of Peers hurried back to Paris to declare the illegality of the forced registration in the lit de justice in Versailles. Their declaration was clearly an act of rebellion, said Robert D. Harris.

On August 15, 1787, King Louis XVI temporarily exiled the members of the Parliament of Paris to Troyes in Champagne Province where he believed they would be less subject to pressure exerted by the popular elements of Paris. Instead, the order by King Louis XVI to exile the Parliament of Paris to Troyes caused the popular elements of Paris to riot, which necessitated intervention by royal military troops and the police. Meanwhile, the members of the Parliament of Paris stranded in Troyes sent directives to all Parliaments in the French Provinces to *refuse to enforce* the tax reforms issued by King Louis XVI. Most of the Parliaments in the French Provinces complied with the directive issued by the exiled Parliament of Paris in Troyes.

The serious problems between the Parliament of Paris and King Louis XVI continued for many months until May 8, 1788, when King Louis XVI summoned the former to a second lit de justice to register five new edicts—the infamous Edicts of May 1788. These edicts did not abolish the Parliament of Paris; rather, they neutered its traditional political functions. King Louis XVI entrusted the power of registering royal edicts and laws to a new court that he named the Plenary Court. "All acts of the royal government that applied *throughout the kingdom* [emphasis added] would be registered by the Plenary Court, so that all the other Parliaments and sovereign courts were similarly divested of their function of registration of such acts, and along with it, the function of judicial review of these acts," noted Robert D. Harris. In addition, "the Parliaments would still retain the function of registration of royal acts that pertained only to their jurisdictions...The Edicts of May 1788 took away all claims of the Parliaments to act as the defenders of the Nation," explained Robert D. Harris.[53]

During the four months following King Louis XVI's issue of

the Edicts of May 1788, the Provincial Parliaments, as well as public opinion, rejected the reforms ordered by King Louis XVI. Historian Robert Roswell Palmer wrote, "If the revolution means a concerted defiance of government, the French Revolution began in the summer of 1788."[54]

In June 1788, the Roman Catholic Church convened its leaders in France in the Assembly General of the Clergy of France, which met every five years. One of the tasks of this organization was to vote a fiscal contribution to the French Crown in the form of a free grant. During prosperous times, the Catholic Church paid the free grant to the French Crown in annual allotments of about ten million livres.[55] However, on June 15, 1788, the Assembly General of the Clergy of France denied the French Crown's request for eight million livres and instead offered a paltry one million eight hundred thousand livres.[56]

King Louis XVI could do nothing about this offer of only one million eight hundred thousand livres, because the clergy, alone in the Kingdom of France, had retained the right to vote taxes. On June 15, 1788, the Assembly General of the Clergy of France also declared that the French Crown could not impose a general tax on Church lands, insisted on the complete autonomy of the Church and retention of its ancient privileges and immunities, denounced the Edicts of May 1788, and called upon King Louis XVI to convene the Estates-General.

Meanwhile, in Alsace in 1788, Cerf Berr requested the initiation by the Alsatian Council of Jewish Communities (Nation Juive) of a Jewish Registry of births, marriages, and deaths. Four years earlier, after the Jewish census of 1784, observers had suggested the need for a Jewish État-civil in France. Recall that in November 1787, King Louis XVI had established an État-civil for the Protestants in France.[57] Zosa Szajkowski described the deficient types of registries that existed among the Ashkenazim in Alsace:

> With a few exceptions and unlike such Jewish registries in other French Provinces, most of these registries of Alsace were never kept by Jews, but by the civil authorities who kept track

of the number of the Jews…Of the few registries kept by the Jews themselves, it is worthy to note the one of Bieschheim [*sic*] with two hundred and twelve entries of circumcision; of these, two hundred and nine were copied from a Hebrew pinkas [a Jewish communal record] dating back to 1669. After the registry was deposited with the authorities in 1792, three new entries of circumcisions in 1780, 1790, and September 14, 1790 were added. The departmental archives of [Lower Alsace] had only one Jewish registry—that of Mutzig (1784–1790). Some cities, e.g., Haguenau [Lower Alsace] kept a list containing the same information as the Jewish État civil.[57]

In July 1788, the Intermediary Commission of Alsace levied yet another new tax on Jews. It charged the Alsatian Council of Jewish Communities (Nation Juive) almost sixty-four hundred pounds for road repairs. On July 18, 1788, the Ashkenazi Syndics of Alsace appealed to King Louis XVI, explaining that their economic situation was extremely tenuous and that most of their possessions consisted of debts owed to them by Alsatian peasants who refused to repay them. On July 27, 1788, someone in Versailles sent the Jewish appeal for relief from the road repair tax back to the Intermediary Commission of Alsace, where a committee presided over by Joseph Schwendt again considered it. "On August 28, 1788, the Intermediary Commission of Alsace informed Paris that not only the Jews, but intellectuals and other merchants as well protested against the service duty imposed on them. Indeed, it would be difficult to consider this particular case as an expression of a special anti-Jewish policy." King Louis XVI's Council of State then rejected the Jewish plea for relief from the road repair tax. However, on October 14, 1788, the Jews appealed again.[58]

On July 13, 1788, a severe hailstorm swept across France, from Normandy to Toulouse, destroying hundreds of square miles of crops on the eve of the harvest. The hailstorm caused France's worst harvest since 1748.[59]

King Louis XVI and his ministers were committed to convening the Estates-General, but refused to set a time, hoping that the reforms, if only the Parliament of Paris would register them, would so improve the nation's financial situation that an Estates-General would be unnecessary. Then, in early August 1788, Finance Minister Loménie Brienne learned that the French Crown's treasury was empty. "The reason for the financial crisis was the loss in confidence of investors and bankers in the financial soundness of the government," declared Loménie Brienne in his memoires. In financial language:

> The drop in value of government securities on the [Bourse, the Paris stock exchange] meant that financiers, who normally granted short-term credit in the form of expectations of future tax revenue, were unable to come forth with more money from such short-term loans. The receivers-general and the farmers-general who were the main source of expectations were dependent upon the government's credit in order to raise that capital in the money markets.[60]

King Louis XVI Agrees to Convene Estates-General, 1788

On August 8, 1788, in an attempt to improve the French Crown's credit on the Bourse and restore the flow of expectations, Finance Minister Loménie Brienne, on behalf of King Louis XVI, dispatched a royal decree that fixed the date for the convocation of the Estates-General for May 1, 1789.[50] "It was a rear-guard action," observed Robert D. Harris. "The government's credit did not improve [with the declaration of the convocation of the Estates-General set for May 1, 1789] and it became increasingly apparent that it would not as long as the detested ministers… remained at their posts. By the middle of August [1788] the government was in desperate straits, [Loménie Brienne] even appropriating funds ordinarily earmarked for relief of the indigent and those ruined by the hailstorms of July [1788]." Robert D. Harris continued:

A loan [to the French Crown] was out of the question. On August 16 [1788], the government passed a decree-in-council suspending amortization payments on certain exigible debts, amounting to one hundred and forty-four million livres per year. In addition, and what created the greatest sensation, was the announcement that the government would temporarily make some of its payments in the form of notes bearing five percent interest. It is usually estimated that about three-fifths of the regular payments of the royal treasury were to be made by these notes, which in fact were paper money. The preamble of the decree attempted to mitigate the impact on public opinion by stating that the financial emergency was only temporary, until the end of the year [1788], and that the forthcoming national assembly of estates, promised for May 1, 1789, would be a guarantee of the financial solvency of the government.[60]

On August 24, 1788, King Louis XVI and Queen Marie Antoinette invited Loménie Brienne to submit his resignation. King Louis XVI then requested the return of Jacques Necker, who reluctantly agreed. Jacques Necker "turned the situation around almost overnight. This was his second ministry; he left his first ministry because King Louis XVI and Queen Marie Antoinette did not much like him. His appointment in itself was greeted with great enthusiasm, the government paper on the Bourse leaping about thirty percent on the day after." Robert D. Harris continued:

The sudden turnabout in the financial situation of the royal treasury was due to the resumption of the flow of expectations made possible because of the confidence Necker was able to inspire in the financiers. Of course such a dramatic change might also have given some credence to the allegations of Necker's enemies that a "Necker cabal" had deliberately withheld credit from the Brienne ministry, a charge that was made a year earlier…when the government notes on the Bourse also took a plunge at the time the Parliament of Paris was exiled to Troyes…But the new finance minister was able to dispense with the paper notes used by Brienne and to meet all government payments in specie."[61]

Nevertheless, the public was aroused against King Louis XVI. Malesherbes strongly urged King Louis XVI to give up his plans for convening the Estates-General and instead to convene an assembly and *immediately grant a French Constitution*. King Louis XVI responded that he could not renege on his promise to his subjects to convene an Estates-General. The process of organizing the colossal event began in earnest.

Cerf Berr Resigns as General Syndic of Alsace, November 10, 1788

On November 10, 1788, the Ashkenazim in Alsace attended a meeting of the Council of the Alsatian Jewish Communities (Nation Juive) held in Obernai, Lower Alsace. The social inequality between the wealthiest Jews in Alsace, who were also the ruling class, and the rest of the impoverished Ashkenazim population caused unrest at this meeting. The poor Ashkenazim objected to the paternalistic ways of their General Syndics, even though the latter were trying to protect their co-religionists from adverse external forces while bearing the burden of financing worship, education, social work, hospitals, and hospices for elderly people in the far-flung Ashkenazi communities in Alsace.

Nevertheless, the majority of Ashkenazim attending the November 10, 1788 meeting in Obernai strenuously contested the management of the affairs of the Nation Juive and forced the three long-serving Ashkenazi General Syndics—Aaron Mayer of Mutzig, Lehmann Netter of Rosheim, and Cerf Berr—immediately to resign their positions. The assembly then elected twenty-eight-year-old Samuel Seligmann

Wittersheim (1760–1831) of Mutzig and thirty-year-old Max Berr (Cerf Berr's oldest son) in their places.

Aaron Mayer and Lehmann Netter were pleased to resign, said Robert Weyl. However, Cerf Berr was angry and briskly departed Alsace, first living in his estate in Tomblaine and then moving to Paris, where he audaciously appointed himself Ashkenazi Grand Syndic of the Three Provinces—Alsace, Lorraine, and the Three Bishoprics. Cerf Berr's prestige was so great in the Kingdom of France that even though the Ashkenazim in Northeastern France had not officially elected him Grand Syndic of the Three Provinces (indeed, there was no such position until Cerf Berr invented it), Cerf Berr was able to represent the Ashkenazim in France to the French Crown, at least for awhile.[62]

In December 1788, as winter descended on Alsace, the Sovereign Council of Alsace published an order expelling all Ashkenazim whose names were not on the list compiled during the royal census of 1784. The order said that identified foreign Jews must leave within the month. The two new Ashkenazi General Syndics protested the expulsion order, stating that its intent was to expel Jews "during the cold winter, when they might perish before being able to find new places of residence. Therefore, on December 13, 1788, the [Sovereign] Council [of Alsace] decided that the order of expulsion was to be enforced during the month of May 1789. But this was somehow delayed, and the [French] Revolution broke out before the expulsion order was actually carried out."[27]

Many people in Paris and in the provinces were starving during the extremely harsh winter of 1788/1789, which followed the ruinous hailstorm of July 1788. Twenty-eight-year-old Lippman Berr, who ran his father's textile factory in Tomblaine, granted the City of Nancy a loan of fifty thousand livres to buy wheat. He also promised personally to purchase wheat for the city. The wheat was late in arriving. The people of Nancy then accused Cerf Berr of hiding the wheat in his storehouses in Nancy for the purpose of speculation. They then attacked his storehouses in Nancy, which resulted in city and provincial authorities placing Cerf Berr's storehouses under government protection.[63]

In summary, the period 1784–1788 was turbulent for the vast majority of Ashkenazim in Alsace who faced ruin both because of the case of the counterfeit receipts and King Louis XVI's onerous new Jewish regulation of July 10, 1784. The period was also turbulent for King Louis XVI, who faced the imminent bankruptcy of the French Kingdom in large part because of his decision to help fund the American Revolutionary War. In late 1788, King Louis XVI called for the convocation of the Estates-General as a desperate last measure to raise the money necessary to save the French Kingdom from bankruptcy.

Cerf Berr was not immune to the social and financial upheaval in Alsace. He remained extremely wealthy. He still owned a hotel-sized home in Strasbourg while continuing to oppose the will of the Strasbourg authorities who refused to honor his naturalization papers from King Louis XVI. In 1786, he transferred most of his businesses to his sons and sons-in-law and set up a philanthropic foundation that funded a yeshiva in Bischheim, among other good works.

However, in November 1788, Cerf Berr's own co-religionists ousted him and the two other Ashkenazi Alsatian General Syndics from their positions as leaders of the Council of the Alsatian Jewish Communities (Nation Juive). Cerf Berr took this rejection badly and immediately left Strasbourg and Bischheim to live on his estate in Tomblaine, Lorraine. In early 1789, he moved to Paris where he audaciously proclaimed himself Grand Syndic of the Three Provinces—Alsace, Lorraine, and the Three Bishoprics.

Chapter Five Notes:

1. Moses Ginsburger: *Cerf-Berr et son Époque*. Société d'Histoire des Juifs d'Alsace-Lorraine. Guebwiller, Alsace, France: J. Dreyfus, 1908, p. 21. Available at http://gallica.bnf.fr/ark:/12148/bpt6k5427849p/f8.image; accessed November 17, 2011.

2. Abbé Joseph Lémann: *L'Entrée des Israélites dans La Société Francaise et Les États Chrétiens d'apres des Documents Nouveaux*. Paris, France: Librairie Victor Lecoffre, 1886, pp. 30–31.

3. Ibid, pp. 34–36.

4. Lee Kennett: *The French Armies in the Seven Years' War*. Durham, North Carolina: Duke University Press, 1967, pp. 10–11.

5. Abbé Joseph Lémann: *L'Entrée des Israélites dans La Société Francaise et Les États Chrétiens d'apres des Documents Nouveaux*. Paris, France: Librairie Victor Lecoffre, 1886, pp. 37–45.

6. Zosa Szajkowski: "The Jewish problem in Alsace, Metz, and Lorraine on the eve of the Revolution of 1789." In *Jews and the French Revolutions of 1789, 1830 and 1848*. New York City, New York: Ktav Publishing House, 1970, pp. 315–316.

7. "Oath More Judaico." *Jewish Virtual Library*. Available at http://www. jewishvirtuallibrary.org/jsource/judaica/ejud_0002_0015_0_14995. html; accessed November 14, 2011.

8. Arthur Hertzberg: *The French Enlightenment and the Jews*. New York City, New York: Columbia University Press, 1968, pp. 319–322.

9. Robert Badinter: *Free and Equal: Emancipating France's Jews 1789–1791*. Translated into English from the French by Adam Simms. Teaneck, New Jersey: Ben Yehuda Press, 2010, pp. 47–48.

10. The data collected during the Jewish census of 1784 is available in *Denombrement des Juifs d'Alsace, 1784*. Strasbourg, Alsace, France: Cercle de Généalogie Juive, Editions du Cédrat, no date. The book is available for purchase at http://www.genealoj.org/New/ ENtexte/page06.php; accessed December 1, 2011. See also Simon Schwarzfuchs: "Alsace and Southern Germany: the creation of a border." In *Jewish Emancipation Reconsidered*. Michael Brenner, Vicki Caron, and Uri R. Kaufmann (eds.). London, England, United Kingdom: Leo Baeck Institute, 2003, p. 9.

11. Charles Friedemann: "Bischheim." 1959. Available at http://judaisme. sdv.fr/synagog/basrhin/a-f/bischhei.htm; accessed November 14, 2011.

12. Frances Malino: *A Jew in the French Revolution: the Life of Zalkind Hourwitz*. Oxford, England, United Kingdom: Blackwell Publisher, 1996, p. 21.

13. Zosa Szajkowski: "Sephardim, Ashkenazim and Avignonese Jews." In *Jews and the French Revolutions of 1789, 1830 and 1848*. New York City, New York: Ktav Publishing House, 1970, p. 248.

14. Abbé Joseph Lémann: *L'Entrée des Israélites dans La Société Francaise et Les États Chrétiens d'apres des Documents Nouveaux*. Paris, France: Librairie Victor Lecoffre, 1886, pp. 109–114.

15. Ibid, pp. 118–125.

16. Ibid, pp. 125–131.

17. Ibid, p. 139.

18. Moses Ginsburger: *Cerf-Berr et son Époque.* Société d'Histoire des Juifs d'Alsace-Lorraine. Guebwiller, Alsace, France: J. Dreyfus, 1908, pp. 31–33; available at http://gallica.bnf.fr/ark:/12148/bpt6k5427849p/ f8.image; accessed November 17, 2011; and Jean Daltroff: "Les Ratisbonne, notables et financiers Strasbourgeois au XIX siècle." *Revue des Études Juives*, Volume 159, Numbers 3–4, July–December 2000, p. 469.

19. "Tomblaine: Son histoire." Available at http://www.tomblaine.fr/ tomblaine/historique-de-la-commune/article/tomblaine-son-histo ire?PHPSESSID=c6c9b7e4f79e3ec5488cb6d24f65d589; accessed November 29, 2011.

20. E. Grosse: *Dictionnaire Statistique du Département De La Meurthe: Contenant une Introduction Historique sur le Pays.* Volume 1. Lunéville, France, 1836, p. 501; and Henri Lepage: *Les Communes de la Meurthe.* Volume 2. Nancy, France: A. Lepage, 1853, p. 555.

21. Arthur Hertzberg: *The French Enlightenment and the Jews.* New York City, New York: Columbia University Press, 1968, pp. 135–136; Zosa Szajkowski: "Sephardim, Ashkenazim and Avignonese Jews." In *Jews and the French Revolutions of 1789, 1830 and 1848.* New York City, New York: Ktav Publishing House, 1970, p. 251–252; Jacqueline Thibaut-Payen: *Les Morts, l'Église et l'État.* Paris, France: Institutions Société Histoire, 1977, p. 201; and Robert Weyl: "Chronique des juifs a Rosheim." In *Saisons d'Alsace*, Number 66, 1978. Available at http:// judaisme.sdv.fr/synagog/basrhin/r-z/rosheim/chroniq.htm; accessed February 2, 2012.

22. Maurice Liber: *Les Juifs et la Convocation des États généraux (1789).* Louvain-Paris, France: E. Peeters, 1989, p. 18, Note #5; and Simon Schwarzfuchs: "Alsace and Southern Germany: the creation of a border." In *Jewish Emancipation Reconsidered.* Michael Brenner, Vicki Caron, and Uri R. Kaufmann (eds.). London, England, United Kingdom: Leo Baeck Institute, 2003, p. 16.

23. Robert Badinter: *Free and Equal: Emancipating France's Jews 1789–1791.* Translated into English from the French by Adam Simms. Teaneck, New Jersey: Ben Yehuda Press, 2010, p. 14.

24. Alyssa Goldstein Sepinwall: "L'Abbé Grégoire and the Metz contest: the view from new documents." *Revue des Études Juives,* Volume 166, Numbers 1–2, 2007, pp. 243–258; and Michael Goldfarb: *Emancipation.* New York City, New York, 2009, pp. 5–6. See also Abraham Cahen: "L'émancipation des Juifs devant la Société royale des sciences et des arts de Metz en 1787 et M. Roederer." *Revue des Études Juives,* Volume 1, Number 1, 1880, pp. 83–104.

25. See Frances Malino: *A Jew in the French Revolution: the Life of Zalkind Hourwitz.* Oxford, England, United Kingdom: Blackwell Publisher, 1996.

26. See Ruth F. Necheles: *The Abbé Grégoire, 1787-1831: the Odyssey of an Egalitarian,* Westport, Connecticut: Greenwood Publishing, 1971; and Alyssa Goldstein Sepinwall: "L'Abbé Grégoire and the Metz contest: the view from new documents." *Revue des Études Juives,* Volume 166, Numbers 1–2, January-June 2007, pp. 243–258.

27. Zosa Szajkowski: "The Jewish problem in Alsace, Metz, and Lorraine on the eve of the Revolution of 1789." In *Jews and the French Revolutions of 1789, 1830 and 1848.* New York City, New York: Ktav Publishing House, 1970, p. 318.

28. Robert D. Harris: *Necker and the Revolution of 1789.* Lanham, Maryland: University Press of America, 1986, pp. 85–86.

29. Ibid, pp. 91–93.

30. Ibid, pp. 103–104.

31. See Michael Hayden: *France and the Estates-General of 1614.* Cambridge, United Kingdom: Cambridge University Press, 2008.

32. John M. S. Allison: *Lamoignon de Malesherbes.* New Haven, Connecticut: Yale University Press, 1938, pp. 119–120.

33. Zosa Szajkowski: *Franco-Judaica: an Analytical Bibliography of Books, Pamphlets, Decrees, Briefs and Other Printed Documents Pertaining to the Jews in France 1500–1788.* New York City, New York: American Academy for Jewish Research, 1962, p. 65, #680.

34. Moses Ginsburger: "Une fondation de Cerf Berr." 1923. Available at http://judaisme.sdv.fr/perso/cerfberr/fondat.htm and athttp://judaisme.sdv.fr/perso/cerfberr/fondat2.htm; accessed November 29, 2011; Max Warschawski: "Rabbinats et Rabbins." Available at http://judaisme.sdv.fr/histoire/rabbins/rabbinat/index.htm; accessed January 26, 2012. Max Warschawski: "David Sintzheim." Available at http://judaisme.

sdv.fr/histoire/rabbins/sintzhei/sintzhei.htm; accessed January 26, 2012. For details about Cerf Berr's specifications for dowries for poor girls and alms for the poor, see http://judaisme.sdv.fr/perso/cerfberr/fondat2.htm; accessed January 26, 2012.

35. Zosa Szajkowski: "Introduction," In *Jews and the French Revolutions of 1789, 1830 and 1848*. New York City, New York: Ktav Publishing House, 1970, p. xvii.

36. Robert D. Harris: *Necker and the Revolution of 1789*. Lanham, Maryland: University Press of America, 1986, pp. 103–143.

37. John Hardman: *King Louis XVI: the Silent King*. London, England, United Kingdom: Arnold Press, 2000, pp. 216–217.

38. Zosa Szajkowski: "The reform of the état-civil of the French Jews during the Revolution of 1789." In *Jews and the French Revolutions of 1789, 1830 and 1848*. New York City, New York: Ktav Publishing House, 1970, pp. 358–370.

39. Geoffrey Adams: *The Huguenots and French Opinion, 1685–1787: the Enlightenment Debate on Toleration*. Toronto, Ontario: Canadian Corporation for Studies in Religion, 1991, p. 302. See also Arno J. Mayer: "The perils of emancipation: Protestants and Jews." *Archives des Science Socials des Religion*. Volume 90, Issue 90, 1995, pp. 5–18. Available at http://www.persee.fr/web/revues/home/prescript/article/assr_0335-5985_1995_num_90_1_982; accessed November 14, 2011.

40. Robert Badinter: *Free and Equal: Emancipating France's Jews 1789–1791*. Translated into English from the French by Adam Simms. Teaneck, New Jersey: Ben Yehuda Press, 2010, pp. 83–86.

41. Arthur Hertzberg: *The French Enlightenment and the Jews*. New York City, New York: Columbia University Press, 1968, pp. 324–325.

42. Pierre-Louis Lacretelle: *Plaidoyer pour Deux Juifs de Metz contre l'Hôtel de Ville et le Corps des Marchands de Thionville, Textes de 1777 et de 1823*. Paris, France: Librairie Lipschutz, 1928, pp. 219–220; and Zosa Szajkowski: "The Jewish status in 18th century France and the 'Droit d'aubaine.'" In *Jews and the French Revolutions of 1789, 1830 and 1848*. New York City, New York: Ktav Publishing House, 1970, pp. 230–231.

43. "Berr Isaac Berr of Turique." *Jewish Encyclopedia*, 1906. Available at http://www.jewishencyclopedia.com/articles/3158-berr-isaac-berr-of-turique; accessed January 12, 2012.

44. Cerf Berr had once impressed King Louis XVI in Versailles in a similar way. Cerf Berr had traveled to tell Louis about a problem in Alsace. When Cerf Berr arrived to the chateau he found assembled a large number of ministers and courtesans and thought that he would be waiting a long time before seeing Louis. Thus, he went to a corner of the antechamber to say his evening prayers. Soon a servant called his name. Cerf Berr did not let this trouble him and finished his prayer. When he was introduced to His Majesty, Cerf Berr said, "I just made a request of the King of Kings, which is why I am late." King Louis XVI knew about the piety and fidelity of Cerf Berr and was not offended. Source: Moses Ginsburger: *Cerf-Berr et son Époque*. Société d'Histoire des Juifs d'Alsace-Lorraine. Guebwiller, Alsace, France: J. Dreyfus, 1908, p. 18. Available at http://gallica.bnf.fr/ark:/12148/bpt6k5427849p/f8.image; accessed November 3, 2011.

45. Simon Schwarzfuchs: "Alsace and Southern Germany: the creation of a border." In *Jewish Emancipation Reconsidered*. Michael Brenner, Vicki Caron, and Uri R. Kaufmann (eds.). London, England, United Kingdom: Leo Baeck Institute, 2003, pp. 15–16.

46. Robert Badinter: *Free and Equal: Emancipating France's Jews 1789–1791*. Translated into English from the French by Adam Simms. Teaneck, New Jersey: Ben Yehuda Press, 2010, pp.16–17. See also (for the verbatim French) Frances Malino: *A Jew in the French Revolution: the Life of Zalkind Hourwitz*. Oxford, England, United Kingdom: Blackwell Publisher, 1996, p. 229, Note #116.

47. Robert D. Harris: *Necker and the Revolution of 1789*. Lanham, Maryland: University Press of America, 1986, p. 231. For a detailed discussion of the fifteen months of Brienne's tenure as finance minister, see pp. 219–259.

48. James Van Horn Melton: *The Rise of the Public in Enlightenment Europe*. Cambridge, United Kingdom: Cambridge University Press, 2001, pp. 59–61.

49. Zosa Szajkowski: "The case of the counterfeit receipts in Alsace, 1777–1789." In *Jews and the French Revolutions of 1789, 1830 and 1848*. New York City, New York: Ktav Publishing House, 1970, pp. 213–241, 607.

50. Zosa Szajkowski: "The Jewish problem in Alsace, Metz, and Lorraine on the eve of the Revolution of 1789." In *Jews and the French Revolutions of 1789, 1830 and 1848*. New York City, New York: Ktav Publishing House, 1970, pp. 298, 326.

51. Robert D. Harris: *Necker and the Revolution of 1789*. Lanham, Maryland: University Press of America, 1986, p. 231.

52. Ibid, p. 242–244.

53. Ibid, pp. 252–255.

54. Robert Roswell Palmer: *The Age of the Democratic Revolution*. Princeton, New Jersey: Princeton University Press, 1989, p. 458.

55. Adrien Dansette: *Religious History of Modern France. Volume I: from the Revolution to the Third Republic*. Edinburgh, Scotland: Nelson Publisher, 1961, pp. 8–9.

56. John McManners: *The French Revolution and the Church*. Westport, Connecticut: Greenwood Press, 1982, pp. 2–3.

57. Zosa Szajkowski: "The reform of the état civil of the French Jews during the Revolution of 1789." In *Jews and the French Revolutions of 1789, 1830 and 1848*. New York City, New York: Ktav Publishing House, 1970, pp. 361–362.

58. Zosa Szajkowski: "The Jewish problem in Alsace, Metz, and Lorraine on the eve of the Revolution of 1789." In *Jews and the French Revolutions of 1789, 1830 and 1848*. New York City, New York: Ktav Publishing House, 1970, pp. 331–332.

59. Simon Schama: *Citizens: a Chronicle of the French Revolution*. New York City, New York: Vintage, 1989, p. 305.

60. Robert D. Harris: *Necker and the Revolution of 1789*. Lanham, Maryland: University Press of America, 1986, pp. 264–265.

61. Ibid, pp. 272–273.

62. Robert Weyl: "Les Juifs à Rosheim." In *Saisons d'Alsace*, Number 66, 1978. Available at http://judaisme.sdv.fr/synagog/basrhin/r-z/rosheim.htm; accessed January 22, 2012.

63. Zosa Szajkowski: "French Jews in the armed forces during Revolution." In *Jews and the French Revolutions of 1789, 1830 and 1848*. New York City, New York: Ktav Publishing House, 1970, pp. 567–568.

CHAPTER SIX:

Cerf Berr Besieges King Louis XVI, 1788–1789

———◆———

On August 25, 1788, the day after Jacques Necker succeeded Finance Minister Loménie Brienne, Pierre-Louis Roederer of the Metz Royal Society of Sciences and Arts announced not one, but three, winners of the Metz Royal Society's long-running essay contest. Recall that the contest question in 1785 was, "Are there means to render the Jews happier and more useful in France?" In 1787, when the contest was initially expected to end, the Metz Royal Society leaders felt that none of the entries merited the prize. However, the Metz Royal Society leaders invited some of the entrants to revise and re-submit their essays no later than August 23, 1788. The second phase of the contest lasted from 1787 to 1788. Then the Metz Royal Society leaders selected the three winners, who were Abbé Henri Grégoire, Zalkind Hourwitz, and Claude-Antoine Thiéry (a Protestant lawyer from Nancy).

In 1750, Henri Grégoire was born in Vého Village in Lorraine amid poor French peasants, although his father was not a poor peasant, but a poor artisan (a tailor). A Jesuit priest discovered young Henri Grégoire's intellectual aptitude and enrolled him on scholarship at the nearby Jesuit Collège in Nancy where he studied until 1763, when King Louis XV closed all the Jesuit schools in France. Henri Grégoire studied elsewhere. In 1775, he was ordained a Roman Catholic priest at the relatively young age of twenty-five years.

"After his ordination, Henri Grégoire restlessly alternated between literary and religious pursuits, submitting secular reform projects to academic contests while he traced his father's pilgrimages through Central Europe," said historian Ruth F. Necheles. Recall that in 1778 and 1779, Henri Grégoire lived in the City of Strasbourg where he belonged to the Société des Philantropes and learned about the plight of the Ashkenazim in Alsace. In 1782, Roman Catholic Church authorities appointed Abbè Henri Grégoire curé (priest) of the Village of Emberménil about two miles from his birthplace.[1] He could have spent his entire professional life ministering to the Catholics in rural Lorraine, but he felt destined to do more. He signed his name during this time as Monsieur Grégoire, Curé du Diocese de Metz (Mr. Grégoire, curé of the Diocese of Metz).

Abbè Henri Grégoire's belief system was complex. Ruth F. Necheles explained that Abbè Henri Grégoire believed that Roman Catholics needed Jews, who were God's chosen people, to create the True Church. In addition, he believed that God did not exclude the Nation Juive because of its alleged responsibility for the death of Christ; rather God saved people one individual at a time. Furthermore, God intended Jews to lead the True Christian Church. Therefore, Christians should use preaching, prayer, and charity to persuade Jews to adopt Christianity.

Abbè Henri Grégoire also believed that giving Jews civil rights in France might hasten the Millennium, i.e., the end of time, when Christ would return to gather the just, annihilate the evil, and reign as King on earth for at least one thousand years. Abbè Henri Grégoire believed in Jewish conversion to Christianity *before* the return of the Messiah. Hence, he preached a loving relationship with the Jews and believed that loving Jews was one of the most important ministries of a Catholic priest.[2]

However, Abbè Henri Grégoire also viewed the contemporary Roman Catholic Church as so corrupt and intolerant that no sane Jew would ever want to join it. For centuries, Catholic priests had condoned discrimination of Jews, although Abbè Henri Grégoire absolved the Church from direct responsibility. Unjust rulers bore blame for spreading anti-Catholicism among the Jews and other persecuted minority groups. Given this state of affairs, Abbè Henri Grégoire argued the following:

> Now the [Church] would have to repair the damage by taking a vigorous stand against all intolerance and by becoming a leading force for social and economic change. Before the [Church] could alter its policy so drastically, it would have to sever its ties with secular interests of state governments and the Roman administration [the Pope]. Only then would the [Church] respond to popular needs [welcoming Jews into the Catholic fold]. The first struggle would have to take place within the [Church] itself where power would have to be wrested from the aristocratic hierarchy. In preparation for assuming broader responsibility, priests would have to receive a better education.[2]

Abbè Henri Grégoire's set of beliefs led him to participate in the lower clergy's pre-revolutionary struggle against the episcopacy in Northeastern France and to play a leading role during the French Revolution. The two main elements of his reform agenda were to reform the Church in France and to emancipate the Jews. "With or without internal reform, the Catholic Church could not hope to win Jewish converts until Jewish hostility towards Christians subsided. Jews would accept Christ's divinity only if practicing Catholics gave the Jews an opportunity to observe the glories of Christianity. This would require civil emancipation," he declared.[2]

The title of Abbé Grégoire's award winning two hundred-and-fifty-seven-page entry to the Metz Royal Society of Sciences and Arts contest was titled *An Essay on the Physical, Moral, and Political Regeneration of the Jews (L'Essai sur la Régénération Physique, Morale et Politique des Juifs)*.[3] The Metz Royal Society did not pay for the publication of the Abbé Grégoire's treatise; however, he found a sponsor to publish his essay in March 1789.[4]

What did Abbè Henri Grégoire's essay say about the Ashkenazim? He agreed with Christian William Dohm's essay of 1781 that the degraded moral and physical condition of Jews resulted from lack of opportunity caused by Christian discrimination and persecution beginning by the fifth century AD. Abbè Henri Grégoire also blamed the Talmud, rabbis, and Jewish ghettos for keeping Jews in their degraded condition. His plan for Jewish regeneration (his word) was to undo the chaos of Talmudic traditions, which he believed had become the theology of the Jews (i.e., the Talmud had replaced the Torah); give Jews limited citizenship rights, including the right to own property, but not to serve in certain offices; and evict Jews from their ghettos.

Abbè Henri Grégoire also advocated dissolution of Ashkenazi semi-autonomous communities and elimination of the role of Ashkenazi Syndics; limitation of the oversight of rabbis to religious matters only; increasing the rights of Jewish women; and eradication of "that Tudesco-Hebraico-Rabbinical jargon [his words]" (Yiddish). Moreover, Jews must obey the laws of the nations in which they lived and must speak the national language. Their children must receive secular education. The biggest obstacle to the regeneration of the Ashkenazim was their rabbis, who ruled the synagogues. However, if the rabbis corrupted the Jewish Nation, they also had the power to reform it, he reasoned.[5]

During the interval between his first Metz essay paper, when the contest holders deemed that no essay was good enough for the prize, and his second Metz essay, which won a prize, Abbè Henri Grégoire had sought friendships with Ashkenazi leaders to obtain "material to lend his essay a greater air of authenticity," averred Alyssa Goldstein Sepinwall.[1] The Jews befriended by Abbè Henri Grégoire were Isaiah Berr Bing, Moses Ensheim, Simon von Geldern, Zalkind Hourwitz, Abraham Furtado, Michel Berr, and Berr Isaac Berr.[1] These seven Ashkenazim lived in Lorraine. Abbè Henri Grégoire apparently did not befriend Cerf Berr, who was living in Paris at this time.

Some historians believe that the Lorraine Ashkenazim listed above actually co-authored Abbè Grégoire's final contest submission, although Abbè Grégoire generally thanked them only in footnotes to his *Essai*. Evidence indicates that Abbè Grégoire first met Isaiah Berr Bing in

1787. Isaiah Berr Bing (1759–1805) was born in Metz. He was a wealthy, well-educated author and translator who published French and Hebrew translations of *Phaedon; or the Death of Socrates* by Moses Mendelssohn and writings of great medieval Jewish authors, such as Jedaiah ben Abraham Bedersi (circa 1270–1340) and Judah Halevi (circa 1075– 1141). Isaiah Berr Bing treasured Spanish Judaism during the Middle Ages, a time when men could retain their individual religions yet be tolerant and accepting of each other. Isaiah Berr Bing operated a large industrial salt works in Eastern France. He was married to Eve Eva [*sic*] Goudchaux Cahen-Silny (1761–1796) with whom he had thirteen children between 1777 and 1793.

Isaiah Berr Bing helped Abbè Grégoire, but decried the Abbé's negative view of Jews as usurers and Judaism as spiritually bankrupt in his *Essai*. Alyssa Goldstein Sepinwall wrote:

> Though Bing never spoke publicly of this tension, the abbé himself revealed it in the *Essai's* footnotes, which offer a surprisingly frank glimpse into their conversations. In these notes, Grégoire offered a running apology to Bing whenever he made a particularly negative comment about Jews. Indeed, nearly every time Grégoire cited Bing, it was to beg his friend's forgiveness for some disparaging remark he was making about Jews or Judaism. This highly unusual string of apologies suggests that Grégoire felt guilt at having heard, and ignored, his new friend's advice.[1]

Ashkenazim Excluded from the Estates-General, 1789

In a letter dated January 24, 1789, King Louis XVI convoked the Estates-General for April 27, 1789 in Versailles.[6] King Louis XVI also sent a Rule consisting of fifty-one articles and countersigned by Pierre Charles Laurent of Villedeuil (1742–1828, henceforth, Villedeuil), Secretary of State, which established the conditions of election to the Estates-

General, the order of the convocations, and the form of the assemblies. The King's Rule for the Estates-General instructed local government units to elect deputies to three separate assemblies, corresponding to the three social classes of France—the clergy (the First Estate), the nobility (the Second Estate), and the people (the Third Estate). The assemblies of the First, Second, and Third Estates were to meet concurrently, but separately, in Versailles. In prior meetings of the Estates-General, each assembly voted as a single unit. Thus, there were three votes per law—one vote from the First Estate, one from the Second Estate, and one from the Third Estate. The combined two votes of the privileged First and Second Estates (the clergy and nobility) easily outweighed the single vote of the Third Estate (the people) in this system.

All French Catholic ecclesiastics were eligible for election to the assembly of the First Estate. All nobles who possessed fiefs; nobles without fiefs, but born French or naturalized; nobles who were resident in the district from which they might be elected; nobles whose age was twenty-five years or older; and nobles who possessed acquired or transmissible nobility were eligible for election to the assembly of the Second Estate. All people who were nobles not possessing transmissible nobility and who were born or naturalized in France, twenty-five years of age or older, living in France, and registered on the tax rolls were eligible for election to the assembly of the Third Estate.

King Louis XVI's Rule of January 24, 1789 doubled the number of deputies that local government units elected to the Third Estate assembly. However, his Rule did not specify how the three estates would vote on issues. Would the three estates vote as they had in the past, one vote per estate-assembly, or would head count determine the outcome of voting?

King Louis XVI's Rule provided for very nearly universal manhood suffrage.[6] The most glaring exception to universal manhood suffrage was the failure to include representation for the Ashkenazim in France. King Louis XVI did not invite the Ashkenazim to elect deputies to send to the Estates-General or even to participate in the election of non-

Ashkenazi deputies to the Third Estate from the towns and regions in Alsace, Lorraine, and the Three Bishoprics.

On February 7, 1789, the Intendants in Alsace, Lorraine, and the Three Bishoprics received their letter of convocation and the King's Rule.[6]

In early February 1789, Abbé Henri Grégoire was managing an epidemic among his parishioners in Emberménil while eyeing possible election as a deputy of the First Estate to the Estates-General on behalf of Lorraine. For the first time, priests from across Lorraine (not only those in Metz) gained admission to Lorraine's Provincial Assembly of the three orders (estates), which selected deputies to serve in the Estates-General.

The change that allowed priests from across Lorraine to compete for a deputy spot was a boon for the lower clergy of which Abbè Henri Grégoire was a member. The upper clergy were clerical nobility whose families belonged to the Second Estate. During the reign of King Louis XVI, every bishop in France was a nobleman. The lower clergy were parish priests, monks, and nuns, who made up about ninety percent of the First Estate and numbered around one hundred and thirty thousand individuals in France in 1789. "Abbé Grégoire belonged both to the Lorraine clergy and to the Metz clergy and he played a leading role in the struggle for the rights of the lower clergy in both dioceses. As a reward for his efforts, the priests of the district of Nancy elected him as one of their two representatives to the First Estate," wrote Ruth F. Necheles.[4]

Around February 14, 1789, King Louis XVI issued a belated invitation to certain large cities to select their own separate delegates to send to the Estates-General. The Strasbourg authorities received news of the invitation through a letter from Crolbois, the city's charge d'affaires in Paris.[7]

On February 23, 1789, Abbé Henri Grégoire wrote the following note to Isaiah Berr Bing:

* * * * * * * * *

Note from Abbé Henri Grégoire to Isaiah
Berr Bing, February 23, 1789

Emberménil, February 23, 1789

Tell me, my dear, on the eve of the Estates-General, shouldn't you be consulting with the other members of your nation [i.e., Berr Isaac Berr and Cerf Berr?] to claim the rights and benefits of citizens? This is the time. You already have the King asking Malesherbes to produce a memoire on the Jewish people…[8]

* * * * * * * * *

Isaiah Berr Bing followed the advice of Abbé Henri Grégoire. The Syndics of the Ashkenazim of Northeastern France communicated and decided on joint action, which they charged to the most influential among them, Cerf Berr of Médelsheim. "He was big enough to take on the initiative," said historian Maurice Liber, who continued:

> Although [Cerf Berr] was the last to become one of the three (General) Syndics of Alsace, he was active and dedicated like no other. Thanks to his wealth and his connections, he enjoyed a certain credibility, which he put in the service of his brothers. He was deeply involved in the scandal of the false receipts and suppression of the Jewish body tax. He was furious at François Hell and was ready to run to the aid of his co-religionists if he could achieve something. Cerf Berr, who was at the time living in Paris, was not one to overlook a favorable circumstance, such as the convening of the Estates-General.[8]

On February 25, 1789, Secretary of State Villedeuil dispatched letters of invitation to the Sephardi Jews residing in Bordeaux to participate in the election of electors from their area. Secretary of State Villedeuil did not send a similar letter to the Ashkenazi Jews residing in the three provinces in Northeastern France. The French Crown regarded the Sephardim, but not the Ashkenazim, as native Frenchmen.

Around February 28, 1789, Cerf Berr heard about the royal invitation to the Sephardim of Bordeaux. On March 6, 1789, Police Chief Rolland of Étain (Lorraine) made an inquiry on behalf of the Ashkenazim as to whether they would be permitted to participate in the assemblies outlined in the King's Rule of January 24, 1789. The reply from Paris was "strictly negative," noted Zosa Szajkowski.[10]

On March 10, 1789, the Strasbourg authorities published a special electoral plan, which endorsed the guild voting system of twenty corporations to elect electors to select the two deputies for the Third Estate to represent the City of Strasbourg in the Estates-General. Meanwhile, the Catholic clergy of Strasbourg Diocese elected their own deputies for the First Estate in a separate district meeting held in the City of Haguenau, Alsace. City of Strasbourg authorities agreed to admit one representative from the city's Lutheran University and two each from the Lutheran Kirchenkonvent and the Chapter of St. Thomas to participate in the electoral process. The Strasbourg authorities viewed Cerf Berr and his family as foreign to the city's civic organization and excluded them from the electoral process.[7]

On Tuesday, March 23, 1789, one hundred and twenty-six electors of Strasbourg convened at the Miroir (the Mirror) establishment, which was home to the anti-Jewish merchants' guild. The electors named a commission of thirty-two people to draft the city's cahier de doléances, or list of grievances (henceforth, cahier), and to elect two deputies to represent the City of Strasbourg in the Estates-General.[7] Cahiers were a required and time-honored part of the Estates-General process, as noted earlier.

On April 8, 1789, the electors completed their Strasbourg cahier and the electoral assembly reconvened at the Miroir in the presence of the full governance of Strasbourg. The cahier was one hundred and thirty-five articles in length. Historian Franklin L. Ford summarized what he believed were the three most important sections of the Strasbourg cahier:

> Section one, relating to the kingdom as a whole, charged the city's two delegates with a number of aims to be pursued at Versailles: full representation for commoners through voting by head [i.e., not by assembly/estate] in the Estates-General; a constitutional charter for all of France; guarantees of civil liberty and freedom of the press; universal and proportional taxes; an end to excessive pensions; abolition of the General Tax Farm; creation of uniform provincial estates; application to the public debt of revenue from the royal domain; [and] unrestricted admission of commoners to the higher military ranks; and several others of less general interest.
>
> In section two, limited to provincial issues, the initial appeal to national solidarity received some hasty qualifications: all special rights enjoyed by Alsatians must be confirmed, and Alsace must remain, for customs purposes, "effectively foreign." Under section three, on Strasbourg in relation to the kingdom, the familiar demands of particularism were set forth even more explicitly: confirmation of all privileges granted in 1681; retention of previous criminal and civil jurisdiction; recognition of municipal properties, taxes, and tolls; [and] exemption from militia service, anywhere in France, for citizens of Strasbourg.[7]

In addition, the cahier of Strasbourg advised regulation of the Jews in Alsace by adopting provisions developed by François Hell for his special project (his Statute for the Alsatian Jews) as a member of the Intermediary Commission of Alsace, which was located in Strasbourg. Recall that the electors of Haguenau and Wissembourg elected François Hell to represent them in the Third Estate of the Estates-General.[11] However, he was not a member of the electors who drafted the cahier of Strasbourg. Nevertheless, he inserted himself into the process, as described by Zosa Szajkowski:

The Jewish Problem is laid down in a sample of a cahier of February 1789, published by the Alsatian leader [François] Hell. He proposed measures against usury and Jews; the annulment of all debts of over twenty pounds owed by peasants to Jewish and Christian creditors if these debts were not contracted with the written agreement of seven members of each debtor's family; the abolishment of the Jewish communities and the Rabbinical Courts; the restriction of marriages among Jews; etc...

The Mayor of Strasbourg, de Dietrich, sent a copy of Hell's sample [cahier] to [Secretary of War Puységur] in Paris, but at the [War] Ministry, Hell's sample was strongly criticized because no samples of cahiers were to be circulated and because Hell's proposals were a result of scandals and intrigues...Hell at that time favored autonomous rights for Alsace, which was not in accordance with the Government's views.[7]

Sometime during March or early April 1789, Cerf Berr launched his siege of King Louis XVI and his ministers to gain representation for the Ashkenazim in France in the Estates-General. Cerf Berr began his siege by writing a memorandum to King Louis XVI's Council of State that posited the rights the Ashkenazim in France to have representation in the Estates-General. In this memorandum, Cerf Berr, for the first time, described the Ashkenazim as régnicoles. The Sephardim in Bordeaux were known to the French Crown as régnicoles. A régnicole was a native-born resident of France who was obedient to the French Crown, as opposed to an aubaine, who was not born in the Kingdom of France or any country, lands, or seigneuries that were obedient to the French King.[9]

Before the French Revolution, the French Crown had tried, usually unsuccessfully, to assert its right of aubaine (droit d'aubaine) over the Jews and other aliens in France. Under the right of aubaine, "the government took possession, in whole or in part, of the estate of a deceased alien... These frequent but isolated attempts of the French monarchy to declare certain deceased Jews to be aubaines and to confiscate their estates aroused all French Jews, for they rightly viewed these cases as a threat to their economic and legal status," explained Zosa Szajkowski.[9]

Cerf Berr's letter to King Louis XVI and his Council of State in spring 1789 on behalf of the Ashkenazim in Alsace, Lorraine, and Metz follows:

* * * * * * * *

Memorandum from Cerf Berr to King Louis XVI Positing the Rights of the Ashkenazim in France to have Representation in the Estates-General, Spring 1789

The purpose of the convocation of the Estates-General is to manage the debt of the state with the consent and participation of the taxpayers. It follows from this that any class of taxpayers in the Kingdom has the right to have one or more representatives in the Estates-General. The Jews of Metz, Alsace, and Lorraine form in each province a community whose incorporation comes from the King...The Jewish Nation established in these three provinces is under the protection of the King...and claims that no régnicole shall be deprived of the right to contribute to the rehabilitation of public affairs. Here are their rights to appear in the Estates-General:

1. The Jewish Nation of the three provinces contains about five thousand families; this class of men, who are not at present allowed to join the convocations to elect deputies to the Estates-General, is large enough not to be forgotten.

2. The Jews who are régnicoles are French, i.e., the King's subjects, and have long been allowed, under the protection of sovereign authority, to keep their religious rites and their particular jurisdiction. This régnicole Jewish Nation benefits from the civil laws of the Kingdom, which include passing on their property successively, or by will, which is a right deprived to aliens.

3. A difference of religion cannot be a reason to exclude the King's subjects from the Estates-General since contributions by all classes of citizens have nothing to do with their [religious] dogma.

4. The new and infinitely wise laws for non-Catholic sects benefit all non-Catholics [i.e., including Jews] by creating a state whose main purpose is to allow [non-Catholic sects] to contribute to the prosperity of the Kingdom.

5. The Jewish Nation provides considerable services to the nation, including being most responsible for the supply of arms and possessing an indefatigable pro-government zeal in the interior of the country.

The scrupulous nature [of the Jewish Nation], which has often been applauded and rewarded with privileges, is a source of encouragement to those who have had hopes of receiving these distinctions. If this industrious [Jewish Nation] manages to make its voice heard in the Estates-General, it will make efforts to help the public good by extending northward the commerce of France [into Saarland and the Palatine?]. Finally,…the Jewish Nation asks to be represented by one or more [Christian] deputies to the Estates-General, who are to be chosen by the Jewish Nation. The Jewish Nation will provide these representatives with the necessary authorizations for them to be able to act in the name of all the Jewish régnicoles who contribute to the general prosperity of the State.[8]

* * * * * * * *

Maurice Liber noted that this letter provided valuable information about the way the Ashkenazim perceived their legal status in France. The Ashkenazim viewed themselves as régnicoles who were subject to the laws of the Kingdom of France, which included the right to participate in the Estates-General. The French Crown recognized Ashkenazi worship and rabbis. The Ashkenazim belonged to a religious sect, it was true, but the King's Edict of Toleration of 1787, which granted partial civil rights to French Protestants, lowered, if not eliminated, the barriers to non-Catholics in France, including the Ashkenazim.

In any case, the difference of religion did not prevent non-Catholics from contributing to the tax burdens of the state. If the Jews were correct in this assessment, they also had an interest in representation in the Estates-General. The Ashkenazim intended to grant subsidies to the government, which was the purpose of convening the Estates-General. The Ashkenazim were taxpayers, large enough for the state to notice them. Finally, the country should be interested in the Jewish Nation because, if the Jewish Nation received encouragement, it would expand its trade to benefit France. Not all Jews were as productive as Cerf Berr was, but they did contribute in a significant way to the economic prosperity of France.[8]

Maurice Liber continued: The Ashkenazim did not ask for representation in the Estates-General in the same way that other subjects were going to be represented. Indeed, Ashkenazi participation already had been ruled out of the electoral process by the way King Louis XVI had summoned his subjects to the Estates-General in his Rule of January 24, 1789. The Ashkenazim asked only that the French Crown allow them to entrust their interests to one or more Christian deputies (Henri Grégoire? Pierre-Louis Roederer?) to whom the Ashkenazim would give their cahiers. The method devised by Cerf Berr and his colleagues, declared Maurice Liber, was ingenious.[8]

Cerf Berr's memorandum was not dated, but it was contemporaneous with (or a few days earlier than) a note sent by Cerf Berr to King Louis XVI's ministers on April 9, 1789.[8]

On April 8, 1789, one hundred and twenty-six electors of Strasbourg elected their two deputies. The first deputy was thirty-nine-year-old Strasbourg Ammeister Jean Turckheim. Recall that he was founder and president of the Société des Philantropes and an original member of the Provincial Assembly of Alsace. King Louis XVI authorized him via letters patent to assume common status for political purposes in France even though Jean Turckheim was landed nobility in the Holy Roman Empire.[8] Thus, Jean Turckheim joined the Third Estate assembly. The second deputy chosen by the Strasbourg electors was the anti-Jewish lawyer Joseph Schwendt, who also was an original member of the Provincial Assembly of Alsace.[8] He also joined the Third Estate assembly.

Meanwhile, the electors of Colmar and Schlettstadt (Sélestat) chose anti-Jewish Jean-François Reubell (Rewbell) as one of their deputies to the Estates-General. Zosa Szajkowski described Jean-François Reubell as follows:

> A man of great influence, energetic, and cultured, he regarded as lawful any means that furthered his purpose and availed himself of every legal trick to carry through his ideas…Rewbell, a lawyer and the son of a notary, grew up in the Alsatian atmosphere, where every Jew was looked upon as a usurer. He appeared before Alsatian courts in cases involving Jews and Christians…[W]e know that Rewbell disliked Switzerland because he lost a lawsuit in which he defended Jews against the Grand Conseil of the Berne canton.[10]

The electors of Haguenau and Wissembourg elected anti-Jewish zealot François Hell to represent them in the Third Estate of the Estates-General.[11]

On April 9, 1789, Cerf Berr wrote again to the King's Council of State about representation for the Ashkenazim in the Estates-General. He was anxious to hear back from the French Crown.

* * * * * * * * *

Cerf Berr's Letter to King Louis XVI's Council of State, April 9, 1789

9 April 1789

Should we ask for an order [for] the Jews in Alsace, Lorraine, and the Three Bishoprics to select among themselves two deputies and two others in Paris to represent the Jews of the Kingdom, except for the Jews of Bordeaux and Bayonne? These members would assemble in the home in Paris of Cerf Berr, their [Grand] Syndic, who is well known to the administration and would deliberate with him to form their cahiers and then give the cahiers to one or more [Christian] deputies of the Estates-General, as well as provide the authorization to these one or more deputies to represent the Jewish Nation. If it is not possible to get an order from the Council of State to convene the members in the home of Cerf Berr in Paris to develop a cahier together, would it be possible to allow Cerf Berr and the Jews of the three provinces to choose representatives who would then travel to Paris to deliberate with Cerf Berr in the interests of the Jewish Nation, which are the same as the rest of the Kingdom.[8]

* * * * * * * * *

Cerf Berr received no response to the above letter. He grew more worried than ever when he learned that some cahiers in Alsace, Lorraine, and the Three Bishoprics, written by anti-Jewish elements, denounced the Ashkenazim. What did these cahiers say about the Jews?

David Feuerwerker studied three hundred and seven Christian cahiers in France that mentioned the Ashkenazim as problematic. These cahiers came from localities in Alsace (nineteen cahiers), Flandre-Maritime (one), Lorraine and Barrois (one hundred and thirty-eight),

Paris (one), Rouen (two), and the Three Bishoprics (one hundred and forty-six).[8] David Feuerwerker identified six anti-Jewish themes in the group of cahiers as a whole.

The first grievance against the Ashkenazim pertained to local taxes, which the Christians, but not the Ashkenazim, were required to pay. However, the Ashkenazim paid other taxes (e.g., right of habitation, protection, industry, and capitation) that were crushing and that were at least as much as the local taxes levied by King Louis XVI on his subjects. Of the three hundred and seven cahiers studied, twenty-four (almost eight percent) mentioned this grievance. The second and third grievances were a paucity of currency in circulation (about eighteen percent of cahiers mentioned this grievance), suggesting that the Jews hoarded currency, and stressful commercial competition (twenty-six percent). The fourth and fifth grievances were hoarding of merchandise by the Jews (five percent) and usury (sixty-eight percent). The sixth grievance was religious hatred (four percent).[8]

Six measures proposed by the authors of some of the cahiers to solve the Jewish problem in their localities were to extend the Jewish Regulation of July 10, 1784 beyond Alsace, restrict Jews to ghettos, limit the number of Jews in the locality, disperse the Jews in the French Kingdom, expel Jews from localities, and destroy Jews' places of worship.[8]

Four arguments mentioned in some of the cahiers exonerated the Jews. There was a real need for credit, Christians also committed usury, Christians also hoarded currency, and Christians prohibited all honest trades to the Jews. The seven measures mentioned in some of the cahiers to help the Jews were to make the Jews more useful, permit Jewish commerce, permit Jewish agriculture, open the trades to the Jews, open the liberal arts to the Jews, integrate the Jews, and give Jews' civil rights.[8]

When Cerf Berr did not hear back from the Council of State following his April 9, 1789 letter reproduced above, he sent the following impassioned letter directly to the King's all-powerful Finance Minister Jacques Necker on April 15, 1789.

Cerf Berr's Letter to Finance Minister Jacques Necker, April 15, 1789

Paris
April 15, 1789

Monseigneur,

The Jews of the three provinces of Alsace, Lorraine, and the Three Bishoprics had flattered themselves that the Council of State of His Majesty would respond favorably to the letter that the Jews had taken the liberty to address to you. We are alarmed, Monseigneur, by the silence of the Council of State and by the news spreading through the three provinces that the Christian cahiers contain proposals that would tighten the strings of the Jewish Nation. I come [to Paris] in the name of the Jewish Nation and as Syndic of these three provinces [recall that Cerf Berr appointed himself Grand Syndic in November 1788] to implore on behalf of them the justice of the King and you. The degradation and stigma to which the Jews are subjected does not satisfy the fanaticism of the Christian deputies. They will continue their course until the Jews are exterminated. Hidden under the appearance of doing the public good, the Alsace deputies will take advantage of the situation and therefore will be more dangerous unless someone is responsible for defending the Jews against the charges made by the Alsatian deputies.

It is with this view, Monseigneur, that the Jews seek a decree of the Council [of State] ordering them to appoint deputies to come along with me to discuss the interests of the Jewish Nation and priority to one or more deputies of the Estates-General to defend the rights of the Jewish Nation, which are those of an oppressed humanity.

There is still time, Monseigneur, to save a [Nation Juive] that has always given the greatest proofs of fidelity and zeal for its country [France] and that has done good every time it has not been prevented from doing so. Even those who cause the destruction of the Jewish Nation will be surprised by the evil that they have done. Hasten, then, Monseigneur, to stop the destructive effects of intolerance, and save the unfortunate Jews who will be useful to the State when it gives them a political existence.

Justice, humanity, and the national interest militate in favor of the Jews. Can one, dare one, condemn them without hearing from them? No, Monseigneur, future races will not condemn a gentle and humane people, a beneficent King, and his just ministers; the cause of intolerance will not prevail.

Will you deign, Monseigneur, to have mercy on us and authorize me by an order of the Council of State signed by you to allow the Jews of the three provinces to assemble and appoint members who, jointly with me, identify one or more deputies to the Estates-General to represent us so that we do not become the victims of fanaticism?

I am, with the most profound respect, Monseigneur, your very humble and very obedient servant,

Cerf Berr[8]

* * * * * * * *

In other words, Cerf Berr pleaded with Finance Minister Jacques Necker to permit a form of indirect participation wherein one or more deputies to the Estates-General would represent Ashkenazi interests.[12] Indefatigable and thorough, Cerf Berr sent a letter similar to the one above on the same day to the Secretary of War Puységur.[8]

On April 19, 1789, the two deputies from Strasbourg, Joseph Schwendt and Jean Turckheim, set out for Paris. Their Strasbourg agent in Paris, Crolbois, greeted them in Paris.[13]

On April 21, 1789, Secretary of War Puységur forwarded the letter he had received from Cerf Berr on April 15, 1789 to Finance Minister Jacques Necker and attached a note that read as follows:

* * * * * * * * *

Note from Secretary of War Puységur to
Finance Minister Jacques Necker, April 21, 1789

Versailles
April 21, 1789

I have the honor, Sir [Jacques Necker], of communicating a letter to you from Mister Cerf Bèerr [*sic*], Jewish Syndic in the domiciles of Alsace, Lorraine and the Bishoprics. He requests, in their name, that we authorize first, to name deputies to deliberate with him on the demands, or, second, to give the results of these deliberations to one or more deputies of the Estates-General who can defend the interests of the Jews in the Estates-General.

It seems to me that there is nothing wrong with their being heard and that it would be unfair to them if they were not.

If that is your opinion, it would be necessary to determine how they will elect the deputies who will defend them in the Estates-General and where they will meet.

Puységur.[8]

* * * * * * * * *

On April 23, 1789, King Louis XVI agreed to Cerf Berr's request for some kind of participation for the Ashkenazim in the Estates-General. King Louis XVI's Keeper of the Seals sent a letter to the Intendants in Alsace, Lorraine, and the Three Bishoprics instructing them to tell the

Jews to choose two Jewish deputies per province. The Keeper of the Seals cautioned the Ashkenazim to act discreetly to avoid stirring up problems with local anti-Jewish Christians.

The six delegates selected by the Ashkenazim in Northeastern France were Berr Isaac Berr and Isaac Mayer Marx to represent the Ashkenazim in Lorraine Province; Goudchaux Mayer Cahen (1742–1815) and Louis Wolff (1746–1814) to represent the Ashkenazim in Metz; and David Sinzheim and Samuel Seligmann Wittersheim to represent the Ashkenazim in Alsace Province.[14] The meetings held between the Ashkenazi delegates and their constituents in Alsace Province wrapped up on May 25, 1789. Ashkenazi Deputies David Sinzheim and Samuel Seligmann Wittersheim worked with thirty-seven Ashkenazi electors to develop their Alsatian Ashkenazi cahier in the home of Max Berr, i.e., in the former Hotel Ribeaupierre at number nine Quai Finkwiller in Strasbourg.[15] The Ashkenazi deputies of Lorraine Province and Metz likewise worked with their electors to develop cahiers specific to those two generalities.

What did the Ashkenazi cahiers from the three provinces in Northeastern France say? The cahiers were couched in the spirit and values of Cerf Berr, averred historian Lionel Kochan. He continued:

> [The Ashkenazi cahiers] formulate[d] a policy in keeping with [Cerf Berr's] earlier support for a strengthened [self-governing] communal body in Alsace and for the retention of communal institutions [i.e., courts, schools] as earlier propounded by Christian Dohm. *Cerf Berr, it is said, was even ready to sacrifice emancipation to the maintenance of communal autonomy* [emphasis added]. But for the moment at least, between full citizenship and communal autonomy, no incompatibility was envisaged. The three generalities [Alsace, Lorraine, and the Three Bishoprics]…demand[ed] an end to enforced protection payments, and uniformity of taxation with other citizens; [that] the Jews should be able to practice all arts and crafts, acquire fixed property, cultivate the land, and enjoy

the freedom of movement without being required to live in segregated districts; [and that] they should be free to practice their religion, retain their rabbis, Syndics and communities, "and their jurisdiction…without any change in their present constitution in everything which might refer to their religion and the Jewish law."

The Jews in Alsace asked for permission to employ Christian servants for help with agriculture and for freedom to marry (that is, without the need for royal permission) subject to the self-imposed condition of owning [twelve hundred] livres in town and four hundred in the countryside. The Jews of Metz argued for an end to the Brancas tax [more below] and for the right to participate in communal facilities. The cahier from Lorraine spoke of the demand for synagogues with no external sign to mark them out as places of worship; for rabbis empowered to pronounce divorces, administer estates, and serve as judges of first instance in cases of Jew versus Jew; for the right to enter colleges and universities; and [for the right to require] that every Jew seeking to establish residence in Nancy show assets of one hundred thousand livres (three thousand [livres] elsewhere in Lorraine and [twelve hundred livres] in the villages)—this would keep at bay paupers and vagabonds. The Jews of Nancy enjoyed an unusual degree of affluence; about half the ninety-seven families were prosperous.[16]

In early June 1789, the six Ashkenazi delegates from Northeastern France sent their three cahiers to King Louis XVI's Keeper of the Seals, but he did not immediately print them, said David Feuerwerker.[8] In fact, the first time any printed communication from the Ashkenazi deputies reached the great body of deputies meeting in Versailles was almost three months later, on August 31, 1789.

Estates-General Opens in Versailles, May 4, 1789

On May 4, 1789, the Estates-General opened in Versailles with a dramatic religious procession, described by historian John McManners as follows:

> On the morning of 4 May [1789], at Versailles, the deputies to the Estates-General marched behind a processional cross to the church of Saint Louis—first the [Third Estate], followed by the nobles, then the clergy; after that, under a rich canopy, the Blessed Sacrament, carried by the Archbishop of Paris, and finally, the King, wearing the coronation mantle. At the church, a mass of the Holy Spirit was sung, and the Bishop of Nancy preached a sermon, full two hours long, to match the uniqueness and dignity of the occasion. An observer among the crowds that thronged the decorated streets, had he been cynical enough, might have observed signs of approaching disharmony in the national unity, which these glittering ceremonies proclaimed. The [Third Estate], in black and unadorned, resented the black and white satin, gold lace, and plumes of the nobility, which the curés, in ordinary cassocks, saw a deep design in the arrangements which put the musicians between them and the bishops, resplendent in their purple and walking alone. This division, said an angry parish priest, was "doubtless necessary to the dignity of prelates, so that distant spectators would not confuse them with the lower clergy."[17]

In his sermon, the Bishop of Nancy mentioned the barbarities of tax collectors, the extravagances of Queen Marie Antoinette, the iniquity of the writings of the philosophes, such as the late Voltaire (1694–1778), the necessity for religion as the continuing basis of the national life, and the need for voluntary renunciation of exemptions from taxation.[17]

On May 5, 1789, the three Estates of the Estates-General convened but were unable to reach consensus on the verification of powers of the electoral credentials of the deputies. John McManners explained:

> The [Third Estate], doubled in numbers by the royal regulations, was determined, from the very start, to force united deliberations in which its numerical weight would prevail…Throughout the month, negotiations proceeded in an attempt to end the deadlock. The nobles were intransigent, the clergy moderate and fearful. On [May 28, 1789], when the nobles proclaimed that the distinction of orders was a fundamental law of the monarchy, the clergy suggested that the three estates might cooperate in measures to deal with the shortage of bread—a crafty proposal which the [Third Estate] countered by arguing that this could best be done in a united assembly.[17]

From September 1788 to December 1789, a bread crisis had been undermining the political and social stability of France. Recall that the bread shortage resulted in part from the poor weather and harvests in 1787 and 1788, followed by the winter of 1788/1789, which was so severe that ice floated in the Seine River flowing through Paris.

The dearth of bread for the six hundred thousand permanent Parisian residents weighed heavily on Jacques Necker, who became even more concerned when starving peasants from the surrounding provinces began to show up in the Paris streets. "The capitol city [became] a haven for the unemployed and the starving who flocked in from the immediately surrounding provinces. During the severe winter of 1788/1789, about one hundred and twenty thousand poor came from these regions searching for work and relief." The transients lived on the streets where they built open fires to warm themselves. Food became so scarce that prices rose despite a decree by the Parliament of Paris that forbade bakers from selling bread for more than the price set by the Chief of Police.[18]

The bread shortage also affected Alsace and Lorraine. The bread crisis in Strasbourg lasted from August 1789 to March 1790. During that time, "a Jewish secret agent of the wheat-commission of Mayence [Mainz] helped to import wheat from Germany to Strasbourg." In 1789, Berr Isaac Berr made a loan of six thousand livres to Nancy for the purchase of sacks of wheat, and Cerf Berr of Médelsheim saved Lorraine from starvation by importing wheat from Germany, noted Zosa Szajkowski.[19]

On May 25, 1789, the Military-governor of Strasbourg, Marshal of Stainville, died. His death created a vacuum in military leadership in the city, because both the offices of Governor-general and Provincial commandant had been vacant since 1788. François-Joseph Louis, Baron of Klinglin (1740–1792; henceforth, Klinglin), field marshal of the camp, replaced the Marshal of Stainville as the most senior ranking military commander of the French Army garrisoned in Strasbourg.[13]

On June 17, 1789, the Third Estate deputies in Versailles famously declared themselves the National Assembly (l'Assemblée nationale). Their behavior so angered King Louis XVI, that, on June 20, 1789, he locked the Third Estate deputies out of their assembly hall. Undeterred, the National Assembly instead convened that same day in King Louis XVI's indoor tennis court where they swore to uphold the Tennis Court Oath, which committed everyone present to produce a French Constitution for their nation.

On June 22, 1789, the National Assembly, joined by a majority of the ecclesiastics of the First Estate, convened in the church of Saint Louis in Versailles. At the same time, King Louis XVI ordered the Swiss regiment of Reinach to move from the Strasbourg garrison to Paris. King Louis XVI was clearly preparing for all eventualities. On June 23, 1789, during a royal session of the combined Estates, King Louis XVI rejected the Third Estate's claim that it could constitute a National Assembly. King Louis XVI also declared null resolutions passed by the fledgling National Assembly and reiterated that each deputy represented only the Estate that had elected him. However, King Louis XVI allowed that all deputies could meet and debate in common upon matters concerning all three Estates, especially royal fiscal policy. This royal compromise tacitly accepted some of the Third Estate's arguments for a single combined assembly of all participants originally elected to the Estates-General.

On June 26, 1789, King Louis XVI summoned to Paris more regiments of infantry and three regiments of cavalry from frontier provinces.[20] King Louis XVI ordered these troops to surround Paris.

On June 27, 1789, when the nobles of the Second Estate showed interest in the National Assembly, King Louis XVI ordered the three Estates to join together as the National Assembly.

On June 28, 1789, King Louis XVI appointed forty-year-old Strasbourg-born Protestant, Baron Frederic of Dietrich (1748–1793, henceforth, Frederic Dietrich) as Royal Praetor of Strasbourg. Frederic Dietrich was the son of Jean Dietrich, the foe of Cerf Berr mentioned earlier, who became the largest landowner of Alsace by the acquisition of estates and who built an industrial empire through the acquisition of forges and blast furnaces. Royal Praetor Frederic Dietrich was "to observe and be sure that nothing occurs contrary to His Majesty's interests," said Franklin L. Ford.[13]

Parisians Revolt against King Louis XVI, July 1, 1789

On July 1, 1789, King Louis XVI's Secretary of War ordered additional troops to surround Paris—bringing the total number to between twenty-five thousand and thirty thousand soldiers. All the troops were scheduled to be in place by July 16, 1789. King Louis XVI placed the troops under the command of Secretary of War Marshal of Broglie (Victor François of Broglie, Second Duke of Broglie, 1718–1804), who had distinguished himself during the Seven Years' War and had succeeded Secretary of War Puységur.

On July 8, 1789, the pro-Jewish Deputy Honoré Mirabeau, who had been elected to the Third Estate, delivered a famous speech in which he fervently denounced the troops that King Louis XVI was placing around both Paris and Versailles. King Louis XVI replied to the charge by saying that the troops were necessary because of the disorder in Paris. He denied any intention to interrupt the work of the National Assembly in Versailles. However, some observers believed that King Louis XVI was planning to crush the popular movement in Paris *and* dissolve the National Assembly.[17]

On July 9, 1789, the deputies of the National Assembly renamed the body the National Constituent Assembly. However, the deputies and the populace continued to call the body by its first name, i.e., the National Assembly.

On July 11, 1789, King Louis XVI suddenly dismissed Finance Minister Jacques Necker and several other ministers with whom Jacques Necker had been working closely. King Louis XVI did not tell the French people why he did so or what he proposed to do now that the ministers were gone. "The people were left to draw their own conclusions and that was that the thirty-thousand-man army had *not* [emphasis added] been assembled outside Paris for a peaceful exercise," observed Robert D. Harris.[17] Parisians replied to the sudden actions of King Louis XVI by an instinctive rising of all classes, noted John McManners.[16]

On July 12, 1789, King Louis XVI ordered one hundred German mercenary cavalry to enter Paris to occupy the Place King Louis XV. As the cavalrymen sat on their horses, a crowd gathered. At first, the crowd simply stared agape at the mounted soldiers, but then threw rocks at them. The soldiers charged the people who were throwing the rocks and a mêlée ensued in which three cavalrymen died and the rest withdrew to the main body of troops stationed at Champ de Mars in Paris. The Champ de Mars was the large marching ground in Paris, northwest of the École Militaire. The Champ de Mars received its name from Campus Martius (Mars Field) in Rome, built by the Romans to honor the Roman God of War.

After the stoning of the King's troops in Place King Louis XV, the aroused Parisian mob proceeded to ransack gun shops, tool sheds, and homes in search of arms to defend themselves against what they perceived as threatening behavior exhibited by King Louis XVI and his foreign mercenary troops. On July 13, 1789, a de novo National Guard unit comprised of middle class men from Paris organized to compel the creation of a constitutional monarchy. Members of the new National Guard unit subsequently blended into the crowds and various citizen militia groups. The citizen militia groups had been formed by the various electors from the districts of Paris who had selected as deputies to represent Paris in the Estates-General (now the National Assembly).

The violence of July 12, 1789 in Paris stunned the moderate deputies of the National Assembly in Versailles. On July 13, 1789, they sent a petition and deputation to King Louis XVI to point out the alarming situation in the French Kingdom, "the danger of the movement in Paris spreading to other cities, [and] the need to pacify Paris by sending away the foreign troops and allowing the formation of a bourgeois militia to maintain order."

The National Assembly deputies recognized that King Louis XVI had the prerogative to choose his ministers, but said, "The assembly cannot conceal that the change of ministers is the actual cause of the present misfortunes." The National Assembly deputation pleaded with King Louis XVI to agree to the above principles and to allow a deputation from the National Assembly to go to Paris, announce the King's concessions, and thereby attempt to appease the troubles.[17] King Louis XVI refused all requests and instructed the deputies to return to writing a French Constitution.

On July 14, 1789, the Parisian crowds, fuming over the dismissal of Finance Minister Jacques Necker, the presence of mercenary foreign soldiers in Paris, and the scarcity of food, increasingly viewed King Louis XVI as their mortal enemy. The Paris mob stormed Saint-Lazare (the motherhouse of the all-male Vincentian religious order), customs houses, the Invalides Fortress, and the Bastille Fortress in search of arms, ammunition, grain and produce. On July 15, 1789, Marie-Joseph Paul Yves Roch Gilbert of the Motier, Marquis of La Fayette (1757–1834; henceforth, Lafayette), a military hero of the American Revolution, took command of the fledgling Paris National Guard.

On July 16, 1789, King Louis XVI relented to his subjects by recalling Finance Minister Jacques Necker to service and sending away the mercenary foreign soldiers. The riots in Paris stopped. After his earlier dismissal, Jacques Necker had returned to his home in Geneva. He now prepared to make the long trip back to Paris.

The Great Fear, Summer 1789

In 1789, news took about four days to travel between Paris and Strasbourg, which are about two hundred and forty miles apart. News of King Louis XVI's dismissal of Finance Minister Jacques Necker on July 11, 1789 reached Alsace on July 15, 1789. On that day, violence erupted against the Ashkenazim residing in Upper Alsace (the Sundgau region). Peasants looted and destroyed Jewish homes. Approximately one thousand Jews did not perish of hunger and misery because the people of Basel and Mulhouse gave them asylum and care. When Cerf Berr in Paris heard of the anti-Jewish crimes in Alsace, he addressed a letter of thanks to the authorities of Basel and Mulhouse and begged the National Assembly to take steps to protect his co-religionists in Alsace.[20]

On July 16, 1789, the same day that King Louis XVI recalled Jacques Necker from Geneva to Versailles, he (the King) responded to Cerf Berr's request for help for the Ashkenazim in Alsace by dispatching to the Strasbourg garrison Royal Commandant Jean-Baptiste Donatien of Vimeur, Count of Rochambeau (1725–1807, henceforth, Rochambeau). Like General Lafayette, Rochambeau was a military hero of the American Revolution; however, he was thirty-two years older than General Lafayette and sixty-four-years-old when he accepted command of the troops garrisoned in Strasbourg.

On July 18, 1789, four days after the storming of the Bastille Fortress, the news of the Bastille rout reached Strasbourg and electrified her residents, just as Count Rochambeau ambled into the city. On July 20, 1789, the official accounts of the troubles in Paris, penned by Strasbourg Deputies Jean Turckheim and Joseph Schwendt, reached

Strasbourg.[13] The Revolution in Paris rapidly spread eastward leaping over the Vosges to infect Strasbourg, just as envisioned by the moderate deputies of the National Assembly who had warned King Louis XVI in their petition and visit of July 13, 1789.

On Sunday, July 19, 1789, the day after the news of the storming of the Bastille Fortress reached the City of Strasbourg, a mob of Strasbourg residents besieged the home of Ammeister Lemp with the clear intention of hanging "that particularly haughty oligarch."[13] The people bore a grudge against the Strasbourg authorities for their tardiness in sharing with the Third Estate electors the results of their deliberations over the Third Estate cahier of Strasbourg.[21] The crowds organized an Assembly of Burgesses, which, on behalf of the people of Strasbourg, elected (by universal suffrage) a new government.[22] Klinglin, who had replaced the dead Marshal of Stainville, as noted above, dispersed the crowd by telling them, "Go home, my children, to where your wives and mistresses await you!"[13]

On July 20, 1789 in Strasbourg, Royal Praetor Frederic Dietrich announced his unqualified pledge to speedily correct all abuses specified in the cahier submitted by the City of Strasbourg to the Estates-General (now the National Assembly) in Versailles. Franklin L. Ford wrote, "Instantly, the threatening shouts became cheers of triumph. An exultant throng surged off to launch an all-night celebration, amid cries of 'Long live Necker! Long live Klinglin! No more taxes!'"[13]

However, on July 21, 1789, the Strasbourg authorities refused to honor the mob's demands, which triggered a brutal attack on Strasbourg Town Hall where negotiations were taking place between the Strasbourg authorities and the revolutionary representatives.[21] The crowd perceived that the royal troops of the Strasbourg garrison would not attack them, except in words and menaces. The crowd thus grew bolder and more violent.

English tourist Arthur Young was caught amid the chaos that day in Strasbourg. He famously documented the attack on Strasbourg's Town Hall as follows:

[The crowds] furiously attempted to beat doors in pieces with iron crows; placing ladders to the windows. In about a quarter of an hour, which gave time for the assembled authorities to escape by a back door, they burst all [doors] open, and entered like a torrent with a universal shout of the spectators. From that minute a shower of casements, sashes, shutters, chairs, tables, sofas, books, paper, pictures, etc., rained incessantly from all the windows of the house, which is seventy to eighty feet long, and which was then succeeded by tiles, skirting boards, banisters, framework, and every part of the building that force could detach…I was for two hours a spectator at different places of the scene, secure myself from the falling furniture, but near enough to see a fine lad of about fourteen crushed to death by something as he was handing plunder to a woman, I suppose his mother, from the horror which was pictured in her countenance. I remarked several common soldiers, with their white cockades [symbolic of the King], among the plunderers, and instigating the mob even in sight of [garrison] officers of the detachment.[13]

On the evening of July 21, 1789, two colonels of the French Army in Strasbourg carefully advanced on their horses to clear away the exhausted mob. No one was hurt. The next morning, the astonished Rochambeau issued arms to a hastily organized citizen's guard (which became Strasbourg's National Guard unit), whose role was to quash looting and protect citizens' homes from further mob attacks. On July 23, 1789, the Strasbourg authorities hoped to set an example for the mobsters by trying and hanging Christian Volkmar in the Place d'Armes for stealing coins from Strasbourg Town Hall.[13]

On July 27, 1789, Jacques Necker reached Versailles after the long trip from Geneva. Recall that King Louis XVI had fired him on July 11, 1789 and recalled him to service on July 16, 1789. During his trip, Jacques Necker observed that anarchy was spreading throughout the French Kingdom and that it was not limited to the cities. In 1789, the vast majority of the French population lived as peasants in the countryside. On July 20, 1789, the so-called Great Fear erupted among the peasants across rural France because of the grain shortage, banditry, and the presence of local militias attempting to guard grain supplies. Peasants attacked their lords' manor houses and outbuildings in search of food and arms. The peasant uprising attained its greatest vigor both in Dauphiné and Northeastern France, i.e., in the three provinces of Alsace, Lorraine, and the Three Bishoprics.

The Great Fear sent nobles fleeing France as the pitchfork-wielding peasantry trashed their estates. Finance Minister Jacques Necker declared that he furnished six thousand passports to "the richest inhabitants in a fortnight. Switzerland was inundated" with the émigrés from Northeastern France and Dauphiné.[23]

Robert D. Harris described the anarchy in France during the summer of 1789:

> While the deputies of the National Assembly had been quite properly engrossed in laying the foundations of the future [French Constitution], there had arisen "a covert but painful anxiety which pervade[d] the nation." Popular uprisings were occurring in almost all cities of the kingdom. "Terror is spreading, property is being destroyed or appropriated without restraint, the law is without power, the courts are supine." The Keeper of the Seals urged the [National Assembly] to accelerate its work in building the new institutions to replace those that had been destroyed. [He said,] "The circumstances require that you take measures immediately to repress the alarming impulse to pillage with impunity, and that you restore to public institutions the power that has been lost."[23]

The peasant uprisings were not simply a "violent, unreasonable explosion of popular wrath." Rather, the peasants carefully sought out and destroyed all records of the various taxes and dues they owed to their lords. The deputies of the National Assembly concluded that the peasants' goals were rational and deserved a rational response. One deputy said, "There are only two ways to calm an excited populace, either by armed force or by persuasion. We have no force; we must try persuasion."[23]

On the night of August 4, 1789, the National Assembly deputies, faced with the specter of a continuing peasant revolt, voted to *abolish the feudal system without indemnification* in a decree comprising nineteen articles.[24] One of the elements of the decree was abolition of all seigniorial courts, including the one in which François Hell worked for the Countess of Sénozan, Périgord, of Miramond and of Veyne. The decree of August 4, 1789 replaced all seigniorial courts (without compensation) with a new system of royal courts that would provide justice free of the exorbitant fees of the seigniorial courts. Cerf Berr must have been elated.[24]

French historian Ernest Labrousse called the Decree of August 4, 1789 "the theatrical demolition of the Ancien Régime."[24] The Decree of August 4, 1789 denounced the tax exemption of the nobility and the clergy and replaced it with taxes that the state would levy on all classes and in the same manner. This long overdue tax reform had been proposed previously without success by Finance Ministers Calonne and Brienne.

The Decree of August 4, 1789 renounced church tithes and all special privileges by treaty enjoyed by Alsace and other provinces. All French subjects, without distinction of birth, now were eligible for ecclesiastical, civil, or military office.[24] The National Assembly's Decree of August 4, 1789 was the first step in the transformation of the French body politic from an absolute monarchy into a republic.

On August 6, 1789, amid the Great Fear, David Sinzheim and some of the other Ashkenazim deputies from Alsace, Lorraine, and Metz rode to Paris to meet with Cerf Berr to compose a joint cahier or Adresse [*sic*] for presentation to the National Assembly.

On August 7, 1789, Finance Minister Jacques Necker appeared before the National Assembly deputies to tell them to complete the new French Constitution as soon as possible to quell the Great Fear. The deputies must have wondered what more they could do after issuing the Decree of August 4, 1789, which essentially abolished feudalism, quipped Robert D. Harris. He continued:

> The most imminent and dangerous threat of all [to the Kingdom of France] was bankruptcy. If the government were unable to meet its financial commitments, the social and political order would break down completely. If the troops could not be paid, the frontiers [e.g., Alsace and Lorraine] would be unguarded...[I]f the government could no longer meet its obligations to creditors...the ensuing financial panic would ensure the ruin of confidence in the political order... The mounting exodus of wealthy landowners and others of property was gravely undermining the economy, causing more unemployment, which in turn increased the expenditures of the government...to care for the destitute.[23]

Where could the French Crown turn to find cash to shore up its economy? On August 10, 1789, Deputy Honoré Mirabeau told his fellow deputies, "We must as of today take back the lands of the Clergy." The nationalization of Roman Catholic Church lands in France could provide the collateral for the government's future credit operations. However, the deputies who seized upon this quick remedy for the immediate financial crisis of the government probably had not thought very carefully about the seriousness of the step, declared Robert D. Harris. Should the State nationalize the entire Church and take over its administration? "Few realized at the time how this would involve the State in the spiritual realm, and the difficulties the spiritual would have in accepting such an intrusion of the secular. Here was to become the most serious schism in the national revolutionary movement, even more serious than the alienation of the 'aristocrats.'"[25]

On August 14, 1789, the Sephardi Jews of Bordeaux asked Deputy Abbé Henri Grégoire, who had been selected by the Ashkenazim to represent their interests in the National Assembly, to cease talking about the Ashkenazim. The Sephardi Jews "were not unsympathetic to the problems their co-religionists faced; they were even more concerned, however, that the accusations of usury leveled against the [Ashkenazim] might lead the revolutionaries to restrict the commercial activities of all Jews," including those of the Sephardim.[26]

On August 20, 1789, the National Assembly created an Ecclesiastical Committee to frame a nationalized church for France.

The Rights of Man and Religious Freedom

On August 22, 1789, the National Assembly deputies were debating aspects of the Rights of Man when Deputy Boniface Louis André, Marquis of Castellane (1758–1837; henceforth, Castellane), who was elected to the Second Estate by the nobility of the territory of Châteauneuf-en-Thymerais, rose to make the following motion: "No man should be harassed for religious opinions."

Deputies Honoré Mirabeau and Rabaut of Saint-Étienne (1743–1793) then arose to speak with great eloquence against religious intolerance, noted historian Léon Kahn. Deputy Honoré Mirabeau protested against any dominant religion in France. Nothing except justice must prevail, he declared. Deputy Rabaut Saint-Étienne announced he did not preach tolerance; rather he preached unlimited freedom of religion, which was a right so sacred to him that he disparaged use of the word tolerance as tyrannical. He asked his fellow deputies to grant liberty and equal rights to both French Protestants and all other non-Catholics of the realm.[27]

On August 26, 1789 in Versailles, the National Assembly ratified the Declaration of the Rights of Man and of the Citizen (henceforth, Declaration of the Rights of Man). The same day, the combined Ashkenazi and Sephardi Jews of Paris (between five hundred and one thousand Jews made up this group in Paris), encouraged by the sympathy expressed by Deputies Honoré Mirabeau and Rabaut Saint-Étienne and by the motion made by the Deputy Castellane, submitted a written Adresse to the National Assembly. In their Adresse, they asked for the same civil rights enjoyed by French Protestants and all other Frenchmen, knowing well that the law passed by King Charles IV banning Jews from living in France had never been repealed.[28]

On August 26, 1789, Cerf Berr, Berr Isaac Berr, and the other deputies representing the Ashkenazim of Northeastern France finished working on their own Adresse. In it, they requested the intervention of the National Assembly in favor of a "proscribed people"; retention of "our synagogues, our rabbis and our Syndics, in the same manner as existed today"; and continuing "the free exercise of our laws, rites, and usages."[29] In addition, they called for freedom of residence, abolition of arbitrary taxation, and freedom of religion with particular reference to the retention of the Metz Synagogue. Cerf Berr and the Ashkenazi representatives had been prepared to send their Adresse to the National Assembly, but delayed its release because of the impending momentous proclamation by the National Assembly of the Declaration of the Rights of Man.

On August 26, 1789, King Louis XVI placed the Ashkenazim in France under his protection. However, sporadic violence against them continued.[28]

On August 27, 1789, the National Assembly proclaimed the Declaration of the Rights of Man, whose unabridged preamble and articles follow:

* * * * * * * * *

Declaration of the Rights of Man and of the Citizen, August 27, 1789, Versailles, France

The representatives of the French people, organized as a National Assembly, believing that the ignorance, neglect, or contempt of the rights of man are the sole cause of public calamities and of the corruption of governments, have determined to set forth in a solemn declaration the natural, unalienable, and sacred rights of man, in order that this declaration, being constantly before all the members of the Social body, shall remind them continually of their rights and duties; in order that the acts of the legislative power, as well as those of the executive power, may be compared at any moment with the objects and purposes of all political institutions and may thus be more respected, and, lastly, in order that the grievances of the citizens, based hereafter upon simple and incontestable principles, shall tend to the maintenance of the constitution and redound to the happiness of all. Therefore, the National Assembly recognizes and proclaims, in the presence and under the auspices of the Supreme Being, the following rights of man and of the citizen:

1. Men are born and remain free and equal in rights. Social distinctions may be founded only upon the general good.

2. The aim of all political association is the preservation of the natural and imprescriptible rights of man. These rights are liberty, property, security, and resistance to oppression.

3. The principle of all sovereignty resides essentially in the nation. No body nor individual may exercise any authority which does not proceed directly from the nation.

4. Liberty consists in the freedom to do everything which injures no one else; hence the exercise of the natural rights of each man has no limits except those which assure to the other members of the society the enjoyment of the same rights. These limits can only be determined by law.

5. Law can only prohibit such actions as are hurtful to society. Nothing may be prevented which is not forbidden by law, and no one may be forced to do anything not provided for by law.

6. Law is the expression of the general will. Every citizen has a right to participate personally, or through his representative, in its foundation. It must be the same for all, whether it protects or punishes. All citizens, being equal in the eyes of the law, are equally eligible to all dignities and to all public

positions and occupations, according to their abilities, and without distinction except that of their virtues and talents.

7. No person shall be accused, arrested, or imprisoned except in the cases and according to the forms prescribed by law. Any one soliciting, transmitting, executing, or causing to be executed, any arbitrary order, shall be punished. But any citizen summoned or arrested in virtue of the law shall submit without delay, as resistance constitutes an offense.

8. The law shall provide for such punishments only as are strictly and obviously necessary, and no one shall suffer punishment except it be legally inflicted in virtue of a law passed and promulgated before the commission of the offense.

9. As all persons are held innocent until they shall have been declared guilty, if arrest shall be deemed indispensable, all harshness not essential to the securing of the prisoner's person shall be severely repressed by law.

10. *No one shall be disquieted on account of his opinions, including his religious views, provided their manifestation does not disturb the public order established by law* [Emphasis added].

11. The free communication of ideas and opinions is one of the most precious of the rights of man. Every citizen may, accordingly, speak, write, and print with freedom, but shall be responsible for such abuses of this freedom as shall be defined by law.

12. The security of the rights of man and of the citizen requires public military forces. These forces are, therefore, established for the good of all and not for the personal advantage of those to whom they shall be intrusted.

13. A common contribution is essential for the maintenance of the public forces and for the cost of administration. This should be equitably distributed among all the citizens in proportion to their means.

14. All the citizens have a right to decide, either personally or by their representatives, as to the necessity of the public

contribution; to grant this freely; to know to what uses it is put; and to fix the proportion, the mode of assessment and of collection, and the duration of the taxes.

15. Society has the right to require of every public agent an account of his administration.

16. A society in which the observance of the law is not assured, nor the separation of powers defined, has no constitution at all.

17. Since property is an inviolable and sacred right, no one shall be deprived thereof except where public necessity, legally determined, shall clearly demand it, and then only on condition that the owner shall have been previously and equitably indemnified.[30]

* * * * * * * *

Berr Isaac Berr learned about the proclamation of the Declaration of the Rights of Man "with much joy."[31] The principles enunciated in the Declaration of the Rights of Man went farther than what he, Cerf Berr, and the other members of their group in Paris had dared to put in their Adresse. Berr Isaac Berr exclaimed:

All men are born equal and free. We [he and his fellow Ashkenazi deputies] found then that not only was our mission pointless but we judged that this decree…granted us rights far beyond those that our cahiers entrusted us with requesting… We decided by general demand to obtain the rights and title of citizen.[32]

Indeed, historian Adam Simms deduced the following from his reading of the Declaration of the Rights of Man:

If, as the Declaration of the Rights of Man declared, "Men are born and remain free and equal in rights, social distinctions may be based only on common utility," and if Jews were part of mankind, several significant questions confronted the National Assembly in the months and years following the charter's adoption: Could some "men" [e.g., Jews] be excluded from citizenship? If so, on what basis? What would such exclusion say about the reformers' claims that the rights recognized as those of French citizens were universal and applicable to all mankind? And could a nation exist and its people attain happiness if some of its inhabitants were citizens and others were excluded from citizenship?[32]

On August 28, 1789, anti-Jewish riots broke out in Lorraine Province. The Intermediary Commission of Lorraine sent a decree to non-affected localities in Lorraine where Ashkenazim resided to denounce "the excesses committed in several communes of the [Lorraine Province] against Jewish families that [were] settled there." The Intermediary Commission of Lorraine urged local authorities to grant Jews shelter and assistance, and "to make sure that when they returned to their homes they would be sheltered from the persecutions they have suffered."[29]

The Ashkenazi and Sephardi Jews residing in Paris moved quickly to spell out the implications of the Declaration of the Rights of Man for their own group:

> We are henceforth certain to lead an existence different from that to which we have hitherto been dedicated. In this empire, which is our homeland, the title of man guarantees us that of citizens; and the title of citizens will give us all the rights of the city and the civil facilities which we see are enjoyed, alongside with us, by the members of a society of which we form part.[31]

The Paris Jews, in return for the rights of citizenship, were willing to renounce their own jurisprudence, police, laws, tribunals, and their own Jewish leaders.

On August 31, 1789, Cerf Berr, Berr Isaac Berr, David Sinzheim, and other representatives of the Ashkenazim in Northeastern France finally submitted their first communication to the National Assembly. They had read that the Declaration of the Rights of Man prohibited discrimination on religious grounds and provided for the exercise of religion as long as it did not disturb public order. Thus, in their updated Adresse, the Ashkenazi leaders asked the National Assembly, as had the Parisian Jews, to "speak specifically to the plight of the Jews by giving them the status and rights of citizens," for "when popular fury recently sought out victims, it turned against the Jews." Only an explicit declaration that Jews enjoyed all the rights of citizens would save them from "attacks of prejudice or the traps of fanaticism."[29,31]

However, Cerf Berr and his colleagues still insisted on retaining the Talmudic system of jurisprudence, police, laws, tribunals, and Syndics, which they believed stabilized their communities. Robert Badinter observed, "This deep, almost visceral, attachment to the traditional institutions could only serve to offend the [National] Assembly."[29]

Alert deputies of the National Assembly, upon reviewing the Adresse submitted by Ashkenazi deputies of Northeastern France, immediately raised concerns about the agenda outlined in it. First, they said, "At a time when feudal privileges were abolished, was it not provocative to seek to retain the judicial administrative privileges of the Jewish communities? Second, the Metz community, concerned about the problem of its debts, sought to prevent its members from leaving Metz [without paying their debts]. How could this be reconciled with the freedom of residence that was also sought?"[31] Third, the Declaration of the Rights of Man made the French Kingdom's laws uniform. Why should the Jews be able to preserve their [Talmudic laws], along with their own communal structure?[29]

Michael Goldfarb observed that the difference between the communications of the Parisian Jews and the Ashkenazim of Alsace, Lorraine, and Metz made clear that "there were actually two

Emancipation debates going on. The first was legislative. The National Assembly had to decide whether to grant Jews citizenship and civil rights. The second was being conducted within the Jewish community."[28] The Ashkenazim struggled over the demand by deputies to relinquish their semi-autonomous communities in exchange for obtaining full citizenship in an untested new abstraction called the French nation.

In late August 1789, two Ashkenazi communities in Lorraine—Lunéville and Sarreguemines—broke ranks with their Ashkenazi deputies (Berr Isaac Berr and Isaac Mayer Marx) and asked the National Assembly that "in the future, the Jews settled in Lunéville and Sarreguemines no longer be set apart from other citizens of their cities. May they cease to be organized as a separate corporation and thus be foreigners in their cities."[29] The Jews in the Cities of Lunéville and Sarreguemines no longer wanted to be part of the system of Ashkenazi semi-autonomous communities. They were prepared to take the leap to citizenship in France.

On September 2, 1789, Deputy Abbé Henri Grégoire was about to formally present the Ashkenazi situation to the National Assembly, when a mischievous deputy suddenly renewed a motion to refer Ashkenazi issues to a committee.[33] Deputy Abbé Henri Grégoire was unable to discuss the plight of the Ashkenazim. This was his third failed attempt to do so. He also had tried unsuccessfully on August 3, 1789 and August 14, 1789.[34]

On September 4, 1789, the *Journal de Paris* reported that the National Assembly had adjourned until seven p.m. Believing that this was to hear a request from the Jews for civil status, the notice added: "The success of such a demand can hardly be doubted in the National Assembly of 1789."[26] Frances Malino described what happened next:

> Attempts to raise the issue of the Jews, however, met with little success. Instead, the deputies in Versailles found themselves confronting fundamental constitutional questions, such as the creation of an upper chamber (voted down on September 10 [1789]). But failure to discuss the demands of the Jews neither

diminished public interest nor dissuaded attempts to influence public opinion. On September 15, [1789], for example, a pamphlet circulated accusing the [Sephardi] Jews of Avignon of plotting against many of the city's dignitaries. The intention was obvious—to ignite popular passions against the Jews in preparation for the discussion in the National Assembly.[26]

The third week of September 1789 was High Holidays for the Ashkenazim. Many Jews who had fled Northeastern France during the pogroms in July and August 1789 returned to Alsace, Lorraine, and Metz to attend the religious festivals. They feared reprisals from their adversaries. Cerf Berr notified Deputy Abbé Henri Grégoire that the Ashkenazim in Alsace needed prompt and effective orders to protect them during the High Holidays. On September 27, 1789, new hostilities erupted against the Alsatian Jews. Deputy Abbé Henri Grégoire shared the information and Cerf Berr's urgent request with the National Assembly.

Deputy Clermont-Tonnerre's Speech, September 28, 1789

On September 28, 1789, Stanislas-Marie-Adélaide, Count of Clermont-Tonnerre (1757–1792, henceforth, Clermont-Tonnerre), interrupted a debate on the payment of State pensions to bring to the floor the request from Deputy Abbè Henri Grégoire to protect the Ashkenazi Jews from Christian adversaries.[28] In the following speech, Deputy Clermont-Tonnerre affirmed the important role played by Deputy Abbé Henri Grégoire as a pro-Jewish spokesman[34] and the dangers faced by the Jews because Yom Kippur (Day of Atonement) was fast approaching:

* * * * * * * * *

Opinion of Deputy Clermont-Tonnerre relating to the Persecutions Threatening the Jews in Alsace, September 28, 1789

For a long time, gentlemen, the Jews domiciled…if we can call "domiciled" men who aren't citizens, who don't enjoy the same rights of man, and who, sometimes tolerated and sometimes persecuted, have only a precarious existence and residency. For a long time, I say, the Jews in Alsace, Lorraine, and the Bishoprics await the moment when your important occupations will allow you to hear them. This moment has not yet arrived. I will not anticipate the truths their defender will present to you. It was reserved to this century of toleration and reason to see a respectable minister [Abbé Henri Grégoire] raise his voice in this tribune in favor of the unhappy remainders of Israel. I will not usurp the holy work he reserved to himself. I will not plead this cause in which there are no objections to be combated, in which there are an abundance of choices of the truths to be established, and which can be reduced to one word: proving that it suffices to be a man—a civilized man— to enjoy the rights of a citizen. But what it is not allowed me to put off, gentlemen, is the positive demand for your protection of the Jews. The greatest dangers surround them; the hatred of the people pursues them, and they have deserved this hatred. Such is the effect of oppression and opprobrium: the oppressed man becomes unjust and the degraded man base. The people cannot follow the chain of truths; their vision stops at what wounds them. They don't try to learn if the man of whom they are victim is not himself the victim of other men, and if the immediate cause of his ills is not itself the effect of another cause, a cause distant yet imperious. But you, gentlemen, whose wisdom and prudence will not fail to recognize the true source of the wrongs imputed to the Jews, you will not want them to perish from the effects of the oppressive regime they've lived under among you. You don't want the decree you will pronounce in their favor making citizens of them do nothing but console their memory. Their houses have already been pillaged, their persons exposed to outrages and violence. The upcoming festival of expiation [Yom Kippur], by bringing them together in their synagogues, leaves them defenseless before popular hatred, and their place of worship can become that of their death.

I ask that the president be authorized to inform the municipalities and public officers of the province of Alsace that the National Assembly places the persons and property of the Jews under the protection of the law, and I would like it to be finally recognized that a man, even if he is not a citizen, cannot be murdered with impunity.[35]

* * * * * * * * *

On September 28, 1789, the National Assembly authorized its President to write a letter "making special note that the Declaration of the Rights of Man was a statement of universal principles and applied to every person in the world." The National Assembly quickly dispatched the letter bearing the King's seal to authorities in Alsace, Lorraine, and Metz. "A precedent had been set. A first legal right had been extended to the Jews: that of the new government's protection," averred Michael Goldfarb.[28]

The National Assembly's decision of September 28, 1789 to protect the Ashkenazim did not affect their legal status because it did not modify any existing restrictions. The letter of protection was a stopgap measure. The deputies of the National Assembly refused to listen to any more of Deputy Abbé Henri Grégoire's requests for pro-Jewish action since "it was senseless to discuss Jews until the [National] Assembly defined the nature of citizenship."[29,36]

On October 1, 1789, Deputy Abbé Henri Grégoire, upset that the National Assembly had once again prevented the Ashkenazim from making their address, published *Motion en faveur des Juifs*, which was a summary of the ideas he had developed in his *Essai* of 1788.[36–37]

On October 3, 1789, the National Assembly legalized lending

money at interest, which, during the Ancien Régime, was lawful only in certain parts of the country, although the practice of usury was widespread.[38]

On October 6, 1789, King Louis XVI and the National Assembly dramatically departed Versailles under crushing pressure from a threatening throng of Parisian women who had marched to Versailles on October 5, 1789 to contest the scarcity and high price of bread. The National Assembly moved to Paris where the deputies occupied the Salle du Manège, a former indoor riding arena behind the Tuileries Palace. King Louis XVI and his family occupied the Tuileries Palace.

Deputy Berr Isaac Berr's Speech, October 14, 1789

On the evening of October 14, 1789, the National Assembly finally agreed to hear a speech by an Ashkenazi deputy. Recall that the Ashkenazi deputies had given a copy of their Adresse to the National Assembly on August 31, 1789. Berr Isaac Berr, not Cerf Berr, spoke on behalf of his Ashkenazi brethren, saying, "In the name of the eternal, author of all justice and truth, in the name of God who has given everyone the same rights, we come before you today to ask you to take into consideration our deplorable destiny."[28] His *Discours des Députés des Juifs des Provinces des Evêches, d'Alsace et de Lorraine Prononcé à la Barre de l'Assemblée Nationale Par le Sieur Berr-Isaac-Berr*, published in Paris in 1790, was "simple, eloquent, and brief," noted historian Frances Malino. "[Berr Isaac Berr] hoped that in the midst of its important work, the [National] Assembly would listen with interest to the 'timid request' that the Jews dared make. That men will regard us as their brothers... and that the ignominious institutions to which we are enslaved will be reformed."[26]

The words spoken by Berr Isaac Berr deeply moved many deputies in the National Assembly arena. "A rare silence fell across the hall as reality silenced prejudice," opined Michael Goldfarb. "Many in the [National] Assembly had never encountered a Jew, and here was one whose presence belied all the stereotypes. He was clean shaven, dressed well, spoke elegant French, and made a simple and compelling case for his people."[28]

On October 14, 1789, the President of the National Assembly, Emmanuel Fréteau of Saint-Just (1745–1794, not to be confused with the fanatical Jacobin Louis Antoine Léon of Saint-Just [1767–1794]), invited the Ashkenazi visitors to remain for awhile, "promising them that their requests would be taken under consideration and that the affair of the Jews would be dealt with in the present term. There had been no promise, however, of equal rights." On the contrary, Berr Isaac Berr had spoken of tolerance and pity. Recall how Deputy Rabaut Saint-Étienne, himself a Protestant, renounced the word tolerance during the National Assembly debates of August 1789. Indeed, after Berr Isaac Berr again used the word tolerance in his speech before the National Assembly, Deputy Rabaut Saint-Étienne again declared, "I demand that [the word tolerance] be proscribed and it will be, this unjust word which represents us only as citizens worthy of pity, as guilty ones whom one pardons."[26]

On November 2, 1789, the National Assembly nationalized all land in France. John McManners estimated the amount of land owned by the Roman Catholic Church in France:

> The Church had vast landed possessions, ranging from the garths and gardens of curés to the great seigneurial complexes farmed out by bishops and the Benedictine monasteries. Rumour inflated the extent of these holdings…to about a quarter, or even a third, of the whole country…A modern estimate goes no higher than six to ten percent. Even so the income from property was immense: a mean among guesses by well-informed contemporaries would put the annual total at one hundred million livres.[16]

In November 1789, Aaron Mayer of Mutzig, now treasurer of the Council of the Alsatian Jewish Communities (Nation Juive) initiated repayment of interest on the loans owed by the Council to eight creditors, all of them Christians. In 1789, the Alsatian debts of the Nation Juive totaled more than one hundred and eighty thousand livres, said Zosa Szajkowksi.[39]

On December 14, 1789, the National Assembly substantially completed the important Law of Municipalities. This law required that a municipality elect an administration that included a mayor, a city attorney and his deputy, seventeen councilmen, and a consultative body of thirty-six notables, with the franchise (those who could vote for the municipal leaders) extended to include all active citizens. The National Assembly defined active citizens in 1789 as royal subjects paying an equivalent of at least three days' wages in direct taxes, said Franklin L. Ford.[40]

On December 21, 1789, as the National Assembly deliberated on eligibility rules for French subjects seeking civil and military positions, Deputy Pierre Brunet of Latuque (1757–1824), a royal judge in Puch-de Gontaud and the deputy from Nérac, asked about the eligibility of non-Catholics, meaning (to him) Protestants, to civil and military positions. The majority of deputies in the National Assembly agreed on the eligibility of Protestants for civil and military positions. However, non-Catholics could also mean Jews. Some Catholic clergy and the anti-Jewish deputies from Alsace recoiled at the thought that eligibility to civil and military positions might extend to Jews.

Debate on the eligibility of non-Catholics continued non-stop for three days. On December 23, 1789, *Le Courier de Provence* reported Deputy Honoré Mirabeau's famous statement on Jews and citizenship: "In church men are Catholics and in synagogues Jews, but in all civil matters patriots are of the same religion."[41]

Deputy Clermont-Tonnerre's Speech, December 23, 1789

On December 23, 1789, at the height of the debate on eligibility of non-Catholics for military and civil positions, Deputy Clermont-Tonnerre enlightened his fellow deputies with the following speech:

* * * * * * * * *

Deputy Clermont-Tonnerre's Speech on Religion and Civil Eligibility, National Assembly, December 23, 1789, Paris

Sirs, in the [Declaration of the Rights of Man] that you believed you should put at the head of the French Constitution you have established, consecrated the rights of man and citizen. In the constitutional work that you have decreed relative to the organization of the municipalities, a work accepted by the King, you have fixed the conditions of eligibility that can be required of citizens. It would seem, Sirs, that there is nothing else left to do and that prejudices should be silent in the face of the language of the law; but an honorable member has explained to us that the non-Catholics of some provinces still experience harassment based on former laws, and seeing them excluded from the elections and public posts, another honorable member has protested against the effect of prejudice that persecutes some professions [executioners and actors]. This prejudice, these laws, force you to make your position clear. I have the honor to present you with the draft of a decree, and it is this draft that I defend here. *I establish in it the principle that professions and religious creed can never become reasons for ineligibility* [emphasis added]...

I come to the subject of religion, without doubt much more important...There is no middle way possible: either you admit a national religion, subject all your laws to it, arm it with temporal power, exclude from your society the men who profess another creed and then erase the article in your Declaration of Rights [of Man]; or you permit everyone to have his own religious opinion, and do not exclude from public office those who make use of this permission.

Every creed has only one test to pass in regard to the social body: it has only one examination to which it must submit, that of its morals. It is here that the adversaries of the Jewish people attack me. This people, they say, is not sociable. They are commanded to loan at usurious rates; they cannot be joined with us either in marriage or by the bonds of social interchange; our food is forbidden to them; our tables prohibited; our armies will never have Jews serving in the defense of the fatherland. The worst of these reproaches is unjust; the others are just specious. Usury is not commanded by their laws; loans at interest are forbidden between them and permitted with foreigners...This usury so justly censured is the effect of our own laws. Men who have nothing but money can only work with money: that is the evil. Let them have land and a country and they will loan no longer: that is the remedy. As for their unsociability, it is exaggerated. Does it exist? What do you conclude from it in principle? Is there a law that obliges me to marry your daughter? Is there a law that obliges me to eat hare [rabbit] and to eat it with you? No doubt these religious oddities will disappear; and if they do survive the impact of philosophy and the pleasure of finally being true citizens and sociable men, they are not infractions to which the law can or should pertain.[42]

* * * * * * * *

Deputy Clermont-Tonnerre then turned to admonish the Ashkenazim, especially Berr Isaac Berr and Cerf Berr, for their unreasonable and unjust demand to retain their own laws, judges, and courts while simultaneously asking for French citizenship:

But, they say to me, the Jews have their own judges and laws. I respond that is your fault and you should not allow it. *We must refuse everything to Jews as a nation and accord everything to Jews as individuals* [emphasis added; this is a famous utterance]. We must withdraw recognition from their judges; they should have our judges. We must refuse legal protection to the maintenance of the so-called laws of their Judaic organization; they should not be allowed to form in the state either a political body or an order. They must be citizens individually. But, some will say to me, they do not want to be citizens. Well then! If they do not want to be citizens, they should say so, and then, we should banish them. It is repugnant to have in the state an association of non-citizens, and a nation within the nation...In short, Sirs, the presumed status of every man resident in a country is to be a citizen.[42]

The deputies who passionately supported citizenship for the Jews of France were Deputies "Robespierre, Barnave, Beaumets, Regnault, Pethion of Villeneuve, Clermont-Tonnerre and Mirabeau." The major adversaries of granting citizenship to the Jews of France were Deputies Abbé Jean-Sifrein Maury (1746–1817), Reubell of Colmar, Anne Louis Henri of La Fare (Bishop of Nancy, served 1787–1816), and other obscure representatives, reported Leon Kahn.[43]

On December 23, 1789, Deputy Abbé Jean-Sifrein Maury told his fellow deputies, "The Jews formed not only a religious sect, but a separate nation with its own laws. In these conditions, to grant citizenship to the Jews would be exactly the same as granting French citizenship to Englishmen and Danes without asking them to cease being Englishmen and Danes."[44]

Deputy Adrien Duport's Amendment, December 23, 1789

Deputy Adrien Duport (1759–1798), originally elected to the Second Estate, a future president of the National Assembly (February 15–26, 1791), and a legislative organizer of the left, proposed to amend the wording in Deputy Clermont-Tonnerre's original motion. "Let's simply reinforce the principle without mentioning form of worship or profession," he said. "His amendment called for any person born in France to be given citizenship and eligibility for public offices."[28] Deputy Clermont-Tonnerre agreed to the change in wording.

The debate on the Jewish question and the role of religion in France continued. "The radical left wanted the [Roman Catholic Church] to have no political role in the state, while the hard-liners on the right wanted to preserve the Catholic Church's place at the heart of government." Finally, someone demanded a vote on Deputy Adrien Duport's amendment calling for citizenship and eligibility for public offices for any person born in France. The final vote was four hundred and eight votes against the amendment and four hundred and three for the amendment. By a razor-thin margin, the National Assembly voted down Deputy Adrien Duport's pro-Jewish amendment.[28]

On December 24, 1789, the deputies of the National Assembly voted for citizenship and eligibility of Protestants for election to public offices. They postponed a ruling on the eligibility of Jews for election to public offices. The leaders of the Parisian Jews dashed off a letter to the National Assembly pleading with it to "consult its accustomed justice, ignore the blandishments of some members, and reverse its decision" about excluding the Jews from citizenship and eligibility for election to public offices.[28]

However, there were not enough votes to merit such a reversal. "This [pro-Protestant] law was ominous for Sephardim and Ashkenazim alike, and its implications were catastrophic for Sephardim because at least those in Bordeaux had voted in the 1789 elections and had regarded themselves as full citizens," continued Ruth F. Necheles. "The

Ashkenazim had not previously participated in French public affairs, and they lost nothing in the ruling. Yet the new law left them worse off than before because they could not anticipate eventual citizenship."[45] December 24, 1789 was a sad day for the Jews of France, as their future prospects appeared grim.

On December 30, 1789, the Sephardim from Bordeaux met. Michael Goldfarb noted:

> From the beginning of the Revolution, the Sephardim in Bordeaux, Bayonne, Avignon, and Paris had feared that the desire of the Ashkenazim in Alsace and Lorraine to maintain communal autonomy would be a roadblock to full equality… Now as the Bordeaux Syndics looked at the reports of the debate, they knew this had been a reason for the defeat, perhaps not the main one, but a useful cover for the hatred motivating the anti-Emancipation vote. They decided the time had come to go it alone.[46]

The Sephardim resolved among themselves to ask the National Assembly to please decree "as precisely" as possible that the Jews of Bordeaux were French citizens. Meanwhile, on the same day (December 30, 1789), the Ashkenazi group in Paris led by Cerf Berr contacted the Paris-based revolutionary Jacques Godard, a young pro-Jewish Christian lawyer from Lorraine, to lobby on behalf of the Ashkenazim and to prepare a detailed response to the disastrous outcome of the pro-Protestant, anti-Jewish National Assembly debates in December 1789.[47]

Back in Alsace, on December 30, 1789, Aaron Mayer requested from the Strasbourg district authorities permission to assemble the Syndics of the Ashkenazi communities to collect taxes. He planned to impose a fine of one hundred livres on Syndics who missed the meeting, which he arranged for April 20, 1790 in Mutzig.[48]

In 1789, Cerf Berr's son-in-law, Wolff Lévy, became involved in a dispute over a delinquent loan owed to him by a noble named Charles-

François-Fréderic, Baron of Haindel (1757–1812; henceforth, Haindel). Haindel filed a factum against Wolff Lévy, who was a Strasbourg banker, in which he asked the judges to prevent Haindel's properties, which had belonged to his family for generations, from falling into the hands of "a Jew." What was this conflict about?

> The Haindel family originated in Styria, Austria and immigrated to Strasbourg in the mid-seventeenth century. In 1659, Christophe-Louis, Baron of Haindel, acquired the villages of Romanswiller and Cosswiller from the City of Strasbourg. At the time, Romanswiller and Cosswiller comprised a few ruins and the run-down Castle of Erlenbourg about fifteen miles west of Strasbourg, nestled in the foothills of the Vosges. Christophe-Louis, Baron of Haindel became seigneur of Romanswiller, Cosswiller, and Erlenbourg. The descendants of Christophe-Louis, including Philippe-Auguste of Haindel, built a new and larger castle up the hill from the Castle of Erlenbourg. When Philippe-August of Haindel died in 1755, he left many debts. His brother, Charles-François-Fréderic, inherited the family property and title of Baron of Haindel, Seigneur of Romanswiller, Cosswiller and Erlenbourg.[49]
>
> Haindel, like his brother, was a reckless spender and incurred a mountain of debt. In 1785, he could not pay his creditors as his debts came due. He printed a memorandum disparaging one creditor named Jean-Frederic Baer of Strasbourg, who was a jeweler and a goldsmith. Haindel called the jeweler and other creditors to whom he owned money a "bunch of Jews." The jeweler replied with his own memorandum, which lambasted Haindel for receiving an inheritance that blinded him with confidence, led him to believe that property he purchased was free, and who, not content with creating so many victims (the people to whom he owed money), sought to lead them to bankruptcy with him.[49] The lawsuits dragged on for three years.

Haindel used psychological warfare in his dealings with his Jewish creditors to increase his chances of winning a dispute, noted Zosa Szajkowski. He did this by calling Wolff Lévy, "a Jew," instead of Wolff Lévy of Strasbourg or the banker Wolff Lévy. Zosa Szajkowski wrote about this denigrating practice:

> In lawsuits between Jews and Gentiles, especially between creditors and debtors, the latters [sic] took advantage of the traditional hatred against Jews. The term "Jew" was used as frequently as possible. The word Juif [Jew] prefixed to a name in court or in everyday life was not parallel to the terms like "the peasant X," "the butcher Y," "the officer Z," "A of Colmar," "B of Huningue," etc., which gave the social status, profession, or place of residence of non-Jews. "Jew" in such cases did nothing to fix the profession or residence of the individual, but merely vented anti-Jewish malice, when for example, Abraham Lévy was "the Jew Abraham Lévy." Jews often protested against this discriminatory practice, which, as a matter of fact, was severely condemned even before 1789.[50]

Cerf Berr's practice of signing his name as Cerf Berr of Médelsheim, Hirtz of Bischheim, and Hirtz of Médelsheim was deliberate. This practice gave him the respect he believed he deserved and signaled the message to a reader, "Do not call me 'Jew.'"

In summary, the National Assembly boldly abolished feudalism in France to quell the rural peasant revolt known as the Great Fear. Cerf Berr successfully argued for representation of the Ashkenazim in the Estates-General after King Louis XVI had excluded them. Despite pronouncement of the Declaration of the Rights of Man and impassioned speeches by Berr Isaac Berr and pro-Jewish deputies of the National Assembly, the National Assembly in late 1789 voted against granting citizenship to Jews in France. The Sephardim decided to break away from the Ashkenazim in their dealings with the National Assembly.

Chapter Six Notes:

1. Ruth F. Necheles: *The Abbé Grégoire, 1787–1831*. Westport, Connecticut: Greenwood Publishing, 1971, pp. xi–xii, 4–5. See also Alyssa Goldstein Sepinwall: *The Abbé Grégoire and the French Revolution: the Making of Modern Universalism*. Berkeley, California: University of California Press, 2005. Alyssa Goldstein Sepinwall also analyzed the Ashkenazi friendships of Abbè Henri Grégoire, in her article, "Strategic friendships: Jewish intellectuals, the Abbé Grégoire, and the French Revolution." In *Renewing the Past, Reconfiguring Jewish Culture*. Ross Brann and Adam Sutcliffe (eds.). Philadelphia, Pennsylvania: University of Pennsylvania Press, 2004, pp. 189–213.

2. Ruth F. Necheles: *The Abbé Grégoire, 1787–1831*. Westport, Connecticut: Greenwood Publishing, 1971, pp. 12–14.

3. The title page of Abbé Grégoire's work reads: Essai Sur La Régénération Physique, Morale et Politique des Juifs; ouvrage couronné par la Société royale des sciences et des arts de Metz, le 23 Août 1788, par M. Grégoire, Curé du Diocese de Metz, actuellement de la même Société. A Metz, de Claude Lamort. Se trouve chez Devilly, Libraire, rue Fournirue. A Paris, Chez Belin, Librairie, Rue Saint-Jacques. A Strasbourg, à la Librairie Academique. Avec Privilege, 1789. Available at http://books.google.com/books?id=or0WAAAAQ AAJ&pg=PA54&source=gbs_toc_r&cad=4#v=onepage&q&f=false; accessed January 27, 2012.

4. Ruth F. Necheles: *The Abbé Grégoire, 1787–1831*. Westport, Connecticut: Greenwood Publishing, 1971, pp. 17, 22 Note #31.

5. Henri Grégoire: *An Essay on the Physical, Moral, and Political Reformation of the Jews*. London, England, United Kingdom, 1789, pp. 199–200, 222. Abbé Henri Grégoire said the Ashkenazi language (Yiddish) was intelligible only to them, and tended "greatly to increase their ignorance, or veil their deception."

6. Beatrice Fry Hyslop: *A Guide to the General Cahiers of 1789 with the Texts of Unedited Cahiers*. New York City, New York: Octagon Books, 1968, pp. 12–13; and David Feuerwerker: "Les juifs en France: anatomie de 307 cahiers de doléances de 1789." *Annales. Économies, Sociétés, Civilisations*. 20e année, Number 1, 1965, pp. 45–61; available at http://www.persee.fr/web/revues/home/prescript/issue/ ahess_0395-2649_1978_num_33_1; accessed March 2, 2012.

7. Franklin L. Ford: *Strasbourg in Transition, 1648–1789*. New York City, New York: Norton, 1958, pp. 237–239; and Zosa Szajkowski: "The Jewish aspect of credit and usury." In *Jews and the French Revolutions of 1789, 1830 and 1848*. New York City, New York: Ktav Publishing House, 1970, pp. 172–173.

8. Maurice Liber: *Les Juifs et la Convocation des États Généraux (1789)*. Louvain-Paris, France: E. Peeters, 1989, pp. 8–9; 68 and Note #1; 69–75; and David Feuerwerker: "Les juifs en France: anatomie de 307 cahiers de doléances de 1789." *Annales. Économies, Sociétés, Civilisations*. 20e année, Number 1, 1965, pp. 45–61; available at http://www.persee.fr/web/revues/home/prescript/issue/ahess_0395-2649_1978_num_33_1; accessed March 2, 2012.

9. Patrick Weil: *Migration Control in the North Atlantic World*. Oxford, England, United Kingdom: Berghahn Books, 2005, p. 14. Zosa Szajkowski: "The Jewish status in 18th century France and the droit d'aubaine." In *Jews and the French Revolutions of 1789, 1830 and 1848*. New York City, New York: Ktav Publishing House, 1970, pp. 220–234; and Zosa Szajkowski: "Discussion on Jewish autonomy during the old regime." In *Jews and the French Revolutions of 1789, 1830 and 1848*. New York City, New York: Ktav Publishing House, 1970, pp. 665–667.

10. Zosa Szajkowski: "The discussion and struggle over Jewish emancipation in Alsace in the early years of the French Revolution." In *Jews and the French Revolutions of 1789, 1830 and 1848*. New York City, New York: Ktav Publishing House, 1970, pp. 342–343.

11. Zosa Szajkowski: "The case of the counterfeit receipts in Alsace, 1777–1789." In *Jews and the French Revolutions of 1789, 1830 and 1848*. New York City, New York: Ktav Publishing House, 1970, p. 214.

12. Lionel Kochan: *The Making of Western Jewry, 1600–1819*. New York City, New York: Palgrave Macmillan, 2004, pp. 252–253; Zosa Szajkowski: "The Jewish problem in Alsace, Metz, and Lorraine on the eve of the Revolution of 1789." In *Jews and the French Revolutions of 1789, 1830 and 1848*. New York City, New York: Ktav Publishing House, 1970, pp. 333–334; Ruth F. Necheles: *The Abbé Grégoire, 1787–1831*. Westport, Connecticut: Greenwood Publishing, 1971, p. 23, Note #35; and Moses Ginsburger: *Cerf-Berr et son Époque*. Société d'Histoire des Juifs d'Alsace-Lorraine. Guebwiller, Alsace, France: J. Dreyfus, 1908, p. 23. Available at http://gallica.bnf.fr/ark:/12148/bpt6k5427849p/f8.image; accessed November 17, 2011.

13. Franklin L. Ford: *Strasbourg in Transition, 1648–1789*. New York City, New York: Norton, 1958, pp. 240–247. Also available in Bernard Vogler: *L'Alsace, une Histoire*. Mulhouse, Alsace, France: Oberlin, 1990, p. 119.

14. Frances Malino: *A Jew in the French Revolution: the Life of Zalkind Hourwitz*. Oxford, England, United Kingdom: Blackwell Publisher, 1996, p. 233, Note #50. See also Moses Ginsburger: *Cerf-Berr et son Époque*. Société d'Histoire des Juifs d'Alsace-Lorraine. Guebwiller, Alsace, France: J. Dreyfus, 1908, p. 23. Available at http://gallica.bnf.fr/ark:/12148/bpt6k5427849p/f8.image; accessed November 17, 2011.

15. Jean Daltroff: "Activités socioprofessionnelles des Juifs de Strasbourg à l'époque de Napoléon 1er." Available at http://judaisme.sdv.fr/histoire/villes/strasbrg/metiers/metiers.htm; accessed November 28, 2011; and Frances Malino: *A Jew in the French Revolution: the Life of Zalkind Hourwitz*. Oxford, England, United Kingdom: Blackwell Publisher, 1996, p. 233, Note #52.

16. Lionel Kochan: *The Making of Western Jewry, 1600–1819*. New York City, New York: Palgrave Macmillan, 2004, pp. 252–255. See also Bernard Vogler: *L'Alsace, une Histoire*. Mulhouse, Alsace, France: Oberlin, 1990, p. 118.

17. John McManners: *The French Revolution and the Church*. Westport, Connecticut: Greenwood Press, 1982, pp. 6–7, 19–23.

18. Robert D. Harris: *Necker and the Revolution of 1789*. Lanham, Maryland: University Press of America, 1986, pp. 548–561.

19. Zosa Szajkowski: "The discussion and struggle over Jewish emancipation in Alsace in the early years of the French Revolution." In *Jews and the French Revolutions of 1789, 1830 and 1848*. New York City, New York: Ktav Publishing House, 1970, p. 352.

20. Moses Ginsburger: *Cerf-Berr et son Époque*. Société d'Histoire des Juifs d'Alsace-Lorraine. Guebwiller, Alsace, France: J. Dreyfus, 1908, pp. 23–24. Available at http://gallica.bnf.fr/ark:/12148/bpt6k5427849p/f8.image; accessed November 17, 2011. See also "Seligmann Alexandre." Available at http://judaisme.sdv.fr/histoire/villes/strasbrg/seligman/seligmanalex.htm; accessed November 27, 2011.

21. Petr Alekseevich Kropotkin: *The Great French Revolution, 1789–1793*. New York City, New York: G. P. Putnam's Sons, 1909, p. 103.

22. Ibid, pp. 126–127.

23. Robert D. Harris: *Necker and the Revolution of 1789*. Lanham, Maryland: University Press of America, 1986, pp. 625–629.

24. "The Decree of August 4, 1789." In J. H. Robinson (ed.): *Readings in European History*, Volume 2. Boston, Massachusetts: Ginn, 1906, pp. 404-409. Available at http://www.historyguide.org/intellect/august4.html; accessed November 24, 2011.

25. Robert D. Harris: *Necker and the Revolution of 1789*. Lanham, Maryland: University Press of America, 1986, pp. 635.

26. Frances Malino: *A Jew in the French Revolution: the Life of Zalkind Hourwitz*. Oxford, England, United Kingdom: Blackwell Publishers, 1996, pp. 72–75.

27. Léon Kahn: *Les Juifs de Paris pendant la Révolution*. Paris, France: Librairie Curlacher, 1898, pp. 16–17. An opinion written by the Marquis of Castellane is available at http://libx.bsu.edu/cdm4/item_viewer.php?CISOROOT=/FrnchRev&CISOPTR=121&CISOBOX=1&REC=7; accessed November 28, 2011.

28. Michael Goldfarb: *Emancipation*. New York City, New York: Simon & Schuster, 2009, pp. 62–70, 76–78.

29. Robert Badinter: *Free and Equal: Emancipating France's Jews 1789–1791*. Translated into English from the French by Adam Simms. Teaneck, New Jersey: Ben Yehuda Press, 2010, pp. 106–108. For more information on the Jewish communities of Lunéville and Sarreguemines, see Maurice Liber: *Les Juifs et la Convocation des États Généraux (1789)*. Louvain-Paris, France: E. Peeters, 1989, pp. 133–139.

30. "Declaration of the Rights of Man – 1789." *Avalon Project*. Available at http://avalon.law.yale.edu/18th_century/rightsof.asp; accessed November 27, 1789.

31. Lionel Kochan: *The Making of Western Jewry, 1600–1819*. New York City, New York: Palgrave Macmillan, 2004, pp. 253–255.

32. Robert Badinter: *Free and Equal: Emancipating France's Jews 1789–1791*. Translated into English from the French by Adam Simms. Teaneck, New Jersey: Ben Yehuda Press, 2010, p. 11.

33. Léon Kahn: *Les Juifs de Paris pendant la Révolution*. Paris, France: Librairie Curlacher, 1898, pp. 22, 25–26.

34. Ruth F. Necheles: *The Abbé Grégoire, 1787–1831*. Westport, Connecticut: Greenwood Publishing, 1971, pp. 46–47, Notes #5 and #6.

35. "Opinion of Count Stanislas de Clermont-Tonnerre Relating to the Persecutions Threatening the Jews in Alsace." Available at http://www.marxists.org/history/france/revolution/1789/jews-stanislas.htm; accessed December 9, 2011.

36. Ruth F. Necheles: *The Abbé Grégoire, 1787–1831*. Westport, Connecticut: Greenwood Publishing, 1971, pp. 27, 29.

37. See "Motion en faveur des juifs." Available at http://judaisme.sdv.fr/histoire/document/jud-chr22/Grégoire/motion.htm; accessed November 27, 2011.

38. Zosa Szajkowski: "Occupational problems of Jewish emancipation in France, 1789–1800." In *Jews and the French Revolutions of 1789, 1830 and 1848*. New York City, New York: Ktav Publishing House, 1970, p. 506.

39. Zosa Szajkowski: "The Alsatian debts." In *Jews and the French Revolutions of 1789, 1830 and 1848*. New York City, New York: Ktav Publishing House, 1970, pp. 700–701; and "Historical sketch." In "An Inventory to the Alsace-Lorraine Collection, 1786–1868." Leo Lichtenberg, N.E. H. Manuscript Processor, Klau Library, Hebrew Union College – Jewish Institute of Religion. Available at http://huc.edu/libraries/collections/inventories/Alsace-Lorraine1786-1868.pdf; accessed January 29, 2012.

40. Franklin L. Ford: *Strasbourg in Transition, 1648–1789*. New York City, New York: Norton, 1958, pp. 253–254.

41. Zosa Szajkowski: "Attacks upon Jewish autonomy during the Revolution." In *Jews and the French Revolutions of 1789, 1830 and 1848*. New York City, New York: Ktav Publishing House, 1970, p. 617 and p. 617, Note #49.

42. Count Clermont-Tonnerre: "Speech in religious minorities and questionable professions, December 23, 1789." In Lynn Hunt (ed.): *The French Revolution and Human Rights: A Brief Documentary History*. Boston, Massachusetts: Bedford, 1996, pp. 86–88. Available at http://chnm.gmu.edu/revolution/d/284/; accessed November 28, 1789.

43. Léon Kahn: *Les Juifs de Paris pendant la Révolution*. Paris, France: Librairie Curlacher, 1898, pp. 33–34.

44. Zosa Szajkowski: "Jewish autonomy debated and attacked during the French Revolution." In *Jews and the French Revolutions of 1789, 1830 and 1848*. New York City, New York: Ktav Publishing House, 1970, pp. 578–580.

45. Ruth F. Necheles: *The Abbé Grégoire, 1787–1831*. Westport, Connecticut: Greenwood Publishing, 1971, p. 30.

46. Michael Goldfarb: *Emancipation*. New York City, New York: Simon & Schuster, 2009, pp. 79–80.

47. Frances Malino: *A Jew in the French Revolution: the Life of Zalkind Hourwitz*. Oxford, England, United Kingdom: Blackwell Publisher, 1996, p. 87.

48. Zosa Szajkowski: "The Alsatian debts." In *Jews and the French Revolutions of 1789, 1830 and 1848*. New York City, New York: Ktav Publishing House, 1970, p. 701.

49. Auguste Philippe Herlaut: *Deux Témoins de la Terreur: le Citoyen Dubuisson, le ci-Devant Baron de Haindel*. Paris, France: Librairie Clavreuil, 1958, pp. 125–135.

50. Zosa Szajkowski: "Psychological propaganda against Jews in the law-courts." In *Jews and the French Revolutions of 1789, 1830 and 1848*. New York City, New York: Ktav Publishing House, 1970, pp. 185–188.

CHAPTER SEVEN:

Jews in France Receive Citizenship Rights, 1790–1791

On January 4, 1790, the Sephardi and Ashkenazi Syndics in Paris met in Cerf Berr's home there to discuss ways to present a united front to the National Assembly to win citizenship for all Jews in France.[1] The meeting followed the dispiriting decree of December 24, 1789, which approved citizenship rights for French Protestants, but postponed ruling on the status of citizenship rights for Jews.

Sephardim Receive French Citizenship Rights, 1790

The meeting between the Ashkenazim and Sephardim in Cerf Berr's Paris home lasted less than two hours. It was the last meeting in which "mutual concerns and fraternal sentiments prevailed," remarked Frances Malino. Cerf Berr and his Ashkenazi colleagues insisted on retaining the semi-autonomous communal structure for all Jews in France. Cerf Berr even advocated the suspension of the Declaration of the Rights of Man for Jews until the Jews of France "by their work and their efforts…will have shown themselves worthy" of the rights and "[were] accustomed to this idea." Frances Malino continued:

> Was this suspension, if not its justification, acceptable to Cerf Berr and the deputies from Alsace and Lorraine? Apparently.

For they admitted to the [Sephardim] that while they would request from the National Assembly full rights of citizenship, they were willing to forgo active citizenship in return for economic equality.[1]

The Sephardi leaders refused to suspend acquisition of the rights of active citizenship for any reason. However, the two groups did agree to work together to enhance the public opinion of Jews. The Sephardim then departed to begin work on their own Sephardi-specific Adresse for presentation to the National Assembly.

On January 17, 1790, the Sephardim completed their Adresse, which they knew would upset Cerf Berr. On January 26, 1790, they again met with Cerf Berr in his Paris home where they shared their Adresse. The Sephardim "dined in luxurious discomfort in the presence of [Pierre-Louis] Roederer, [Henri] Grégoire, [Claude-Antoine] Thiéry, and [Jacques] Godard."[1]

What did the Sephardi Adresse say? "The brief and powerful Adresse…offered the National Assembly a seductive distinction [between the Ashkenazim and the Sephardim]. Could the 'ill-considered requests' of some Jews from Alsace and Lorraine, who enjoyed almost no advantages, deprive them of rights they already possessed?"[1] asked the Sephardim.

Cerf Berr was furious. He contacted Deputy Charles Maurice of Talleyrand-Périgord, First Prince of Bénévent (1754–1838, henceforth, Talleyrand). The National Assembly had assigned the Constitutional Committee, which Deputy Talleyrand headed, to review the Sephardi Adresse and report back to the National Assembly. On January 27, 1790, Deputy Talleyrand told the Sephardi Syndics that the Ashkenazi Syndics had told him that they wanted active citizenship presented to the National Assembly on behalf of *all*, or *no*, Jews. The Ashkenazim also asked Deputy Talleyrand to delay his report about the Sephardi Adresse to the National Assembly until he had received a petition that the Ashkenazim were composing. Deputy Talleyrand refused their request.

On January 28, 1790, the deputies of the National Assembly listened to Deputy Talleyrand's report on the Sephardim Adresse. Deputy Talleyrand concluded by saying that the committee that he headed, without prejudging the wider question of the state of the Jews in general, had decided the Bordeaux Jews were "active citizens," i.e., full citizens. After debates, the motion passed three hundred and seventy-three to two hundred and twenty-five to confer full citizenship on the Sephardim in France.[2]

This decree upon the "privileged" Jews in France endangered the entire struggle for the emancipation of the Ashkenazi Jews, averred Zosa Szajkowski. "It took great courage and patience [for the Ashkenazim] to overcome this danger, and in this struggle for citizenship of all the Jews of France, the Sephardim had no share whatsoever."[3] Zalkind Hourwitz, the Polish Ashkenazim living in Paris, decried the distinction now drawn by the National Assembly between the Sephardim and the Ashkenazim in their right to enjoy the Rights of Man.[3]

The same day that the Bordeaux Sephardim became French citizens (January 28, 1790), the Ashkenazi Syndics placed their one hundred and seven-page *Pétition des juifs établis en France, adressée à l'Assemblée nationale le 28 janvier 1790, sur l'ajournement du 24 décembre 1789*, penned by Jacques Godard, before the National Assembly. In 1790, Théodore Berr, Cerf Berr's son who also had a home in Paris, published the *Pétition*.[4] Isaac Mayer Marx, Berr Isaac Berr, David Sinzheim, Théodore Berr, Lazare Jacob, Trenell père, and Cerf Berr signed the *Pétition*.[1,4]

What did the *Pétition* say? It stated, "Our principal demands are the same as those of the Bordeaux." It summarized all the arguments for and against granting full citizenship to Ashkenazi Jews. However, it lacked "a clear statement concerning the future status of Jewish [semi-autonomous] communities. On the contrary, in true compromise fashion, autonomy was implicitly assumed, implicitly repudiated, and never actually mentioned," declared Frances Malino. "Missing as well was an explicit demand for nothing less than active citizenship."[1] However, the *Pétition* did reveal something new and important: Cerf

Berr signed his name on page 107 of the petition, "Cerf-Berr, ci-devant Syndic Général des Juifs." In English, this phrase reads, Cerf Berr, *heretofore* [until now, emphasis added] Syndic General of the Jews.[4–5]

On January 28, 1790, Jacques Godard began his intensive effort in Paris to increase support for Ashkenazi citizenship at the same time that the Ashkenazi Syndics submitted their *Pétition* to the National Assembly. Jacques Godard and Zalkind Hourwitz went to the Hôtel de Ville in Paris to speak to the General Assembly of the Paris Commune. "Both brought with them the conviction that independent of any decision that day concerning the [Sephardim], the emancipation of the Jews of France now rested with the revolutionaries of Paris."[6]

Jacques Godard reminded the General Assembly of the Paris Commune that it had supported the Jews of Paris in the past. Now the Ashkenazim themselves were pleading for the Commune's continued support for the emancipation of all Jews in France. Jacques Godard declared, "You will have the satisfaction, so sweet for true friends of public well-being, to serve, not only the cause of the Jews of Paris in particular, but that of all the Jews" in the Kingdom of France. When Jacques Godard and Zalkind Hourwitz learned that the National Assembly had voted in favor of granting citizenship to the Sephardim in France, they realized that obtaining citizenship for the Ashkenazim would be a piecemeal process.[2,6]

In response to Jacques Godard's speech, Abbé François-Valentin Mulot (1749–1804), President of the Paris Commune, told the Jews in attendance at the General Assembly of the Paris Commune, "The distance of your religious opinions from the truths that we profess as Christians cannot prevent us, as men, from bringing ourselves nearer to you, and if mutually we believe each other to be in error,…we are nevertheless able to love one another."[6]

On January 30, 1790, Abbé A. R. C. Bertolio[7], a member of the Paris Commune, "demanded equality for the Jews because freedom of conscience demanded it, because to think differently from others neither injured nor harmed them, and because, finally, only in questions of morality could religion interest the government." He continued,

The morals of the Jews were "irreproachable." What essential difference is there between the Jews of Paris and the rest of the [French Kingdom] and their [Sephardi] brothers of Bordeaux? Is it that the one has letters patent [the Sephardim] and the other [the Ashkenazim] has not? The letters patent of the French Jews are in Nature; and the seal of nature is worth more than the seal of all the chancelleries of Europe.

The Paris Commune adopted the opinion of Abbé A. R. C. Bertolio.[6] He then proposed that the Paris Commune postpone issuing its formal support of the Jews' quest for citizenship until after it conducted a survey of the opinions of the sixty districts of Paris. The Paris Commune leadership agreed and set the project in motion.

On February 5, 1790, City of Strasbourg voters elected Royal Praetor Frederic Dietrich as Strasbourg Mayor as part of the implementation of the new Law of Municipalities, described above.[8] On February 7, 1790, the Strasbourg Society of the Friends of the Constitution (i.e., Strasbourg's Jacobin Club, founded January 15, 1790) voted to accept Jewish members and to censure yet another anti-Jewish pamphlet circulating in Alsace.[9]

On February 5, 1790, the National Assembly voted to increase the number of clergy deputies in the Ecclesiastical Committee, which had been working on framing a nationalized French version of the Catholic Church since August 20, 1789.

National Assembly Dissolves All Religious Corporations in France, 1790

On February 13, 1790, the National Assembly voted to dissolve all religious corporations in France. The National Assembly directed the law primarily against Christian monastic orders. However, the law also outlawed the Council of the Alsatian Jewish Communities (Nation Juive), which the National Assembly viewed as a religious corporation. Ruth F. Necheles noted:

[The decree of February 13, 1790] raised questions about the judicial and taxing powers of the [Ashkenazi] northeastern communities, thereby striking at the roots of the corporations' strength. *The Syndics, or heads, no longer had the authority to speak for Ashkenazi interests* [emphasis added]. Because the northeastern Jews had no voice in the selection of local officials, the February law placed them completely at the mercy of locally elected officials who were probably [anti-Jewish].[10]

On February 20, 1790, the Strasbourg Society of the Friends of the Constitution accepted Max Berr as its first Jewish member. The Society then voted to publish Max Berr's speech about, and the Society's statement censuring, the anti-Jewish pamphlet circulating wildly in Alsace. In addition, the Strasbourg Society of the Friends of the Constitution voted to nominate a special commission of five members to study the problems of Alsatian Jewry.[10]

On February 27, 1790, the Strasbourg Society of the Friends of the Constitution reported that it favored granting citizenship to the Ashkenazim and sent this information to the Paris Chapter of the Society of the Friends of the Constitution. Zosa Szajkowski wrote:

The [Strasbourg] report stated that the rich landowners and the officials were against emancipation of the Jews because they were afraid of losing a source of income; the priests circulated [information] that the Jews would buy the nationalized properties and enslave the peasants; and many Christian artisans were afraid of Jewish competition. But the report declared that the Jews would become an economically useful element. "How many villages do not have any shoemaker? Should a Jew take up this trade, he would sell shoes much cheaper to the peasants than the Christian shoemakers of the cities…If we made peasants and handicraftsmen of the Jews, they would expand the industry and commerce of our province." The same meeting of the Society voted that a request be made to the City to discontinue the blowing of the Shofar [Kraeuselhorn or Grusselhorn, a type of horn], a tradition of pre-Revolutionary days, a sign to Jews not authorized to stay in Strasbourg, that they should leave the city."[9]

Moses Ginsburger noted that around this time, Max Berr and some of his friends made a clandestine trip to the heights of Strasbourg Cathedral to permanently disable the Shofar.[2]

In February 1790, Captain Weber of the Strasbourg National Guard accepted Max Berr as a soldier. Previously, no Jews had been permitted to join the Strasbourg National Guard. On February 20, 1790, Max Berr made a gesture of good will to the Strasbourg National Guard by presenting buckles and other silver articles donated by some of the Jews of Bischheim, Turckheim, Wintzenheim, and other communities. A committee of the Society of the Friends of the Constitution wrote a thank you note to Captain Weber for accepting Max Berr to serve in the Strasbourg National Guard.[9]

In February 1790, the Paris Commune reported the decisions of the sixty districts of Paris on whether to support citizenship for the Paris Jews.[7] Of the sixty Paris districts, fifty-nine approved. The citizens of the District of Mathurins disapproved, saying that the Jews were estranged from the body politic, were not really French, never mixed with other people, and were a nation with their own laws, constitution, and even their own king, "whom they still await." The Paris District of Mathurins sent a copy of its disapproval both to the National Assembly and the Paris Commune leaders in the Hôtel de Ville.[11]

Around February 24, 1790, Abbés Mulot and Bertolio and a deputation from the Paris Commune appeared before the National Assembly to voice their support for the emancipation of the Jews in Paris. Jacques Godard read the Adresse of the Paris Commune, which requested that the National Assembly decree citizenship.[12] However, the leaders of the Paris Commune failed to persuade the National Assembly, and even Jacques Godard grew silent.[10]

In February 1790, certain nobles, who had previously owned land in Alsace, sent a protest letter to the National Assembly. Recall that on November 2, 1789, the National Assembly had nationalized all land in France, including the seigneuries of noblemen in Alsace. The Alsatian nobles were unhappy about being dispossessed of their property, which in some cases their families had owned for centuries. The National Assembly referred the nobles' protest letter to the Feudal Committee of the National Assembly for review.

On March 29, 1790, Pope Pius VI (1775–1799) officially condemned the Declaration of the Rights of Man, which the National Assembly of France had proclaimed on August 27, 1789. The National Assembly ignored him. Pope Pius VI was a "weak, vain, [and] worldly" Pope whose greatest revelry was "raising obelisks, building fountains, and purchasing expensive art works," said papal historian Eamon Duffy.[13] "At the crisis of religion in France, he hesitated when decisive action was needed. Certain of his own divinely ordained leadership in the Church, he failed to rise to the challenge of leadership [and] allowed the situation to drift." The pontificate of Pope Pius VI was one of the most disastrous since the papal office began, stated Eamon Duffy.[13]

On April 7, 1790, the Strasbourg authorities voted to petition the National Assembly *against* granting citizenship to the Ashkenazim. On April 9, 1790, a new outbreak of anti-Jewish violence in Strasbourg prompted Ashkenazi Syndic Max Berr to seek the assistance of Mayor Frederic Dietrich to protect his beleaguered co-religionists.[14]

On April 13, 1790, National Assembly Deputy Joseph Schwendt learned that Deputy François Hell had prepared another pamphlet against the Ashkenazim. Cerf Berr obtained the pamphlet and threatened to broadcast the entire sorry story of François Hell's anti-Jewish criminal activities, which persuaded François Hell to cancel publication of his pamphlet. Deputy Joseph Schwendt himself opposed Jewish emancipation, but he also disliked François Hell.[15]

On April 20, 1790, Aaron Mayer convened the following Ashkenazi Syndics in a meeting in Mutzig: Simon Herz of Saverne, Abraham Gabriel Bloch and Mayer Szmul of Soultz, David Scholem of Soutzmatt, David Emanuel of Markolsheim, Abraham Lévy of Dambach, Michel

David of Epfig (who represented also Jacques Lévy of Markolsheim), and Samuel Seligmann Wittersheim and Samuel Loeb of Strasbourg. The purpose of the meeting was to collect taxes to cover expenses already incurred by the Council of the Alsatian Jewish Communities between April 18, 1788 and October 28, 1789.

During the meeting, the attendees re-elected Samuel Seligmann Wittersheim as General Syndic of Alsace. Among the proposed expenses were twenty-two hundred and fifty livres for administrative expenses of the Council; two hundred and sixteen livres, eleven sous, and three deniers for expenses to convene the next two meetings of the Council; an annuity of seven hundred livres, sixteen sous, and six deniers to be paid to the Council's former leader, Aaron Mayer; three hundred livres 'Klaper-Geld'; three hundred livres to the rabbi in Mutzig; and one hundred livres to the rabbi of the episcopate. A much later statement of July 1, 1805, signed by the treasurer, indicated that the group collected no taxes from the Ashkenazim of Alsace between 1788 and 1805.[16]

Meanwhile, various pro-Jewish politicians in the National Assembly continued to raise the question of Ashkenazi citizenship. Each time, the machinations of Deputy Abbé Maury and the threats of Deputy Jean-François Reubell caused referral of the question to the Constitutional Committee for further study.

During April 1790, forty-five-year-old Berr Isaac Berr argued for the traditional Ashkenazi Talmudic corporate model in spite of the new French law of February 13, 1790, which dissolved all religious corporations in France. Berr Isaac Berr's twenty-one-year-old nephew, Dr. Jacob Goudchaux Berr Orchel (1769–1840), a Jewish physician in Nancy, denounced as an "abuse of power" his uncle's offer of a separate regime and the union of civil and religious authority.[15] Zosa Szajkowski explained:

> In a pamphlet [Dr. Jacob Berr] maintained that Berr Isaac Berr wished to keep the Jews in a state of estrangement from non-Jews and to perpetuate their isolation. Jacob Berr held the "despotic

regime" of the Jewish community responsible for many evils and criticized Berr Isaac Berr for his "dangerous" request that the autonomous Jewish communities be maintained.[15]

On April 16, 1790, the National Assembly, on behalf of King Louis XVI, again decreed that the Ashkenazim in Alsace were under the protection of the law as follows:

* * * * * * * * *

Proclamation of the King. Paris. April 16, 1790

Given the decree, whose tenor follows,

Decree of the National Assembly, of April 16, 1790

The National Assembly again places the Jews in Alsace and the other provinces of the Kingdom under the safeguard of the law. It prohibits all persons from attacking their safety; orders municipalities and the National Guard to protect their persons and property with all their power.

The King sanctioned and sanctions said edict and consequently orders the municipalities and National Guard to conform to it and to have it executed and observed.

Executed in Paris, April 18, 1790 and the sixteenth year of our reign.

Signed,

LOUIS [17]

* * * * * * * * *

On May 20, 1790, the Society of the Friends of the Constitution of Epinal (a town in the Vosges) published a pamphlet that railed against the practice of dividing the État-civil according to the religion professed by the person being entered into the Registry. This practice, the Society argued, only helped the old despotic regime separate and isolate Catholic, Protestant, and Jewish groups. Zosa Szajkowski continued:

> "Is it not true—the pamphlet demanded—that all Frenchmen are born and are Citizens before being Christians [Catholics], before being Protestants, before being Jews? Only through the abolition of the distinctions of acts which establish the right of citizenship, by introducing a uniform État-civil, real liberty and equality could prevail." It took over three years before the Revolution deprived the Catholic Clergy of control over France's État-civil.[18]

Civil Constitution of the Clergy Ratified, July 12, 1790

On July 12, 1790, King Louis XVI presided over the National Assembly's ratification of the Civil Constitution of the Clergy. The Ecclesiastical Committee had been working on the Civil Constitution of the Clergy since August 20, 1789. The Civil Constitution of the Clergy framed the new nationalized Gallican (French) Church as the moral bulwark of the new republican order.

On July 14, 1790, France celebrated the Feast of the Confederation (Fête de la Confédération) to commemorate capture of the Bastille Fortress the previous year. The crowds cheered King Louis XVI during the festival.

On July 20, 1790, the National Assembly voted to abolish the odious Brancas tax paid annually by the Ashkenazim of Metz to the Brancas noble family. What was the Brancas tax? In 221 AD, Jews first settled in Metz.[19] The City of Metz passed under French dominion in 1552.

On December 31, 1715, Louis of Brancas, Duke of Villars (henceforth, Louis Brancas) solicited and obtained from French Regent Philippe II, Duke of Orléans (1674–1723, ruled as Regent 1715–1723 for young King Louis XV), the right to levy forty livres from every Jewish family in Metz and its region per year for thirty years (1715–1745). Louis Brancas and the Regent for Louis XV shared a mistress named Countess Marie-Louise-Charlotte of Pelard of Givry (died 1730), who helped arrange the payment scheme.[19] She was married to an officer from the Fontaine House. The purpose of this tax on the Jews was allegedly for their "residency, protection, and toleration." The true reason for this tax was to provide income to support Louis Brancas.

The Brancas tax did not end as planned in 1745. Instead, the tax on the Metz Ashkenazim continued and grew over time. In 1790, the Brancas House levied twenty thousand francs on the Jews of Metz. Between 1715 and 1790, the Jews of Metz paid one million five hundred thousand livres to the Brancas House. "The establishment of the levy in question was one of the most absolute acts of despotism, and the suppression of it is pronounced by all the decrees of the National Assembly sanctioned by [King Louis XVI]," declared Louis Wolff. Recall that Louis Wolff was the Ashkenazi deputy from Metz who was part of Cerf Berr's group in Paris. Louis Wolff continued:

> If one were to ask what advantages the Jews obtained for so onerous a levy, what they have obtained for the sum of one million five hundred thousand livres that they have till now paid to the Houses of Fontaine and Brancas, we would answer that they have obtained and paid for the ability to breathe the air of the country in which they were born, since they do not have the freedom of owning land, or of engaging in commerce, or exercising the arts, none of which prevents them from being forced to pay a surcharge.
>
> Though they don't form an eighteenth of the population of the City of Metz they pay a sixth of the city's capitation, [around eighty-three hundred] livres, plus [around seventy-

seven hundred] livres for the right to work, [around thirty-four hundred] livres for their miserable housing, [around thirteen hundred] for mandatory labor, four hundred and fifty livres for the general hospital, where they are never admitted, two hundred livres for the vicar of the parish, five hundred livres for the housing of soldiers, two hundred livres to the court bailiffs, and finally, in all passive operations they are considered and act as citizens. For the past while, they have contributed three hundred louis to the loan for the acquisition of grains. Finally, the municipal officers of Metz demand of them the declaration of a quarter of their revenues. They would have met this demand if they hadn't hoped to obtain from one day to the next a definitive decision concerning their status. The principles of equality that the National Assembly established would be violated if the Jews, paying a quarter of their revenues, remained subject to specific levies.[19]

What did the Brancas House say in response to the demand of the Jews of Metz to end the Brancas tax? The Brancas House said:

The Jews of Metz should be considered foreigners and the levy as a tax on foreigners. It is as foreigners that they have, from reign to reign, received letters of confirmation. The sovereigns are master of according entry and residence to foreigners and placing on these favors the conditions they please. The concession made to the House of Brancas of a levy of twenty thousand livres had as object the rewarding for services rendered the state by that house.[19]

When a committee of the National Assembly presented a report urging the abolition of the Brancas tax as well as all other taxes on Jews for "the right to live, protection and tolerance" anywhere else in France, all deputies except for one accepted the recommendation of the report. Only Deputy Jean-François Reubell of Alsace voted against the abolition of the Brancas tax. Before the decree could be read into the record, Deputy Reubell asked the following question: "If the Jews were no longer going to pay this special tax, what tax would they pay? They would pay the same taxes as other citizens, came the answer from Deputy DuPont. The speaker had fallen into Reubell's lawyerly trap. The Jews are not citizens, so why should they pay? If you let them pay the same tax as everyone else, aren't you de facto giving them citizenship?"[19] Nevertheless, the National Assembly read the decree into the record, thus formerly abolishing the protection and residence taxes imposed on Jews, including the Brancas tax, although local authorities of the three provinces in Northeastern France variably applied the new law.

On October 28, 1790, the National Assembly's Feudal Committee, which had received a protest letter in February 1790 from nobles who had lost their inherited land in Alsace as described above, finally reported their findings and recommendations before the National Assembly. Recall that on August 4–5, 1789, the National Assembly had voted to abolish feudalism (including all fiefdoms) to quell the peasant revolt called the Great Fear. Ennobled landowners in Alsace protested that the National Assembly could not abolish unilaterally what was their land by treaty.

However, the Feudal Committee, under the influence of Deputy Philippe-Antoine Merlin of Douai (1754–1838), asserted to the National Assembly, "The unity of France and Alsace rested on the unanimous decision of the Alsatians; that ancient treaties and the stipulations of their former rulers [the dynasts of the Holy Roman Empire] could no longer bind a free people." Deputy Honoré Mirabeau saw that "such a declaration could only mean war; and accordingly he persuaded the [National] Assembly to pass a resolution to uphold the sovereignty of France in Alsace, but at the same time to ask [King Louis XVI] to arrange a sufficient indemnity [to] be paid to the Princes of the [Holy Roman] Empire in compensation for their losses."

Unfortunately, this resolution "only postponed the question, for the majority of the Princes refused to accept any monetary compensation for their lost fiefs and took their cases to the Imperial Diet of the

Holy Roman Empire."[20] Among the unhappy princes was Christian of Hesse-Darmstadt (1763–1830), who removed his archives from his birth place in Bouxwiller, Alsace and, along with other nobles, prepared to emigrate. Christian of Hesse-Darmstadt eventually became a lieutenant general who fought *against* France from 1793 to 1794 in the Army of William V, Prince of Orange-Nassau. Another prince, Cardinal of Rohan (1734–1803), pulled up his considerable stakes in Strasbourg and crossed the Rhine River to live in Ettenheim.[21]

On October 28, 1790, David D. Silveyra, a Parisian Ashkenazim, obtained a document from the National Assembly stating that all Jews who had obtained letters patent prior to the French Revolution could now benefit from the law of January 28, 1790. Recall that this law granted citizenship to the Sephardi Jews, as noted above. David D. Silveyra sent a copy of this document to Cerf Berr, who forwarded it to Mayor Frederic Dietrich, "who was among his friends." Mayor Dietrich asked Cerf Berr to send an official copy of the document to his office. "It seems that Cerf Berr wanted to use this statement in his controversy with the city about the right of residence for himself and his family." However, Mayor Dietrich, like his father, Jean Dietrich (who blocked Cerf Berr from gravel mining on the Reid River, as noted above), did not help Cerf Berr, said Zosa Szajkowski.[22]

On November 27, 1790, four months after ratification of the Civil Constitution of the Clergy, the National Assembly ordered all clergy to take an oath to uphold the new Constitution. This order lacked the signature of King Louis XVI, who refused to force clergy to take this oath. On December 27, 1790, Deputy Abbé Henri Grégoire became the first priest to take the oath; only sixty-two other priests in the National Assembly followed his example. This poor showing did not bode well for ecclesiastical support of the Civil Constitution of the Clergy in France.

In November/December 1790, conservative anti-Jewish Catholics, who despised Deputy Abbé Henri Grégoire for leading the church nationalization movement in France, used his unashamed philo-Judaism as a way to combat the ecclesiastical reforms he ardently supported. Ruth F. Necheles explained:

> Conservative opposition to Church reform was a serious threat to [Deputy Abbè Henri] Grégoire's plans. He was certain that unless the Church was purified, it would continue to lose its members and would fail to attract [Jewish] converts. Much as he wanted to assist the Jews, therefore, he could not risk identification with their cause as long as conservative Catholics employed northeastern [anti-Jewish] prejudices to provoke opposition to the entire Revolution, including its program of church reform.
>
> During the period when the ecclesiastical reforms embodied in the Civil Constitution of the Clergy were in the process of development and then while they were being inaugurated, northeastern clerics tried to discredit the changes by identifying them with philo-[Judaism]. Taking Grégoire as their symbol, they...nicknamed [his] diocese...a "little synagogue." Grégoire could not combat such deep-seated prejudices singlehandedly, and, preferring to save the new Church, he temporarily cut his public ties with the Jews.[23]

In December 1790, the selloff of ecclesiastical properties in France began, creating a rush of offers, which caused selling prices to run about a third above the estimations. "The effects of this vast auction on the national life and on the course of the Revolution were incalculable. Inventories, sales, hagglings, demolitions, officials, clubs, and committees installed in ecclesiastical premises—all added a faint, sacrilegious perversity to ordinary existence." The bourgeoisie and richer peasants bought most of the property.[24]

Sometime in 1790 (or possibly earlier), Théodore Berr, Cerf Berr's twenty-four-year-old son, married twenty-four-year-old Jeannette Jendel Yentelé Marx (1766–1829). During the next two years, they had Alphonse Abraham Cerfberr (1791–1859) and Max Cerfberr (1792–

1874). Of Cerf Berr's children by his late wife Jüdel, only Jeanette Berr and Lippman Berr remained unmarried in 1790.

On January 18, 1791, Deputy Abbè Henri Grégoire's first day as President of the National Assembly, he permitted a member of the Ecclesiastical Committee to speak about Ashkenazi issues even though the Ecclesiastical Committee had no jurisdiction over citizenship matters. The speaker proposed enfranchising Jews, regardless of origin and residence, who had received letters patent of naturalization before May 1789. This date qualified Cerf Berr of Médelsheim to become a citizen of France. This motion would have made citizenship dependent upon a legal, rather than on a hereditary distinction, but it would have included few Ashkenazim.[21] President Abbè Henri Grégoire remained silent as the anti-Jewish Deputy Charles Broglie of Alsace lambasted him for admitting such a motion. President Abbè Henri Grégoire referred the motion and abstained from all debates on the Jewish question for the remainder of the existence of the National Assembly.[23]

On April 2, 1791, Deputy Honoré Mirabeau died of natural causes. He had been a dear friend and strong supporter of the Jews of France.

In April 1791, Aaron Mayer, treasurer of the Council of the Alsatian Jewish Communities (Nation Juive) completed payment of around twenty-six thousand livres to the Council's eight Christian creditors. Recall that he had started to repay the Council's debt in November 1789. Most of the money repaid to the Christian lenders was interest on the debts owed by the Nation Juive of Alsace. The names of the eight Christians and the amount that each one loaned the Council of the Alsatian Jewish Communities were Tecomp (loaned twenty thousand livres), Chubel (ten thousand livres), Zollicoffer (ten thousand livres), Chapui (six thousand livres), Dartin (thirty thousand livres), Fried (twelve thousand livres), Striebeck (eighteen thousand livres), and De Salomon (six thousand livres).[25]

King Louis XVI Attempts Escape from France, 1791

On the night of June 20/21, 1791, King Louis XVI and his family attempted to escape from France. However, local revolutionary authorities apprehended them in the Village of Varennes (France) and escorted them back to the Tuileries Palace "amid glacial silence." The escape attempt fanned conspiracy theories of an imminent Austrian invasion, which gripped the hearts of the French people.[26]

On June 24, 1791, members of the Cordeliers Club, which met in the nationalized monastery of the Franciscan Cordeliers, presented a petition to the National Assembly calling for the deposition (removal from authority) of King Louis XVI for trying to escape his Kingdom. While the club members presented their petition, a menacing crowd of about thirty thousand people swarmed outside the Salle du Manège behind the Tuileries Palace. In 1790, Jacobins had founded the Cordeliers Club to prevent the abuse of power and "infractions of the rights of man." The National Assembly pondered the petition.

On July 5, 1791, Holy Roman Emperor Leopold II (1747–1792) issued the Padua Circular, which proposed a coalition of French émigré nobles with the armies of Austria, Prussia, Britain, Spain, and Russia to oppose the French revolutionaries. The Padua Circular set forth the principles for which this alliance would fight—most notably, the restoration of King Louis XVI to his full pre-1789 powers.[27] The various European monarchs pondered the circular.

Massacre at Champ de Mars, July 1791

On July 8, 1791, around fifty thousand people staged a mass demonstration on the Champ de Mars in Paris to urge the removal of King Louis XVI. The members of the National Assembly watched the mass demonstration with horror. Most of them were still unnerved by King Louis XVI's attempted escape seven weeks earlier (June 20/21,

1791). Now they feared that the mob would soon rule France, and the crowned heads of Europe would descend on France.

On July 17, 1791, the National Assembly issued a decree that King Louis XVI would remain monarch under a constitutional monarchy. Jacobin leaders rallied against this decree. The National Assembly then declared martial law in Paris and dispatched the Paris National Guard under the command of Lafayette to disperse the crowd on the Champ de Mars. On July 17, 1791, a volley of gunshots ensued, killing between twelve and fifty demonstrators.[28] The Paris masses had forced the National Assembly to resort to force! Monarchs outside of France erroneously believed that the National Assembly was finally coming to its senses by cracking down on Parisian insurrectionists.

On July 25, 1791, around three weeks after issuing the Padua Circular, Prussia and Austria signed a convention that settled outstanding disputes, pledged cooperation over suppressing the Revolution in France, and paved the way for a formal alliance. On August 27, 1791, Emperor Leopold II and Frederick William II (the Great, 1744–1797, ruled 1786–1797, King of Prussia) met in the Pillnitz Castle in Saxony where they jointly issued the Declaration of Pillnitz, which called on European powers to intervene militarily in the politics of France if the people of France harmed King Louis XVI. The Declaration of Pillnitz specifically called on the crowned heads of Europe "to restore to the King of France complete liberty and to consolidate the bases of monarchical government in accordance with the rights of sovereigns and the welfare of the French nation."

The Prussian and Austrian authors of the Declaration of Pillnitz wholeheartedly believed that the National Assembly in France was moving back to the political center because of foreign intimidation and the crackdown on the mass demonstration on the Champ de Mars on July 8, 1791.

The French émigré nobles were elated over the Declaration of Pillnitz. They redoubled their military preparation to invade France. Meanwhile, the antics of the émigrés and the Declaration of Pillnitz only fed the paranoia of the French revolutionaries and the masses that an international conspiracy directed against the French Revolution would end in the invasion of France. "Nothing could have been further from the truth," said historian T. C. W. Blanning.[28]

French Constitution of 1791 Proclaims Constitutional Monarchy

On September 3, 1791, the National Assembly proclaimed the French Constitution of 1791, which created a constitutional monarchy.[28] The French Constitution of 1791 was not signed by any Founding Fathers, as in the United States of America. Rather, it was proclaimed by the anonymous National Assembly. In addition, the anonymous authors of the French Constitution of 1791 wrote it entirely from the third person point of view.

The French Constitution of 1791 created a unicameral Legislative Assembly and an Executive Branch consisting of the King and his ministers. King Louis XVI was now a constitutional monarch. He supposedly retained the power of the veto over laws promulgated by the Legislative Assembly and of the decision to declare war and make peace. The Judicial Branch of the French Government was separate from the Legislative and Executive Branches. The French Constitution's first guarantee was, "All citizens are admissible to offices and employments, without any distinction other than virtue and talents."[19]

The Declaration of the Rights of Man, ratified on August 26, 1789, became the Preamble to the French Constitution of 1791. The Constitution abolished the feudal geographic divisions of the past and divided France into départements (henceforth, departments). Alsace was divided into two departments—Bas-Rhin and Haut-Rhin. Active citizenship meant a citizen possessed the right to participate in the selection of electors, who chose representatives to the Legislative Assembly. The French Constitution of 1791 required that electors were property owners, as described in chapter 1, section 2, and number 7 of the French Constitution of 1791, reproduced below.

* * * * * * * * *

French Constitution of 1791
Chapter 1, Section 2, Number 7

No one may be chosen as an elector if, in addition to the qualifications necessary for active citizenship, he does not fulfill the following requirements:

In cities of more than six thousand inhabitants, that of being proprietor or usufructuary of a property assessed on the tax rolls at a revenue equal to the local value of two hundred days' labor, or of being tenant of a dwelling assessed on said same rolls at a revenue equal to the value of one hundred and fifty days' labor;

In cities of fewer than six thousand inhabitants, that of being proprietor or usufructuary of a property assessed on the tax rolls at a revenue equal to the local value of one hundred and fifty days' labor, or of being tenant of a dwelling assessed on said same rolls at a revenue equal to the value of one hundred days' labor;

And in rural districts, that of being proprietor or usufructuary of a property assessed on the tax rolls at a revenue equal to the local value of one hundred and fifty days' labor, or of being farmer or *métayer* of properties assessed on said same rolls at the value of four hundred days' labor.

With regard to those who are at the same time proprietors or usufructuaries on the one hand, and tenants, farmers, or *métayers* on the other, their revenues from such divers titles shall be cumulated up to the rate necessary to establish their eligibility.[29]

* * * * * * * * *

317

On September 3, 1791, the National Assembly, despite strong opposition from the Jacobins, established the King's Constitutional Guard for the protection of King Louis XVI and his family. The National Assembly was especially concerned for the safety of the Royal Family after its failed escape, which had aroused deep hatred among the populace. The King's Constitutional Guard was composed of six divisions of infantry (two hundred men per division) and three divisions of cavalry (two hundred men per division), or a total eighteen hundred guards. Louis Hercule Timolon of Cossé, Duke of Brissac (1734–1792), commanded the King's Constitutional Guard.

On September 14, 1791, the National Assembly presented the French Constitution of 1791 to thirty-seven-year-old King Louis XVI for his review and signature. On September 25, 1791, King Louis XVI reluctantly agreed to the French Constitution. King Louis XVI knew that his acceptance of the Constitution would upset the French émigrés, who he still considered as his subjects. He wrote the following letter to the French émigrés:

* * * * * * * *

King Louis XVI Accepts the Constitution of 1791 (September 14–25, 1791)

You have no doubt been informed that I have accepted the Constitution and you are aware of the reasons that I gave to the Assembly. These reasons will not be sufficient for you, so I shall give you all of them.

The condition of France is such that it may end up in total disintegration, and this result will come even more quickly if violent solutions are applied to all the overwhelming ills. The cause of all our problems is the partisanship that divides and destroys governmental authority. There are, however, only two ways to accomplish this: force or reconciliation…Force can only be used by foreign armies and this means resorting to war…I know we flatter ourselves into thinking we control immense forces, and that war will be prevented by the fact that resistance would be seen as futile…But the leaders of the Revolution, they who are able to sway the people, believe they have too much at risk to ever show discretion. They could never be persuaded that they could be forgiven or pardoned for their crimes…They will use the National Guards and other armed citizens…and they will begin by massacring aristocrats…The émigrés want nothing but revenge, and if they cannot make use of foreign arms, they will enter France alone, and will exact that revenge, even if they are all sure to die. War will thus be inevitable, because it is in the interest of those in authority. It will be horrible because it will be motivated by violence and despair. Can a king contemplate all these misfortunes with equanimity and bring them down upon his people?…

I know that my émigré subjects pride themselves on the fact that there has been a great change in people's attitudes. I myself believed for a long time that this change was brewing, but now I see that it was not…

One can never govern a people against its will. This maxim is as true in Constantinople as it is in a republic. Right now, the will of this nation is for the Rights of Man, senseless though they be…

I have carefully weighed the matter and concluded that war presents no other advantages but horrors and more discord. I also believe then that this idea should be put aside and that I should try once again by using the sole means remaining to me, that of joining my will to the principles of the Constitution. I realize how difficult it will be to govern a large nation this way, I will even say that I believe it to be impossible. But the obstacles that I would have put in the way [by refusing to accept the Constitution] would have brought about the war I sought to avoid, and would have prevented the people from properly assessing the Constitution because my constant opposition would have blinded them. By adopting the principles of the Constitution, and executing them in good faith, the people will come to learn the true cause of their misfortunes. Public opinion will change, since without it [my acceptance of the Constitution], only new convulsions could be expected…and I prefer to proceed towards a better order than that which would result from my refusal.[30]

* * * * * * * * *

On September 25, 1791, Strasbourg Mayor Frederic Dietrich demonstrated unity with the National Assembly in Paris by holding a festival in Strasbourg Cathedral to celebrate King Louis XVI's acceptance of the French Constitution of 1791. The festival attracted the attention of French émigrés lingering outside the boundaries of Northeastern France. Mayor Dietrich's name was on the lips of all the sincere friends of the French Constitution who relied on him to form a core of resistance in Northeastern France against the anarchists from elsewhere in Europe who were moving towards France.[31]

In the waning days of September 1791, the National Assembly in Paris prepared to adjourn so that the new Legislative Assembly established by the French Constitution of 1791 could begin its work. "The Legislative Assembly was an entirely new body, for its predecessor [National Assembly] had passed a self-denying ordinance excluding any of its number from continuing in office. As a result, the new deputies were younger, included far fewer members of the privileged orders [nobility and clergy] and were appreciably more radical, in most cases receiving their political education during the previous two years as members of the new local administrations."[32]

Ashkenazim Receive French Citizenship Rights, September 1791

On Thursday, September 27, 1791, as the National Assembly was preparing to adjourn as a body, Deputy Adrien Duport stood up to speak about the subject of citizenship for the Ashkenazim in France, whose fate, he said, was too important an issue to leave unresolved. His brief speech is below.

* * * * * * * * *

Deputy Adrien Duport's Speech on the Jews
before the National Assembly,
September 27, 1791, Paris

I have one very short observation to make to the [National] Assembly, which appears to be of the highest importance and which demands all its attention. You have regulated by the Constitution [of 1791], Sirs, the qualities deemed necessary to become a French citizen, and an active citizen: that sufficed, I believe, to regulate all the incidental questions that could have been raised in the Assembly relative to certain professions, to certain persons. But there is a decree of adjournment that seems to strike a blow at these general rights: I speak of the Jews. To decide the question that concerns them, it suffices to lift the decree of adjournment that you have rendered and which seems to suspend the question in their regard. Thus, if you had not rendered a decree of adjournment on the question of the Jews, it would not have been necessary to do anything; for, having declared by your Constitution how all peoples of the earth could become French citizens and how all French citizens could become active citizens, there would have been no difficulty on this subject.

I ask therefore that the decree of adjournment be revoked

and that it be declared relative to the Jews that they will be able to become active citizens, like all the peoples of the world, by fulfilling the conditions prescribed by the Constitution. I believe that freedom of worship no longer permits any distinction to be made between the political rights of citizens on the basis of their beliefs and I believe equally that the Jews cannot be the only exceptions to the enjoyment of these rights, when pagans, Turks, Muslims, Chinese even, men of all the sects, in short, are admitted to these rights.[33]

* * * * * * * * *

Adversaries of the Jews in the National Assembly were livid. Deputy Reubell "tried to intervene to demand a full debate. [However, a] supporter of [Deputy Adrien] Duport, [Deputy] Michel of Saint-Jean-d'Angely, asked the chair to call Reubell and anyone else to order who spoke against the motion, 'since to speak against it is to speak against the constitution itself.'"[19] Deputy Adrien Duport's motion to grant citizenship to all Jews in France (i.e., the Ashkenazim, since the Sephardim had already received citizenship) passed by a wide margin.

However, on September 28, 1791, anti-Jewish deputies of the National Assembly tried to amend the law to halt citizenship for the Ashkenazim. "As part of the Assembly's usual opening business, a vote to approve of the minutes of the previous session, including the endorsement of Duport's motion, was brought to the floor." Michael Goldfarb continued:

The Prince of Broglie [Charles] demanded the right to speak. Before the minutes were endorsed he insisted on an amendment to the decree moved by [Deputy Adrien] Duport. All citizens had to take an oath of loyalty, and therefore the law should state, said Broglie, that when a Jew takes the oath it should be considered a formal renunciation of his adherence to Jewish communal law.[19,34]

322

The National Assembly approved the amendment. Then Deputy Reubell demanded another amendment, i.e., "The Jews in Alsace submit within one month a list of all debts owed them by Christian creditors." Furthermore, "the Alsatian authorities were requested to study the debtors' abilities to repay the debts." Deputy Reubell was seeking to link emancipation of the Jews to the condition that they liquidate the debts on terms favorable to Christian debtors but ruinous to the Jews themselves. The National Assembly voted in favor of this amendment. However, the Ashkenazim in Alsace refused to submit the list and the demand by Deputy Reubell was never put into effect.[35]

Finally, the National Assembly voted to approve the minutes and to decree that *all* Jews of France now had the right of active citizenship, if they, like all other French citizens, fulfilled the requirements for active citizenship and if they took the oath of citizenship, which now automatically meant that they renounced all previous privileges and exceptions of Jews. Deputy Adrien Duport's wording of the decree that he submitted to the National Assembly for vote on September 27, 1791 read:

> The National Assembly, considering that the conditions necessary to be a French citizen and to become an active citizen are fixed by the Constitution, and that every man meeting the said conditions, who swears the civic oath, and engages himself to fulfill all the duties that the Constitution imposes, has the right to all of the advantages that the Constitution assures; revokes all adjournments, reservations, and exceptions inserted into the preceding decrees relative to Jewish individuals who will swear the civic oath which will be regarded as a renunciation of all the privileges and exceptions introduced previously in their favor.[29]

Berr Isaac Berr of Nancy, upon hearing the news of citizenship and civil rights for all Jews in France, "executed a partial volte-face and at once dispatched a letter of congratulation to his co-religionists, to rouse enthusiasm for their newly-attained freedom, and at the same time incline them to appropriate improvements." He wrote:

> At length the day has arrived on which the veil is torn asunder which covered us with humiliation! We have at last again obtained the rights of which we have been deprived for eighteen centuries. How deeply at this moment should we recognize the wonderful grace of the God of our forefathers! On the 27th of September [1791] we were the only inhabitants of this great realm who seemed doomed to eternal humiliation and slavery, and on the very next day, a memorable day which we shall always commemorate, didst Thou inspire these immortal legislators of France to utter one word which caused sixty thousand unhappy beings, who had hitherto lamented their hard lot, to be suddenly plunged into the intoxicating joys of the purest delight.
>
> God chose the noble French nation to reinstate us in our due privileges, and bring us to a new birth, just as in former days. He selected Antiochus and Pompey to degrade and oppress us...This nation asks no thanks, except that we show ourselves worthy citizens.[36]

Lionel Kochan described the emancipation of the Ashkenazim and Berr Isaac Berr's reaction as follows:

> Not with a bang the struggle [for civil rights] ended, but with a whimper. Until the end, Ashkenazim fought to enforce a conception of citizenship that would be reconcilable with some degree of communal autonomy. They had to yield while leaving details in a sort of limbo. Only during the reaction under Napoleon and his successors did the Jews recover a form of acknowledged self-rule...Berr Isaac Berr...maintained, "[God] has chosen the generous nation and King Louis XVI to reintegrate us into our rights...the title of active citizen

that we have just obtained is without contradiction the most precious quality that a man can possess." This enthusiasm Berr Isaac Berr tempered with the acknowledgement that the Jews must change their manners and customs and acquire a perfect command of the French language, if they were to obtain the esteem of their fellow-countrymen. In respect of religion they must "abandon that esprit de corps and of community for all those civil and political aspects, which are not inherent in our spiritual laws; there we must absolutely be no more than individuals."[37]

The National Assembly decree of September 27, 1791 automatically settled, in Cerf Berr's favor, the herculean sixteen-year legal struggle in which he and the Strasbourg government had engaged over his right to live and own property in that city.

On September 30, 1791, the National Assembly dissolved itself to make way for the Legislative Assembly. From July 1, 1789 to October 1, 1791, the National Assembly had passed more than twenty-five hundred laws.[38]

Legislative Assembly Supersedes National Assembly, War Looms

On October 1, 1791, the seven hundred and forty-five newly-elected members of the Legislative Assembly expressed concerns about the French émigrés, who were threatening to invade Alsace and other French Provinces. Many deputies felt "shame that so many [French émigrés] should be in arms on the eastern frontier, breathing nothing but a desire to fight with and destroy their own countrymen," wrote historian Henry Morse Stephens.[38]

Nevertheless, the French émigré problem required the attention of the Legislative Assembly of the Kingdom of France. On October 20, 1791, the Legislative Assembly began a two-week debate on the émigrés. Deputy Pierre Victurnien Vergniaud (1753–1793) categorized the émigrés into three groups: simple citizens, whose property could be affected if their persons could not be seized; officers on whom the penalties for desertion could be invoked; and princes of the blood.

On November 9, 1791, the Legislative Assembly voted to require the return of all French émigrés to France no later than January 1, 1792. If the French émigrés failed to return to France by that date, the Legislative Assembly would declare them conspirators, condemn them to death, and confiscate their property. King Louis XVI vetoed the decree the same day. King Louis XVI's messenger attempted to provide the Legislative Assembly with the King's reasons for vetoing the act. However, Deputy Pierre Vergniaud, President of the Legislative Assembly, told the messenger that the deputies were obliged to hear that the King had vetoed the decree, but that they were not obliged to listen to his reasons.

On November 13, 1791, King Louis XVI confirmed the full equalization of all French Jews who took the oath to the French Constitution of 1791. The administration of the Bas-Rhin Department took six weeks to promulgate the new royal decree, because it feared the effects of the decree on the anti-Jewish population of Lower Alsace.

On November 29, 1791, the Legislative Assembly requested that King Louis XVI write to the German princes about their harboring of French émigrés. King Louis XVI consented and sent a letter to his brother-in-law, Holy Roman Emperor Leopold II.[39]

On November 29, 1791, the Legislative Assembly decreed the end of the period for Catholic, Protestant, and Jewish clergy to take the oath to the Civil Constitution of the Clergy. All non-juring priests, also known as orthodox or refractory priests, who remained in France were suspect and subject to immediate arrest. Most of the priests in Alsace refused to take the oath to the Civil Constitution of the Clergy. Many orthodox priests emigrated from Alsace, but others remained and went into hiding while continuing to clandestinely minister to faithful Roman Catholics in the province.

On December 14, 1791, King Louis XVI received a reply to his letter from Holy Roman Emperor Leopold II in which the latter declared that his duty was to protect *any* prince of the Holy Roman Empire who appealed to him. King Louis XVI told the Legislative Assembly that he agreed with the rationale provided by Holy Roman Emperor Leopold II.[39]

On December 27, 1791, the Legislative Assembly decreed that King Louis XVI should notify Holy Roman Emperor Leopold II that France would declare war if the French émigrés were not at once expelled from foreign states of the Holy Roman Empire.

On December 28, 1791, the administration of the Bas-Rhin Department issued a public notice, written in French and German, which announced the emancipation of the Ashkenazim in France. The decree officially enabled Jews to vote, run for public office, and serve in the Strasbourg National Guard.[40]

As the year 1791 closed, two groups of French émigré nobles were plotting to attack France. One group convened in Coblenz and the other in Worms. The Coblenz group, led by Count d'Artois (1757–1836, later ruled France as Charles X, 1824–1830), appealed for foreign help. Indeed, Count d'Artois, a younger brother of King Louis XVI, had been present with Holy Roman Emperor Leopold II and German King Frederick William II in Pillnitz on August 27, 1791 when the monarchs issued the Declaration of Pillnitz. The group of princes and nobility in Coblenz was noisy, decadent, selfish, and immersed in intrigue and therefore posed little threat to France as a military force.

However, the Worms group, led by the Prince of Condé, deeply valued the monarchy and the orthodox Catholic religion. Recall that in 1786, the Prince of Condé had hosted a party at Fontainebleau in honor of Finance Minister Calonne. The Prince of Condé was the only Bourbon Prince to possess military experience, which he had acquired during the Thirty Years' War. The Prince of Condé assembled approximately twenty-three thousand soldiers in Worms. He planned to invade the City of Strasbourg and use it as his headquarters in France. He also planned to call on Germany's help, if needed, to suppress the French Revolution.[41]

The Prince of Condé expected the officers garrisoned in Strasbourg, with whom he was communicating, to stage an uprising in Strasbourg sometime between December 28, 1791 and January 10, 1792. During that window of time, he planned to lead his soldiers from Worms to Strasbourg. However, the uprising never happened, because the Strasbourg military officers hesitated to commit themselves. The Legislative Assembly in Paris learned about the plot, which confirmed the deputies' worst suspicions about the activities and intentions of the French émigrés.[41]

In December 1791, the first three great France Armies formed as war with Austria and Prussia loomed. Generals Rochambeau and Lafayette, the veterans of the American Revolutionary War, commanded the French Army of the North and the French Army of the Center, respectively. General Nikolaus, Count of Luckner (1722–1794), commanded the French Army of the Rhine. If the Émigré Army of the Prince of Condé in Worms had succeeded in taking Strasbourg as it had planned to do, General Luckner would have been the general responsible for leading around fifteen thousand French soldiers to repel that advance.[42]

Meanwhile, in 1791, Cerf Berr's twenty-five-year-old daughter Jeanette married David Salomon, a banker in Hanover, Germany.[43] After the marriage of Jeanette, the only unmarried child of Cerf Berr and the late Jüdel Berr was Lippman Berr. He finally married in 1800 at age forty years. His bride was fifteen-year-old Sara Berr of Turique (1785–1847), the youngest daughter of the Lorraine Ashkenazi leader, Berr Isaac Berr.[44]

In summary, the Ashkenazim won their civil rights in France on September 27, 1791 for at least two reasons: the skillful and unrelenting leadership of Cerf Berr of Médelsheim and the courageous convictions of Deputies Grégoire, Clermont-Tonnerre, Mirabeau, and Duport. King Louis XVI tried to escape from France, which both disappointed and enraged his subjects. They placed him in the Tuileries Palace under guard and demanded that the National Assembly depose him. It did not, resulting in a massive demonstration on Champ de Mars. The fearful National Assembly used force to crush the demonstration. People died. The French Constitution of 1791 created a constitutional monarchy with a unicameral Legislative Assembly. King Louis XVI reluctantly approved the French Constitution of 1791. Meanwhile, Prussia and Austria threatened retaliation against France for its treatment of King Louis XVI and Queen Marie Antoinette. The Legislative Assembly began to form several French Armies to defend the nation against its adversaries.

Chapter Seven Notes:

1. Frances Malino: *A Jew in the French Revolution: the Life of Zalkind Hourwitz*. Oxford, England, United Kingdom: Blackwell Publisher, 1996, pp. 87–91; and *La Révolution française et l'émancipation des Juifs, Issues 4–5*. Éditions d'histoire sociale, 1789. Ann Arbor, Michigan: University of Michigan, digitalized August 27, 2008. Available at http://books.google.com/books?id=BbptAAAAMAAJ&pg=RA1-P A143&dq=P%C3%A9tition+des+Juifs+Etablis+en+France&source =gbs_selected_pages&cad=3#v=onepage&q=P%C3%A9tition%20 des%20Juifs%20Etablis%20en%20France&f=false; accessed January 29, 2012.

2. Michael Goldfarb: *Emancipation*. New York City, New York: Simon & Schuster, 2009, pp. 79–84.

3. Zosa Szajkowski: "Sephardim, Ashkenazim, and Avignonese Jews." In *Jews and the French Revolutions of 1789, 1830 and 1848*. New York City, New York: Ktav Publishing House, 1970, p. 261.

4. *La Révolution française et l'émancipation des Juifs, Issues 4-5*. Éditions d'histoire sociale, 1789. Ann Arbor, Michigan: University of Michigan, digitalized August 27, 2008. Available at http://books. google.com/books?id=BbptAAAAMAAJ&pg=RA1-PA143&dq=P% C3%A9tition+des+Juifs+Etablis+en+France&source=gbs_selected_p ages&cad=3#v=onepage&q=P%C3%A9tition%20des%20Juifs%20 Etablis%20en%20France&f=false; accessed January 29, 2012; and Zosa Szajkowski: "Bibliography of Books, Pamphlets, and Printed Documents, 1789–1800)." In *Jews and the French Revolutions of 1789, 1830 and 1848*. New York City, New York: Ktav Publishing House, 1970, p. 862.

5. Zosa Szajkowski: "Jewish autonomy debated and attacked during the French Revolution." In *Jews and the French Revolutions of 1789, 1830*

and 1848. New York City, New York: Ktav Publishing House, 1970, p. 579.

6. Frances Malino: *A Jew in the French Revolution: the Life of Zalkind Hourwitz*. Oxford, England, United Kingdom: Blackwell Publisher, 1996, pp. 91–94.

7. Isidore Singer and Israel Lévi: "Abbé Bertolio." *Jewish Encyclopedia*. 1906. Available at http://www.jewishencyclopedia.com/articles/3172-bertolio-abbe; accessed November 28, 2011.

8. Franklin L. Ford: *Strasbourg in Transition, 1648–1789*. New York City, New York: Norton, 1958, pp. 253–254.

9. Friedrich Karl Heitz (ed.): *Les Sociétés Politiques de Strasbourg pendant les Années 1790 à 1795*. Strasbourg, Alsace, France: Frederick-Charles Heitz, 1863, pp. 17–18; and Zosa Szajkowski: "The discussion and struggle over Jewish emancipation in Alsace in the early years of the French Revolution." In *Jews and the French Revolutions of 1789, 1830 and 1848*. New York City, New York: Ktav Publishing House, 1970, pp. 344–346.

10. Ruth F. Necheles: *The Abbé Grégoire, 1787–1831*. Westport, Connecticut: Greenwood Publishing, 1971, p. 31.

11. Frances Malino: *A Jew in the French Revolution: the Life of Zalkind Hourwitz*. Oxford, England, United Kingdom: Blackwell Publisher, 1996, pp. 95–97, 100.

12. Zosa Szajkowski: "Bibliography of Books, Pamphlets, and Printed Documents, 1789–1800)." In *Jews and the French Revolutions of 1789, 1830 and 1848*. New York City, New York: Ktav Publishing House, 1970, p. 872, #152.

13. Eamon Duffy: *Saints and Sinners: a History of the Popes*. New Haven, Connecticut: Yale University Press, 2002, pp. 203–204.

14. Zosa Szajkowski: "The discussion and struggle over Jewish emancipation in Alsace in the early years of the French Revolution." In *Jews and the French Revolutions of 1789, 1830 and 1848*. New York City, New York: Ktav Publishing House, 1970, pp. 336–340, 346–347.

15. Lionel Kochan: *The Making of Western Jewry, 1600–1819*. New York City, New York: Palgrave Macmillan, 2004, p. 258; and Zosa Szajkowski: "Jewish autonomy in France." In *Jews and the French*

Revolutions of 1789, 1830 and 1848. New York City, New York: Ktav Publishing House, 1970, pp. 578–580.

16. Zosa Szajkowski: "The Alsatian debts." In *Jews and the French Revolutions of 1789, 1830 and 1848*. New York City, New York: Ktav Publishing House, 1970, pp. 700–702.

17. Zosa Szajkowski: "The Jewish problem in Alsace, Metz, and Lorraine on the eve of the Revolution of 1789." In *Jews and the French Revolutions of 1789, 1830 and 1848*. New York City, New York: Ktav Publishing House, 1970, p. 339.

18. Zosa Szajkowski: "The reform of the état-civil of the French Jews during the Revolution of 1789." In *Jews and the French Revolutions of 1789, 1830 and 1848*. New York City, New York: Ktav Publishing House, 1970, pp. 359–360. The National Assembly decree of April 16, 1790 is available at http://www.marxists.org/history/france/revolution/1789/jews-proclamation.htm; accessed December 9, 2011.

19. "Metz." *Jewish Encyclopedia*, 1906. Available at http://www.jewishencyclopedia.com/articles/10743-metz; accessed February 12, 2012; Zosa Szajkowski: "The origin of the debts owed by the Jewish community of Metz." In *Jews and the French Revolutions of 1789, 1830 and 1848*. New York City, New York: Ktav Publishing House, 1970, p. 628; Louis Wolff: "Statement in support of the Jews of Metz concerning a levy of twenty thousand francs they annually pay the Duke of Brancas under the title of 'tax for residency, protection, and toleration.'" *Mémoire pour les Juifs de Metz*. Paris, France: Imprimerie P. de Lorimel, no date (probably around 1790). Available at http://www.marxists.org/history/france/revolution/1790/metz-jews.htm#n1; accessed February 12, 2012; and Michael Goldfarb: *Emancipation*. New York City, New York: Simon & Schuster, 2009, pp. 85–87.

20. T. C. W. Blanning: *The French Revolutionary Wars, 1787–1802*. London, England, United Kingdom: Arnold Publisher, 1996, p. 50; and *The Cambridge Modern History*. Volume 8: French Revolution. Cambridge, England, United Kingdom: Cambridge University Press, 1904, p. 398.

21. Louis Spach: *Histoire de la Basse Alsace de la Ville de Strasbourg*. Strasbourg, France: Berger-Levrault, 1858, pp. 289–290.

22. Zosa Szajkowski: "The discussion and struggle over Jewish emancipation in Alsace in the early years of the French Revolution."

In *Jews and the French Revolutions of 1789, 1830 and 1848.* New York City, New York: Ktav Publishing House, 1970, p. 348, Note #50.

23. Ruth F. Necheles: *The Abbé Grégoire, 1787–1831.* Westport, Connecticut: Greenwood Publishing, 1971, pp. 32–33.

24. John McManners: *The French Revolution and the Church.* Westport, Connecticut: Greenwood Press, 1982, p. 30.

25. Zosa Szajkowski: "The Alsatian Debts." In *Jews and the French Revolutions of 1789, 1830 and 1848.* New York City, New York: Ktav Publishing House, 1970, pp. 700–701.

26. John McManners: *The French Revolution and the Church.* Westport, Connecticut: Greenwood Press, 1982, p. 62.

27. The Padua Circular of July 5, 1791 is available at http://chnm.gmu.edu/revolution/d/420/; accessed January 28, 2012; and in John Hall Stewart: *A Documentary Survey of the French Revolution.* New York City, New York: Macmillan, 1951, pp. 221–223.

28. T. C. W. Blanning: *The French Revolutionary Wars, 1787–1802.* London, England, United Kingdom: Arnold Publisher, 1996, pp. 55–58.

29. The text of the French Constitution of 1791 is available at http://sourcebook.fsc.edu/history/constitutionof1791.html; accessed November 29, 2011.

30. Félix-Sébastien Feuillet de Conches (ed.): *King Louis XVI, Marie-Antoinette et Madame Élisabeth,* Volume 2. Paris, France: Plon, 1864, pp. 366–375. Available at http://chnm.gmu.edu/revolution/d/315/; accessed January 1, 2012.

31. Louis Spach: *Histoire de la Basse Alsace de la Ville de Strasbourg.* Strasbourg, France: Berger-Levrault, 1858, pp. 292–293.

32. T. C. W. Blanning: *The French Revolutionary Wars, 1787–1802.* London, United Kingdom: Arnold Publisher, 1996, pp. 59–63.

33. Micheline Ishay: *The Human Rights Reader: Major Political Essays, Speeches, and Documents from Ancient Times to the Present.* New York City, New York: Routledge, 2007, pp. 187–188. See also Frances Malino: *A Jew in the French Revolution: the Life of Zalkind Hourwitz.* Oxford, England, United Kingdom: Blackwell Publisher, 1996, pp. 112–113; and David Feuerwerker: *L'Émancipation des Juifs en France de l'Ancien Régime à la fin du Second Empire.* Paris, France: Editions Albin Michel, 1976, pp. 389–391.

34. David Feuerwerker: *L'Émancipation des Juifs en France de l'Ancien Régime à la fin du Second Empire*. Paris, France: Editions Albin Michel, 1976, pp. 389–391.

35. Zosa Szajkowski: "Introduction." In *Jews and the French Revolutions of 1789, 1830 and 1848*. New York City, New York: Ktav Publishing House, 1970, pp. xxxiv–xxvi; and "The decree of September 28, 1791," p. 875.

36. Heinrich Graetz: *History of the Jews*. Volume V. Philadelphia, Pennsylvania: Jewish Publication Society of America, 1895, pp. 448–449; and Lionel Kochan: *The Making of Western Jewry, 1600–1819*. New York City, New York: Palgrave Macmillan, 2004, pp. 263–265.

37. Lionel Kochan: *The Making of Western Jewry, 1600–1819*. New York City, New York: Palgrave Macmillan, 2004, pp. 263–265.

38. Moses Ginsburger: *Cerf-Berr et son Époque*. Société d'Histoire des Juifs d'Alsace-Lorraine. Guebwiller, Alsace, France: J. Dreyfus, 1908, p. 26. Available at http://gallica.bnf.fr/ark:/12148/bpt6k5427849p/f8.image; accessed November 30, 2011.

39. Henry Morse Stephens: *A History of the French Revolution*. Three volumes. New York City, New York: Charles Scribner's Sons, 1911, Volume 2, pp. 32–33.

40. Rodolphe Reuss: "Seligmann Alexandre." Available at http://judaisme. sdv.fr/histoire/villes/strasbrg/seligman/seligmanalex.htm; accessed December 22, 2011.

41. Henry Morse Stephens: *A History of the French Revolution*. Three volumes. New York City, New York: Charles Scribner's Sons, 1911, Volume 2, pp. 36–37.

42. Ibid, p. 555.

43. Zosa Szajkowski: "Jewish émigrés during the French Revolution." In *Jews and the French Revolutions of 1789, 1830 and 1848*. New York City, New York: Ktav Publishing House, 1970, p. 541.

44. Pierre-André Meyer: "Autour de Michel Wolff (Orchel) de Nancy, et de quelques autres…" *Revue du Cercle de Généalogie Juive*. Number 108, November-December 2011, p. 16.

CHAPTER EIGHT:
Cerf Berr's Waning Days, 1792–1793

In January 1792, pro-monarchy Strasbourg Mayor Frederic Dietrich grew increasingly disturbed over anti-monarchists in the Strasbourg Society of Friends of the Constitution Club. Mayor Dietrich applauded the establishment of a constitutional monarchy by the National Assembly and believed that anti-monarchists associated with the Strasbourg club were undermining the new government and seeking to destabilize the City of Strasbourg.

Recall that the Strasbourg Jacobin Club was "at first a stronghold of constitutional royalism, of which Dietrich…was one of the leading supporters. But from the beginning there was a disturbing element which kept pace with the eddying currents in Paris and ended up dominating the club," noted historian George Peabody Gooch. He continued:

> When [Johann Friedrich] Reichardt [1752–1814], the music composer, visited [Strasbourg] on his way to Paris in the spring of 1792, he found the citizens separating into camps. "On entering the gates I at once donned a tricolor cockade [symbol of the French Revolution and later the French Republic]. Thus constitutionally attired I hurried to the club, of which two meetings were held every week, French and German being used alternately." He recognized the chairman, Laveaux, a

renegade French monk, who had for some years taught French at Berlin and was now engaged in editing a French paper. The club split into two parties: the constitutional royalists, led by [Protestants Frederic] Dietrich and [Jean] Turckheim, the representatives of the old families, while the worthless Laveaux belonged to the republican group, which events in Paris were soon to raise to undisputed power.[1]

In January 1792, Strasbourg Mayor Dietrich formally asked that the Legislative Assembly in Paris declare Strasbourg "in a state of war" (en état de guerre). This declaration, according to the relevant law of July 10, 1791, would empower his government to expel from the City of Strasbourg those men whom they considered security threats.[1] The Legislative Assembly referred the request of Strasbourg Mayor Dietrich to a committee.

On March 1, 1792, Holy Roman Emperor Leopold II unexpectedly died, which "removed the only hand which was capable of restraining and tempering those outbursts of feeling, both in Austria and France, which had for the last two years threatened to plunge Europe into the vortex of war."[2] The death of Emperor Leopold II thrust twenty-four-year-old Franz Joseph Karl (1768–1835, ruled 1792–1835) into power. Franz Joseph Karl was immediately crowned King of Hungary and Bohemia. However, he had to await coronation as Holy Roman Emperor for four months following the death of Holy Roman Emperor Leopold II.

On March 15, 1792, French King Louis XVI appointed Charles-François du Périer Dumouriez (1739–1823) (henceforth, Dumouriez) as Secretary of Foreign Affairs. On March 17, 1792, King Louis XVI appointed Jean-Marie Roland of the Platière (1734–1793, henceforth, Roland) as Secretary of the Interior, in spite of persistent rumors that the pro-monarchy Strasbourg Mayor Frederick Dietrich would receive the post, noted Henry Morse Stephens.[2]

In early April 1792, the anti-monarchy Jacobins in Alsace so feared by Strasbourg Mayor Dietrich created lists of grievances that attacked the administrations of the fledgling Bas-Rhin and Haut-Rhin Departments.

France Declares War on Austria, April 20, 1792

On April 19, 1792, Franz Joseph Karl, the new King of Hungary and Bohemia, sent an ultimatum to the French Legislative Assembly demanding a return of the territories and rights in Alsace to the violated Holy Roman Empire Princes. On April 20, 1792, French King Louis XVI attended the meeting of the Legislative Assembly to hear Secretary of Foreign Affairs Dumouriez announce that France should declare war on Austria. King Louis XVI said a few words and formally declared war on King Franz Joseph Karl. The Legislative Assembly enacted King Louis XVI's decree, thus initiating a ten-year war.[2]

On April 21, 1792, the day after the French Legislative Assembly declared war on King Franz Joseph Karl, Strasbourg Mayor Dietrich arrested the Jacobin Laveaux for condoning the use of force against orthodox priests still active in Alsace who refused to take the oath to the Civil Constitution of the Clergy. A court tried and released Laveaux in May 1792. He then scurried to Paris to agitate for charges against Strasbourg Mayor Dietrich.

On April 24, 1792, Strasbourg Mayor Dietrich "remarked at a great banquet [in Strasbourg] that it was very sad that all the national war songs of France could not be sung by her present defenders, because they all treated of loyalty to [King Louis XVI] and not to the nation as well. One of the guests was a young captain of engineers, [Claude Joseph] Rouget of Lisle [1760–1836], who had in 1791 composed a successful Hymne à la Liberté, and Dietrich appealed to him to compose something suitable." That night, Rouget of Lisle wrote the words and music to the famous war-song of France, subsequently named the Marseillaise by patriots of Marseille, France.[3]

On May 4, 1792, the radical Jacobins in Alsace sent their lists of grievance against the administration of the Bas-Rhin Department to their counterpart Jacobins in Paris, who called for the Legislative Assembly in Paris to try the officers of the Bas-Rhin Department for the alleged grievances. The list of grievances and a petition found their way to French Secretary of the Interior Roland.[1]

On May 30, 1792, the French Legislative Assembly voted to dissolve the short-lived King's Constitutional Guard. Instead, it placed King Louis XVI and his family under the protection of the fledgling National Guard of Paris. King Louis XVI gravely doubted the loyalty of the National Guard of Paris to the Royal Family in an attack on the Tuileries Palace.[4]

On June 8, 1792, the Legislative Assembly approached King Louis XVI about establishing a camp of about twenty thousand soldiers, drawn from departments throughout France, to form outside the walls of Paris. Its alleged purpose was to function as a reserve for the French Armies on the frontier preparing to fight international foes. Approximately eight thousand Parisians signed a petition protesting the camp, which resulted in the resignation of Secretary of Foreign Affairs Dumouriez as Secretary of Foreign Affairs on June 15, 1792. Monsieur Dumouriez failed to understand how anyone could object to a military camp near Paris.[3]

In early June 1792, the French Legislative Assembly declared Strasbourg in a state of war (en état de guerre), which gave Strasbourg Mayor Dietrich the powers that he sought to control the activities of some of the members of the Strasbourg Jacobin Club. Mayor Dietrich's fellow municipal authorities and officials in the Bas-Rhin Department supported his decisions.[1]

Tuileries Palace Cased, June 20, 1792

On June 20, 1792, the one-year anniversary of King Louis XVI's failed escape, a Parisian mob overran the Tuileries Palace allegedly in response to the dismissal of certain royal ministers by Queen Marie Antoinette, but probably to survey the Tuileries Palace for a later operation. The Paris insurrectionists were appalled that King Louis XVI was still in power (and alive) after attempting to flee his own Kingdom, an act that they considered unforgivingly treasonous. Marie-Thérèse Charlotte (1778–1851), a daughter of King Louis XVI and Queen Marie Antoinette who witnessed the mob event, described it as follows:

> Under the circumstances the people took a mania to place in all the public squares and gardens what were called "liberty trees"; these were little trees, or tall poles, at the top of which they put the bonnet rouge [red hat] with tricolor ribbons—that is to say, red, blue, and white. They expressed to my father [King Louis XVI] a wish to plant one [liberty tree] in the garden of the Tuileries, and he acquiesced. The day they planted this tree was made a species of revolutionary fête, somewhat like that formerly given at the planting of the May tree on the first of that month. They triumphed in having wrung this consent from my father, and to celebrate it they chose the 20th of June [1792], the anniversary of our departure for Varennes, and the fête was to take place beneath our windows…On the 20th of June, about eleven o'clock in the morning, nearly all the inhabitants of the faubourgs Saint-Antoine and Saint-Marceau, where the populace chiefly lived, marched in a body to the National [sic] Assembly, to go from there to the garden and plant the liberty tree. But as they were all armed, which gave reason to suspect bad intentions, my father ordered the gates of the Tuileries to be closed. The [Legislative] Assembly showed great dissatisfaction, and sent a deputation of four municipals to induce [King Louis XVI] to order the gates to be opened. These deputies spoke very insolently; said they exacted the opening of the gates in order that those who had come to plant the tree, the sign of liberty, might return that way, inasmuch as the crowd in the rue Saint-Honoré was too great to allow them to pass. My father, however, persisted in his refusal, and they then went and opened themselves the gates of the garden,

which was instantly inundated by the populace; the gates of the courtyards and the château still remained locked. The mob gained access to the palace where they harassed the Royal Family in their royal apartments until that evening when the deputies of the Legislative Assembly finally restored order and dispersed the crowds. No one in the Royal Family received physical injuries.[5]

King Louis XVI resolved against the camp of twenty thousand soldiers beneath the walls of Paris, but consented to the Feast of the Confederation (Fête de la Confédération) to commemorate capture of the Bastille Fortress three years earlier (July 14, 1789) and to celebrate the reconciliation of all the French people who now lived in a constitutional monarchy. Thousands of French Army soldiers camped on the Champ de Mars to celebrate the Feast of the Confederation. Many Parisian men, seeing the French Army regulars camped on the Champ de Mars and sensing war in the air, volunteered to join the French Army.

On July 14, 1792, the City of Frankfurt overflowed with Holy Roman Empire Princes who had converged on the city for the coronation of Francis II (Franz Joseph Karl, King of Hungary and Bohemia) as the new Holy Roman Emperor. Shortly after his coronation, Emperor Francis II met with Prussian King Frederick William II to discuss the invasion of France to save the French monarchy. Prussian King Frederick William II insisted that his Prussian Army advance en masse toward France from Coblenz at the junction of the Moselle and Rhine Rivers. He proposed to invade France by heading in a southwesterly direction for a distance of about one hundred miles to reach Longwy in the iron-ore mining district of Lorraine, France. From Lorraine, the Prussian Army then would advance to Stenay (about twenty-five miles west of Longwy) and then to Verdun (about twenty-five miles south of Stenay). After taking the Verdun Fortress, the Prussian Army would advance rapidly to the French capital, about one hundred and forty miles to the southwest. Some twenty thousand Austrian soldiers and eight thousand French émigré soldiers would defend the flanks of the Prussian Army. The Prussian King appointed Charles William Ferdinand, Duke of Brunswick-Wolfenbüttel (1735–1806) (henceforth, Duke of Brunswick) to lead the vaunted Prussian Army. The Duke of Brunswick was a capable professional soldier. King Frederick William II planned to accompany the Duke of Brunswick and the Prussian Army as far as Verdun.

Brunswick Manifesto, July 25, 1792

On July 25, 1792, Prussian King Frederick William II officially declared war on France and ordered the Duke of Brunswick to lead the Prussian Army in an invasion of France. The same day, the Duke of Brunswick sent a proclamation to the French Legislative Assembly, which struck Paris like a thunderbolt. The residents of Paris expected war with Prussia, but the severe terms of Brunswick's manifesto caused indignation and fear. The Duke of Brunswick was well known for the enlightened rule of his own Holy Roman Empire principality and had been friendly to France before he received orders from Prussian King Frederick William II to invade France.[6]

What did the Brunswick proclamation say that caused such alarm among Parisians? The proclamation announced the Duke of Brunswick's intent to invade Paris for the following reasons:

* * * * * * * * *

Excerpt from the Brunswick Manifesto, July 25, 1792

To put an end to the anarchy in the interior of France, to check the attacks upon the throne and the altar, to reestablish the legal power, to restore to [King Louis XVI] the security and the liberty of which he is now deprived and to place him in a position to exercise once more the legitimate authority which belongs to him. Convinced that the sane portion of the French nation abhors the excesses of the faction which dominates it, and that the majority of the people look forward with impatience to the time when they may declare themselves openly against the odious enterprises of their oppressors, his Majesty the Emperor and his Majesty the King of Prussia call upon them and invite them to return without delay to the path of reason, justice, order, and peace. In accordance with these views, I, the undersigned, the Commander in Chief of the two armies, declare:

1. That, drawn into this war by irresistible circumstances, the two allied courts [Prussia and Austria] entertain no other aims than the welfare of France, and have no intention of enriching themselves by conquests.

2. That they do not propose to meddle in the internal government of France, and that they merely wish to deliver [King Louis XVI, Queen Marie Antoinette, and the Royal Family] from their captivity, and procure for his Most Christian Majesty the necessary security to enable him, without danger or hindrance, to make such engagements as he shall see fit, and to work for the welfare of his subjects, according to his pledges.

3. That the Allied Armies will protect the towns and villages, and the persons and goods of those who shall submit to [King Louis XVI] and who shall cooperate in the immediate reestablishment of order and the police power throughout France.

4. That, on the contrary, the members of the National Guard who shall fight against the troops of the two allied courts, and who shall be taken with arms in their hands, shall be treated as enemies and punished as rebels to their King and as disturbers of the public peace...

5. That the inhabitants of the towns and villages who may dare to defend themselves against the troops of their Imperial and Royal Majesties and fire on them, either in the open country or through windows, doors, and openings in their houses, shall be punished immediately according to the most stringent laws of war, and their houses shall be burned or destroyed...

6. The City of Paris and all its inhabitants without distinction shall be required to submit at once and without delay to [King

Louis XVI], to place that prince in full and complete liberty, and to assure to him, as well as to the other royal personages, the inviolability and respect which the law of nature and of nations demands of subjects toward sovereigns...*Their said Majesties declare, on their word of honor as emperor and king, that if the Chateau of the Tuileries is entered by force or attacked, if the least violence be offered to their Majesties the King, Queen, and Royal Family, and if their safety and their liberty be not immediately assured, they will inflict an ever memorable vengeance by delivering over the City of Paris to military execution and complete destruction, and the rebels guilty of the said outrages to the punishment that they merit* [emphasis added].[7]

* * * * * * * * *

On July 30, 1792, the Prussian Army left Coblenz and marched to Trier via Wittlich, on the north side of the Moselle River. They arrived in Trier on August 4, 1792. The Prussian Army rested in Trier for eight days and then left on August 12, 1792 to reach Luxembourg on August 14, 1792.

On August 4, 1792, while the Prussian Army was resting in Trier, the anti-Jewish Baron Haindel, seigneur of Romanswiller, Cosswiller, and Erlenbourg in Alsace, cowered when one hundred and fifty-two creditors conjointly sued him for payment of his outstanding debts in the Court of the District of Strasbourg. Recall that in 1789, Haindel had called Strasbourg banker Wolff Lévy "a Jew" in a factum while trying to avoid paying his debt to the banker. The Court of the District of Strasbourg began the process of verifying the claims of the one hundred and fifty-two creditors. On September 1, 1792, the creditors assembled to demand the execution of a judgment against Haindel. On October 9, 1792, the Court of the District of Strasbourg completed verification of the claims of the creditors of Haindel and proceeded to liquefy his assets, including his castle in Romanswiller, to pay his creditors.

Cerf Berr apparently followed the proceedings against Hainsdel. When Hainsdel's Romanswiller's Castle in the Vosges was put on sale,

Cerf Berr successfully purchased it. The purchase occurred sometime in October, November, or December 1792. The castle still stands today (Chateau du Haut Barr). Cerf Berr and his descendants owned the castle for ten years.[8–9] In late 1792, Cerf Berr lived in the Romanswiller Castle.[10]

On August 8, 1792, Strasbourg Mayor Dietrich and his fellow administrators in Strasbourg and in the Bas-Rhin Department sent a letter to the French Legislative Assembly warning that if any harm came to King Louis XVI, Strasbourg would secede from France.[1] This letter sealed the already tenuous fate of Strasbourg Mayor Dietrich.

Tuileries Palace Attacked, August 10, 1792

On August 9, 1792, the leaders of the Paris Commune, angered and scared by the Brunswick Manifesto, changed the name of the commune to the Revolutionary Commune of Paris and prepared to overthrow King Louis XVI. King Louis XVI received this ominous information and alerted the nine hundred Swiss Guards then guarding the Tuileries Palace. He also alerted a number of nobles loyal to him, including former National Assembly Deputy Clermont-Tonnerre, who joined King Louis XVI in the Tuileries Palace.

At midnight on August 9, 1792, leaders of the Revolutionary Commune of Paris signaled the mob to fire on the Tuileries Palace. One of the first shots killed former Deputy Clermont-Tonnerre. For part of the night, the tumult continued outside the Tuileries Palace. Reinforcements from the Paris National Guard arrived to defend King Louis XVI. "Unfortunately, most of them were already seduced and treacherously inclined," noted King Louis XVI's daughter.[5]

On August 10, 1792, the Revolutionary Commune of Paris overthrew King Louis XVI in the following manner. During the morning of August 10, 1792, King Louis XVI and his family fled the Tuileries Palace through its garden, which abutted the Salle du Manège of the Legislative Assembly in the rear of the Tuileries Palace. The

Legislative Assembly deputies who met the Royal Family asked it to wait in the hallway while the Legislative Assembly pondered what to do. The deputies of the Legislative Assembly voted to admit King Louis XVI and his family into the Salle du Manège. About thirty minutes after first entering the hallway, King Louis XVI entered the Salle du Manège first, saying loudly that he came to take refuge with his family "in the bosom of the [Legislative] Assembly, to prevent the French nation from committing a great crime," said his daughter.[5]

The Legislative Assembly deputies placed King Louis XVI and his family "at the bar, and they then discussed whether it was proper that [King Louis XVI] should be present at their deliberations. They said, as to that, that it was impossible to let him stay at the bar without infringing on the inviolability of the sovereign people." They then led him and his family into a small journalist's box where reporters with the *Journal Logographique* usually sat to write their reports of the speeches of the Legislative Assembly for reading by the public.[5]

Meanwhile, the mob, made up of sans-culottes (more below), broke down the front door of the Tuileries Palace. The insurrectionists believed that the Swiss Guards might be amenable to fraternization, as had the soldiers of the National Guard of Paris. However, the Swiss Guards fired on the entering insurrectionists, killing some four hundred individuals. Cannons backing the attacking forces of sans-culottes enabled them to advance and to take the Tuileries Palace. The insurrectionists massacred around six hundred Swiss Guards. The deputies of the Legislative Assembly and the Royal Family could hear the clamor of combat in the Tuileries Palace from the Salle du Manège.

The term sans-culotte means literally "a fellow without breeches." It was a name of reproach given by the nobility to the lower class revolutionaries who rejected short breeches as an article of dress unique to the upper classes.[11] The sans-culottes desecrated the corpses of the Swiss Guards—"limbs lopped off, genitals cut out and stuffed in the dying mouth or fed to the scavenging dogs," wrote historian Graeme Fife.[12]

King Louis XVI and his family remained in the journalist's box in the Salle du Manège of the Legislative Assembly for about forty-eight hours. Guards then moved the Royal Family to four cells in the empty Convent of the Feuillants in Paris. Later, the Legislative Assembly voted to imprison King Louis XVI and his family in the Tower of the thirteenth-century Temple Fortress in Paris. The Royal Family remained imprisoned there until their final dispositions.

On August 18, 1792, the advancing Prussian Army invested Longwy in a siege.[13] Investment is the military tactic of surrounding an enemy fort (or city) with armed forces to prevent entry or escape of the enemy.

On August 18, 1792, French Secretary of the Interior Roland denounced Strasbourg Mayor Dietrich, suspended him from office, and ordered him to proceed to Paris for alleged counter-revolutionary activities, including protecting refractory priests and threatening to break off links with France if harm came to King Louis XVI. Frederic Dietrich instead fled to Basel to stay with his half-brother, Peter Ochs (1752–1821), who was a Swiss politician.

On August 23, 1792, the Revolutionary Commune in Paris, whose insurrectionary activities resulted in the imprisonment of King Louis XVI in the Temple Fortress, resolved to eliminate all of his supporters. The leaders of the Revolutionary Commune drew up enemy lists.

On August 23, 1792, the French garrison at Longwy surrendered to the Prussian Army.[13]

On August 25, 1792, Deputy Armand-Guy-Simon of Coetnempren, Count of Kersaint (1742–1793), returned to Paris from Sedan in the Ardennes where he had been on a deputy mission to the French Army of the Center. He told the Legislative Assembly that the Prussian Army would reach Paris in two weeks, i.e., around September 7, 1792. The Legislative Assembly ordered thirty thousand Parisian men to join the French Army.

On August 27, 1792 and on September 2, 1792, six members of the Legislative Assembly conducted elections for deputies to serve in a new body named the National Convention, which soon would replace the Legislative Assembly. The National Convention was the third of the three sequential bodies to govern revolutionary France from 1789 to 1795; the other two were the National Assembly and the Legislative Assembly. The purpose of the National Convention, according to its organizers, was both to abolish the monarchy and to determine a new form of government. The members of the National Convention would draft a new Constitution to replace the constitutional monarchy form of government outlined in the French Constitution of 1791. *Fewer than one in five electors showed up to vote for the new deputies of the National Convention*, in part because of both the horrific carnage on the night of August 28, 1792 and the September Massacres of September 2–7, 1792. Of the seven hundred and forty-nine newly elected deputies to the National Convention, less than two hundred had previous experience in the Legislative Assembly.

What was the horrific carnage on the night of August 28, 1792? That night, the leaders of the Revolutionary Commune in Paris called for seizure and imprisonment of their perceived enemies. The Commune leaders ordered the gates of Paris closed, deployed sentinels on the quays and boats stationed on the Seine River to prevent escape of residents by water, divided the city into circumscriptions and for each division provided a list of suspects, stopped the circulation of vehicles, and ordered every citizen to stay at home.

Jacobins Round Up Enemies in Paris, August 28, 1792

At six p.m. on August 28, 1792, the Paris revolutionaries launched their "Great Domiciliary Visit" to the homes of Paris. Their pretext was to search for muskets, but their real intent was to ferret out nobles, refractory priests and nuns, and anyone else they believed might collaborate with the Prussians, Austrians, and French émigrés who were advancing toward Paris to liberate King Louis XVI and quash the revolutionary movement. Sixty pikemen and seven hundred squads of sans-culottes burst doors with pile drivers, picked locks, sounded walls, searched cellars, seized papers, and confiscated arms. There is no information on the whereabouts of Cerf Berr and other Berr family members that night.

By five a.m. on August 29, 1792, around three thousand perceived enemies of the Revolutionary Commune of Paris were under arrest, noted historian Hippolyte A. Taine.[14] By August 31, 1792, the Revolutionary Commune of Paris had filled all local prisons and makeshift holding areas in numerous emptied nunneries and monasteries with their perceived enemies.

On August 31, 1792, the Prussian Army invested Verdun. On Sunday, September 2, 1792, the Prussians captured Verdun. Prussian King Frederick William II then ordered the Duke of Brunswick to advance on Paris.[13]

September Massacres, September 2–7, 1792

On September 2, 1792, news of the Prussian victory at Verdun reached Paris. The leaders of the Revolutionary Commune of Paris set into action their grisly plot to eliminate their imprisoned perceived enemies before the Prussian Army could reach the city. The leaders of the Revolutionary Commune of Paris dispatched their executioners to conduct mock trials and then slay all the enemies they had rounded up on the night of August 28/29, 1792. The historical name given to this macabre slaughter was the September Massacres.

The September Massacres resulted in part from fear that the Prussian Army would torch Paris when it arrived, as the Duke of Brunswick had threatened in his manifesto of July 25, 1792. Recall that he had promised "une exécution militaire et à une subversion totale." "Of all the counter-productive declarations in history, this must surely take the palm, for it had exactly the opposite effect to that intended," declared T. C. W. Blanning. The Duke of Chartres observed, "This manifesto of the Duke of Brunswick inspired more enthusiasm in France for the defense of the fatherland and national independence than all the patriotic appeals of the National Assembly and the revolutionary societies put together."[13]

The September Massacres began on September 2, 1792, the same afternoon that the news reached Paris that the Prussian Army had reached Verdun, and the same day that electors were supposed to be electing deputies to the National Convention. Only one in five electors showed up to vote for the new deputies, as noted above, suggesting the possibility that one reason for staging the September Massacres on September 2, 1792 was to frighten away electors, thereby providing the opportunity for manipulation of the make-up of the National Convention by revolutionary actors.

On September 2, 1792, Commissar Stanislas-Marie Maillard (1763–1794) of the Revolutionary Commune of Paris and his executioners took their swords, pikes, and guns to three religious houses that were being used as prisons: the Abbey of Saint-Germain-des-Prés (Latin Quarter, number three Place Saint-Germain-des-Prés), the Carmelite Convent at Rue de Vaugirard and Rue d'Assas, and the Vincentian Seminary of Saint Firmin. At each place, they demanded the oath of allegiance to the Civil Constitution of the Clergy from refractory priests and then slew them when they refused. Each priest suffered a gruesome death.

The September Massacres ended on September 7, 1792, although insurrectionists murdered the Duke of Brissac, the former head of the King's Constitutional Guards, on September 8, 1792 in Versailles because of his close personal relationship with King Louis XVI. One story alleged that a drunken mob butchered the Duke of Brissac's body and severed his head, transported his head wrapped in a cloth to the Château de Louveciennes, and threw the head into an open window where it landed at the feet of the Duke of Brissac's lover, Madame du Barry (1743–1793), the former royal mistress of King Louis XV.[15] The executioners working for the Paris Commune insurrectionists killed more than a thousand of their perceived enemies. "The September Massacres demonstrated the kind of fanaticism that the Prussian and Austrian invaders could expect if they ever reached Paris," said T. C. W. Blanning.[13]

Parisian men lined up to volunteer to join the French Armies to fight the Allied Armies of Prussians, Austrians, and French émigrés as they advanced on Paris. The French Armies of General François Christophe Kellermann (1735–1820, French Army of the Center) and General Dumouriez (French Army of the North) swelled to around thirty-six thousand men of dubious quality, compared to the thirty-four thousand professional troops under the command of the Duke of Brunswick.[16]

On September 20, 1792, two weeks after the September Massacres in Paris, the swollen French Army advanced to meet the Prussian Army on the plain at Valmy, a position prepared by the French about one hundred and twelve miles east of Paris and about thirty miles west of Verdun. "Both sides opened a cannonade until [one p.m. in the afternoon], when the Prussian guns fell silent and their infantry, arrayed in two lines, marched forward in attack." French General Kellermann raised his hat on his sword, cried "Vive la Nation!" and watched his valiant men surge forward. The Duke of Brunswick suddenly halted his attack and fell back, stunning the surging French troops. The two sides exchanged only cannonballs until night fell. German writer Johann Wolfgang von Goethe (1749–1832), who was riding with the Prussian Army, declared that the French victory at Valmy saved Paris *and* the French Revolution.[16]

The French Army's victory at Valmy provided an opportunity farther north for French General Adam Philippe, Count of Custine (1740–1793, henceforth, General Custine), who commanded the French Army of the Vosges. French General Custine sought and received permission to invade Germany from his superior, French General Armand Louis of Gontaut, Duke of Lauzun and later Duke of Biron (1747–1793), who commanded the French Army of the Rhine and was a veteran of the American Revolutionary War. The plan was to invade the Palatinate north of Alsace and capture the great German cities along the Rhine River. General Custine's French Army of the Vosges consisted of ten thousand infantry, four thousand cavalry, and forty cannons.

On September 20, 1792, General Custine attacked the City of Speyer, the major base of the Austrian Army. He had started from Landau, located in the Palatinate on the west side of the Rhine River about fifty-five miles northeast of Strasbourg and eighteen miles southwest of Speyer.

In September 1792, Strasbourg voters elected Jean Turckheim to replace the deposed Mayor Frederic Dietrich. Recall that Jean Turckheim had served as a deputy representing the City of Strasbourg in the Estates-General and the National Assembly. He had returned to Strasbourg after the National Assembly dissolved in September 1791. Also recall that on August 18, 1792, Frederic Dietrich fled to Basel after Secretary of the Interior Roland dismissed him and ordered him to Paris.

On September 20, 1792, the French Legislative Assembly, on the last day of its existence, formally transferred responsibility for recording births, marriages, and deaths from the Roman Catholic Church in France to secular municipal authorities across France. "This was an extremely important move because it marked the break between the world and the Church and also marked the introduction of the secular state, definitely discarding the old conception of the Christian monarchy which had given a religious character to all the great events of life," explained historian Adrien Dansette.[17]

On September 21, 1792, the National Convention, which superseded the Legislative Assembly, held its first meeting. During the next few days, the National Convention established the French Republic (later known as the First French Republic), abolished the monarchy, and stripped King Louis XVI of his title, renaming him Citoyen (Citizen) Louis Capet.

On September 30, 1792, French General Custine and the French Army of the Vosges captured the City of Speyer. On October 4, 1792, General Custine captured the City of Worms; on October 21, 1792, the City of Mainz; and on October 23, 1792, the City of Frankfurt am Main.[18] Speyer, Worms, and Mainz were on the west side (left bank) of the Rhine River, while Frankfurt am Main was on the east side (right bank) of the Rhine River and on the north side of the Main River. General Custine was under orders to demonstrate to the residents of these cities that the French had not come as exploitative conquerors but rather as altruistic liberators. A number of anti-monarchical and anti-religious leaders in the City of Mainz convinced the leaders of the

French Army that the Mainz population uniformly detested the tyranny of kings and priests. The anti-monarchical and anti-religious leaders in Mainz wanted to free the City of Mainz from the perceived tyranny of Prussian King Frederick William II.

On November 4, 1792, the Secretaries of War, Interior, and the Marine of the National Convention formed a Military Purchasing Directory (Directoire des Achats) to try to bring order to the chaotic military supply system of the French Armies operating both inside and outside of France. The National Convention, increasingly run by a small cadre of radical Jacobins, had unsuccessfully tried to nationalize the French Army supply systems, but the task had proved beyond their control. The cadre learned that trade in grain, forage and livestock, milling, and transportation was not concentrated in a small number of enterprises that any government could control. In addition, the government's credit was dismal, cash flow to suppliers was slow, and the usual military suppliers resisted providing goods on credit to the National Convention in Paris.

In the last three months of 1792, food in Paris and in the French Provinces was again scarce. To prevent riots in Paris, the National Convention sold bread to Parisians below the cost at which the National Convention purchased the bread from suppliers. At the same time, the National Convention bought scarce grain at a higher price from abroad to supply the French Provinces, which were shipping their grain to Paris. The market had tightened because of the political crisis and the collapse of the assignats, as described elsewhere.[19]

On November 5, 1792, the National Convention named the directors of the new Directoire des Achats: Jacques Biedermann, Professor A. Cousin, and Max Berr (son of Cerf Berr). Jacques Biedermann, a Swiss banker, purchased supplies for the Secretary of War. Professor A. Cousin purchased supplies for the Secretary of the Interior, which meant feeding Paris and other starving cities. Max Berr purchased supplies for the Secretary of the Marine, which meant supplying the storehouses of the major ports of the Channel, the Mediterranean Sea, and the Atlantic Ocean. Max Berr was not very active in supplying the

Marine, according to Charles Poisson. For example, on November 11, 1792, the Directoire des Achats sent Max Berr inland to Alsace to make deals with suppliers who previously had worked under agreements with King Louis XVI. Max Berr was given authority to require the previous royal suppliers to either continue or discontinue their purchases on behalf of the French Republic, said Charles Poisson.[19]

The Directoire des Achats hired hundreds of managers to supply goods to towns and the French Armies in France. For example, for the period November/December 1792, the Directoire des Achats hired four managers to supply the Cities of Landau, Lauterbourg, and Strasbourg in the Bas-Rhin Department. The four managers were Baruch Berr (Cerf Berr's son and Max Berr's brother) for Landau; Savagnier for Lauterbourg; and Ducluzel and Galimart for Strasbourg. For January/February 1793, the Directoire des Achats hired at least eight managers to supply the Cities of Landau, Lauterbourg, Schlettstadt, Strasbourg, Wissembourg, and Haguenau. The eight known managers were Barthelemy, Savagnier, Dagon de la Contrie, Cahen, Galimart, Cucluzel, Quinpel, and the Bertrand brothers.[19]

What did Baruch Berr supply to the City of Landau during November/December 1792? Extraordinarily precious extant records show that he supplied the following goods during that two-month time span. Note that one quintal equals one hundred kilograms, or two hundred and twenty pounds.

Grains:	228,646 quintals
Avoine (oats):	75,509 sacs
Foin (hay):	108,870 quintals
Paille (straw):	374,900 quintals
Légume verts (green vegetables):	5,000 quintals
Riz (rice):	7,000 quintals[19]

The Directoire des Achats also appointed Baruch Berr and Théodore Berr as régisseurs (purchasing managers) for the French Army of the Rhine and Lippman Berr as régisseur for the French Armies of the

Ardennes, Meurthe, Moselle, and the Vosges. Even before Lippman
Berr could begin his work with the French Armies of the Ardennes,
Meurthe, Moselle, and the Vosges, the Directoire des Achats sent him
to Belgium to try to save the disorganized quartermasters of the French
Army of the North commanded by General Dumouriez.

General Dumouriez was frustrated with the army suppliers and
complained mostly about the Jewish ones, including Max, Lippman,
and Théodore Berr. Zosa Szajkowski explained:

> Army contractors were frequently criticized [by their employers
> and their customers], but at that time, the [Directoire des Achats]
> leaders also fell victim to the conflict between [Secretary of War
> J.-N. Pache and Secretary of the Interior Roland]. Pache was
> pushed into the [Ministry of War] by his Girondist friends,
> but when he later went over to the Montagnards [Jacobins],
> Roland took away from the Directory [des Achats] the right
> to supply [Pache's Ministry of War]. Dumouriez was a known
> friend of the Girondists and this strengthened his assaults on
> the Directory [des Achats]. This agency had been created in
> a moment of grave financial crisis, drought, speculation, and
> political conflict. Bankers were active in both factions of the
> Revolution. [Banker Jacques] Biedermann was a friend of both
> the Girondists and the Dantonists, and he was not impartial.
> But the Jews in the Directory [des Achats]—all of them were
> Ashkenazi Jews—did not participate in these factional conflicts.
> Max Berr was undoubtedly a very ambitious banker, but his
> activities were restricted to the contracting business.[19]

Recall that in late 1792, Cerf Berr of Médelsheim left Paris for his
newly purchased property in Romanswiller in the Vosges. Before he left
Paris, Cerf Berr donated the cemetery land, which he had purchased in
1785, to the Paris Jewish community.[20]

In November 1792, Strasbourg authorities asked sixty-six-year-old
Cerf Berr to provide them with data on Ashkenazi births, marriages, and

deaths in Alsace. Recall that on the last day of its existence (September 20, 1792), the Legislative Assembly had turned over the function of registering births, marriages, and deaths to the municipalities of France. The Strasbourg authorities were following up on this new law. Cerf Berr responded to the Strasbourg authorities that to his knowledge no such Ashkenazi Registry existed in the archives of the Alsatian Council of Jewish Communities although he had tried to start one in 1788 before he resigned as one of the three Alsatian Ashkenazi Syndics. In 1793, Strasbourg authorities ordered the Ashkenazim in Strasbourg to comply with the regulations for the état civil.[20]

Fate of Citizen Louis Capet

On November 6, 1792, the deputies of the National Convention began to debate the fate of Citizen Louis Capet (King Louis XVI). On November 13, 1792, twenty-five-year-old Deputy Louis Antoine Léon of Saint-Just (1767–1794) (henceforth, Saint-Just), the lawyer son of a knight and the youngest deputy elected to the National Convention on September 2, 1792, made his maiden speech in the National Convention on what he considered the proper fate of Citizen Louis Capet. Deputy Saint-Just declared with "tranquil inhumanity" the following:

> What I say is that the king must be judged as an enemy, that it is not so much a matter of judging him as of fighting him...Between a king and a people there could be no natural relationship. The very concept of kingship implied the invasion of the social by the political, and any king, by the mere virtue of his office, was guilty of the worst of all crimes. Monarchy was an offence against the law of nature...any citizen would be entitled to murder Louis [King of France].[21]

On November 19, 1792, in response to the mood of triumphalism following the French capture of Speyer and other Rhenish cities by

General Custine and the persuasive reports of repression cited by some Mainz residents, the National Convention issued its Edict of Fraternity, as follows:

* * * * * * * *

Edict of Fraternity, National Convention, November 19, 1792

The NATIONAL CONVENTION declares, in the name of the French nation, that it will grant fraternity and assistance to all peoples who wish to recover their liberty, and instructs the Executive Power to give the necessary orders to the [French Army] generals to grant assistance to these peoples and to defend those citizens who have been—or may be—persecuted for their attachment to the cause of liberty. The National Convention further decrees that the Executive Power shall order the generals to have this decree printed and distributed in all the various languages and in all the various countries of which they have taken possession.[22]

* * * * * * * *

The French Edict of Fraternity of November 19, 1792 had two "baleful effects," said T. C. W. Blanning. "It gave carte blanche to radicals in every country in Europe to subvert the existing regime, whether it was at war with France or not, and it allowed decision makers and public opinion in France to believe that territorial expansion to 'the Alps, the Rhine, and the Pyrenees' was not only good for France but a moral imperative."[22]

On November 25, 1792, in Lixheim, Lorraine, local Christians chased Jews out of a church where the latter were attempting to cast their votes in an election. One of the reasons for the Christians' behavior was that the would-be Jewish voters refused to uncover their heads in the church.[23] This voting place irregularity in Lixheim demonstrated that at least some French Jews in late 1792 were attempting to exercise their newly acquired right as French citizens to vote.

In late November 1792, former Strasbourg Mayor Frederic Dietrich surrendered to the Strasbourg authorities, stood trial before the Criminal Tribune of Bas-Rhin, by order of the National Convention, and received an acquittal. In November 1792, voters elected three Jacobins to the Bas-Rhin Department government. One of them was Pierre Monet (also spelled Monnet), a shadowy Jacobin figure from Savoy.

On December 2, 1792, the Duke of Brunswick, now positioned with his Prussian Army in the Rhine River Valley, confronted General Custine's French Army in the City of Frankfurt am Main, causing the French Army to flee the city and retreat westward to the City of Mainz. In the aftermath of this retreat, General Custine offered his resignation to the National Convention, which promptly refused it and ordered him to defend the Rhine River Valley.

On December 3, 1792, Deputy Maximilien Robespierre (1758–1794, henceforth, Robespierre), a new thirty-four-year-old deputy from Arras in Northern France, delivered to his colleagues of the National Convention the most important speech concerning the fate of Citizen Louis Capet. Deputy Robespierre concurred with the opinion of Deputy Saint-Just, i.e., whether Citizen Louis Capet was guilty of the specific charges against him or not did not really matter; rather, if his death was good for the country, he should die. "His death was a political necessity, not an act of strict justice."[24] The deputies of the National Convention then began the trial of Citizen Louis Capet whose counsel was Malesherbes.

On December 14, 1792, the Duke of Brunswick and the Prussian Army again defeated French General Custine, this time in the City of Hockenheim in the Palatinate. The Prussians then took winter quarters and awaited the arrival of spring to besiege the City of Mainz still held by the French.

On December 17, 1792, Pierre Monet of Savoy requested and received permission from his co-administrators in the Bas-Rhin

Department to invite two National Convention deputies in Paris to visit the department to provide assistance in managing the political unrest in Lower Alsace. The two Jacobin deputies on mission arrived and promptly purged the administrations of the Bas-Rhin Department and the City of Strasbourg of all perceived counter-revolutionaries, i.e., enemies of the French Revolution. In early 1793, they replaced Strasbourg Mayor Jean Turckheim with Pierre Monet.

In 1792, Berr Isaac Berr signed a petition in Nancy to save from demolition the statue of King Louis XV in the Place Royale.[24]

In December 1792, Bas-Rhin Department authorities transferred to the City of Besançon Frederic Dietrich for retrial despite his acquittal in the Bas-Rhin Department trial. On December 23, 1792, Antoine-Melchior Nodier (1738–1808) acquitted Frederic Dietrich. Despite this verdict, Deputy Robespierre in Paris ordered Frederic Dietrich transferred to Paris for a third trial at which he was convicted on December 26, 1793 as "one of the major conspirators of the Republic." Deputy Robespierre declared, "National justice requires that [Frederic Dietrich] be punished, and the interest of the people request that it be done promptly." The Committee of Public Safety condemned Frederic Dietrich to death on December 28, 1793 and guillotined him the next day, December 29, 1793.[58]

The year 1793 was even stormier for the fledgling Republic of France than was the year 1792. On January 20, 1793, the National Convention voted on the fate of Citizen Louis Capet. The final vote was three hundred and sixty-one deputies for regicide; three hundred and nineteen for imprisonment until the peace, followed by banishment; two for life imprisonment in irons; two for execution after the war; twenty-three for death conditioned to a debate on reprieve; and eight for death and expulsion of the entire Bourbon family.[25]

On January 21, 1793, thirty-eight-year-old Citizen Louis Capet made his last confession to an orthodox Roman Catholic priest, and the executioner let fall the guillotine blade across his neck. Throngs of armed sans-culottes cheered as an eighteen-year-old assistant executioner paraded around the scaffold displaying Citizen Louis Capet's severed head.[26]

Deputy Robespierre, immediately following the regicide, solemnly declared the following to his fellow deputies of the National Convention:

* * * * * * * *

Deputy Robespierre's Comments on the Regicide, January 21, 1793

Monday, 21 January at 10h15 in the morning on the Place of the Revolution, the man formerly known as King Louis XVI, the Tyrant, fell under the sword of the Law. This great act of justice has consternated the Aristocracy, brought to naught the superstitions of Royalty, and created the [French] Republic. It stamps greatness on the [N]ational Convention and renders it worthy of the confidence of the French people. It was in vain that an audacious faction and insidious orators exhausted their efforts in calumny, in charlatanism and chicanery [referring to the Girondins, who favored moderation in dealing with the fates of King Louis XVI's and other men, such as Frederic Dietrich]; the courage of the republicans triumphed; the majority of the Convention remained unshakeable in its principles and the genius of intrigue ceded way to the genius of Liberty and to the Ascendancy of virtue.[26]

* * * * * * * *

Foreign monarchs, as well as many Frenchmen, were sickened by the horrific news of the execution of Louis XIV in Paris. The Spanish Crown joined the British Crown's blockade of French Mediterranean ports. Soon after the regicide most monarchs of Europe declared war against the French Republic. On February 2, 1793, the National Convention declared war on England.

On January 25, 1793, the National Convention for unknown reasons placed under arrest the three directors of the Directoire des Achats. A constable followed Max Berr everywhere he went as he continued to supply artillery crews and military convoys with goods. He protested bitterly about the surveillance and his lack of freedom. On June 21, 1793, the National Convention finally released Max Berr from custody.[19]

Two French Army generals complained about Cerf Berr's sons. General Custine accused Baruch and Théodore Berr of provisioning German princes in the various territories under occupation by the French Army, rather than solely provisioning the French Army. General Custine also accused Baruch and Théodore Berr of employing recruits who were evading service in the French Army, noted Zosa Szajowski.[19] Baruch Berr in turn accused General Custine of sabotage. General Dumouriez censured Lippman Berr for problems associated with the directors of the Directoire des Achats, which was supplying certain factions within the French Revolution, as noted earlier. Lippman Berr told the general that he was only trying to serve his country well, "on my honour as a Jew."[27]

On February 12, 1793, the National Convention suspended the Directoire des Achats, only three months after its creation. The Directoire des Achats had not succeeded in controlling costs or improving the supply of the French Armies.

On February 24, 1793, the National Convention passed the Conscription Act, which required three hundred thousand men, ages eighteen to twenty-five years (excluding married men and widowers), to enroll in the French Army by March 10, 1793. The Conscription Act allowed France to build up an army of eight hundred thousand men. The conscription of the French people became an instrument to turn individuals into French citizens of the French Republic, averred historian George Q. Flynn. "The ideology of the [French Revolution] emphasized the rights of man, but threats from foreign foes obligated the leadership to define military service as the sine qua non of full citizenship."[28]

The new Conscription Law was not well received in certain parts of France. On March 4, 1793, thousands of peasants of the rustic Vendée in Pays-de-la-Loire region in Western France rioted in Cholet when conscription agents dispatched by the National Convention appeared in town. Other anti-conscription riots followed in nearby departments. The peasants, who were called counter-revolutionaries by the National Convention revolutionaries, believed in "their own local ideal of 'liberty'—liberty to stay at home and hear mass said by their old familiar priests," averred John McManners. The people of Vendée were devout smallholders, peasant farmers, fishermen, reed-cutters, and charcoal-burners, who were profoundly loyal to their King, country, and Roman Catholic faith. "They had been unfairly taxed under the Ancien Régime in comparison with other areas. Their cahiers for the Estates-General had made simple requests—lower taxation, the repair of their miserable roads, and help for the infirm and indigent, who abounded."[29]

At the beginning of the French Revolution, the Vendeans had rejoiced over the National Assembly's abolition of feudal dues and taxes. However, they soon learned that "what they received from the French Revolution was a new consolidated land tax based on the same unjust assessment, and so arranged that the cultivator [i.e., the Vendean peasant himself] had to pay it all directly, instead of some falling on the proprietor [the Vendean lord], as in the days before the reform." "In the special case of the Vendée, there was a demoralizing impression that they were paying more out of diminished revenue—as indeed they were." The Vendeans were enraged at the French Revolutionary Government in Paris and risked death, rather than serving in the French Revolutionary Armies.[29]

The Jacobins of the National Convention blamed orthodox Catholic priests and nobles who had fled France beginning in 1789 for "lighting torches of fanaticism and civil war" behind the battle lines and for supporting an attack on the French Republic. The Jacobins regarded the Vendeans as fanatics.

On March 6, 1793, two days after the Vendean riot erupted in

Chalot, the leaders of the National Convention deployed eighty deputies to the French Provinces and scenes of "federalist revolts" (Jacobins' term). There the deputies functioned as French Revolutionary Government Bailiffs with full powers to speak and act for the National Convention in Paris. "They became an awesome part of the revolutionary machine," said Graeme Fife, especially after the creation of the Revolutionary Tribunal organ, a criminal court for trying political enemies of the French revolutionaries.

On March 9, 1793, National Convention Deputy Jean-Baptiste Carrier (1756–1794), known for his cruelty to his enemies, especially the clergy, first proposed a Revolutionary Tribunal to try counter-revolutionaries of the French Republic.[30] By creating the Revolutionary Court, the National Convention conflated the Legislative, Executive, and Justice branches of the French Government. Deputy Georges Danton (1759–1794) supported establishing the Revolutionary Court, writing the following:

> An extraordinary criminal tribunal shall be established at Paris which shall have cognizance of all counter-revolutionary activities, of all attacks against the liberty, the equality, the unity, the indivisibility of the Republic, the internal and external security of the state and of all plots tending to re-establishing the monarchy or to establish any other authority inimical to the liberty, equality or sovereignty of the people, regardless of whether the culprits should be employees of the government, military personnel or plain citizens.[30]

On March 12, 1793, the National Convention cleared the names of Baruch and Théodore Berr. Recall that French General Custine had accused them of treason.[31]

On March 18, 1793, French General Dumouriez retreated with his troops during the critical Battle of Neerwinden, thus earning him the undying enmity and wrath of the Jacobin leaders of the National Convention.

On March 21, 1793, in response to the Vendean and other departmental revolts, the National Convention voted to form the Committee for General Security, "a central police administration for all activities coming within the definition of counter-revolutionary activities…to investigate all matters pertaining to [French] émigrés, foreign nationals and those already declared outside revolutionary law." [30] Surveillance committees were set up in every section of the French Republic's cities and communes to arrest anyone who "by their behavior, their contacts, their words or their writings showed themselves to be supporters of tyranny, federalism, or else to be enemies of liberty. Thus definition of 'enemy of the people' was left to the caprice, or interpretation of those keeping watch on their fellow citizens."[31]

In March 1793, the Prussian Army left its winter quarters, crossed the Rhine River (from east to west), and attacked the City of Mainz while French General Custine was in the City of Worms. General Custine advanced to the front, retreated after some early setbacks, and finally pulled his soldiers back to Landau Fortress, claiming to be massively outnumbered. On March 30, 1793, the formidable coalition of Prussia, Austria, and French Emigré Armies surrounded the City of Mainz, which still contained French Army troops.

French General Custine became deeply dejected after falling back on Landau Fortress at the end of March 1793. The combination of an overwhelming number of Austrian and Prussian forces and his own disorganized French Army made him consider the necessity of evacuating the Palatinate. However, the Austrian and Prussian Armies did not pursue him.[32]

Thus, French General Custine directed the energies of the French Army of the Rhine to repairing the fortifications on the Lines of Wissembourg, which are entrenched works (an earthen rampart dotted with small outworks) along the Lauter River. The Lines of Wissembourg generally follow the northern boundary of Alsace. The Lines of Wissembourg are about twelve miles in length and stretch from Wissembourg on the west end to Lauterbourg on the east end.

French General Custine also ordered his troops to strengthen

?yhyg

Bitche Fortress, which commanded a main pass across the Vosges, to secure his communications with the French Army of the Moselle.[33] Wissembourg is the northernmost city in Lower Alsace; it is about thirty miles north of Strasbourg and fifteen miles south of Landau. Bitche is in the northernmost part of Lower Alsace, about twenty miles west of Wissembourg. French General Custine fortified Bitche and the Lines of Wissembourg in anticipation of an Allied Armies' advance on Alsace and capture of Strasbourg.

On April 1, 1793, Deputy Georges Danton of the National Convention exclaimed, "All patriots must rally…to save the Republic and purge the Convention of *cowardly intriguers*" (emphasis in original).[34]

On April 4, 1793, French General Dumouriez defected to Austria following publication of a letter in which he threatened to march the French Army on Paris if the National Convention did not accept his leadership. The Jacobin revolutionaries in Paris despaired that the Allies were close to defeating the French Revolution. On April 6, 1793, the Jacobins in the National Convention formed a War Cabinet, which they called the Committee of Public Safety. They subordinated the Committee for General Security to the new Committee of Public Safety and appointed Deputy Georges Danton as a member. "Across France, many communes [including Strasbourg] established their own [Committee of Public Safety/Revolutionary Tribunal], largely at the behest of local Jacobins," explained Graeme Fife.[35]

On April 12, 1793, twenty-two anti-Jacobin Girondin deputies voted to impeach Jacobin President Jean-Paul Marat (1743–1793) of Neuchâtel. They voted to impeach him because he had signed a decree accusing the Girondins of being "disloyal deputies" and a "sacrilegious cabal."[35] The Jacobins counter-demanded expulsion of the twenty-two Girondin deputies from the National Convention. On April 24, 1793, the National Convention deputies voted to acquit President Jean-Paul Marat of the impeachment charge. On May 31, 1793, the Girondins referred the matter to the Committee of Public Safety.

On April 14, 1793, the Allied Armies of Prussians, Austrians, and

French émigrés surrounded the City of Mainz and began to build their siege works.

On April 30, 1793, Esther Cerfberr Sinzheim of Bischheim, the sister of Cerf Berr and the wife of Rabbi David Sintzheim, died. She was buried in a new section of Rosenwiller Jewish Cemetery.[36] Jewish decedents of Bischheim usually received burial either in the Ettendorf Jewish Cemetery (founded in the fifteenth century), about fifteen miles northwest of Bischheim, or in the Rosenwiller Jewish Cemetery, about fifteen and one-half miles southwest of Strasbourg. The first historical mention of Rosenwiller Jewish Cemetery was in 1349.

In mid-May 1973, the National Convention transferred General Custine from the French Armies of the Rhine and the Moselle to the French Army of the North.

On June 2, 1793, a group of sans-culottes served a petition to the National Convention to demand dismissal of the twenty-two Girondin deputies. A clutch of deputies then attempted to leave the building. However, they were met by more than seventy-five thousand Paris National Guard troops, commanded by street orator and September Massacres' veteran, François Hanriot (1761–1794). The troops brandished their sabers, causing the alarmed deputies to retreat into the building. Street Commander François Hanriot refused to disperse his troops even when asked to do so by National Convention President Marie-Jean Hérault of Séchelles (1759–1794), who was also a member of the Committee of Public Safety.[37]

Commander Hanriot told the deputies of the National Convention to send the twenty-two Girondin deputies outside within the hour or he would raze the National Convention building. The Committee of Public Safety refused to arrest the twenty-two Girondin deputies. However, the rest of the deputies of the National Convention, who were anxious to go home, voted to indict the twenty-two Girondin deputies plus seven other deputies who had investigated insurrectionary activity in Paris. Commander Hanriot then permitted all the deputies to leave the building unharmed. Later the National Convention arrested and outlawed the twenty-nine deputies.[37]

On June 8, 1793, sixty-three members of the National Convention signed a protest against the popular violence led by François Hanriot on June 2, 1793. However, Deputy Robespierre acted to consolidate his power by calling on the Committee of Public Safety to prosecute the twenty-nine Girondin deputies and "then proceed to the banishment of all foreigners from French soil."[37] Deputy Robespierre despised the French émigrés who he believed were inflaming French emotions in Alsace and other outlying French Provinces. The National Convention complied with Deputy Robespierre's request and placed the twenty-nine deputies under house arrest.

On June 5, 1793, the Allied Armies began their bombardment of the outer defenses of the City of Mainz. On June 18, 1793, the Allied Armies began their main bombardment of the city, seriously damaging the massive red sandstone Saint Martin's Cathedral and many other city structures. Saint Martin's Cathedral served as the camp for the French Army, whose soldiers wrote profanities on its walls, sold its artifacts, and burned its interior wood for heat.

On June 24, 1793, the National Convention ratified the French Constitution of 1793—allegedly written solely by Deputy Saint-Just of the Committee of Public Safety. However, the National Convention set aside the French Constitution of 1793 and instead decreed rule solely by the French Revolutionary Government until peace resumed in France.

By June 27, 1793, the number of soldiers in the French Armies of the Rhine and Moselle under General Alexander François Marie of Beauharnais (1760–1794, he was the first husband of Napoleon's first wife, Joséphine) and French General Jean Nicholas Houchard (1739–1793), increased to sixty thousand and forty thousand strong, respectively. However, most of the French soldiers were raw recruits and thus both French Armies remained inactive until mid-July 1793.[33] The French Army of the Rhine was garrisoned at the Landau Fortress in the Palatinate while the French Army of the Moselle was garrisoned in Saarbrücken, Saarland.

On July 10, 1793, the Committee of Public Safety, under pressure from the Jacobins of the National Convention, replaced its original fourteen members with nine members. Of these nine members, at least five were extremists in favor of crushing (de-Christianizing) the provincial revolts. The Jacobins continued to believe that underground orthodox Roman Catholic priests and French émigrés were leading the provincial revolts.

On July 17, 1793, the French Army still inside the gates of the City of Mainz began negotiations to surrender to the Allied Armies. On July 23, 1793, the French Army in Mainz accepted the Prussian Army's terms and marched unharmed out of Mainz with the honors of war on the condition that they did not serve against France's external enemies for at least one year. However, the National Convention refused to accept the terms presented by the Allied Armies and ordered all of the French officers released from Mainz to return to Paris for trial. The National Convention wanted to set an example for officers and soldiers in the fortresses in Northeastern France, which were under attack by the resurgent Allied Armies. Among the officers involved in the surrender of the City of Mainz was General Jean Baptiste Kléber (1753–1800), who the National Convention re-instated (rather than standing trial) and sent with many of his troops to Western France to help put down the Vendée revolt.[37]

With the City of Mainz freed from French occupation, Austrian General Dagobert Sigismund, Count of Wurmser (1724–1797, henceforth, Wurmser), a native of Strasbourg, positioned his Austrian Army in the Palatinate between the Vosges and the Town of Edenkoben. From his position in the Palatinate, General Wurmser was able to block the French Army of the Rhine positioned at Landau Fortress, about seven miles south of Edenkoben, from advancing northward to attack the Prussian Army commanded by the Duke of Brunswick. The Prussian Army was encamped in the Vosges in the City of Kaiserslautern, about twenty miles northwest of Edenkoben.

Austrian General Wurmser's intent was to wrest Alsace from France and return her to her wronged Holy Roman Empire Princes. However, the Prussian Army was not keen on the Austrian Army's plan to retake Alsace for herself.

On July 19, 1793, French General Beauharnais led the French Army of the Rhine northward toward Edenkoben and, on July 24, 1793, forced General Wurmser's Austrian troops to evacuate Edenkoben. This evacuation left the road open to Neustadt, the next town north along the foothills of the Vosges. French General Beauharnais also successfully cut the communications between Austrian General Wurmser and the Prussian Duke of Brunswick.

On July 22, 1793, the National Convention arrested French General Custine, in part because of the fall of the City of Mainz for which the Jacobin leaders blamed him. The Committee of Public Safety found him guilty on a trumped up charge of treason.[36] The Committee of Public Safety named French General Houchard of the French Army of Moselle as General Custine's replacement for the French Army of the North. In addition, the Committee on Public Safety shifted thirty thousand soldiers from the French Armies of the Rhine and Moselle to reinforce the French Army of the North, thus leaving the French Army of the Moselle at the mercy of the Prussian Army led by the Duke of Brunswick. However, the Duke of Brunswick did not attempt to annihilate the French Army of the Moselle. Meanwhile, Austrian General Wurmser pushed the French Army of the Rhine southward toward the Lines of Wissembourg, which the troops of the condemned French General Custine recently had re-enforced.

On July 27, 1793, Deputy Robespierre became a member of the Committee of Public Safety by replacing another member who resigned because of ill health.

On July 27, 1793, the Strasbourg Jacobin Club refused admission to Cerf Berr and Berr Isaac Berr.[38] The request for admission places Cerf Berr in the City of Strasbourg on July 27, 1793, rather than in Romanswiller where he had been living since late 1792. It is unknown why Cerf Berr and Berr Isaac Berr sought admission to the Strasbourg Jacobin Club on July 27, 1793.

Cerf Berr may have been in Strasbourg in July 1793 to conduct business relating to the Council of the Alsatian Jewish Communities. The National *Convention* treated the Ashkenazim *not* as individual enfranchised Frenchmen of the "Mosaic Persuasion", but as members of religious corporations, even though the National *Assembly* had officially outlawed religious corporations in France in February 1792.[39] The National Convention held the Jewish religious corporations responsible for the debts that they had incurred before the emancipation of the Jews in France on September 27, 1791.

In the last year of his life, Cerf Berr of Médelsheim volunteered as the principal creditor of the Council of the Alsatian Jewish Communities, whose debts now totaled more than one hundred and eighty thousand livres. In 1793, Cerf Berr made one forced payment to the principal creditors of the Council of the Alsatian Jewish Communities of one hundred and thirty thousand livres using his own money in assignats (paper money).[39]

Deputy Robespierre rapidly made changes to the Committee of Public Safety to improve its efficiency. His first change was to require all trials of the Revolutionary Tribunal to end within a maximum three days. In addition, on August 1, 1793, only four days after Deputy Robespierre joined the Committee of Public Safety, "the full force of [Jacobin] republican violence was unleashed on the provincial rebels, its focus trained ruthlessly on the Vendée," said Graeme Fife.[36]

On August 14, 1793, the Committee of Public Safety added two military engineers, Claude Antoine, Count Prieur-Duvernois, commonly known as Prieur of the Côte-d'Or, who was responsible for providing the material for war, and Lazare Nicolas Marguerite, Count Carnot (1753–1823), who exercised complete authority over French Army personnel.

On August 24, 1793, Austrian General Wurmser forced the French Army of the Rhine southward into the Lines of Wissembourg. Upon learning this news, the Committee of Public Safety replaced French General Beauharnais with General Landremont and then General Carlens, in rapid succession. "The French were very strongly posted along the Lines of Wissembourg; their right being unturnable, lying as it did on Lauterbourg and the Rhine [River], while their left rested on Wissembourg and the [Vosges]. It was quite evident that, without concerted action with the Prussians, [General] Wurmser with thirty thousand Austrians would be unable to dislodge the [French] Army of the Rhine, which was about thirty-five thousand strong."[33] However, the Prussian Duke of Brunswick said he was busy and made the Austrian General Wurmser await his help.

On August 28, 1793, the French Revolutionary Government executed French General Custine in Paris.

On September 4, 1793, the Paris mobs demanded bread from the National Convention deputies. Food was becoming scarcer as European powers embargoed France's ports and French farmers in the provinces fought the French revolutionaries in their midst instead of growing crops.

Reign of Terror Begins, September 5, 1793

On September 5, 1793, Deputy Robespierre declared terror "the order of the day" in response to yet another riot in Paris near the National Convention, staged by the ultra-left wing political faction of the Paris Revolutionary Commune known as the Hébertists. Their leader was journalist Jacques René Hébert (1757–1794). His newspaper, *Le Père Duchesne*, appeared in November 1790 and soon became the most widely read newspaper of the French Revolution, attacking the church and the aristocracy.[40]

Historian Robert Roswell Palmer described the Hébertists this way:

> The Hébertists were partisans of the guerre à outrance [war to the uttermost], war to the knife upon the enemies of the human race. The Hébertists, or at least certain ones in the vague group so named, were the party of unmitigated violence, of war upon tyrants, war upon Christianity, war upon the

starvers of the people. Historians of many shades of thought have agreed in calling them demagogues...[T]hey rejoiced that the misfortunes of the people helped them to exterminate their enemies...Hébertism was a form of extremism, but was only an extreme version of the Jacobin orthodoxy of 1793. Followers of Hébert and of Robespierre might easily fuse together. They used the same phrases and had the same enemies. It was easy for Robespierre to appropriate Hébert's program, and it not inconceivable that Hébert might one day oust Robespierre in turn. Therein lay a great danger to the [Committee of Public Safety]. Whether from Hébertist influence or from voluntary decision, and probably from both, the [Committee of Public Safety] after September 5, [1793] took the Hébertist view of the war.[40]

National Convention Deputy Jean-Baptiste Carrier, the person who first proposed a Revolutionary Tribunal as a means to control perceived counter-revolutionaries of the French Revolution, was a devoted Hébertist.[40]

On September 5, 1793, the Hébertists and radical Jacobins of the National Convention insisted that a vigorous government and liberal use of the guillotine could set right a French Revolution that they perceived was in danger of faltering. "The National Convention [Jacobins] capitulated and tried to salvage something out of the confrontation [with the Hébertists] by directing the Terror themselves lest it fall into the hands of the sectional militants" and be turned against the deputies of the National Convention."[40]

Meanwhile, on September 10, 1793 in Strasbourg, four residents named Edelmann, Fischer, Grün, and Weyher published an accusation against Cerf Berr. The existence of the notice places Cerf Berr in Strasbourg around this date. The announcement is reproduced below:

* * * * * * * * *

Accusation against Cerf Berr, Strasbourg, September 10, 1793

By an invitation made to Cerf Berr and other wealthy citizens of this commune by the commission charged with supplying the newly formed battalion, Cerf Berr sent twenty-three bottles of wine. However, the quality of the wine was so bad that it was not fit for the brave defenders of the homeland to drink and we sent it back right away. We strongly hope that the good citizens of Strasbourg will never let their brothers suffer privations, marching to the field of battle and of victory. At the same time we informed the above-mentioned citizen that we do not deem him worthy to take part any longer in the contribution to the maintenance of freedom and that we refuse any subsequent help from him. The commission decided to punish him by advertising the vile conduct of one of the wealthiest citizens of the city and to make it known publicly through this posting. Strasbourg, September 10, 1793
Edelmann, Fischer, Grün, and Weyher.[41]

* * * * * * * * *

Moses Ginsburger noted that the truth of this accusation is impossible to determine. However, after all that is known about Cerf Berr and his character, the accusation must be considered calumny.[41] The accuser named Edelmann may be Jean-Frédéric Edelmann (1749–1794) of Strasbourg who became administrator of the Bas-Rhin Department in 1789. In 1790, his good friend Strasbourg Mayor Frederic Dietrich and he worked side-by-side. However, in 1792, they joined opposite political factions, implying that Edelmann joined the radical Jacobins since Mayor Dietrich was a monarchist. Jean-Frederic Edelmann testified against his former friend Frederic Dietrich during his trial in Alsace. Jean-Frederic Edelmann was also a well-known composer of instrumental music for harpsichord with string accompaniment.[41] On September 22, 1793, the National Convention sent Deputy Joseph Fouché (1759–1820) to terrorize Christians of the Nièvre Department of France. He initiated terror by holding a festival in honor of the Roman Brutus (85–42 BC) inside the Catholic Church of Saint-Cyr, Nevers. He personally preached a sermon against "religious sophistry" and afterwards presided over a ceremony in honor of married love.

On September 25, 1793, Deputy Joseph Fouché "denounced ecclesiastical celibacy and ordered unmarried priests to adopt a child or an old person." On September 26, 1793, he told the people of the City of Nevers that the National Convention had instructed him "to substitute for the hypocritical and superstitious worship to which the people still unhappily cling, that of the Republic and of natural ethics."[42]

In September and October 1793, the National Convention deputies on mission in Strasbourg and Strasbourg Mayor Monet organized a Committee of Surveillance and General Safety charged with terrorizing the inhabitants of Alsace. They created a Mobile Revolutionary Tribunal composed of a president, two assessors (judges), and a civil commissar who functioned as the public accuser. In addition, they created a Mobile Revolutionary Army made up of elite soldiers who were devoted to the French Republic. The National Convention deputies and Mayor Monet appointed as civil commissar Euloge Schneider (1756–1794), a Hebrew-speaking immigrant monk originally from Germany. Taffin became president and Wolf and Clavel became assessors (judges) of the Mobile Revolutionary Tribunal. The Mobile Revolutionary Tribunal, supported by the Mobile Revolutionary Army, traveled through the scattered villages of Alsace with a portable guillotine. The purpose of the Mobile Revolutionary Tribunal was to terrorize people by accusing, arresting, condemning, and executing some unfortunate souls.[43]

On October 10, 1793, Deputy Joseph Fouché, who had returned to Paris from the City of Nevers, published his de-Christianization decree, which ordered the French people to recognize no religion except that of morality and no dogma except that of France's own sovereignty. All decedents were to receive burial in civil, not religion-affiliated, cemeteries. He outlawed all religious cemeteries. To that end, Deputy Joseph Fouché ordered destruction or removal and sale of all religious symbols from Catholic, Protestant, and Jewish cemeteries throughout France. He instructed National Convention deputies and local authorities in the provinces to transfer all statues, crosses, and other symbols that had monetary value to the treasury of the National Convention. Finally, he ordered National Convention and local authorities to attach a sign to the gate of every cemetery in France that read, "Death is an eternal sleep."[42]

In October 1793, Austrian General Wurmser finally received Prussian Army support to force the Lines of Wissembourg. On October 13, 1793, General Wurmser stormed the Lines of Wissembourg in the First Battle of Wissembourg, while the Prussian Army under the command of the Duke of Brunswick protected the western flank of the Austrian Army by marching southward from the City of Zweibrücken (Deux Ponts) to Bitche. Recall that the late General Custine earlier had fortified Bitche Fortress in expectation of such a Prussian Army advance. The City of Zweibrücken was about twenty miles southwest of the City of Kaiserslautern and fourteen miles north of the City of Bitche. Austrian General Wurmser, in spite of faulty arrangements, managed to penetrate the French lines at Wissembourg. The French Army retreated southward toward Strasbourg. The Austrian Army encamped in Brumath, about ten miles north of Strasbourg.

On October 17, 1793, Austrian General Wurmser ordered one of his lieutenants, Friedrich Karl August, the German Prince of Waldeck (1743–1812), to seize the Wantzenau, a town only five miles northeast of Strasbourg. Meanwhile, wounded soldiers, peasants, and curious city dwellers peered out of Strasbourg's north gate as the Strasbourg National Guard swarmed the city's ramparts intent on defending the city despite the calumnies hurled at them from Paris. The enemy, eager for plunder, demolished the houses, fruit trees, and walkways in the areas surrounding Strasbourg.[43]

Austrian General Wurmser postponed an attack on Strasbourg to instead lay what he considered was the foundation of a new

Austrian regime in Alsace. His delay in attacking Strasbourg caused the inhabitants of Alsace to forget their dislike of the French in their hatred of the Austrian invaders, who destroyed their homes and gardens. Meanwhile, the Prussian Army, reproachful of Austrian intentions to retake Alsace for Austria, refused to move eastward from Saverne to help advance General Wurmser's Austrian goals.[33]

The news of the successful Austrian invasion of Alsace caused a profound sensation in Paris.[39] On October 17, 1793, the Committee of Public Safety dispatched Deputy Saint-Just, who was now Robespierre's closest ally, and Deputy Philippe-François-Joseph Le Bas (1762–1794, henceforth, Le Bas) to Strasbourg to motivate the French Army of the Rhine to push the Austrian and Prussian Armies out of Alsace and back into Germany.

On October 20, 1793, as Deputies Saint-Just and Le Bas made their way from Paris to Strasbourg, the Mobile Revolutionary Tribunal of Alsace wandered through the countryside, imposing special taxes on the rich, requisitioning supplies, inflicting heavy penalties on traders who disregarded price controls, and intermittently accusing, trying, and executing alleged counter-revolutionary Alsatians.[44]

On October 22, 1793, Deputies Saint-Just and Le Bas reached Strasbourg where they installed themselves in the Hotel La Prévôté, according to historian Louis Spach.[43] On their arrival, a new phase of the Reign of Terror began in Strasbourg. They immediately removed General Carlens from his command of the French Army of the Rhine and called up Jean-Charles Pichegru (1761–1804) to replace him. On October 26, 1793, they set up a Supreme Military Tribunal to restore discipline in the French Army of the Rhine.

The Supreme Military Tribunal "had power to deal summarily with all cases sent before it, and at once began to make examples of officers and private soldiers who either shirked their duties or were at all insubordinate." The Supreme Military Tribunal used terror to shock into submission the soldiers and officers of the French Army of the Rhine. The Supreme Military Tribunal executed General Eisenberg for running away at the skirmish of Bischwiller, two colonels, one captain, three non-commissioned officers, one private, a French Army administrator, and one war contractor (not a Cerf Berr family member).[45-46] Deputy Saint-Just especially detested dishonest army purveyors. The Supreme Military Tribunal shot army purveyors who it judged guilty and imprisoned in the interior of France other army purveyors who were only suspected of dishonesty, noted Robert Roswell Palmer.[46]

Deputy Saint-Just requisitioned new provisions and clothes for the bedraggled soldiers of the French Army of the Rhine by ordering stunned Strasbourg residents to produce within mere days ten thousand pairs of shoes, two thousand beds, and fifteen thousand shirts.[33,44] He enforced the Law of the Maximum, which set price ceilings on goods, including meat, grain, soap, and firewood, and made price gouging and food hoarding crimes. The Law of the Maximum rarely worked where it was enacted in France. Deputy Saint-Just ordered adjoining departments of Bas-Rhin to furnish fodder for all the military horses within twelve days. Deputy Saint-Just forced all peasants living along the roads of Alsace to provide the horses and wagons needed by the French Army of the Rhine.[43] Cerf Berr and his sons must have watched this spectacle with interest.

On October 28, 1793, Austrian General Wurmser, for unknown reasons, advanced the Austrian Army to Haguenau, about six miles northeast of Brumath, towards the Lines of Wissembourg. Haguenau is about fifteen miles north of Strasbourg.[47] The residents of Haguenau received General Wurmser as a liberator.[48]

On October 29, 1793, Charles Pichegru arrived in Strasbourg to take command of the French Army of the Rhine. On October 31, 1793, Louis Lazare Hoche (1768–1797) arrived to take command of the French Army of the Moselle.

On October 31, 1793, Deputy Saint-Just levied a tax of nine million livres on one hundred and ninety-three wealthy citizens of Strasbourg, including Cerf Berr and members of his extended family.[47]

On November 2, 1793, Deputy Saint-Just dissolved the governments of the Bas-Rhin Department and the City of Strasbourg. He was unsure of the loyalty of their elected officials. He surrounded himself with a handpicked band of adherents. The only survivor of the purge was Strasbourg Mayor Pierre Monet.

On November 3, 1793, the one hundred and ninety-three wealthy Strasbourg citizens whose names appeared on Deputy Saint-Just's taxation list received a curt letter demanding immediate payment of the tax. Deputy Saint-Just taxed Strasbourg resident Seligmann Alexandre, a tobacco and cloth manufacturer, son-in-law of Cerf Berr, and husband of Rebecca Berr, the huge sum of two hundred thousand livres.

On November 5, 1793, Deputy Saint-Just still had received nothing from Seligmann Alexandre. Secretary Carnier of the Committee for General Security in Strasbourg threatened Seligmann Alexandre with imprisonment if he did not pay the money within twenty-four hours. Seligmann Alexandre could not pay this sum and instead spent two months in prison. The French Revolutionary Government also confiscated part of his property and arrested his partner, Abraham Auerbach, the son-in-law of Rabbi David Sintzheim.[49]

Deputy Saint-Just taxed Max Berr twenty-five thousand livres. Max Berr appealed. On the following November 15, 1794, the tax was reduced to ten thousand livres. When Baruch Berr asked for reduction of *his* tax, the Committee for General Security of Strasbourg refused saying, "[Baruch Berr] never showed any proofs of patriotism." Thirty-one Ashkenazim were among the one hundred and ninety-three wealthiest people of Strasbourg who Deputies Saint-Just and Le Bas forced to pay a compulsory tax of a total nine million livres. Of the nine million livres, the thirty-one Ashkenazim contributed slightly more than one million four hundred thousand livres, said Zosa Szajkowski. Cerf Berr paid the colossal sum of three hundred thousand livres.[49]

On November 8, 1793, Deputy Saint-Just ordered the execution of Old Mayno (also spelled Maino), one of the wealthiest merchants in Strasbourg, because he would not pay the assessed tax of three million livres. Deputy Saint-Just used Old Mayno as an example to encourage other wealthy citizens to pay the tax he demanded of them.[50]

On November 16, 1793, Deputies Saint-Just and Le Bas temporarily left Strasbourg to attend meetings in Paris. In their absence, a political crisis erupted between Strasbourg Mayor Pierre Monet and Civil Commissar Euloge Schneider of the Mobile Revolutionary Tribunal in Alsace.[50] Robert Roswell Palmer described the two men as follows:

> Monet and Schneider detested each other, and were detested by the great majority of Alsatians. Neither was French in background, though Monet was French in language. They were foreign adventurers of the kind dreaded by Robespierre, seeing the Revolution partly as the local maneuvers in which they were engaged, partly as a worldwide movement in which men of all nationalities might share. They had little sense of solidarity with the rest of France, or of allegiance to the National Convention.[51]

On the morning of November 20, 1793, Mayor Pierre Monet led a Festival of Reason in Strasbourg. He was mimicking the Festival of Liberty held the same day in Notre Dame Cathedral in Paris. Historian François-Alphonse Aulard described the Festival of Liberty in Notre Dame Cathedral in Paris as follows:

> An actress from the Opera personified [the goddess] Liberty. The "Torch of Truth" was seen to burn on the "Altar of Reason." Then the department and the [Paris] Commune repaired to the bar of the [National] Convention. [Pierre Gaspard] Chaumette [1763–1794, a Hébertist] declared that the people wanted no more priests; no other gods than those whom Nature offers us. He said, "We, the people's magistrates, have verified its decision, and we bring it to you from the Temple of Reason." And Chaumette demanded that the Church of Notre Dame should thenceforth bear the name of the Temple of Reason. A decree to that effect was immediately passed. The actress who figured as Liberty stood at the desk and received the embraces of the [National Convention] President, [Pierre Antoine]

Laloy [1749–1846], and the secretaries. Then the [National] Convention proceeded to Notre Dame, where the ceremony was recommenced in its honour.[52]

In Strasbourg, the Festival of Reason began with an elaborate procession, which formed at nine o'clock in the morning. The procession approached the Temple of Reason (Strasbourg Cathedral) decorated with a large tricolor flag and a placard reading, "Light after darkness." More flags draped the interior of the Strasbourg Cathedral/Temple of Reason, and in the nave stood the usual symbolic mountain, with statues of Nature and Liberty at the summit, said Robert Roswell Palmer. "On the mountainside were portrayed 'monsters with human face, reptiles half buried in fragments of rock,' symbolizing the frustrated powers of superstition." Strasbourg Mayor Pierre Monet then made a speech in praise of Reason. The Surgeon-general of the French Army of the Rhine made a speech in which he denounced priests, tyrants, rascals, aristocrats, intriguers, and moderates, while Bas-Rhin Civil Commissar of the Mobile Revolutionary Tribunal, Euloge Schneider, publicly abdicated his priesthood. In the street outside Strasbourg Cathedral, revolutionaries burned fifteen cartloads of documents removed from the archives of the Strasbourg Roman Catholic Diocese.[43,52]

On the morning after the Festival of Reason in Strasbourg (November 21, 1793), Strasbourg Mayor Pierre Monet launched a vicious anti-Jewish diatribe to the so-called Provisional Commissioners of the District of Strasbourg. The time had arrived to terrorize the Jews. Mayor Monet execrated the Ashkenazim as enemies of the French Republic, because they continued their barbaric customs in the face of Nature and despite everything that the French Revolution had produced of benefit to them (i.e., political emancipation). He condemned the Jews for still circumcising their male infants, as if Nature was not perfect! The Jews were in contempt of the Deity. He condemned the Jews for still wearing long beards, because, he said, they wanted to be ostentatious and sing praises to their Patriarchs, whose virtues they did not inherit. The Jews continued to speak Hebrew, which they did not even use or understand.

Therefore, said Mayor Monet, "I request the Provisional Commission [of the District of Strasbourg] to prohibit the Jews from these uses and direct burning of all Hebrew books, including the Talmud."[50]

Mayor Monet's address persuaded the members of the Provisional Commission of the District of Strasbourg, said historian Rodolphe Reuss. The Provisional Commission ordered that "the proposals contained in the indictment [to] be implemented by the respective municipalities of residence of the citizens professing the Law of Moses."[50]

On November 21, 1793, the Provisional Commissioners read the indictment to assembled Ashkenazim and ordered them to shave their beards, perform no more circumcisions, and refrain from speaking Hebrew "under penalty of being treated as suspects," which implied imprisonment, at a minimum.[50]

On November 24, 1793, Deputies Saint-Just and Le Bas returned to Strasbourg in time to witness the acme of anti-religion frenzy precipitated by the Festival of Reason four days earlier. They personally ordered the destruction of freestanding statues around Strasbourg Cathedral, but forbade destruction of statues on the exterior and interior of the structure. In this way, the twin allegorical statues of Ecclesia and Synagoga escaped damage. The two deputies shared the religious policy of Deputy Robespierre, which was "a strain of reverence that was stifled at the sight of Catholicism in practice, but awakened at the sight of vandalism and 'philosophic masquerades.'" Deputy Saint-Just then quashed further excesses of the anti-religious frenzy. For example, he instructed Strasbourg officials to treat prisoners with humanity.[52]

On November 25, 1793, the Commissioners of the District of Strasbourg imprisoned for unknown reasons the following Ashkenazim: Cerf Berr of Médelsheim, Léopold Samuel, Isaac Waltenheim (Isaac Leyser of Waldenheim), Salomon Lévi, Abraham Cahn, Meyer Vetel (Nettel), and Meyer Dreyfus.[53] Perhaps these men still wore beards. Cerf Berr and his co-religionists probably served their sentences either in the vacant Jesuit Seminary or in the Darmstadt Hotel in Strasbourg, said Louis Spach. These places combined male and female prisoners of all ages and of all classes of society. Some prisoners died in the dank, dirty, and cold quarters. Some prisoners were transferred to other prisons in the Cities of Metz, Besançon, and Chalon-sur-Saône. During the transfer, prisoners were vulnerable to summary execution by the local populations along the way who railed against the "traitors of the Rhine frontier."[54]

On the night of November 24, 1793, several Provisional Commissioners of the District of Strasbourg, Commissar Nicholas Oberlin of the District of Strasbourg, and two men on horseback (probably gendarmes) entered and destroyed the Rosenwiller Jewish Cemetery, according to Robert Weyl. The group removed all religious symbols from the cemetery and destroyed the headstones.[47]

Civil Commissar Euloge Schneider of the Mobile Revolutionary Tribunal continued his travels to Alsatian villages, portable guillotine in tow. For example, on November 30, 1793, the residents of Rosheim (about thirteen miles southwest of Strasbourg and one mile from Rosenwiller Jewish Cemetery) were awakened at four o'clock in the morning to the sound of drum rolls. At eight o'clock in the morning, gendarmes marched the entire population of Rosheim south more than two miles to the Town of Obernai where Euloge Schneider was waiting. He extended his usual welcome. The guillotine had already been set up. The Mobile Revolutionary Army that accompanied Civil Commissar Euloge Schneider also had gathered residents of neighboring towns in the same way they had amassed the terrified residents of Rosheim. Commissar Euloge Schneider demanded that all clergy present, including priests, ministers, and one rabbi, abjure their faith, as he had done during the Festival of Reason in Strasbourg Cathedral on November 20, 1793.[46]

On December 4, 1793, the National Convention passed the Law of Frimaire, which ordered the centralization of political power and forbade deputies on mission in the provinces from taking action without the authority of the Committee of Public Safety in Paris. Deputy Saint-Just used this law to demand a public explanation from Euloge Schroeder for his sadistic conduct. On December 7, 1793, Commissar Schneider replied the following to Deputy Saint-Just: "The sans-culottes have bread, and the people bless the guillotine that has saved them." Between

November 5, 1793 and December 12, 1793, the Mobile Revolutionary Tribunal had executed twenty-eight people from Strasbourg, Mutzig, Barr, Obernai, Epfig and Sélestat.[52]

On December 7, 1793, Civil Commissar Euloge Schneider, apparently in a last-minute attempt to gain respect, married Mademoiselle Stamm of the Town of Barr, about four miles southwest of Obernai. Deputy Saint-Just was unimpressed and sent Euloge Schneider to Paris for trial, saying "Let us have no faith in cosmopolitan charlatans, but trust only to ourselves...The Revolution had become a national enterprise; foreign enthusiasts were not wanted."[52] The revolutionary authorities in Paris tried, convicted, and executed Euloge Schneider in Paris on April 1, 1794.

Cerf Berr Dies, December 7, 1793

On December 7, 1793 at one o'clock in the afternoon, Cerf Berr of Médelsheim died in his multi-storied, black-and-white, timber-framed home at number nine Quai Finkwiller in Strasbourg. The date of his release from prison is unknown.

An extant document numbered 1869 in the archives of the Strasbourg État Civil recorded Cerf Berr's death. By chance, the Strasbourg État Civil first began to record the births and deaths of Ashkenazim near the end of 1793. The record of Cerf Berr's death reads as follows (the French version and a photo of the actual record are available elsewhere[55]):

* * * * * * * *

Cerf Berr's Death Record, Number 1869,
Strasbourg Registry, December 7, 1793

This day 17 Frimaire of the second year of the French Republic [December 7, 1793], seen by Mr. Charles Frederic Schneider, member of the Council General of the Commune of Strasbourg,

Department of the Bas-Rhin, was elected to record acts designed to enter the État civil of citizens. The copy of the Procès verbal of this day, made by Jean Michel Aumond, Commissar of Police of the Third Arrondissement of Strasbourg Commune, noted that Clerk Hermann Engel, aged twenty-six years, and Samuel Levy Portier, aged thirty years, both domiciled in the City of Strasbourg and who were deemed competent before Commissar Aumond, have declared that Cerf Berr, aged sixty-eight years, banker, legitimate husband of Anne Brill [sic], died today at one hour after noon in his house on Finkwiller and that the said Commissar came and made sure of that death. I, Charles Frederic Schneider, after Hermann Engel and Samuel Levy, certify the verity of this declaration, that I have prepared this document, and that the declaration is signed by me. Made in the Common House of Strasbourg, the day, month and the year above.

Hermann Engel – Salomon Levy – Schneider[55]

* * * * * * * * *

Cerf Berr of Médelsheim died about sixteen days after Strasbourg Mayor Pierre Monet terrorized the Ashkenazim in the District of Strasbourg on November 21, 1793. There is no cause of death reported for Cerf Berr. However, he was sixty-eight-years-old, which was an advanced age for French men of his era. Indeed, the average life expectancy was around twenty-five years for French people born around the same time as Cerf Berr was born (the early 1700s).[56] Cerf Berr outlived his predicted life expectancy by around forty-three years. However, the proximity in time between Cerf Berr's imprisonment and his death suggests that his death may have been due in part to the suffering associated with his imprisonment and persecution, said historian Renée Neher-Bernheim.[57]

Cerf Berr died at the height of the Cult of Reason, when every French person was supposed to receive burial in a state-approved civic cemetery.

The devout Cerf Berr would never have agreed to this blasphemy. Burial in the Ettendorf Jewish Cemetery would have satisfied him and his kin, but Austrian and Prussian Armies blocked the road to the Ettendorf Jewish Cemetery.

Rosenwiller Jewish Cemetery was another possibility for Cerf Berr's burial. His sister Esther was buried there. However, representatives of the French Revolutionary Government had destroyed Rosenwiller Jewish Cemetery thirteen days earlier (November 24, 1793), as noted above, and theoretically no Jew was supposed to receive burial there.

In summary, in 1792, the French Revolution spun badly out of control. Deputy Robespierre launched the Reign of Terror to try to regain control of the French Revolution. On December 7, 1793, Cerf Berr of Médelsheim died after a cruel imprisonment for being an Ashkenazim. French Revolutionary Government actors had desecrated and closed down the Rosenwiller Jewish Cemetery near Strasbourg weeks earlier, and Austrian and Prussian Armies blocked the road to the Ettendorf Jewish Cemetery. The old man of Alsace, Cerf Berr of Médelsheim, needed a final resting place. What would his family do?

Chapter Eight Notes:

1.   George Peabody Gooch: *Germany and the French Revolution*. London, England, United Kingdom: Longmans, Green and Co., 1920, p. 350; Hugh Gough: "Politics and power: the triumph of Jacobinism in Strasbourg, 1791–1793." *The Historical Journal*: 1980, Volume 23, Number 2, pp. 327–352; and Henri Wallon: "Dietrich." In *Histoire du Tribunal Révolutionnaire de Paris avec le journal de ses actes*. Volume 2, Paris, France: Librairie Hachette, 1880, pp. 294–302. Available at http://www.archive.org/stream/histoiredutribu06wallgoog#page/n306/mode/2up; accessed December 26, 2011.

2.   Henry Morse Stephens: *A History of the French Revolution*. Three volumes. New York City, New York: Charles Scribner's Sons, 1911, Volume 2, pp. 54–55, 62–63, 115.

3.   Ibid, pp. 79–82.

4. Jean Tulard, Jean Arthême Fayard, and A. Fierro: *Histoire et Dictionnaire de la Révolution Française: 1789–1799*. Paris, France: Robert Laffont, 1998.

5. "Narrative of Marie-Thérèse de France." Available at llhttp://digital.library.upenn.edu/women/wormeley/princess/princess-3.html; accessed November 30, 2011.

6. Henry Morse Stephens: *A History of the French Revolution*. Three volumes. New York City, New York: Charles Scribner's Sons, 1911, Volume 2, pp. 105–106.

7. "The Proclamation of the Duke of Brunswick." In J. H. Robinson (ed.): *Readings in European History*, Volume 2. Boston, Massachusetts: Ginn, 1906, pp. 443–445. Available at http://history.hanover.edu/texts/bruns.htm; accessed October 30, 2011.

8. Auguste Philippe Herlaut: *Deux Témoins de la Terreur: le Citoyen Dubuisson, le ci-Devant Baron de Haindel*. Paris, France: Librairie Clavreuil, 1958, pp. 125–135.

9. "Commune de Romanswiller: Histoire." Available at http://romanswiller.fr/?page_id=13; accessed January 22, 2012.

10. Robert Weyl: "Les Juifs à Rosheim." In *Saisons d'Alsace*, Number 66, 1978. Available at http://judaisme.sdv.fr/synagog/basrhin/r-z/rosheim.htm; accessed January 22, 2012.

11. "Sans-culotte." *Webster's New International Dictionary of the English Language*, Second Edition, Unabridged. Springfield, Massachusetts: Merriam, 1941, p. 2214.

12. Graeme Fife: *The Terror: the Shadow of the Guillotine*. New York City, New York: St. Martin's Press, 2004, pp. 61–62.

13. T. C. W. Blanning: *The French Revolutionary Wars, 1787–1802*. London, England, United Kingdom: Arnold Publisher, 1996, pp. 71–73. For more information on the September Massacres, see the following works: Frédéric Bluche: *Septembre 1792, Logiques d'un Massacre*. Paris, France: Robert Laffont, 1986; Pierre Caron: *Les Massacres de Septembre*. Paris, France: Maison du Livre français, 1935; Paul Girault de Coursac: *September 1792, la Mort Organisee*. Paris: Editions F. X. de Guibert, 1994; Louis Léon Théodore Gosselin: *Les Massacres de Septembre*. Paris, France: Perrin, 1907; and Georges Soria: *Grande Histoire de La Révolution Francaise*. Paris, France: Bordas, 1988 (Three volumes: 1: L'embrasement, 2: Les paroxysms, 3: L'irréversible).

14. Hippolyte Adolphe Taine: *The French Revolution*. Volume 2. Translated by John Durand. New York City, New York: Henry Holt and Company, 1892, p. 164.

15. Joseph Tylenda: *Jesuit Saints & Martyrs*. Chicago, Illinois: Loyola Press, 1998, par. 275; "Dukes of Brissac." In Hugh Chisholm (ed.): *Encyclopaedia Britannica*. Volume 4, 11th edition. New York City, New York: Encyclopaedia Britannica Company, 1910, p. 574; and Joan Haslip: *Madame du Barry: the Wages of Beauty*. New York City, New York: Tauris Parke, pp. 177–178.

16. Gregory Fremont-Barnes: *The French Revolutionary Wars*. Oxford, England, United Kingdom: Osprey Publishing, 2001, p. 26.

17. Adrien Dansette: *Religious History of Modern France. Volume I: from the Revolution to the Third Republic*. Edinburgh, Scotland: Nelson Publisher, 1961, p. 82.

18. Adolphus W. Ward (ed.): "The French Revolution." In *The Cambridge Modern History*. London, England, United Kingdom: C. J. Clay and Sons, Volume 8, pp. 413–414. See also Arthur Chuquet: *The Wars of the Revolution, VII: The Siege of Mainz and the French Occupation of the Rhineland, 1792–1793*. Paris, France: Plon-Nourrit et Cie, The Nafziger Collection, 2006.

19. Charles Poisson: *Les Fournisseurs aux Armées sous la Révolution Française: Le Directoire des Achats* (1792–1793). Paris, France: Librairie Historique A. Margraff, 1932. The information on supplies provided by Baruch Berr to the French Army of the Rhine in Landau during November/December 1793 is on p. 129. See also Zosa Szajkowski: "The discussion and struggle over Jewish emancipation in Alsace in the early years of the French Revolution." In *Jews and the French Revolutions of 1789, 1830, and 1848*. New York City, New York: Ktav Publishing House, 1970, pp. 352–353; and Zosa Szajkowski: "French Jews in the armed forces during the Revolution of 1789." In *Jews and the French Revolutions of 1789, 1830, and 1848*. New York City, New York: Ktav Publishing House, 1970, pp. 569, 573–574.

20. Robert Weyl: "Les Juifs à Rosheim." In *Saisons d'Alsace*, Number 66, 1978. Available at http://judaisme.sdv.fr/synagog/basrhin/r-z/rosheim.htm; accessed January 31, 2012; and Zosa Szajkowski: "The reform of the État-Civil of the French Jews during the Revolution of 1789." In *Jews and the French Revolutions of 1789, 1830 and 1848*. New York City, New York: Ktav Publishing House, 1970, pp. 363–364.

21. Norman Hampson: *Saint-Just*. Oxford, England, United Kingdom: Basil Blackwell, 1991, pp. 82–83.

22. T. C. W. Blanning: *The French Revolutionary Wars, 1787–1802*. London, England, United Kingdom: Arnold Publisher, 1996, pp. 91–92.

23. Zosa Szajkowski: "The Jewish problem in Alsace, Metz, and Lorraine on the eve of the Revolution of 1789." In *Jews and the French Revolutions of 1789, 1830 and 1848*. New York City, New York: Ktav Publishing House, 1970, p. 337.

24. Henry Morse Stephens: *A History of the French Revolution*. Three volumes. New York City, New York: Charles Scribner's Sons, 1911, Volume 2, p. 214. The source of the quote on Berr Isaac Berr is Lionel Kochan: *The Making of Western Jewry, 1600–1819*. Houndmills, Basingstoke, Hampshire, England: Palgrave-MacMillan, 2004, pp. 265–266.

25. Graeme Fife: *The Terror: the Shadow of the Guillotine*. New York City, New York: St. Martin's Press, 2004, p. 93; and Henry Morse Stephens: *A History of the French Revolution*. Three volumes. New York City, New York: Charles Scribner's Sons, 1911, Volume 2, p. 216.

26. Graeme Fife: *The Terror: the Shadow of the Guillotine*. New York City, New York: St. Martin's Press, 2004, p. 96.

27. See "Observations pour le citoyen Lipman-Cerfberr en réponse au rapport fait, le 25 janvier [1793], par les commissaires de la Convention nationale, a l'armée de la Belgique." Available at http://gallica.bnf.fr/ark:/12148/bpt6k44054p/f1.image; accessed December 24, 1793.

28. George Q. Flynn: *Conscription and Democracy: the Draft in France, Great Britain, and the United States*. Westport, Connecticut: Greenwood Press, 2002, p. 15.

29. John McManners: *The French Revolution and the Church*. Westport, Connecticut: Greenwood Press, 1982, pp. 82–84.

30. Graeme Fife: *The Terror: the Shadow of the Guillotine*. New York City, New York: St. Martin's Press, 2004, pp. 87–88.

31. Zosa Szajkowski: "French Jews in the armed forces during the Revolution of 1789." In *Jews and the French Revolutions of 1789, 1830, and 1848*. New York City, New York: Ktav Publishing House, 1970, pp. 569, 573–575.

32. Graeme Fife: *The Terror: the Shadow of the Guillotine*. New York City, New York: St. Martin's Press, 2004, p. 139.

33. Adolphus W. Ward (ed.) "The French Revolution." In *The Cambridge Modern History*. London, England, United Kingdom: C. J. Clay and Sons, Volume 8, p. 423–426.

34. Graeme Fife: *The Terror: the Shadow of the Guillotine*. New York City, New York: St. Martin's Press, 2004, p. 96.

35. Ibid, pp. 125–127; and "Cimetière juif de Rosenwiller." Available at http://www.lieux-insolites.fr/basrhin/rosenwiller/rosen.htm; accessed March 10 2012.

36. Avraham Malthete: *Registre du Cimetière Israélite de Rosenwiller, 1753–1980*. Paris, France: Cercle de Généalogie Juive, 2004, p. 168. Available for purchase at http://www.genealoj.org/New/texte/page08.php; accessed December 12, 2011.

37. Graeme Fife: *The Terror: the Shadow of the Guillotine*. New York City, New York: St. Martin's Press, 2004, pp. 128–129.

38. Zosa Szajkowski: "Gli Ebrei nei club dei Giacobini durante la rivoluzione francese del 1789." In *Jews and the French Revolutions of 1789, 1830 and 1848*. New York City, New York: Ktav Publishing House, 1970, p. 416.

39. Zosa Szajkowski: "The Alsatian debts." In *Jews and the French Revolutions of 1789, 1830 and 1848*. New York City, New York: Ktav Publishing House, 1970, pp. 703–704; and "Historical sketch." In "An Inventory to the Alsace-Lorraine Collection, 1786–1868." Leo Lichtenberg, N.E. H. Manuscript Processor, Klau Library, Hebrew Union College – Jewish Institute of Religion. Available at http://huc.edu/libraries/collections/inventories/Alsace-Lorraine1786-1868.pdf; accessed January 29, 2012.

40. "Jacques Hébert Archive (1757–1794)" in *The History of the French Revolution*, available at http://www.marxists.org/history/france/revolution/hebert/index.htm; accessed March 12, 2012; and Robert Roswell Palmer: *Twelve Who Ruled: the Year of the Terror in the French Revolution*. Princeton, New Jersey: Princeton University Press, 1941, pp. 58–59; and David P. Jordan: *The Revolutionary Career of Maximilien Robespierre*. Chicago, Illinois: University of Chicago Press, 1985, p. 179.

41. Moses Ginsburger: *Cerf-Berr et son Époque*. Société d'Histoire des Juifs d'Alsace-Lorraine. Guebwiller, Alsace, France: J. Dreyfus, 1908, pp.

25–26. Available at http://gallica.bnf.fr/ark:/12148/bpt6k5427849p/ f8.image; accessed November 30, 2011. The source of the information on Jean-Frédéric Edelmann is available at http://www.operas.com. ar/Music-Encyclopedia/24530/Edelmann,-Jean-Frederic-[Johann-Friedrich].htm; accessed February 6, 2012.

42. John McManners: *The French Revolution and the Church*. Westport, Connecticut: Greenwood Press, 1982, pp. 87–88; William Doyle: *The Oxford History of the French Revolution*. Oxford, England: Oxford University Press, 2003, p. 259; and Sylvia Neely: *A Concise History of the French Revolution*. Lanham, Maryland: Rowman & Littlefield, 2008, p. 199.

43. Louis Spach: *Histoire de la Basse Alsace de la Ville de Strasbourg*. Strasbourg, France: Berger-Levrault, 1858, pp. 302–305.

44. Henry Morse Stephens: *A History of the French Revolution*. Three volumes. New York City, New York: Charles Scribner's Sons, 1911, Volume 2, pp. 437–441; and Norman Hampson: *Saint-Just*. Oxford, England, United Kingdom: Basil Blackwell, 1991, pp. 154–155.

45. Norman Hampson: *Saint-Just*. Oxford, England, United Kingdom: Basil Blackwell, 1991, pp. 148–149.

46. Robert Roswell Palmer: *Twelve Who Ruled: the Year of the Terror in the French Revolution*. Princeton, New Jersey: Princeton University Press, 1941, pp. 184–185.

47. Robert Weyl: "Les funérailles de Cerf Berr de Médelsheim à Rosenwiller." *Revue des Études Juives*, Volume 136 (1–2), January-June, 1977, pp. 157–158.

48. Robert Weyl: "Chronique des juifs Rosheim." In *Saisons d'Alsace*, Number 66, 1978. Available at http://judaisme.sdv.fr/synagog/basrhin/ r-z/rosheim/chroniq.htm; accessed January 31, 2012.

49. Zosa Szajkowski: "The Jewish aspect of levying taxes in the French Revolution." In *Jews and the French Revolutions of 1789, 1830, and 1848*. New York City, New York: Ktav Publishing House, 1970, pp. 527–529, including footnote#19, p. 529.

50. Rodolphe Reuss: "Seligmann Alexandre ou les tribulations d'un Israelite strasbourgeois pendant la Terreur." Available at http:// judaisme.sdv.fr/histoire/villes/strasbrg/seligman/seligmanalex.htm; accessed December 25, 2011.

51. Robert Roswell Palmer: *Twelve Who Ruled: the Year of the Terror in the French Revolution.* Princeton, New Jersey: Princeton University Press, 1941, pp. 186–191.

52. François-Alphonse Aulard: *The French Revolution: a Political History, 1789–1804,* Volume 3. Translated from the French of the third edition by Bernard Miall. New York, New York: Charles Scribner's Sons, 1910, p. 160.

53. Moses and Ernest Ginsburger: "Contributions à l'histoire des Juifs d'Alsace pendant la terreur" *Revue des Études Juives.* Volume 47, Paris, France: Librairie Durlacher, 1903, pp. 285–286.

54. Louis Spach: *Histoire de la Basse Alsace de la Ville de Strasbourg.* Strasbourg, France: Berger-Levrault, 1858, pp. 308–309.

55. Renée Neher-Bernheim: "Note sur la date de la mort de Cerfberr de Médelsheim." *Revue des Études Juives.* Volume 132, January-June, 1973, p. 142.

56. Data on French life expectancies from 1740 to 2005 is from the Institute national d'études démographiques (INED). Available at http://www.ined.fr/en/everything_about_population/graph_month/life_expectancy_france/; accessed December 23, 2011.

57. Renée Neher-Bernheim: "Note sur la date de la mort de Cerfberr de Médelsheim." *Revue des Études Juives.* Volume 132, January-June, 1973, p. 141.

Epilogue

The death of Cerf Berr of Médelsheim was heartbreaking for his large and devoted family. They likely gathered in the inner courtyard of the former Hotel Ribeaupierre to mourn his passing. In a room separate from Cerf Berr's death chamber, several rabbis likely were praying. In the death chamber itself, Cerf Berr may have been placed on a wooden board at the foot of his bed, as was the Alsatian Jewish custom, while a few women sewed his shroud. The Cerf Berr family may have performed the rite of the Mehila (forgiveness), described by Jewish Alsatian historian Daniel Stauben as follows:

> All relatives entered the mortuary chamber. They were ushered...and lined...up in front of the board upon which the dead [person] was lying...One by one, the desolate people bent down to the deceased and, lifting the shroud around him, they held his two cold feet in their hands, while with a choking voice they muttered the prescribed formula, imploring him to forgive them in heaven, whatever pain they may have caused him on earth. The casket was then temporarily nailed.[1]

Jewish funerals in Alsace did not display pomp, even for someone of the stature of Cerf Berr of Médelsheim. For example, there was no Requiem or Mass for the dead. Four men wearing round hats as their only adornment may have carried Cerf Berr's black cloth-draped coffin on their shoulders to a nearby horse-drawn vehicle. Cerf Berr's family had decided to transport him secretly and under cover of night to Rosenwiller Jewish Cemetery despite prohibition of further burials there by the French Revolutionary Government.

Near the entrance to Rosenwiller Jewish Cemetery was a little building called Metare Hüss, or the house of purification.[2] Cerf Berr would have received his last washing and dressing in the Metare Hüss. However, French revolutionaries earlier had damaged the Metare Hüss during the desecration of the cemetery, so whether Cerf Berr received the traditional sacred rites in this building is unknown. According to these rites, he would have been washed with tepid water, his nails cut and his hair combed, and his body dressed in his shroud. A shawl called a tallit would have been placed around his shoulders with its ends laced around his fingers in such a way that one could discern in each hand the three Hebrew letters: shin, daled, yad. The three letters combined convey the name of the Eternal, the God of the dead and the living.[1]

Cerf Berr's relatives were concerned about where to bury him in the Rosenwiller Jewish Cemetery. If adversaries ever located his gravesite, they would desecrate it. Cerf Berr's kin also had to perform the burial quickly and return to Strasbourg before dawn. The first place considered for Cerf Berr's grave was in the new part of the cemetery, which the Ashkenazim had acquired in 1763. In April 1793, Cerf Berr's sister Esther had been buried in the new part of the cemetery.[2] The second place considered for Cerf Berr's gravesite was near the damaged Metare Hüss. Cerf Berr's kin decided to bury him there. If a headstone of wood or stone ever was erected over the site, it did not survive into the nineteenth century.[3] Yet, a Registry existed of the individuals buried in Rosenwiller Jewish Cemetery beginning in 1753. Oddly, the Rosenwiller Jewish Cemetery Registry did not contain the name of Cerf Berr of Médelsheim, Hirtz of Médelsheim, Hirtz of Bischheim, or any other moniker that might describe the hero of this book. However, the Registry did record the following note for a grave near the old Metare Hüss: "A poor nameless woman of the province of Médelsheim and of Bischheim, who lived in Strasbourg." Eventually, six graves appeared in the area near the old Metare Hüss. The six graves belonged to the following decedents:

Number 1 – Mordekhai ha-Cohen, a late eighteenth-century rabbi of Rosheim, who was listed in the royal census of 1784 under the name of Marx Cahn, rabbi, and who died in 1816.

Number 2 – Israel Tergheim, rabbi and mohel of Mutzig, son-in-law of Rabbi Simon Moyse Horchheim, rabbi of Mutzig. He died in 1816.

Number 3 – Simon Moyse Horchheim, rabbi of Mutzig, by letters patent of the Prince Bishop of Strasbourg. He died in 1805.

Number 4 – Edel, the wife of Rabbi Simon Horchheim. She was the daughter of Rabbi Loeb. She died in 1817.

Number 5 – The wife of Abraham Wingersheim of Strasbourg, who died in 1800.

Number 6 – A poor nameless woman of the province of Médelsheim and of Bischheim, who lived in Strasbourg.[4]

By 1908, Cerf Berr's grave was marked with a headstone, which mentioned his name and read:

> Here is buried the body of one who was faithful to his people, sought the good for the community, and cherished justice. He was perfect in his conduct and friendly toward the poor. He protected the needy against the storm, feared God, and made Israel a good house. The powerful, sublime, honorable, and distinguished Rabbi Naftali Hirz Médelsheim…May his soul be bound in the bundle of life with the soul of the righteous and pious, where he awaits his fate at the end of days.[5]

Between 1930 and 1935, Alsatian Jews undertook restoration of the old headstones of Rosenwiller Jewish Cemetery. Cerf Berr's headstone stated his name, but listed an erroneous date of death—September 20, 1794. Endless confusion ensued as to what was the true date of Cerf

Berr's death. Cerf Berr's death record in the Strasbourg État Civil, cited above, finally resolved the discrepancy.[5] Cerf Berr of Médelsheim died on December 7, 1793.[6]

Nothing in Cerf Berr's epitaph suggests his role as the consistent driving force behind the emancipation of the Ashkenazim in France. Heinrich Graetz appreciated Cerf Berr's seminal contribution to history. Heinrich Graetz wrote:

> The freedom of the French Jews did not fall into their laps like ripe fruit, in the maturing of which they had taken no trouble. They made vigorous exertions to remove the oppressive yoke from their shoulders...The most zealous energy in behalf of the liberation of the French Jews was displayed by a man, whose forgotten memory deserves to be transmitted to posterity. Herz Médelsheim or Cerf Berr was the first to exert himself by word and deed to remove the prejudices against his co-religionists, under which he himself suffered severely. He was acquainted with the Talmud, in good circumstances, warm-hearted enough to avoid the selfishness bred by prosperity, and sufficiently liberal to understand and spread the new spirit emanating from [Moses] Mendelssohn.[7]

Cerf Berr of Médelsheim was an even greater personage than suggested by Heinrich Graetz, in the opinion of the author. Before September 27, 1791, the Ashkenazim in Europe had survived for almost sixteen centuries as a disenfranchised and oppressed minority population that lived outside of all prevailing political orders in Europe. For almost five hundred years, Jews had lived tenuously in France because of a long-standing law prohibiting their residence in the Kingdom of France. For four hundred years, the Ashkenazim in Alsace had been degraded by an onerous body tax required for them to enter Lower Alsace and the City of Strasbourg. Cerf Berr of Médelsheim tenaciously and single-handedly led the demolition of this status quo. He never gave up on his quest to forge economic and political freedom for his people. Because of his efforts, his adversaries hunted him during life and after death so that his name—Cerf Berr of Médelsheim—and his remarkable role in the emancipation of the Jews in France remained hidden from posterity, until now.

Epilogue Notes:

1.   Daniel Stauben: *Scenes of Jewish Life in Alsace.* Edited and translated by Rose Choron. London, England: Joseph Simon Pangloss Press, 1991, pp. 47–50.

2.   Robert Weyl: "Les funérailles de Cerf Berr de Médelsheim à Rosenwiller." *Revue des Études Juives*, Volume 136 (1–2), January-June, 1977, p. 156.

3.   "Rosenwiller." Cercle de Genealogie Juive JGS cemetery information. Available at http://www.iajgsjewishcemeteryproject.org/france/ rosenwiller-bas-rhin-departement-alsace-region.html; accessed March 12, 2012.

4.   Robert Weyl: "Les funérailles de Cerf Berr de Médelsheim à Rosenwiller." *Revue des Études Juives*, Volume 136 (1–2), January-June, 1977, pp. 160–161.

5.   Moses Ginsburger: *Cerf-Berr et son Époque.* Société d'Histoire des Juifs d'Alsace-Lorraine. Guebwiller, Alsace, France: J. Dreyfus, 1908, p. 34. Available at http://gallica.bnf.fr/ark:/12148/bpt6k5427849p/f8.image; accessed November 30, 2011.

6.   Renée Neher-Bernheim: "Note sur la date de la mort de Cerfberr de Médelsheim." *Revue des Études Juives*. Volume 132, January-June, 1973, pp. 142–143.

7.   Heinrich Graetz: *History of the Jews.* Volume V. Philadelphia, Pennsylvania: Jewish Publication Society of America, 1895, p. 430.

BIBLIOGRAPHY

Israel Abrahams: *Jewish Life in the Middle Ages*. Philadelphia, Pennsylvania: Jewish Publication Society of America, 1993.

Geoffrey Adams: *The Huguenots and French Opinion, 1685–1787: the Enlightenment Debate on Toleration*. Toronto, Ontario: Canadian Corporation for Studies in Religion, 1991.

Elkan Nathan Adler: *Jewish Travellers [sic] in the Middle Ages: 19 Firsthand Accounts*. New York City, New York: Dover, 1987.

Ken Alder: *Engineering the Revolution: Arms and Enlightenment in France, 1763–1815*. Chicago, Illinois: University of Chicago Press, 1997.

Sholom Aleichem: *The Bloody Hoax*. Translated by Aliza Shevrin. Bloomington, Indiana: Indiana University Press, 1991.

Jean Le Rond d'Alembert: *An Account of the Destruction of the Jesuits of France*. London, England, United Kingdom: T. Becket & P. A. De Hondt, 1766.

John M. S. Allison: *Lamoignon de Malesherbes*. New Haven, Connecticut: Yale University Press, 1938.

Alexander Altmann: *Moses Mendelssohn: a Biographical Study*. Oxford, England, United Kingdom: Littman Library of Jewish Civilization, 1998.

Anonymous: *La Révolution Française et l'Emancipation des Juifs, Issues 4-5.* Éditions d'histoire sociale, 1789. Ann Arbor, Michigan: University of Michigan, digitalized August 27, 2008. Available at http://books. google.com/books?id=BbptAAAAMAAJ&pg=RA1-PA143&dq=P% C3%A9tition+des+Juifs+Etablis+en+France&source=gbs_selected_p ages&cad=3#v=onepage&q=P%C3%A9tition%20des%20Juifs%20 Etablis%20en%20France&f=false; accessed January 29, 2012.

Nigel Aston: *Religion and Revolution in France, 1780–1804.* Washington, D.C.: Catholic University of America Press, 2000.

Augustine of Hippo: *The City of God.* New York City, New York: Penguin Classics, 2003.

François-Alphonse Aulard: *The French Revolution: a Political History, 1789–1804.* Four volumes. Translated by Bernard Miall. New York City, New York: Charles Scribner's Sons, 1910.

Bernard S. Bachrach: *Early Medieval Jewish Policy in Western Europe.* Minneapolis, Minnesota: University of Minnesota Press, 1977.

Robert Badinter: *Free and Equal: Emancipating France's Jews 1789–1791.* Translated into English from the French by Adam Simms. Teaneck, New Jersey: Ben Yehuda Press, 2010.

Henry Martyn Baird: *The Huguenots and the Revocation of the Edict of Nantes.* Two volumes. New York City, New York: Charles Scribner's Sons, 1895.

Sabine Baring-Gould: *The Book of the Rhine from Cleve to Mainz.* New York City, New York: Macmillan, 1906. Available at http://www. archive.org/details/abookrhinefromc00barigoog; accessed January 1, 2012.

Salo Wittmayer Baron: *Social and Religious History of the Jews.* Eighteen volumes. Philadelphia, Pennsylvania: Columbia University Press and the Jewish Publication Society of America, 1952–1983.

Rita Hermon Belot: *L'Abbé Grégoire: la Politique et la Vérité*. Paris, France: Seuil, 2000.

Benjamin of Tudela: *The Itinerary of Benjamin of Tudela: Travels in the Middle Ages*. Cold Spring, New York: Nightingale Resources, 1983. Available at http://depts.washington.edu/silkroad/texts/tudela. html#itinerary_1; accessed November 6, 2011.

Esther Benbassa: *The Jews of France: a History from Antiquity to the Present*. Princeton, New Jersey: Princeton University Press, 2001.

Jay R. Berkovitz: "The French Revolution and the Jews: assessing the cultural impact." *Association for Jewish Studies*. Volume 20, Number 1, 1995.

Jay R. Berkovitz: *Rites and Passages: the Beginnings of Modern Jewish Culture in France, 1650–1860*. Philadelphia, Pennsylvania: University of Pennsylvania Press, 2004.

Jay R. Berkovitz: "Ritual and modernity: rethinking Jewish emancipation." Available at http://www.umass.edu/judaic/ anniversaryvolume/articles/03-A1-Berkovitz.pdf; accessed December 12, 2011.

Jay R. Berkovitz: *The Shaping of Jewish Identity in Nineteenth Century France*. Detroit, Michigan: Wayne State University: Wayne State University Press, 1989.

Oliver Bernier: *Louis the Beloved: the Life of King Louis XV*. New York City, New York: Doubleday, 1984.

James H. Billington: *Fire in the Mind of Men*. New Brunswick, New Jersey: Transaction Publishers, 1999.

T. C. W. Blanning: *The French Revolutionary Wars, 1787–1802*. London, England, United Kingdom: Arnold, 1996.

François Bluche: *King Louis XV*. Paris, France: Editions Perrin, 2000.

Frédéric Bluche: *Septembre 1792, Logiques d'un Massacre*. Paris, France: Robert Laffont, 1986.

Poul Borchsenius: *The Chains are Broken; the History of the Jewish Emancipation*. Volume IV, *The History of the Jews*. New York City, New York: Simon and Schuster, 1965.

Mary C. Boys: *Has God Only One Blessing? Judaism as a Source of Christian Self-Understanding*. Mahwah, New Jersey: Paulist Press, 2000.

Martin Brecht: *Martin Luther: the Preservation of the Church, 1532– 1546*. Minneapolis, Minnesota: Fortress Press, 1993.

Michael Brenner, Vicki Caron, and Uri R. Kaufmann (eds.): *Jewish Emancipation Reconsidered*. London, England, United Kingdom: Leo Baeck Institute, 2003.

Dewey A. Browder: *Zweibrücken: Yesterday and Today*. Zweibrücken, Germany: Pfaelzischer Merkur, 1976.

Raymond E. Brown: *An Introduction to the New Testament*. New York City, New York Doubleday, 1997.

Reed Browning: *The War of the Austrian Succession*. New York City, New York: St. Martin's Press, 1993.

Geoffrey Bruun: *Saint-Just: Apostle of the Terror*. Hamden, Connecticut: Archon Books, 1966.

James Bryce: *The Holy Roman Empire*. London, England, United Kingdom: Macmillan and Co., 1873.

Julius Caesar: *The Conquest of Gaul*. New York City, New York: Penguin Classics, 1983.

Abraham Cahen: "L'émancipation des Juifs devant la Société royale des sciences et des arts de Metz en 1787 et M. Roederer." *Revue des Études Juives*, Volume 1, Number 1, 1880, pp. 83–104.

The Cambridge Modern History. Volume 8: French Revolution. Cambridge, England, United Kingdom: Cambridge University Press, 1904.

Michelle Cameron: *The Fruit of her Hands: the Story of Shira of Ashkenaz.* New York City, New York: Pocket Books,

Pierre Caron: *Les Massacres de Septembre.* Paris, France: Maison du Livre français, 1935.

Alphonse Cerfberr de Médelsheim: *Les Juifs: leur Histoire, leur Moeurs.* Paris, France: Albert Frères, 1847.

M. Chahin: *The Kingdom of Armenia: a History.* Surrey, England, United Kingdom: Curzon, 2001.

Robert Chazan: *In the Year 1096: the First Crusade and the Jews.* Philadelphia, Pennsylvania: Jewish Publication Society of America, 1996.

Arthur Chuqet: *L'Expédition de Custine.* Paris, France: Librairie Plon, 1913.

Jeremy Cohen: *The Friars and the Jews: the Evolution of Medieval Anti-Judaism.* Ithaca, New York: Cornell University Press, 1982.

Jeremy Cohen: *Living Letters of the Law: Ideas of the Jews in Medieval Christianity.* Berkeley, California: University of California Press, 1999.

Patrick Collinson: *The Reformation.* London, England, United Kingdom: Phoenix, 2003.

Yves Combeau: *Le Comte d'Argenson, 1696–1764: Ministre de King Louis XV.* Paris, France: Mémoires et Documents de L'École nationale des chartes, 55, 1999.

Martin van Creveld: *Supplying War: Logistics from Wallenstein to Patton.* Cambridge, United Kingdom: Cambridge University Press, 2004.

Derek Croxton: "The peace of Westphalia of 1648 and the origins of sovereignty." *International History Review*, Volume 21, 1999, pp. 569–591.

Derek Croxton and Anuschka Tischer: *The Peace of Westphalia: a Historical Dictionary*. Westport, Connecticut: Greenwood Publishing, 2001.

Jean Daltroff: "Activités socioprofessionnelles des Juifs de Strasbourg à l'époque de Napoléon 1er." Available at http://judaisme.sdv.fr/histoire/villes/strasbrg/metiers/metiers.htm; accessed November 28, 2011.

Jean Daltroff: "Les Ratisbonne, notables et financiers Strasbourgeois au XIX siècle." *Revue des Études Juives*, Volume 159, Numbers 3–4, July–December 2000, pp. 461–477.

Adrien Dansette: *Religious History of Modern France*. Volume I. Freiburg, Germany: Herder, 1961.

Norman Davies: *Europe: a History*. New York City, New York: Oxford University Press, 1996.

"Declaration of the Rights of Man–1789." *Avalon Project*. Available at http://avalon.law.yale.edu/18th_century/rightsof.asp; accessed November 27, 1789.

Pierre Delaunay: "Hirsch Hirtz Cerf Naftali (Le Grand Cerf Berr) Berr Cerf Berr of Médelsheim." Available at http://gw3.geneanet.org/delaunaypierre?lang=en&p=hirsch+hirtz+cerf+naftaly+le+grand+cerf+berr&n=berr+cerf+berr+Médelsheim; accessed January 20, 2012.

Denombrement des Juifs d'Alsace, 1784. Strasbourg, Alsace, France: Cercle de Généalogie Juive, Editions du Cédrat, no date. The book is available for purchase at http://www.genealoj.org/New/ENtexte/page06.php; accessed December 1, 2011.

Charles Dickens: *All the Year Round: a Weekly Journal.* Volume 4, from June 4–November 26, 1870. London, England, United Kingdom: Chapman and Hall, 1870.

William Doyle: *Jansenism: Catholic Resistance to Authority from the Reformation to the French Revolution.* New York City, New York: Palgrave Macmillan, 2000.

Eamon Duffy: *Saints & Sinners: a History of the Popes.* New Haven, Connecticut: Yale University Press, 1997.

Richard van Dülmen and Richard Klimmt: *Saarländische Geschichte. Eine Anthologie.* St. Ingbert/Röhrig, 1995.

Hastings Eells: *Martin Bucer.* New Haven, Connecticut: Yale University Press, 1931.

Shlomo Eidelberg: *The Jews and the Crusades: the Hebrew Chronicles of the First and Second Crusades.* Hoboken, New Jersey: Ktav Publishing House, 1996.

Saadia R. Eisenberg: *Reading Medieval Religious Disputation: the 1240 "Debate" between Rabbi Yehiel of Paris and Friar Nicholas Donin.* University of Michigan dissertation, 2008. Available at http://deepblue.lib.umich.edu/handle/2027.42/60741; accessed December 17, 2011.

Eusebius: *Life of Constantine.* Oxford, England, United Kingdom: Oxford University Press, 1999.

Rémi Fabre: *Les Protestants en France depuis 1789.* Paris, France: La Découverte, 1999.

Pascal Faustini: "Entrepreneurs juifs en Sarre dans la second moitié du XVIIIᵉ siècle: Éléments généalogiques concernant les familles Alexander, Blien, et Beer." Available at http://judaisme.sdv.fr/histoire/historiq/fer/fer.htm; accessed November 6, 2011.

David Feuerwerker: *L'Emancipation des Juifs en France*. Paris, France: Albin Michel, 1976.

David Feuerwerker: "Les juifs en France: anatomie de 307 cahiers de doléances de 1789." *Annales. Économies, Sociétés, Civilisations.* 20e année, Number 1, 1965, pp. 45–61; available at http://www.persee.fr/web/revues/home/prescript/issue/ahess_0395-2649_1978_num_33_1; accessed March 2, 2012.

David Feuerwerker: "The abolition of body taxes in France." *Annales. Économies, Sociétés, Civilisations*, 1962, Volume 17, Number 5. Available in English (translator: Mitchell Abidor) at http://www.marxists.org/history/france/annales/1962/body-taxes.htm; accessed January 16, 2012.

Heinrich Fichtenau: *Living in the Tenth Century: Mentalities and Social Orders*. Translated from the German by Patrick J. Geary. Chicago, Illinois: University of Chicago, 1991.

Graeme Fife: *The Terror: the Shadow of the Guillotine*. New York City, New York: St. Martin's Press, 2004.

Louis Finkelstein: *The Jews: their History, Culture, and Religion*. 4th edition. New York City, New York: Schocken Books, 1970.

Franklin L. Ford: *Strasbourg in Transition, 1648–1789*. New York City, New York: Norton, 1958.

Gregory Fremont-Barnes: *The French Revolutionary Wars*. Oxford, England, United Kingdom: Osprey Publishing, 2001.

Charles Friedemann: "Bischheim." 1959. Available at http://judaisme.sdv.fr/synagog/basrhin/a-f/bischhei.htm; accessed November 14, 2011.

Kirsten A. Fudeman: *Vernacular Voices: Language and Identity in Medieval French Jewish Communities*. Philadelphia, Pennsylvania: University of Pennsylvania Press, 2010.

François Louis Ganshof: *Frankish Institutions under Charlemagne.* Providence, Rohde Island: Brown University Press, 1968.

J. Gayot et H. Herly: "La métallurgie des pays de la Saare moyenne jusqu'en 1815." In *Les Cahieris Sarrois* #4, Berger-Levrault, 1928.

Noel Gerson: *The Edict of Nantes.* New York City, New York: Grosset and Dunlap, 1969.

Moses Ginsburger: *Cerf-Berr et son Époque.* Société d'Histoire des Juifs d'Alsace-Lorraine. Guebwiller, Alsace, France: J. Dreyfus, 1908, p. 21. Available at http://gallica.bnf.fr/ark:/12148/bpt6k5427849p/f8.image; accessed November 17, 2011.

Moses Ginsburger: *Les Familles Lehmann et Cerf Berr.* Paris, France: Cerf in Versailles, 1910. Available at http://sammlungen.ub.uni-frankfurt.de/freimann/content/titleinfo/277414; accessed November 12, 2011.

Moses Ginsburger: "Une fondation de Cerf Berr." 1923. Available at http://judaisme.sdv.fr/perso/cerfberr/fondat.htm; accessed November 29, 2011.

Moses and Ernest Ginsburger: "Contributions à l'histoire des Juifs d'Alsace pendant la terreur." *Revue des Études Juives.* Volume 47, Paris, France: Librairie Durlacher, 1903, pp. 283–299.

Patrick Girard: *Les Juifs de France de 1789 à 1860.* Paris, France: Calmann-Lévy, 1976.

Paul Girault de Coursac: *September 1792, la Mort Organisee.* Paris: Editions F. X. de Guibert, 1994.

Leonard B. Glick: *Abraham's Heirs: Jews and Christians in Medieval Europe.* Syracuse, New York: Syracuse University Press, 1998.

Michael Goldfarb: *Emancipation.* New York City, New York: Simon & Schuster, 2009.

George Peabody Gooch: *Germany and the French Revolution*. London, England, United Kingdom: Longmans, Green and Co., 1920.

Louis Léon Théodore Gosselin: *Les Massacres de Septembre*. Paris, France: Perrin, 1907.

Robert S. Gottfried: *The Black Death: Natural and Human Disaster in Medieval Europe*. New York, New York: The Free Press, 1983.

Hugh Gough: "Politics and power: the triumph of Jacobinism in Strasbourg, 1791–1793." *The Historical Journal*: 1980, Volume 23, Number 2, pp. 327–352.

Heinrich Graetz: *History of the Jews*. Six volumes. Philadelphia, Pennsylvania: Jewish Publication Society of America, 1895.

Michael Graetz: *The Jews in Nineteenth-Century France*. Translated from the German by Jane Marie Todd. Stanford, California: Stanford University Press, 1996.

Michael Grant: *Constantine the Great*. New York City, New York: L. Scribner's Sons, 1998.

Henri Grégoire: *An Essay on the Physical, Moral, and Political Reformation of the Jews: a Work Crowned by the Royal Society of Arts and Sciences at Metz*. London, England, United Kingdom: C. Forster, Poultry, 1789.

Gregory of Tours: *History of the Franks*. New York City, New York: Penguin Classics, 1776.

E. Grosse: *Dictionnaire Statistique du Département De La Meurthe: Contenant une Introduction Historique sur le Pays*. Volume 1. Lunéville, France, 1836.

Andre Hallays: *The Spell of Alsace*. Boston, Massachusetts: The Page Company, 1919.

William W. Hallo, David B. Ruderman, and Michael Stanklawski (eds.): *Heritage: Civilization and the Jews: Source Reader.* Westport, Connecticut: Praeger, 1984.

John Hardman: *King Louis XVI: the Silent King.* London, England, United Kingdom: Arnold Press, 2000.

Robert D. Harris: *Necker and the Revolution of 1789.* Lanham, Maryland: University Press of America, 1986.

Thierry Hatt: "Cerf Baer un Juif revendiquant d'être 'citoyen' en 1789; localisation de son habitation a l'aide du plan de 1725." Contribution a l'exposition "Les Juifs a Strasbourg." December 2002. Available at http://thierry.hatt.gps.free.fr/01-site-acad-tous-pdf/cerf-baer-02.pdf; accessed March 11, 2012.

Michael Hayden: *France and the Estates-General of 1614.* Cambridge, United Kingdom: Cambridge University Press, 2008.

Richard Hayman: *Ironmaking: the History and Archaeology of the Iron Industry.* Stroud, Gloucestershire, United Kingdom: History Press, 2011.

Friedrich Carl Heitz: *Les Sociétés Politiques de Strasbourg pendant les Années 1790 à 1795.* Strasbourg, Alsace, France: Frederic-Charles Heitz, 1863.

Robert Heitz: *Strasbourg.* Paris, France: Librairie Hachette, 1961.

Jonathan I. Helfand: "The symbiotic relationship between French and Germany Jewry in the age of emancipation." *Leo Baeck Institute Yearbook, 1984.* Volume 29, Issue 1, pp. 331–350. Available at http://leobaeck.oxfordjournals.org/content/29/1/331.extract; accessed March 2, 2012.

Auguste Philippe Herlaut: *Deux Témoins de la Terreur: le Citoyen Dubuisson, le ci-Devant Baron de Haindel.* Paris, France: Librairie Clavreuil, 1958.

Arthur Hertzberg: *The French Enlightenment and the Jews.* New York City, New York: Columbia University Press, 1968, pp. 319–322.

P. Hildenfinger: *Documents sur les Juifs à Paris au XVII Siècle.* Paris, France: Champion, 1913. Available at http://scans.library.utoronto. ca/pdf/5/14/documents27sociuoft/documents27sociuoft_bw.pdf; accessed January 5, 2012.

Kurt Hoppstädter: *Der Jude in der Geschichte des Saarlands.* Kaiserslautern, 1943.

G. Huffel: *La Forêt Sainte de Haguenau en Alsace.* Nancy-Paris-Strasbourg: Berger-Levrault, 1920.

Lynn Hunt (ed.): *The French Revolution and Human Rights: A Brief Documentary History.* Boston, Massachusetts: Bedford, 1996.

Paul E. Hyman: *The Emancipation of the Jews in Alsace.* New Haven, Connecticut: Yale University Press, 1984.

Paula Hyman: *The Jews of Modern France.* Berkeley, California: University of California Press, 1998, pp. 10–11.

Beatrice Fry Hyslop: *A Guide to the General Cahiers of 1789 with the Texts of Unedited Cahiers.* New York City, New York: Octagon Books, 1968.

Walter Isaacson: *Benjamin Franklin: an American Life.* New York City, New York: Simon & Schuster, 2004.

Micheline Ishay: *The Human Rights Reader: Major Political Essays, Speeches, and Documents from Ancient Times to the Present.* New York City, New York: Routledge, 2007.

Ernst Johann: *The Rhineland-Palatinate and Saar.* Frankfurt am Main, Germany: Umschau Verlag, 1979.

Paul Johnson: *A History of the Jews.* New York City, New York: Harper Perennial, 1988.

Peter M. Jones: *Reform and Revolution in France: the Politics of Transition, 1774–1791*. Cambridge, England, United Kingdom: Cambridge University Press, 1995.

David P. Jordan: *The Revolutionary Career of Maximilien Robespierre*. Chicago, Illinois: University of Chicago Press, 1985.

Josephus: *Antiquities of the Jews*. Translated by William Whiston, Book 14, chapter 4, available at http://www.gutenberg.org/ebooks/2848; accessed December 23, 2011.

Léon Kahn: *Les Juifs de Paris pendant la Révolution*. Paris, France: Librairie Curlacher, 1898.

Aryeh Kaplan: *Handbook of Jewish Thought*. Volume 1, Brooklyn, New York: Moznaim Publishing, 1990.

Jonathan Karp and Adam Sutcliffe: *Philosemitism in History*. New York City, New York: Cambridge University Press, 2011.

J. E. Kaufmann and H. W. Kaufmann: *The Medieval Fortress: Castles, Forts, and Walled Cities of the Middle Ages*. Cambridge, Massachusetts: Da Capo Press, 2004.

Lee Kennett: *The French Armies in the Seven Years' War*. Durham, North Carolina: Duke University Press, 1967.

Kathleen M. Kenyon: Jerusalem: Excavating 3000 Years of History. New York City, New York: McGraw-Hill, 1967.

Martin Klewitz: *Das Saarland*. Munich, Germany: Deutscher Kunstverlag, 1982.

Franz Kobler: *Napoleon and the Jews*, New York City, New York: Schocken Books, 1976.

Lionel Kochan: *The Making of Western Jewry, 1600–1819*. New York City, New York: Palgrave-Macmillan, 2004.

Roger Kohn: *Les Juifs de la France du Nord dans la Seconde Moitie du 14th Siècle*. Louvain-Paris, France: E. Peeters, 1988.

D. G. Kousoulas: *The Life and Times of Constantine the Great*. Bethesda, Maryland: Rutledge Books, 1997.

Petr Alekseevich Kropotkin: *The Great French Revolution, 1789–1793*. New York City, New York: G. P. Putnam's Sons, 1909.

Tony Kushner and Nadia Valman: *Philosemitism, Antisemitism, and the Jews: Perspective from the Middle Ages to the Twentieth Century*. Aldershot, Hampshire, England, United Kingdom: Ashgate Publishing, 2004.

Lazare Landau: "Le massacre de la Saint-Valentin." Available at http://judaisme.sdv.fr/histoire/historiq/stval/stval.htm; accessed November 6, 2011.

André Latreille: *L'Eglise Catholique et la Révolution Française: Le Pontificat de Pie VI et La Crise Française (1775–1799)*. Paris, France: Librairie Hachette, 1950.

Stephen J. Lee: *The Thirty Years War*. New York City, New York: Routledge, 1991.

Rosanne and Daniel N. Leeson: *Index de Memoire Juive en Alsace: Contrats de Mariage au XVIIIème Siecle par A. A. Fraenckel*. Volume I, Bas-Rhin. Strasbourg, Alsace, France: Cercle de Généalogie Juive, Editions du Cédrat, 1997, p. 6. The book is available for purchase at http://www.genealoj.org/New/ENtexte/page06.php; accessed December 1, 2011.

Arsène Legrelle: *Louis XIV et Strasbourg: Essai sur la réunion de Strasbourg à la France*. Paris, France: Librairie Hatchette, 1881.

Edna Hindie Leman, Alison Patrick, and Joel Felix: Revolutionaries at Court: Constituent Assembly 1789–1791. Oxford, England, United Kingdom: Voltaire Foundation, 1996.

Joseph Lémann: *L'Entrée des Israélites dans La Société Francaise et Les États Chrétiens d'apres des Documents Nouveaux*. Paris, France: Librairie Victor Lecoffre, 1886.

Yves Lemoine: *Malesherbes (1721–1794): Biographie d'un Homme dans sa Lignée*. TUM/Editions Michel de Maule, 1994.

Henri Lepage: *Les Communes de la Meurthe*. Volume 2. Nancy, France: A. Lepage, 1853.

Jean-Denis G. G. Lepage: *Vauban and the French Military under Louis XIV*. Jefferson, North Carolina: McFarland, 2009.

Randall Lesaffer: *Peace Treaties and International Law in European History*. New York City, New York: Cambridge University Press, 2004, pp. 9–44.

Paul Leuilliot: *L'Alsace au Début du XIX Siècle: Volume III: Religions et Culture*. Paris, France: S. E. V. P. E. N., 1960.

Roger Lévylier: *Notes et Documents sur la famille Cerf-Berr*. Three volumes. Paris, France: Plon, 1902–1906.

Maurice Liber: *Les Juifs et la Convocation des États Généraux (1789)*. Louvain-Paris, France: E. Peeters, 1989. Available at http://www.archive.org/stream/revuedestudesj64soci#page/318/mode/2up; accessed January 7, 2012.

Isidore Loeb: "La controverse de 1240 sur le Talmud." *Revue des Études Juives*. Paris, France: Librairie Durlacher, Number 4, April-June 1881, pp. 248–270. Available at http://www.archive.org/stream/revuedestudesju00fragoog#page/n435/mode/2up; accessed January 7, 2012.

Isidore Loeb: "Rabbi Joselmann de Rosheim." *Revue des Études Juives*, Paris, France: Librairie Durlacher, Number 4, April-June 1881, pp. 271–277. Available at http://www.archive.org/stream/

revuedestudesju00fragoog#page/n461/mode/2up; accessed January 7, 2012.

Andrew Lossky: *Louis XIV and the French Monarchy*. New Brunswick, New Jersey: Rutgers University Press, 1994.

Steven M. Lowenstein: *The Berlin Jewish Community: Enlightenment, Family, and Crisis, 1770–1830*. New York City, New York: Oxford University Press, 1994.

Barbara Luttrell: *Mirabeau*: Carbondale, Illinois: Southern Illinois University Press, 1990.

John A. Lynn: *The Wars of Louis XIV, 1667–1714*. Harlow, Essex, United Kingdom: Pearson Education, 1999.

Frances Malino: *A Jew in the French Revolution: the Life of Zalkind Hourwitz*. Oxford, England, United Kingdom: Blackwell Publisher, 1996.

Avraham Malthete: *Registre du Cimetière Israélite de Rosenwiller, 1753–1980*. Paris, France: Cercle de Généalogie Juive, 2004. Available for purchase at http://www.genealoj.org/New/texte/page08.php; accessed December 12, 2011.

Jacob Rader Marcus: *The Jew in the Medieval World: a Source Book: 315–1791*. Cincinnati, Ohio: Hebrew Union College Press, 1990.

Marie-Thérèse of France: "Narrative of Marie-Thérèse of France." Available at llhttp://digital.library.upenn.edu/women/wormeley/princess/princess-3.html; accessed November 30, 2011.

Walter Marsden: *The Rhineland*. London, England, United Kingdom: B. T. Batsford, 1973.

Albert Marx: *Die Geschichte der Juden im Saarland vom Ancien Regime bus zum Zweiten Weltkrieg*. Saarbrücken, 1992.

Donald K. McKim: *The Cambridge Companion to John Calvin.* Cambridge, United Kingdom: Cambridge University Press, 2004.

John McManners: *The French Revolution and the Church.* Westport, Connecticut: Greenwood Press, 1969.

Robert Michael: *A History of Catholic Antisemitism: the Dark Side of the Church.* New York City, New York: Palgrave Macmillan, 2008.

Jules Michelet: *Histoire de la Révolution Française.* Volume I. Paris, France: Chamerot, Libraire-éditeur, 1847. Available at http://www.archive.org/details/histoiredelarev08unkngoog; accessed February 6, 2012.

Roland E. Mousnier: *The Institutions of France under the Absolute Monarchy, 1598–1789.* Translated from the French by Brian Pearce. Chicago, Illinois: University of Chicago Press, 1979.

Ester Muchawsky-Schnapper: *Les Juifs d'Alsace.* Jerusalem, Israel: Musée d'Israel, 1991.

Ruth F. Necheles: *The Abbé Grégoire, 1787–1831: the Odyssey of an Egalitarian.* Westport, Connecticut: Greenwood Publishing Company, 1971.

Renée Neher-Bernheim: *Les Juifs en France de la Révolution à nos Jours.* Collection Classique Judaica. Paris, France: Fondation Sefer, 1981.

Renée Neher-Bernheim: "Note sur la date de la mort de Cerfberr de Médelsheim." *Revue des Études Juives.* Volume 132, January-June 1973.

David Nicolle: *Poitiers AD 732: Charles Martel Turns the Islamic Tide.* Oxford, England, United Kingdom: Osprey Publishing, 2008.

A Nineteenth Century Miracle: the Brothers Ratisbonne and the Congregation of Notre Dame de Sion. (no author listed) Translated from the French by L. M. Leggatt. London: Burns Oates & Washbourne, 1922.

Hilda Rodwell Ormsby: *France: a Regional and Economic Geography.* London, England, United Kingdom: Methuen and Company, 1968.

Robert Roswell Palmer: *The Age of the Democratic Revolution.* Princeton, New Jersey: Princeton University Press, 1989.

Geoffrey Parker: *The Military Revolution: Military Innovation and the Rise of the West, 1500–1800.* Cambridge, United Kingdom: Cambridge University Press, 1996.

Geoffrey Parker: *The Thirty Years' War.* New York, New York: Routledge, 1997.

Boris B. Piotrovsky: *The Ancient Civilization of Urartu.* New York City, New York: Cowles Book Company, 1969.

Iwo Cyprian Pogonowski: *Jews in Poland.* New York City, New York: Hippocrene Books, 1993.

Charles Poisson: *Les Fournisseurs aux Armées sous la Révolution Française: Le Directoire des Achats* (1792–1793). Paris, France: Librairie Historique A. Margraff, 1932.

Munro Price: *The Road from Versailles: King Louis XVI, Marie Antoinette, and the Fall of the French Monarchy.* New York City, New York: St. Martin's Griffin, 2004.

Ruth Putnam: *Alsace and Lorraine: From Cæsar to Kaiser, 58 B.C.-1871 A.D.* New York City, New York: Putnam's Sons, 1915.

Louis I. Rabinowitz: *Jewish Merchant Adventures: A Study of the Radanites.* London, England, United Kingdom: Edward Goldston, 1948.

Pierre Rétat: *Le Dernier Règne: Chronique de la France de King Louis XVI, 1774–1789.* Paris, France: Librairie Artheme Fayard, 1995.

Rodolphe Reuss: *Histoire d'Alsace*. Paris, France: Ancienne Librairie Furne: Boivin, 1918.

Rodolphe Reuss: *L'Alsace pendant la Révolution Français*. I. Correspondance des Députés de Strasbourg à l'Assemblée Nationale. Paris, France: G. Fischbacher, 1980.

Rodolphe Reuss: "L'Antisémitisme dans le Bas-Rhin pendant la Révolution (1790–1793)." *Revue des Études Juives*, Volume 68. Paris, France: La Librairie Durlacher, 1914, pp. 246–263. Available at http://www.archive.org/stream/revuedestudesj68soci#page/262/mode/2up; accessed March 1, 2012.

Rodolphe Reuss: *La Cathédrale de Strasbourg pendant la Révolution. Études sur l'histoire politique et religieuse de l'Alsace (1789-1802)*. Paris, France: Fischbacher, 1888. Available at Project Gutenberg at http://www.gutenberg.org/catalog/world/readfile?fk_files=228202&pageno=2; accessed March 3, 2012.

Rodolphe Reuss : *La Constitution Civile Du Clergé Et La Crise Religieuse En Alsace (1790-1795) d'après des documents en partie inédits*. Strasbourg, France: Imprimerie Alsacienne, 1922.

Rodolphe Reuss: "Seligmann Alexandre." Available at http://judaisme.sdv.fr/histoire/villes/strasbrg/seligman/seligmanalex.htm; accessed December 22, 2011.

I. S. Robinson: *Henry IV of Germany, 1056–1106*. Cambridge, England, United Kingdom: Cambridge University Press, 1999.

Nils Roemer: *German City, Jewish Memory: the Story of Worms*. Lebanon, New Hampshire: University Press of New England, 2010.

James C. Riley: *The Seven Years War and the Old Regime in France: the Economic and Financial Toll*. Princeton, New Jersey: Princeton University Press, 1986.

J. H. Robinson (ed.): "The Proclamation of the Duke of Brunswick." In *Readings in European History*, Volume 2. Boston, Massachusetts: Ginn, 1906, pp. 443–445.

Clifford J. Rogers (ed.): *The Military Revolution Debate*. Boulder, Colorado: Westview Press, 1995.

Nina Rowe: *The Jew, the Cathedral, and the Medieval City: Synagoga and Ecclesia in the Thirteenth Century*. Cambridge, United Kingdom: Cambridge University Press, 2011.

William Russell: *The History of Modern Europe*. Volume 2. Philadelphia, Pennsylvania: Robert Carr, 1802.

Hayim Ben Sasson (ed.): *A History of the Jewish People*. London, England, United Kingdom: Weidenfeld and Nicolson, 1976.

Simon Schama: *Citizens: a Chronicle of the French Revolution*. New York City, New York: Vintage, 1989.

Michael Schneider: *Der Traum der Vernunft: Roman eins deutschen Jakobiners*. Köln, Germany: Verlag Kiepenheuer & Witsch, 2001.

Simon Schwarzfuchs: "Alsace and Southern Germany: the creation of a border." In *Jewish Emancipation Reconsidered*. Michael Brenner, Vicki Caron, and Uri R. Kaufmann (eds.). London, England, United Kingdom: Leo Baeck Institute, 2003.

Simon Schwarzfuchs: *Napoleon, the Jews, and the Sanhedrin*. New York City, New York: Oxford University Press, 1984.

E. Seinguerlet: *Strasbourg pendant la Révolution*. Paris, France: Berger-Levrault, 1881.

Alyssa Goldstein Sepinwall: "L'Abbé Grégoire and the Metz contest: the view from new documents." *Revue des Études Juives*, Volume 166, Numbers 1–2, 2007, pp. 243–258.

Alyssa Goldstein Sepinwall: *The Abbé Grégoire and the French Revolution: the Making of Modern Universalism*. Berkeley, California: University of California Press, 2005.

Alyssa Goldstein Sepinwall: "Strategic friendships: Jewish intellectuals, the L'Abbé Grégoire, and the French Revolution." In *Renewing the Past, Reconfiguring Jewish Culture*. Ross Brann and Adam Sutcliffe (eds.). Philadelphia, Pennsylvania: University of Pennsylvania Press, 2004, pp. 189–213.

J. H. Shennan: *The Parlement of Paris*. Thrupp, Stroud, Gloucestershire, United Kingdom: Sutton Publishing, 1998.

Sister Marie Ida de Sion: *Sion! Long May Her Banner Wave! Memories of Notre Dame de Sion in Kansas City 1912–1965 and the Fifty Golden Years of Sister Marie Ida de Sion 1915–1965*. Yearbook House: Kansas City, Missouri, April 22, 1965.

Morris Slavin and Agnes Monroe Smith (eds.): *Bourgeois, Sans-Culottes, and other Frenchmen: Essays on the French Revolution in Honor of John Hall Stewart*. Waterloo, Ontario, Canada: Wilfrid Laurier University Press, 1981.

Norman Solomon: *The Talmud: a Selection*. London, England, United Kingdom: Penguin, 2009.

Roger Henry Soltau: *The Duke de Choiseul: The Lothian Essay*. Oxford, England, United Kingdom: B. H. Blackwell, 1908.

George Soria: *Grande Histoire de la Révolution Francaise*. Three volumes. Paris, France: Bordas, 1988.

Louis Spach: *Histoire de la Basse Alsace de la Ville de Strasbourg*. Strasbourg, France: Berger-Levrault, 1858.

Daniel Stauben: *Scenes of Jewish Life in Alsace*. Edited and translated by Rose Choron. London, England: Joseph Simon Pangloss Press, 1991.

Henry Morse Stephens: *A History of the French Revolution*. Three volumes. New York City, New York: Charles Scribner's Sons, 1911, Volume 2.

Selma Stern: *The Court Jew: a Contribution to the History of the Period of Absolutism in Central Europe*. Translated from the German by Ralph Wieman. Philadelphia, Pennsylvania: Jewish Publication Society of America, 1950.

Selma Stern: *Josel of Rosheim*. Philadelphia, Pennsylvania: Jewish Publication of American, 1965.

Hermann L. Strack: *Introduction to the Talmud and Midrash*. New York City, New York: Meridian Books, 1931.

Antoine Sutter: *Les Années de Jeunesse de l'Abbé Grégoire: son Itinéraire jusqu'au Début de la Révolution*. Paris, France: Éditions Pierron, 1992.

Franz A. Szabo: *The Seven Years War in Europe 1756–1763*. Harlow, England, United Kingdom: Pearson Education, 2008.

Zosa Szajkowski: *Franco-Judaica: an Analytical Bibliography of Books, Pamphlets, Decrees, Briefs and Other Printed Documents Pertaining to the Jews in France 1500–1788*. New York City, New York: American Academy for Jewish Research, 1962.

Zosa Szajkowski: *Jewish Education in France, 1789–1939*. New York City, New York: Columbia University Press, 1980.

Zosa Szajkowski: *Jews and the French Revolutions of 1789, 1830, and 1848*. New York City, New York: Ktav Publishing House, 1970.

Hippolyte Adolphe Taine: *The French Revolution*. Two volumes. Translated by John Durand. New York City, New York: Henry Hold and Company, 1892.

Joseph Telushkin: "The Shulkhan Arukh." In *Jewish Literacy*. New York City, New York: William Morrow and Company, 1991.

Alan M. Tigay: *The Jewish Traveler*. Northvale, New Jersey: Jason Aronson, 1994.

Jean Tulard, Jean Arthême Fayard, and A. Fierro: *Histoire et Dictionnaire de la Révolution Française: 1789–1799*. Paris, France: Robert Laffont, 1998.

Christopher Tyerman: *God's War: a New History of the Crusades*. London, England, United Kingdom: Penguin Books, 2007.

James Van Horn Melton: *The Rise of the Public in Enlightenment Europe*. Cambridge, United Kingdom: Cambridge University Press, 2001.

Bernard Vogler: *L'Alsace, Itineraires de Decouvertes*. Rennes, Brittany, France: Ouest-France, Edlarge, 2007.

Bernard Vogler: *L'Alsace, une Histoire*. Mulhouse, Alsace, France: Oberlin, 1990.

Henri Wallon: *Histoire du Tribunal Révolutionnaire de Paris avec le journal de ses actes*. Six volumes, 1880-1882. Paris, France: Librairie Hachette, 1880.

Max Warschawski: "David Sintzheim." In "*L'Almanach du KKL-Strasbourg 1749-1989*." Available at http://judaisme.sdv.fr/histoire/rabbins/sintzhei/sintzhei.htm; accessed February 4, 2012.

Max Warschawski: "Histoire des Juifs de Strasbourg." Available at http://judaisme.sdv.fr/histoire/villes/strasbrg/hist/hist2.htm; accessed November 6, 2011.

C. V. Wedgwood and Anthony Griffin: *The Thirty Years War*. New York City, New York: 2005.

Patrick Weil: *Migration Control in the North Atlantic World*. Oxford, England, United Kingdom: Berghahn Books, 2005.

Max Weinreich: *History of the Yiddish Language*, Volume 1. Chicago, Illinois: University of Chicago, 2008.

Robert Weyl: "Les funérailles de Cerf Berr de Médelsheim à Rosenwiller." *Revue des Études Juives*, Volume 136 (1–2), January-June, 1977, pp. 155–161.

Robert Weyl: "Chronique des juifs Rosheim." In *Saisons d'Alsace*, Number 66, 1978. Available at http://judaisme.sdv.fr/synagog/basrhin/r-z/rosheim/chroniq.htm; accessed January 31, 2012.

Robert Weyl: "Les juifs d'Alsace et les droits de l'homme." 1984. Available at http://judaisme.sdv.fr/histoire/historiq/droitsh/drh1.htm; accessed November 6, 2011.

Robert Weyl: "Les Juifs a Rosheim." In *Saisons d'Alsace*, Number 66, 1978. Available at http://judaisme.sdv.fr/synagog/basrhin/r-z/rosheim.htm; accessed January 22, 2012.

Christie Sample Wilson: *Beyond Belief: Surviving the Revocation of the Edict of Nantes in France*. Plymouth, United Kingdom: Lehigh University Press, 2011.

James E. Wilson: *Terroir: The Role of Geology, Climate, and Culture in the Making of French Wines*. University of California at Berkeley: Berkeley, California, 1998.

INDEX

Enlightenment, French *See* French
Enlightenment.

Enlightenment, Jewish *See* Jewish
Enlightenment.

Ensheim, Moses 238

Entrepreneur 26, 104, 109, 110

Epidemic 60, 63, 241

Equipment 107

Erkanbald 30

Erlenbourg, Alsace 288, 343

Escape (failed) from France, Royal
Family (June 20/21, 1791) 314,
318, 328, 338

Essay (contest) 149, 150, 151, 201,
202, 213, 235, 237, 238

*Essay on the Physical, Moral, and
Political Regeneration
of the Jews (L'Essai sur la
Régénération Physique, Morale et
Politique des
Juifs)* 237

Estates, Three 204, 240, 258 259,
260 *See also* First Estate, Second
Estate, Third Estate.

Estates-General 204, 205, 210, 219,
221, 223, 225, 227, 239, 240, 241,
242, 243, 244, 245, 246, 247,
248, 249, 250, 252, 253, 254, 257,
258, 260, 262, 264, 289, 351, 361

Estates-General religious procession
(May 4, 1789) 257

Esther Berr *See* Berr, Esther.

Esther Cerfberr Sinzheim *See* Berr,
Esther.

Esther, Queen (Biblical) 37

État-civil 211, 212, 221, 307

Etienne-François, Count of
Stainville, Duke of Choiseul *See*
Choiseul.

Ettendorf Jewish Cemetery 206,
365, 384

Ettenheim 311

Eucharist 38, 49

Exceptional laws, Jewish *See* Jewish
exceptional laws.

Expense/expenditure 40, 56, 136,
142, 144, 145, 154, 168, 205, 209,
216, 218, 268, 305

Eve Berr *See* Berr, Eve.

Exile 39, 58, 69, 105, 148, 220, 225

Fabrics 200

Fachon Berr *See* Berr, Fradel.

Factory 126, 184, 186, 187, 200,
226

False receipts *See* Counterfeit
receipts.

Famine 125

Fanaticism 191, 252, 253, 275, 349,
361

Farming (agricultural) 92, 140

Farming (tax) 91, 93, 111, 117, 118,
244

Faustini, Pascal 103

Feast of Pentecost 95

Feast of the Confederation 307, 340

Feast of Weeks 95

Fecundity 150

Ferdinand II of Aragon 6

Festival of Liberty (Paris) 378

Festival of Reason (Strasbourg) 379

Fête de la Confédération 307, 340

Feudal Committee, National
Assembly 304, 310

Feudalism, abolition without
indemnification 267, 268, 269,
275, 289, 310, 316, 361

Feudal social order, Christian 69

Feuerwerker, David 92, 154, 167,
170, 250, 251, 256

Fife, Graeme 345, 362, 364, 369,

Financial reform 153, 203, 209, 216,
218, 219, 220, 221, 223

Grégoire, Henri 149, 150, 151, 202, 235, 236, 237, 238, 239, 241, 242, 248, 269, 276, 277, 278, 279, 298, 311, 312, 313, 328

Grégoire, Henri, belief system of 236–237

Grusselhorn 68, 303

Guild 55, 58, 65, 213, 243

Guillotine 358, 371, 373, 381

Gustavus Adolphus, King (Sweden) 72

Hadrian 13–14

Haguenau 59, 67, 72, 92, 140, 143, 162, 163, 222, 243, 244, 249, 353, 376

Haguenau property 140

Hailstorm (July 1788) 222, 223, 226

Haindel, Charles François-Fréderic, Baron of 288, 289, 343

Haindel, Christophe-Louis, Baron of 288

Haindel, Philippe-Auguste 288

Hakhnassat Kalla 207

Halevi, Judah 239

Ham 28, 79, 80

Haman 37

HaMe'assef 169

Hampson, Norman 5

Hanau-Lichtenberg 72, 74, 90

Hanover (Germany) 135, 169, 195, 328

Hanriot, François 365, 366

Harpsichord 373

Harris, Robert D. 168, 203, 205, 209, 220, 223, 224, 261, 266, 268

Harun-al-Rashid, Caliph 27

Harvests 96, 222, 258

Hasmonean 12

Haut-Rhin Department 4, 316, 337

Hay 22, 92, 108, 110, 140, 353

Hébert, Jacques René 370

Hébertist 370, 371, 378

Hebrew 6, 11, 12, 13, 15, 23, 28, 29, 37, 39, 44, 45, 48, 49, 76, 96, 97, 119, 141, 143, 147, 157, 169, 187, 202, 222, 239, 373, 380, 392

Hebrew Bible 15, 28, 37, 44, 45, 48, 49, 76, 97, 202

Hebrew characters 143

Hebrew letters 392

Hegmann 63

Hell, François 130, 131, 145, 146, 147, 148, 209, 217, 242, 244, 245, 249, 267, 304, 365

Henry IV 30–33

Herodotus 28

Hertzberg, Arthur 111, 185, 186, 188, 200, 214

Hesse 4, 99

Hesse-Darmstadt 8, 100, 311

High Middle Ages 11, 28–55, 70, 76, 95

Hildegard 28

Hippo 21

Hirtz of Bischheim 95, 289, 392 *See also* Cerf Berr of Médelsheim.

Hirtz of Médelsheim 95, 289, 392 *See also* Cerf Berr of Médelsheim.

Holy Ark 169

Holy Roman Emperor 28, 30, 31, 33, 43, 46, 53, 59, 60, 65, 66, 71, 74, 100, 156, 157, 314, 326, 327, 336, 340

Holy Roman Empire 7, 28, 31, 38, 43, 51, 53, 59, 68, 70, 72, 75, 94.111, 156, 157, 249, 310, 311, 327, 337, 341, 367

Holy Spirit 257

Horses 22, 44, 55, 56, 75, 92, 101, 107, 108, 109, 110, 138, 145, 161, 205, 261, 265, 376, 381, 391

Modern Period, Early *See* Early Modern Period.

Monet, Pierre 1, 357, 358, 373, 377, 378, 379, 380, 383

Monk Rigord 40

Monsieur of Ris 75

Montagnard 354

Montbarrey, Alexander Marie Leonor of Saint-Mauris of *See* Alexander Marie Leonor of Saint-Mauris of Montbarrey.

Monteynard 104, 127–129

Montrouge 200

Moral imperative 356

Morale, Jewish 50–51

Morality 48, 201, 207, 238, 284, 300, 301, 307, 356, 373

Moselle River 11, 28, 29, 32, 35, 39, 150, 152, 181, 340, 343, 354, 364, 365, 366, 368, 376

Moses 39, 40, 50, 62

Moses Blien *See* Blien, Moses.

Mouches, Henri 143

Mount Sinai 95, 50

Mullenheim family 58

Mulot, Francois-Valentin 300, 303

Municipal Assemblies 216

Municipalities, Law of *See* Law of Municipalities.

Munitionnaire 107, 108, 110

Musket 347

Muslim 22, 25, 26, 31, 35, 36, 37, 76, 211, 322

Mutzig 93, 94, 100, 103, 125, 141, 199, 206, 222, 225, 226, 282, 287, 304, 305, 382, 393

Nancy (Lorraine) 135, 140, 141, 163, 188, 199, 226, 235, 241, 256, 257, 259, 285, 305, 323, 358

Napoleon Bonaparte 119, 324, 366

Napoleon, Joséphine 366

Nassau-Saarbrücken 8, 99, 100, 105, 111

National Assembly 7, 16, 217, 224, 259–289, 297–313, 315–329, 344, 345, 347, 348, 350, 361, 369

National Constituent Assembly 261

National Convention 346, 347, 349, 351, 352, 355, 356, 357, 358, 359, 360, 361, 362, 363, 364–371, 373, 374, 378, 379, 381

National Guard (Paris) 262, 263, 315, 319, 338, 342, 344, 345, 365

National Guard (Strasbourg) 265, 303, 306, 319, 327, 342, 374

Nationalization of Roman Catholic Church in France 268

Nationalization of Roman Catholic Church land in France 268, 281–282

Nation Juive 75, 103, 123, 125, 136, 141, 142, 167, 196, 221, 222, 225, 227, 236, 253, 282, 301, 313

Necheles, Ruth F. 236, 241, 286, 301, 312

Necker cabal 224

Necker, Jacques 140, 142, 153, 156, 168, 216, 224, 235, 251, 252, 253, 254, 258, 261, 262, 263, 264, 265, 266, 268

Neher-Bernheim, Renée 383

Nérac 282

Netter, Lehmann 103, 125, 141, 142, 225, 226

Netter, Mariam 142, 207

Neustadt 368

Nevers 373

New Testament 13, 15, 19, 20, 44

Nicolas III of Corberon 130

Nicolas of Bulach 65

Nicolas Prosper Bauyn of Angervilliers 93

441

Prussia 103, 104, 110, 218, 314, 315, 328, 329, 340–343, 346–350, 352, 357, 363, 364, 366, 367, 368, 370, 374, 375, 378
Prussian Army 340, 341, 343, 346, 348, 349, 350, 357, 363, 367, 368, 374, 375, 384
Psalm 20, 36, 37, 41, 97
Psychological warfare 299
Puch de Gontaud 282
Purchasing Directory, Military See Military Purchasing Directory.
Purchasing manager 353
Puységur, Louis Pierre of Chastenet 138, 245, 253, 254, 260
Quadratus 14
Quai Finkwiller 1, 4, 124, 255, 382, 383
Queen Blanche of Castille 47
Queen Marie Antoinette See Marie Antoinette, Queen.
Quien, Jean-Clément 100
Rabaut of Saint-Étienne 269–270, 281
Rabbi Aberlin 101
Rabbi Caro See Caro, Rabbi Joseph ben Ephraim.
Rabbi Jacob Perle 141
Rabbi Joseph Steinhardt 118
Rabbinical Court 92, 118, 155, 201, 245
Rabbi, Patent See Patent Rabbi.
Rabbi Peyret, See Peyret, Rabbi.
Rabbi, sous See Sous-Rabbi.
Rabbi Tudela See Tudela, Rabbi.
Rabbi Yechiel See Yechiel, Rabbi.
Radanites 26–27
Radius, Casimir-Henry 126
Radulf 36–37
Rappoldstein 59
Ratisbon 29, 194

Ratisbonne, Auguste 194
Ratisbonne, Louis 194
Ratisbonne, Sophie (Zardlé)
  See Regensburger, Zardlé and Ratisbonne, Zardlé.
Ratisbonne, Zardlé (Sophie) 194
Reb Leima (Bischheim) 155
Refractory priest 326, 346, 347, 349
Regensburg 29, 39, 71, 194
Regensburger, Jacob Hirsch 194
Regensburger, Jacob Sussmann 194
  See also Ratisbonne, Auguste.
Regensburger, Wolff 194 See also Ratisbonne, Louis.
Regensburger, Zardlé See Ratisbonne, Zardlé.
Regicide 358, 359
Régisseurs 353
Registry 211, 221, 222, 307, 355, 382, 392
Reichardt, Johann Friedrich 335
Reid River 158, 311
Reign of Terror 1, 370, 375, 384
Reims 23, 101
Religious creed 283–284
Remi 23
Remigius 23, 24, 101
Renaissance 54
Republic, French 267, 307, 319, 335, 336, 351, 353, 358, 359, 360–364, 369, 373, 379, 382
Republic, Roman 12
Reubell (Rewbell), Jean-François 217, 249, 285, 305, 309, 310, 322, 323
Réunions 73, 74
Revolutionary Commune of Paris 344, 348, 349
Revolutionary Court 362
Revolutionary Tribunal 362, 364, 373, 375, 378, 381, 382

Saarland 5, 32, 74, 75, 89, 94, 95, 99, 100, 101, 103, 105, 111, 117, 247, 366
Saarlouis 89, 164
Saint-Antoine faubourg (Paris) 339
Saint-Étienne , Rabaut of 269–270, 281
Saint-Germain, Claude Louis, Count of 138
Saint Germain-des-Prés (Paris) 109, 349
Saint Just, Emmanuel 281
Saint Just, Louis Antoine Léon 1, 281, 355, 357, 366, 375, 376, 377, 380, 381, 382
Saint Louis Roman Catholic Church (Strasbourg) 142
Saint Marceau faubourg (Paris) 339
Saint Martin's Cathedral (Mainz) 366
Saint-Maur, Nicolas-François Dupré of 212
Saint Valentine's Day Massacre 65, 66, 101
Salle du Manège 280, 314, 344, 345, 346
Salomon, David 328
Salt works 239
Samuel, Léopold 380
Sanhedrin 13
sans-culotte 345, 347, 358, 365, 381
Sarreguemines 105, 163, 276
Saverne 3, 154, 304, 375
Savoy 57, 60, 61, 147, 357
Scheidterbach River Valley 100
Schlettstadt (Sélestat) 67, 163, 249
Schneider, Charles Frederic 382–383
Schneider, Euloge 373, 378, 379, 381, 382
Schutzbrief 60

Schwarber, Berthold 60
Schwarber, Peter 64–65
Schwarzfuchs, Simon 73, 103
Schwendt, Joseph 217, 222, 249, 253, 264, 304
Second Crusade 36, 37
Second Estate 240, 241, 260, 269, 286
Secretary of War (France) 93, 94, 104, 105, 106, 108, 109, 112, 122, 123, 127, 128, 137, 138, 148, 155, 156, 158, 159, 165, 180, 245, 253, 254, 260, 352, 354
Secular 268, 351, 201, 203, 236, 237, 238
Sedan 94, 164, 346
Seed 144
Ségur, Philippe Henri, Marquis of 138, 155, 156, 158, 159, 165
Seigniorial judge See Judge, seigniorial.
Seigniorial court See court, seigniorial.
Seine River 39, 258, 347
Sejanus 12
Sélestat (Schlettstadt) 59, 65, 67, 382
Seligmann Berr See Berr, Seligmann.
Seljuq Turks 31
Semi-autonomous community 90, 91, 92, 217, 276, 297, 299
Semitic 28, 217
Sephardim 6, 7, 8, 9, 29, 152, 200, 213, 214, 243, 245, 269, 286, 287, 289, 297, 298, 299, 300, 301, 322
Sepinwall, Alyssa Goldstein 149, 151, 201, 238, 239
September Massacres 348, 349, 350, 365
Serge (fabric) 200

Made in the USA
Coppell, TX
06 August 2020

31734289R00251